THE GOOD REBEL

THE GOOD REBEL

Understanding Freedom and Morality

Louis Groarke

Fairleigh Dickinson

Madison • Teaneck
Fairleigh Dickinson University Press
London: Associated University Presses

Associated University Presses
2010 Eastpark Boulevard
Cranbury, NJ 08512

Associated University Presses
16 Barter Street
London WC1A 2AH, England

Associated University Presses
P.O. Box 338, Port Credit
Mississauga, Ontario
Canada L5G 4L8

The paper used in this publication meets the requirements of the American National Standard for Permanence of Paper for Printed Library Materials Z39.48-1984.

Library of Congress Cataloging-in-Publication Data

Groarke, Louis.
 The good rebel : understanding freedom and morality / Louis Groarke.
  p. cm.
 Includes bibliographical references and index.
 ISBN 0-8386-3899-6 (alk. paper)
  1. Autonomy (Philosophy). 2. Ethics. I. Title.
 B808.67 .G76 2002
 170—dc21

                                                      00-064365

PRINTED IN THE UNITED STATES OF AMERICA

For my father, a good rebel

†John Cuthbert Groarke
August 17, 1922–August 25, 2000

What is a rebel? A man who says No, but whose refusal does not imply renunciation. He is also a man who says Yes, from the moment he makes his first gesture of rebellion.

Rebellion cannot exist without the feeling that, somewhere somehow, one is right.

—Albert Camus, *The Rebel*

Contents

Acknowledgments

I would like to thank Fairleigh Dickinson University Press for this publication opportunity and their expeditious handling of the editorial process. I would also like to thank Julien Yoseloff, Wyatt Benner, Christine Retz, and the staff at Associated University Presses for their patience and their understanding, as well as two anonymous referees for insightful and helpful comments on earlier drafts of this manuscript.

This book has been, to borrow a colloquialism, a long time coming. Dan Lyons at Colorado State University was the first philosophy professor I encountered in my university career and one of the best teachers I have ever known. At the University of Waterloo, Lawrence Haworth introduced me to John Dewey and to a political and moral view that is, broadly speaking, communitarian in character. I have benefited from discussions with many other members of the Waterloo philosophy department, including Margaret Moore, Jim Horne, Bernie Suits, Joseph Novak, Richard Holmes, and Jim Van Evra. Jan Narveson, the tireless champion of a very different view of ethics, has forced me to buttress the details of my argument.

My brothers Leo, a professor at Wilfrid Laurier University, and Paul, now at St. Thomas University and the Atlantic Human Rights Centre, have been exceedingly patient and kind. Jim Robinson at Okanagan University-College provided emotional support at a timely moment, and colleagues at Humber College, Toronto, have shared their intellectual aspirations in many hours of lively discussion. These include: John Elias, Melanie Chaparian, Wendy O'Brien-Ewara, Clive Cockerton, Jonathan Lavery, Colin Pearce, George Bragues, Ray Maher, and Jason Maclean. The philosophy department at Trent University along with Christine McKinnon and Christopher Tindale have also offered me their generous hospitality and helpful advice.

Brian Merrilees and the Northrop Frye Centre of Victoria University at the University of Toronto provided me with a quiet refuge for the final stage of rewriting.

Let me also thank my many friends at Waterloo and elsewhere: Debbie, Linda, Anne, Pamela, Jean, Carlos, Stuart, Jason, Meg, Carla, Tom, Neb, Nirmalya, Gary and Gary, Ken, Teena, Glenda, Laura, Paul, Gloria, Glen, Sheena, Burt, Malcolm, Craig, Corina, and Raymond.

Pour conclure, j'aimerais remercier ma femme, Marie-Andrée, et nos enfants pour leur patience et leur appui. Cela est peut-être intéressant mais aussi compliqué d'avoir un philosophe comme mari ou comme père. En acceptant mes longues absences de la maison, ils ont fait preuve d'une grande générosité.

Introduction

FREEDOM AND MORALITY

This book presents a moral theory of personal autonomy or individual freedom. Although freedom is often divorced from morality in modern discourse, I will argue that a closer study of pertinent issues reveals that serious human endeavor always has a moral aspect, that morality cannot be separated from freedom, and that only a moral person can be truly free.

One may advance, as the paradigm case of human freedom, the image of the good rebel, the person who rebels against an oppressive system for the sake of the good. Good rebels are conspicuously moral and conspicuously free. It is not simply their nonconformism we admire. We admire the intrinsic worth of their actions. Their nonconformism has a moral base. It is exerted in the direction of some recognizable good. While good rebels present epic examples of moral achievement, ordinary individuals provide more modest examples of the kind of good rebellion that must characterize any autonomous agent.

Modernity stresses values of authenticity, interiority, self-expression, personal autonomy, and individualism. The resulting emphasis on the self may monopolize our philosophy. Though we cannot ignore the realm of subjective experience, I will argue that notions about personal achievement must, at the same time, be based on objective moral criteria. Good rebels provide compelling examples of human endeavor because they satisfy objective standards of achievement, standards that are valid or true, not because the agent believes they are valid or true, but because they are, in some independent sense, reasonable and compelling.

Philosophical discourse about individual freedom is fraught with moral implications that go unrecognized, in part, because of an "official" view of morality that does not recognize the full extent of moral striving. If we hope to successfully govern ourselves, we must be moral. This is more

11

than just a pious platitude. To speak of an immoral autonomous individual is not just distasteful or morally repugnant. It is conceptually incoherent. We must disapprove of immoral acts, not only because they violate widely shared notions of goodness but also because, properly understood, they make us "unfree."

THE GOOD REBEL

Let us begin by looking at a specific example of "good rebellion." From 1960 to 1963 Stanley Milgram carried out a series of experiments on human obedience to authority. The experiments are old hat to social psychologists, but they provide a timeless and disturbing commentary on the human capacity for submissive behavior.[1]

An advertisement was placed in a local newspaper, asking lay volunteers to participate in scientific research on the effects of punishment on learning. Each volunteer was introduced to an actor playing the part of another volunteer. It was explained that one volunteer would be required to teach the other a simple task involving word associations. The subject and the stooge drew lots to determine who would be teacher and who would be pupil. The selection procedure was fixed so that the volunteer always became the teacher and the stooge always became the pupil. The stooge was then strapped to a chair in an adjacent room and hooked up to an electrical apparatus. The volunteer was led into another room with an electric shock generator.

Supervised by a distinguished-looking older man in a lab coat, the volunteer was asked to instruct the pupil in a simple method of word-pairing by means of a question-and-answer technique. Every time the pupil made a mistake at his assigned task, the teacher was to administer an electric shock by flicking a switch on the generator. The switches were arranged in groups from 15 volts to 450 volts, and the last ones were labeled: *Intense Shock, Extreme Intensity Shock, Danger: Severe Shock, XXX.* No shocks were, of course, administered, but everything possible was done to make it seem that they were.

At the very beginning of the experiment, the volunteer received a sample 45-volt shock. Each time he or she pressed a switch on the mock electric generator, a blue light flashed, a pilot light came on, there was an audible buzzing and the sound of various relay clicks, and the dial on a voltage meter swung to the right. Throughout the sessions, the volunteer could hear the voice of the pupil in the adjacent room, whose response to individual shocks progressed from mild grunts to painful groans, to agonized screams or shrieks, to dead silence. In some variations of the experiment, the victim would pound on the wall and complain of a heart condition. But to no avail.

Milgram discovered that almost two-thirds of the volunteers were willing to continue shocking the stooge whenever they were instructed to do so by the uniformed authority figure. As the experimenter summed up his findings: "Many subjects will obey the experimenter no matter how vehement the pleading of the person being shocked, no matter how painful the shocks seem to be, and no matter how much the victim pleads to be let out. . . . The extreme willingness of adults to go to almost any lengths on the command of an authority . . . constitutes the chief finding of the study."[2]

Although a majority of Milgram's subjects obeyed the unconscionable demands of authority, a smaller number refused to go along with the procedure. Call this type of subject the good rebel. Under conditions of extreme duress, some people refuse to break the moral code. They will "not inflict suffering on a helpless person who is neither harmful nor threatening to [themselves]."[3] They will not allow themselves to be controlled or manipulated by others. In displaying such independence and self-reliance, these good rebels supply us with a paradigmatic example of heroic human achievement. They stand out as an example par excellence of personal autonomy.

This is a book about personal autonomy. According to the philosopher Meir Dan-Cohen, "The core idea behind the ideal of autonomy is that of the self-governing person, who can effectuate his will and thus exercise control over his life."[4] One can trace the etymology of the word "autonomy" to the Greek concept of the self-governing city-state. Autonomy is "the condition of living according to laws one gives oneself." Or, expressed negatively, it is the condition of "not being under control of another."[5] Because autonomous agents are "self-directed," they are able to preserve their independence, to assume responsibility for their actions and, in this case, disobey the authority figure in a laboratory coat.

I want to base a theory of personal autonomy on the model of the good rebel. As Milgram insists, in such trying circumstances rebellion cannot be construed in exclusively negative terms: "[Disobedience] is not a negative conclusion, but has the character of an affirmative act, a deliberate bucking the tide."[6] Like Camus's rebel, Milgram's good rebels say "yes and no simultaneously."[7] They say no to the experimenter and yes to the victim; yes to morality and no to corrupt authority; yes to conscience and no to an oppressive society. Good rebels do not merely rebel *against* something. They replace the experimenter's commands with a higher scheme of personal values and act accordingly.[8]

Milgram, in a discussion of his experiment, distinguishes between "autonomous" agents and "systemic" or "agentic" agents,[9] between agents who are "self-directed"[10] and agents who define themselves "as an instrument for carrying out the wishes of others."[11] In criticizing the agentic model, Milgram denounces moral concepts of obedience, authority, loyalty, duty, and discipline, because they refer "to the adequacy with which a subordinate fulfils his socially defined role."[12] But to discard such moral virtues out of hand begs the question. One cannot make sense of moral achievement without making at least implicit reference to such notions. Good rebels *obey* the moral law. They submit to the *authority* of their individual conscience. They are *loyal* to a humanitarian creed. They champion their *duty* to the victim. They exhibit self-*discipline*, not by doing what the experimenter says, but by a public act of disobedience. It is not that these moral concepts are intrinsically flawed. It is that they are often misapplied and misconstrued.

Good rebels act under duress. There are at least two components to their rebellion: (1) they act on their own initiative; (2) they act in accordance with the good. And so it is with personal autonomy. There are, I will argue, two necessary conditions for the achievement of autonomy: (1) autonomous agents must govern themselves; (2) autonomous agents must achieve the good. Although autonomy does not always entail an overt act of rebellion against an evil authority, the good rebel typifies, in the most conspicuous way possible, the act of successful self-government. Autonomy becomes, in such trying circumstances, a heroic task.

According to one contemporary view, agents are autonomous if and only if they express their individuality. This is an integral and important component of personal autonomy. But it needs to be supplemented by a second requirement. I will argue that agents are autonomous if and only if they express their individuality *and* achieve the good. Autonomous agents must not only display individuality. They must be moral people. It is not enough to act on one's own initiative. One must, like the good rebel, act in the direction of an authentic good. Autonomy does not only mean doing what one wants to do. It also means satisfying objective criteria of excellence.

Autonomous agents must satisfy subjective and objective criteria of achievement. On the one hand, they must be true to themselves. On the other hand, they must do that which is really, truly good. Autonomy is both an expression of individuality and an expression of a recognizable good. Throughout the rest of this book, I mean to argue that this twofold notion of individual achievement provides the best explanation of human freedom.

One may try to reconcile modern accounts of freedom with the claims of morality by distinguishing between negative and positive theories of freedom. Roughly put, negative freedom is about removing obstacles to action. Positive freedom is about empowering or enabling an agent. An agent who enjoys negative freedom exists in an environment that offers no resistance to intended action; an agent who is positively free is able to act in accordance with his or her deepest aspirations. In this book I will argue that positive accounts of freedom are logically prior to negative accounts of freedom. Positive accounts of liberty provide a justification for negative liberty. Although immoral agents can enjoy negative liberty, they cannot be, in a positive sense, free.

CONTRIBUTING TO A TRADITION

Gaylin and Jennings have critiqued "a powerful and often arrogant culture of autonomy,"[13] which they identify as a "phase of decadent individualism"[14] But while their criticisms resonate with many of the concerns raised here, they propose a different conceptual solution. These authors argue that we must resist the "seductive voice of autonomy"[15] and "reach for a form of moral life richer than the one autonomy alone can supply."[16] Gaylin and Jennings argue that there is "a moral horizon beyond autonomy,"[17] but I want to argue that morality is not something separate and apart from freedom, something that limits or restricts the development or flourishing of human agents. Morality must be understood as an integral part of the freedom phenomenon itself.

The contemporary Canadian philosopher Charles Taylor explains: "Where . . . we are quite self-deceived, or utterly fail to discriminate properly the ends we seek, or have lost self-control, we can quite easily be doing what we want . . . without being free; indeed, we can be further entrenching our unfreedom."[18] This book may be understood as an attempt to elaborate extended philosophical support for this basic insight. Like Taylor, I argue for the objective nature of moral values and provide a sympathetic historical account of a morality of self-realization while criticizing reductionist views of ethics and any exclusive preoccupation with negative liberty. While Taylor's work is steeped in Hegel, Heidegger, and the Continental tradition, I have been personally inspired by Lawrence Haworth's work on autonomy, which finds its inspiration in John Dewey and American pragmatism. Pragmatism, in this original form, remains close to ordinary practice; it is fallibilistic, antiskeptical, nonanalytic, coherentist. It proposes a political and moral view that is, broadly speaking, communitarian in character.

Contemporary authors such as Alasdair MacIntyre, Michael Sandel,

Christine Swanton, Martha Nussbaum, Iris Murdoch, Nel Noddings, and John Keykes elaborate philosophical views that evince similar concerns. An "altruistic liberal" like Joseph Raz claims that freedom "is valuable only if it is exercised in pursuit of the good."[19] I want to go one step further and argue that freedom has an inalienable moral component. My views differ, in important ways, from those of some of these authors, but I have consulted their works at length and offer, in many ways, a similar perspective.

This book also consults the history of philosophy. The account of personal autonomy I advance is not a contemporary invention. Classical authors in the Western tradition typically argue that serious immorality is a fetter, a chain, something that enslaves us and makes us unfree. At the end of the *Republic,* for example, Socrates argues that the tyrant who is able to do whatever he wants is still not free.[20] Dragged this way and that by the many-headed monster of his appetites and the untamed lion of his renegade will, he is enslaved to his lower parts. Although Socrates' view of human nature seems excessively rationalistic, his claim that someone who does what he wants is not necessarily free is in line with the position taken here.

The concept of moral autonomy I invoke can be traced back, more precisely, to Dewey's threefold account of morality, to John Locke's romantic account of human individuality, to Kant's conception of the relationship between autonomy, morality, and rationality, to the account of natural law found in Aquinas and the Stoics, and, most centrally perhaps, to Aristotle's moral philosophy as expressed in the *Nicomachean Ethics.* In the later chapters of the book, I propose a positive account of successful self-government based on the Aristotelian conception of *akrasia* (weakness of will) and the Platonic notion of moral ignorance.

METAETHICS, NOT NORMATIVE ETHICS

Although I argue that human flourishing has an inalienable moral component, I do not offer a definitive account of human flourishing. If autonomy requires morality, we cannot determine who is autonomous unless we understand what morality, in a normative sense, entails. But this is a work of metaethics, not normative ethics. I do not defend any specific normative view, derive a conclusive set of moral rules, or elaborate a complete set of moral principles that will tell us the difference between right and wrong. I do not champion a Christian, an Islamic, or a Jewish morality, a secular humanist morality, a pacifist morality, a capitalist or a socialist morality, a

Stoic morality, and so on. I will not produce a normative account of morality here. If I am able to establish the connection between morality and autonomy, that will be more than enough.

Though I do not intend to present a normative account of morality, I will assume that ordinary moral feelings are, in the main, correct. We may be wrong about particular details, but decent human beings have a basic grasp of what is right and wrong. This may seem to presume too much. Social scientist James Wilson claims that modern Western society has lost confidence in morality.[21] Moral discourse is considered, at best, a tenuous endeavor. To insist on any robust, objective sense of morality has become an intellectual faux pas, an embarrassing admission of simplemindedness or naïveté. Ordinary citizens are "nervous or on guard when hearing someone speak of virtue."[22] When they speak of moral character, "they must do so privately, in whispers, lest they be charged with the grievous crime of being 'unsophisticated' or, if they press the matter, 'fanatics.'"[23]

Wilson attributes this crisis of moral confidence to the intellectual elements of modern civil society. Adepts of Marxian dialectics, Freudian psychoanalysis, secular humanism, and modern philosophy have done their best to talk us out of having strong moral opinions. Intellectuals have insisted, ad nauseam, "that morality has no basis in science or logic.[24] Philosophers have claimed that "no rational foundation can be given" for particular moral judgments.[25] Social scientists have presented morality as an atavism, a degeneration to an earlier type, a thinly disguised fundamentalism, or a social construct. "To defend morality is," it seems, "to defend the indefensible."[26]

Wilson sets out to rehabilitate the moral impulse. He wants "to help people recover the confidence with which they once spoke about virtue and morality[,] . . . to re-establish the possibility and the reasonableness of speaking frankly and convincingly about moral choices."[27] Situating his own work in a philosophical tradition that stretches from Aristotle to Aquinas to Adam Smith, Wilson argues that we have an innate moral sense including a pronounced capacity for sympathy, a theme developed by eighteenth-century British and Scottish thinkers like Butler, Hutcheson, Hume, and Smith. In the face of a fashionable relativism, he claims that this older view of human nature is the more correct one, that human beings have a common moral nature to which we all appeal when making moral judgments, and that the findings of modern science do not support a relativistic conception of morality. In the course of his study, he marshals an impressive array of evidence from biology and social science, from child psychology, evolutionary biology, and cultural anthropology.

Wilson is a social scientist rather than a philosopher. Although one may dispute his account of the origins of morality, he makes an important point: an awareness of goodness and evil is not something we have to argue our way to but something we begin with. We do not believe in Mount Everest because a philosopher somewhere has elaborated an argument proving its existence. We believe in Mount Everest because Mount Everest is there. In a similar sense, morality is there. It exists as an immovable feature of any human landscape. Even in an age of pluralism, there is still residual agreement about the basic issues of morality.

Modern authors tend to overemphasize normative disagreement about morality. Montaigne assures us that the "The murder of children, the murder of fathers, traffic in stolen goods, there is nothing, in short, so extreme, that it cannot be found as a received custom of some nation."[28] William Graham Sumner, the American social Darwinist, goes so far as to proclaim that "mores can make anything right."[29] But is this really so?

William Gass invokes a paradigmatic case of immorality.[30] Suppose someone were to lure a cooperative stranger into striking distance with requests for help, knock him over the head with an ax, tie him up on a spit, and leave him baking in an oven while he, the malefactor, goes off to play poker. We can all appreciate the wickedness of this act, whatever our ethnic background, our religion, our political persuasion. Indeed, this kind of act is so blatantly immoral that attempts by philosophers to explicate its wrongness seem wholly beside the point. As Gass expresses the thought: "Cases, like that of the obliging stranger, are cases [we can] call clear. They have the characteristic of moral transparency, and they comprise the core of our moral experience. When we try to explain why they are instances of good or bad, of right or wrong, we sound comic, as anybody does who gives elaborate reasons for the obvious, especially when such reasons are so shamefaced before reality, so miserably beside the point."[31]

One of the most serious objections to any ethical theory is that it contradicts commonly held moral intuitions. Experience teaches us that there are moral landmarks, examples, principles, sentiments, or dispositions that cannot be ignored. These inalienable features of human experience are self-evident. Small numbers of subjects may be so damaged, mentally and morally, that they do not recognize the most basic norms of human civility. Perhaps they can be cured. Perhaps they cannot. One way or the other, this moral deafness has no philosophical merit. In this book I will not argue for a specific normative account of morality, but I will assume that we can appeal to a basic fund of human wisdom on moral matters.

Even if one disputes the possibility of consensus on normative manners, the relationship between morality and freedom still holds. People who embrace different moral views advance different views of freedom precisely *because* their moral views influence and predetermine their views of liberty. As we shall see, disagreement about freedom is often rooted, on a deeper level, in disagreement about morality.

The task of this book is inevitably unsatisfying. This project sets the scene for a different kind of discussion: a discussion about the normative content of morality, about human achievement, about the kinds of life that are worth living. I make a more modest point. I want to argue that morality and freedom are inextricably linked. We must investigate the normative nature of morality, not only to be moral but also in order to be free. Liberty, properly understood, presses upon us the urgency of the moral task. If I were to advance a particular normative view, this would necessitate a different set of arguments and a different focus.

THE PLAN OF THE BOOK

In this book I will argue that good rebellion is a model par excellence for autonomy. This argument can be unpacked into three claims: a claim about rationality, a claim about morality, and a claim about rebellion. So the book is divided into three parts. The first part, entitled *Rationality*, argues that the good rebel, or more generally the good person, is a rational agent. The second part, entitled *Morality*, argues that individual freedom or personal autonomy is a moral achievement. And the third and final part, entitled *Rebellion*, argues that rebellion, or more specifically good rebellion, offers an illuminating account of human freedom.

In making the case that moral agents are rational, I will argue for a specific view of rationality. One widespread conception of rationality has its origins in an economic conception of humanity and in a familiar contractarianism. If, however, we do not think of rationality in terms of the utility calculus, but as the practice of a wide-ranging coherence, it will be easier to accept that morality is, in its own right, a form of rationality.

In arguing that autonomous agents must be moral, I will in turn invoke a specific conception of morality. According to one popular view that has its historical origins in Puritan theology, morality is an external constraint on a wayward human nature. There is, however, a different view that has it origins in Aristotle, the Stoics, Augustine and Aquinas and is taken up by later thinkers like Locke, Rousseau, Dewey, and Taylor. Viewed from the perspective of these authors, morality is a form of self-realization. It is not an obstacle but an aid to individual human flourishing. I will argue that if this traditional account of moral accomplishment is accurate, we cannot be free in a positive sense without being moral.

The notion of rebellion has been maligned in traditional literature and uncritically celebrated in popular culture. I will argue that authentic rebellion incorporates moral aspirations. It entails a resolute exercise of the will in the direction of the good. Without morality, rebellion is unfulfilling. Faced with human imperfections, our slaveries and our idolatries, good rebellion provides a fitting archetype of human flourishing.

Good rebellion is perhaps the supreme moral achievement. Good rebels do the right thing under duress. If, however, good rebellion necessitates morality, negative liberty, properly understood, is a necessary precondition for moral achievement. I will argue that we can best secure a strong liberal defense of negative liberty if we construe negative liberty as a means to personal autonomy, understood in moral terms.

RATIONALITY, MORALITY, AND AUTONOMY

The first part of my argument reduces to the Kantian claim that autonomous agents must be both moral and rational. I will argue that there is a necessary link between autonomy, morality and rationality. These three terms are not, however, synonymous. They refer to different kinds of things. In what sense then, can they refer to the very same agent?

Philosophers, down through history, have dealt with similar problems. Mediaeval metaphysicians, for example, argued that the transcendental predicates of existence, unity, truth, and goodness all referred to the same thing. If something had existence, it had to have some kind of unity. It also had to be true. (It was not an illusion, a mere deception.) And it had to be valuable. (In a metaphysical sense, existence is the most valuable attribute, more valuable than non-existence.) But how could four different predicates—*ens, unum, verum,* and *bonum*—all apply to the same thing? Philip the Chancellor initiated a Scholastic tradition when he argued that the transcendental predicates were extensionally equivalent but intensionally or conceptually distinct.[32] They were different ways of thinking about the very same thing. We might offer a similar account of the relationship between autonomy, morality and rationality. These three concepts may be understood as providing three different outlooks on human action.

The terms "autonomy," "morality" and "rationality" signify, in metaphysical terms, a modal distinction. They do not describe a substance or a thing. They describe a particular kind of human behavior.[33] The same act may, however, be moral, rational, and free. Suppose I pay the cashier at the grocery store two dollars for a carton of milk. We might say that this is a rational act. It would be irrational to pay the cashier 3 million dollars for a carton of milk. Or if I were to get on all fours and bark like a dog, that would be irrational. Paying two dollars is a rational act. But it is also a moral act. It would be immoral to steal the milk, to grab the carton and run out of the store without paying. To pay two dollars is to fulfill my moral obligations, to pay the store owner what I owe. But the same act is also free. Although I have satisfied my ethical obligations, no one held a gun to my head and forced me to pay two dollars to the cashier. I did it voluntarily, on my own initiative. It follows that the act of paying two dollars for a carton of milk is simultaneously rational, moral, and free.

I will argue that autonomy, morality, rationality are three different characteristics we can apply to the conduct of a fully autonomous agent. These distinctions come about because we look at the same act from three different perspectives, not because we look at three different things. Such distinctions are logical rather than existential in nature. Traditional Thomists differentiate between distinctions made according to the mind *(secundum rationem)* and those made according to reality *(secundum rem)*. When we differentiate between autonomy, morality, and rationality, we are making a distinction in the former sense, *secundum rationem*. The distinction resides in the mind or the understanding. We can *think* about the acts of an autonomous agent in three different ways. But, as Dewey points out, the acts themselves make up one seamless unified whole.[34] The reality itself is one.

Nietzsche, in the *Genealogy of Morals*, argues that there is "only a perspective seeing, only a perspective knowing."[35] Any assertion, truthful or otherwise, must always be identified with a specific human perspective. We may emphasize perspective while disputing the relativism of contemporary perspectivists.[36] Different perspectives on reality may provide equally truthful and informative accounts of reality. For instance, although the concepts of "rationality," "morality," or "autonomy" provide us with three alternative descriptions of the same act, all three descriptions may be equally truthful and informative.

Suppose three observers look at a small red circle. The first says it is red; the second says that it is a circle; the third says it is small. The color "red," the shape "circle," and the size "small" are all different features or properties of the same thing. So each statement is equally true and informative. In the same way, I will argue that the conduct of a fully autonomous agent may be simultaneously rational, moral, and free. This is true even if, in the sense already explained, these terms have different meanings.

To argue for perspectivism is to argue that the human mind cannot take in reality all at once. Because of our position within the world, we view events from one particular position or angle. Reality unfolds one aspect at a time. I do not argue, like Parmenides, for any indivisible monism.

Conceptually, we can break an act or an event into parts. We can view it from different perspectives. It is not that these perspectives are all the same. It is that they logically entail one another. In the case of an autonomous agent, we have behavior which is simultaneously rational, moral, and free. This behavior must be rational and moral, for rationality and morality are necessary and sufficient conditions for autonomy.

To assert that the concepts "rationality," "morality," and "autonomy" are *necessarily* connected is not to posit a physical connection between three separate objects. It is to posit a logical connection between three different ways of viewing the world. These three concepts allow us to isolate different features of human conduct. They provide three different measuring sticks that we can use to evaluate behavior. Rational acts are consistent with the nature of the world. Moral acts are consistent with the moral law or with ethical aspirations. Free acts are consistent with the will of the subject. Human subjects may then succeed in three different ways: their conduct may be rational, moral, or free. And they may fail in three different ways: their conduct may be irrational, immoral or unfree. In so much as autonomy entails both rationality and morality, it may be considered as the acme of human achievement.

Freedom, the ability to exercise one's will, is a precondition for rationality and morality. A person who is not—to any degree—free cannot act rationally or morally. Rational or moral actions must originate within the agent in some rational or moral faculty. The actions of agents who lack all freedom do not originate in the individual. They are like stones kicked this way and that by external forces. They do not act on their own initiative; they are acted upon by the world outside themselves. So they cannot act in a rational or a moral manner.

Individual freedom is a necessary precondition for rationality and morality, but I will argue for the more controversial claim that rationality and morality are necessary preconditions for freedom. Irrationality and immorality are foreign forces that imprison the agent. Human beings inevitably strive not just to be rational but, with equal urgency, to be moral. It is not that human agents are always moral. It is that human beings are evaluators. They consciously evaluate action. They admire or despise, praise or critique, censure or encourage their own and other people's behavior. There may be serious disagreement about the substantive content of morality but the very act of evaluation presupposes some objective basis for value. Moral judgments are implicit in the types of evaluations all functioning human beings make. If we separate personal evaluations from moral evaluations, this is an artificial distinction. The act of evaluation that underlies human striving presupposes rationality and, more importantly, morality.

FREE WILL

This is a book about personal autonomy, not a metaphysical treatise on free will. Nonetheless, hard-core determinism seems to take the bite out of personal autonomy. George Santayana protests: "Let it not be said that the zest of life is gone when we know that all is fixed. Do we read a story with less interest because the last page was written long ago?"[37] But the problem with determinism is not that future events are fixed. The problem is that if all our actions and choices are predetermined, we do not choose for ourselves. Genes, sexual drives, childhood experiences, societal expectations, the laws of physics, or blind inexorable destiny do all the work of choosing. The self is a channel through which these outside factors work their irresistible influences. To speak of autonomy or *self*-government is fundamentally misguided.

Santayana claims that the man who knows that all his actions are predetermined can still rejoice in "what he is to accomplish."[38] But the man whose actions are determined by forces outside of himself accomplishes nothing. The word "accomplishment" is, in this instance, a misnomer if not an oxymoron. If we are to take charge of our lives in any meaningful way, our choices must somehow derive from ourselves. We must be able to initiate action, to deliberate and choose in some meaningful way.

There are, in any case, two serious problems with hard-core determinism. Firstly, it does not seem to be a verifiable hypothesis. There are many different constraints on our actions, but none of them militates decisively against the notion of free will. Even if I am not totally free to do anything, I do seem to enjoy a certain freedom. As William James points out, we do have the subjective experience of freedom.[39] We feel that the future is open and that past events could have been different.

Secondly, and more importantly, we cannot make sense of human endeavor unless we assume that individual human beings can, in some important sense, decide for themselves. Hard-core determinism bears little relation to the way we actually live our lives. We treat people *as if they were free*. We say that Susan is an autonomous individual, that Tom is a conformist, that Nirmalya does what he wants, that Alexander caves in under pressure, that Paul is a rugged individualist. We criticize those who are enslaved to passions, appetites, individuals, or ideologies. We want to master our own faults, to decide for ourselves, to take charge of our destinies. In our daily lives, we continue to presuppose the existence of free will.

The modern age is an age of individualism. Other ages were not. Paul Feyerabend writes that ancient peoples did not recognize individuality. They saw themselves as "exchange station[s] of material and spiritual, but always objective causes," existing without an "I," without an ego. In their literature, "Such an I is neither mentioned nor is it noticed. It is nowhere to be found." Their texts depict an individual who is a mere "assemblage of limbs, . . . a puppet set in motion by outside forces such as enemies, social circumstances, feelings."[40]

Such ideas, whatever their historical validity, present an instructive foil to modern beliefs. In everyday life we assume, unless we have evidence the contrary, that agents are able to choose for themselves. Their acts are not fully predetermined, either sociologically, psychologically, or through some divine or material agency. There is an "I" that chooses, directs and implements action. In light of such strongly held convictions, metaphysical arguments about the existence of freedom seem beside the point.

A belief in freedom is itself a liberating force. If we are free, we are responsible. We must undertake, not with solemnity but with seriousness, the work of freedom—choosing, deliberating, and initiating action. We must accord one another the dignity that can only be accorded to free-willing selves. It is up to us to make life worth living. Perhaps this is reason enough to reject determinism. For the purposes of the present discussion, I will assume that as human beings we possess some residue of free will without developing further any kind of metaphysical argument.

Part I:
Rationality

1

Morality and Rationality

I will argue that the autonomous agent must be rational and moral. Irrationality naturally springs to mind as something that restricts freedom. If human beings are, as the traditional formula has it, "rational animals," seriously irrational subjects have lost touch with their own nature. They are no longer themselves. In obeying an irrational will, they are losing themselves in neurosis, in meaningless, self-defeating, or inauthentic behavior.

Serious irrationality destroys personal identity. In curing neurosis, we restore personal identity. We help afflicted subjects be themselves. To be autonomous is to act in accordance with one's own will. Those who are insane have, however, lost sight of their own will. Their personal identity has been obscured and undermined by serious irrationality. So they cannot be free. To the extent that they are less than rational, they lack autonomy.

In this section I explore the relationship of rationality to autonomy. If, however, we hope to produce an account of rationality that is compatible with a moral account of autonomy, we must first consider the relationship of rationality to morality. In this section I will demonstrate that rationality is compatible with the practice of morality, and that autonomy, construed as a moral ideal, entails the practice of rationality.

Contemporary philosophers often question the compatibility of morality and rationality. David Gauthier informs us that: "The reconciliation of morality with rationality is the central problem of modern moral philosophy."[1] David Schmidtz laments that "we have taken the 'why be moral?' question so seriously for so long."[2] Kurt Baier, who finds moral talk "rather repugnant," claims that "the very best reasons are required" if we hope to establish "the necessity and justifiability of morality."[3] Contemporary authors such as Gauthier, Schmidtz, Baier, J. L. Mackie, Jan Narveson, Peter Vallentyne, Peter Danielson, and Paul Viminitz set out to demonstrate the

27

rationality of morality.[4] Let us consider the standard argument. After demonstrating what is wrong with this account, I will try to demonstrate, in a
different way, why rationality requires morality.

The Utility Model

Although philosophers such as Mackie, Gauthier, Narveson, et al. claim to
reconcile morality and rationality, their focus is, in fact, much narrower.
They do not want to reconcile all conceptions of morality with all conceptions of rationality. Rather, they want to reconcile a *social* view of morality
with an *economic* interpretation of rationality. If they define rationality in
terms of self-interest, they define morality in terms of social restrictions on
individual actions. Rationality means maximizing the satisfaction of one's
preferences. Morality means respecting one's duties and obligations to others. But defining morality and rationality in these terms has troubling consequences. If rationality means pursuing my own self-interest and morality
means (loosely put) caring for the interests of others, why should I, as a
rational (self-interested) agent, act morally? This is the question that has
preoccupied these contemporary philosophers.

Members of what I will call this "why-you-should-be-moral" school
claim that they can demonstrate that it is in the agent's self-interest to act
morally. Properly construed, morality is a profitable enterprise, a paying
proposition. Even if we were nonmoral beings, we could "jump-start"
morality solely on the basis of self-interest. John Rawls, in a different debate, provides a similar argument in favor of justice.[5]

These authors want to provide an amoral justification for morality.
They want to argue that someone who is neither moral or immoral has
good reasons for acting in a moral manner. If agents already have a preference for morality, then, obviously, they can best satisfy their preferences
by acting morally. The reverse is also true. Immoral agents will only be
able to satisfy their (immoral) preferences by acting immorally. If then we
wish to determine whether morality is rational, we need to appeal to an
objective judge, to an agent who does not lean one way or the other, to an
agent in a premoral (and a preimmoral) state. Philosophers in the why-be-
moral school address their arguments to this kind of hypothetical amoral
judge. It is generally assumed that if we can convince an amoral but rational agent that it is in his or her self-interest to act morally, we will have
secured the rationality of morality.

Philosophers in the why-be-moral tradition rely on a standard formula for rational decision-making. Suppose an agent must decide whether or not to do X. If we want to determine the rationality of his or her decision, we can draw up a decision-making matrix, map out possible outcomes, and award utiles to these outcomes. A utile is a measure of the quantity of individual happiness, pleasure or preference-satisfaction procured. Rational agents always maximize the number of utiles procured; that is, they will always choose those outcomes which promise to produce the most utiles, those outcomes with the highest "expected utility."

Consider a specific example. Suppose that doing X gives me great pleasure. But suppose that doing X also harms other people. Should I do X? We might schematically represent my choice as shown in table 1.

Table 1. Should I Do Immoral Action X?

Possible Course of Action	Expected Utility to Agent
Immorality: Go ahead and do X	25
Morality:	(0 + -5 =) -5

The precise numbers used are arbitrary. The idea is to acquire a general overview of the situation. As the table indicates, if I do X, I procure for myself a substantial amount of pleasure (+25 utiles). If I do not do X, I lose this pleasure (0 utiles) and experience a certain discomfort at this loss (-5 utiles). Should I do X? Rationality indicates that I should, for rationality (on this model) always tends toward the maximization of utiles. Morality, on the other hand, indicates that I should not do X. I should refrain from harming other people. In these circumstances, then, morality seems to be an irrational venture.

Philosophers in the why-be-moral tradition hope to demonstrate that, appearances to the contrary, morality is a rational (or self-interested) endeavor. The only way they can do this is by demonstrating that the numbers in the previous table are somehow mistaken. The moral option "not doing X" must somehow possess more utiles than the immoral option "doing X." Authors usually attempt to show that this is the case by expanding the original decision-matrix to represent, not only the choices of the isolated individual, but the choices of the other members of society.

I may choose to be moral or not moral, and other members of society are faced with the same choice. If I can decide whether or not I will morally cooperate with other people, other people can decide whether they will morally cooperate with me. The expanded decision-making matrix will be as in table 2.

Table 2. What about the Actions of the Rest of Society?

	Morality Everyone else cooperates (Everyone else refrains) from doing X)	Immorality: No one else cooperates (Everyone does X)
Morality I cooperate (I refrain from doing X	-5 + 6 + 15 = 16 [A1]	-5 + 0 – 25 = -30 [A2]
Immorality I do not cooperate (I do X)	25 – 10 + 15 = 30 [B1]	25 + 0 – 25 = 0 [B2]

We are left with a Prisoner's Dilemma. Consider the possible outcomes:

A1] I refrain from doing X and everyone else refrains from doing X. This is essentially the same situation as in table 1, except that my discomfort at my loss of the pleasure (-5 utiles) may be offset by the pleasure I get from some strong sense of social approval (+6 utiles). (A moral society commends moral actions and the people that do them.) I will also enjoy the peace and security that comes from living in a moral society where my rights will be respected by other people (+15 utiles). This results in a total score of +16 utiles.

A2] I personally refrain from doing X while everyone else does X. This is the worst possible outcome. To begin with, I receive no moral approbation (0 utiles). (A society of immoral people does not praise virtuous actions.) Secondly, I experience the loss of pleasure (-5 utiles). And thirdly, *comble de malheurs*, I find myself living in a state of nature, a lawless situation where no one fulfills his or her moral obligations, where life is unregulated, brutal, nasty, and short (-25 utiles). This results in a net loss, for a score of -30 utiles.

B1] I do X and everyone else refrains from doing X. This is the best possible outcome. I receive 25 utiles of pleasure (+25 utiles). I live, however, in a lawful society (+15 utiles). If I am discovered I will not only suffer the moral disapprobation of my colleagues. I will be punished. The riskiness of the act makes me somewhat nervous (-10 utiles). This results in a total score of +30 utiles.

B2] I do X in a society where everyone else does X. I still receive my 25 utiles of pleasure (+25 utiles); I receive no moral disapprobation (0 utiles) but am forced to live in a lawless state (-25 utiles) for a total score of 0 utiles.

These different outcomes can be ranked as in table 3.

Table 3. Ranking Outcomes

Rank	Outcome	Expected Utility
1	[B1]: An immoral agent in a moral society	+30
2	[A1]: A moral agent in a moral society	+16
3	[B2]: An immoral agent in an immoral society	0
4	[A2]: A moral agent in an immoral society	-30

Outcome B1 is the best. If I can be immoral in a moral society, I will procure the largest number of utiles. If, however, we all aim at outcome B1, if we all do X hoping no one else does X, we will end up with the second-worst outcome, B2; that is, we will end up living in a society where everyone is immoral. There is a better way. Suppose each of us agrees to refrain from immorality just so long as everyone else agrees to refrain from immorality. If everyone agrees, we will end up with outcome A1; that is, we will end up acting morally in a moral society. But this is the second-best outcome. Considered from this wider viewpoint, morality is then a rational option. If we all agree to be moral agents together, this will lead to the maximization of private utility. All-round morality is better than all-round immorality, for outcome A1 is better than outcome B2.

CHEATING

Philosophers in the why-be-moral tradition argue that social cooperation is a paying proposition, that it is in our interest to be moral just so long as everyone else is moral. But the argument has a fatal flaw. Individually, the best way to maximize utility is not to refrain from immorality while living in a moral society but to practice immorality without getting caught. Master maximizers will make a great pretense of morality so as to be admitted into the company of the moral. But once admitted into their company, they will act immorally whenever they can get away with it.

So the utility model establishes that the rational course of action is not to be a moral cooperator, but a patient, skillful cheater. When the chance comes, the rational agent will, metaphorically and literally, make a killing. The why-be-moral argument provides a rationale, not for morality, but for cheating. It does not teach us that it is rational to be moral or to desist from crime. It teaches us to commit crime in such a way that we cannot get caught.

The why-be-moral model does not provide a definitive barrier to immorality. If you are never caught, crime is to your own advantage. This is hardly breaking news. Antiphon, the ancient Greek Sophist, distinguishes between the laws of men *(nomos)* and the laws of nature *(physis)*. The man who follows the laws of nature ignores the restrictions of morality, relentlessly pursuing his own advantage, fulfilling his own self-interested desires. Antiphon suggests a strategy for social success: "A man will be just, then, in a way most advantageous to himself if, in the presence of witnesses, he holds the laws of the city in high esteem, and in the absence of witnesses, when he is alone, [he holds] those of nature [in high esteem]."[6] In other words, the successful agent will be moral in public, but privately he will do whatever is in his interest, for "he who breaks the rules . . . and escapes detection . . . incurs no shame or penalty."[7] So the master maximizer will be an immoral person who compounds his or her own immorality by acting in a hypocritical manner!

One may try to shore up the utility model by instituting sanctions against cheaters. Thomas Hobbes recommends setting up a sovereign, an enforcer who has the power to punish anyone who does not refrain from acting immorally. If the penalties for acting immorally are severe enough, they will provide an effective incentive against such action. But here again, punishment only makes a difference *if you get caught.* Policing systems can never be foolproof. There will always be individuals who can escape punishment. Master criminals have friends in high places; they pay people off; they have charming personalities; they are unusually intelligent; they know things no one else knows; they have more powerful weapons; they school themselves in the art of deception; and so on. For such individuals, morality will be an irrational venture.

Hobbes's solution to the problem of cheating is, in the long run, rather unattractive. In modern liberal society, we value individual liberty. But the more individual liberty there is, the easier it will be for cheaters to break the law. Even if a police state could deter all crime (it cannot), instituting a police state is not, it seems, a good way to secure a prosperous liberal society.

Gauthier proposes a different strategy. Rather than instituting a police force, we might internalize the policing agency. If we inculcate in every citizen a clear sense of right and wrong, individual agents can police themselves. If, for example, I feel guilty every time I do X, this will seriously detract from the utility of X. The more stringent my conscience, the smaller the expected utility of X. If I feel good about myself every time I refrain from doing X, this will add to the expected utility of not doing X. And if people police themselves, this will avoid expense and trouble. There will be no need for an authoritarian policing apparatus. And it will ensure that anyone who cheats will get caught. Even if the civil authorities do not catch them, they will be plagued by a bad conscience. They will, so to speak, punish themselves.

There are, however, two problems with Gauthier's approach. To begin with, we cannot inculcate a robust sense of right and wrong in *every* individual. In any society there will always be criminals, sociopaths, cheaters. Secondly, and more importantly, intelligent agents, on this analysis, will come to see the cultivation of conscience as irrational, as something that interferes with the maximization of utility. They may pretend to have a conscience, but privately, they will regard conscience as a serious defect in human nature, a radical softness of the brain, a sissyness, something for the weak and the gullible. They will, like Machiavelli's prince, come to think of morality as a way of regulating, to their own advantage, the behavior of the credulous.

It has, rightly or wrongly, been suggested that modern-day followers of Leo Strauss take precisely this attitude toward morality.[8] Why-be-moral philosophers, on the other hand, want to argue for the rationality of morality. And yet, in mounting a defense, they demonstrate the irrationality, the unintelligence, of the moral life. Gauthier's "internal policing agency" may provide an efficient barrier to immoral acts by some, but gifted agents will be able to overcome this kind of social conditioning and act immorally. They will, of course, support a public morality. They want, after all, to live in a moral society. But secretly, they will regard conscience as a defect in human nature. They will do their best to cultivate *other* people's consciences while divesting themselves of any residual sense of right and wrong.

ANOMALOUS CASES

The why-be-moral argument provides, at best, an inadequate defense of morality. And there are other anomalies. The utility numbers attributed to the outcomes in table 2 accord with orthodox theory. In individual cases, however, specific factors may be inoperative. Suppose I am going to be dead in five minutes. The threat of some future punishment no longer carries any weight. Suppose I am mortally wounded, I have a shotgun in my hands, and I have just the faintest inclination to shoot a bystander. Would this be a rational thing to do? Suppose the decision-matrix is as in table 4.

Table 4. A Near-Death Decision

Possible Course of Action	Expected Utility
Immorality: Shoot the innocent bystander	$+1 - 0 - 0 = +1$
Morality: Refrain from shooting	$-1 + 0 + 0 = -1$

Consider the two outcomes. If I shoot the bystander, I will feel just a hint of momentary pleasure: +1 utile. The threat of punishment is nil (0 utiles). My life is slipping away at this very instant. Even if this act leads to anarchy and ultimately to a state of nature (which seems highly unlikely), I will not be around in any case. If everyone in society embraces immorality, this will not produce any personal disutility for me (0 utiles). So the total utility procured from the act of shooting the innocent bystander is: +1 utile -0 utiles -0 utiles = +1 utile.

If I refrain from shooting this innocent bystander, I will experience a momentary regret at losing this pleasure: -1 utile. The promise of moral approbation is nil (0 utiles). I will not be around to receive the approbation of my fellow citizens. And again, it means nothing to me if society returns or does not return to a state of nature (0 utiles). If then I refrain from shooting the bystander, this will result in a total score of -1 utile + 0 utiles + 0 utiles = -1 utile. If rationality means nothing more than the maximization of utility, it would be irrational to refrain from shooting the innocent bystander. In this specific case, morality is irrational.

Or consider a case of extreme pleasure. If I derive enormous pleasure from the commission of an immoral act, the penalties associated with moral condemnation, punishment, or banishment to a state of nature will pale in comparison to the utility of the crime. Suppose Mr. Malice hates Mr. Nice with an all-consuming passion. He wants to destroy him. This is his only goal in life. With every ounce of his twisted being, this is all he yearns to do. He does not care if he is punished, he is willing to sacrifice everything, if he can actually kill him. We might represent the circumstance as in table 5.

Table 5. Killing Mr. Nice?

Possible Course of Action	Expected Utility
Immorality: Kill Mr. Nice	10,000
Morality: Refrain from killing Mr. Nice	-10,000

If Mr. Malice commits the murder, he will experience vast amounts of the most intense pleasure: +10,000 utiles. Mr. Malice does not care about anything else. Threats of punishment, of moral condemnation, or of a return to the state of nature have no dissuasive force. If, on the other hand, Mr. Malice does not kill Mr. Nice, he will suffer an extremely frustrating loss of pleasure: -10,000 utiles. In these circumstances, immorality will procure 20,000 more utiles of pleasure for Mr. Malice than morality. If Mr. Malice is a rational individual, he will commit the murder. To restrain himself would be (on this account) irrational.

On the why-be-moral model, rationality and morality do not always coincide. Suppose I can steal five hundred dollars *without getting caught*. If we want to defend the rationality of morality, we must demonstrate that, even in this kind of circumstance, it makes sense to refrain from immorality. If, however, there is no chance of being caught, there can be no threat of punishment or moral condemnation. It is implausible to suggest that one act of petty thievery will precipitate a return to the state of nature. Should I commit the robbery? Consider the corresponding decision-matrix in table 6.

Table 6. Stealing without Getting Caught

Possible Course of Action	Expected Utility
Immorality: Steal $500	10
Morality Refrain from stealing $500	-5

If I take the money, I procure 10 utiles. (Money is an extremely useful commodity.) If I do not take the money, I will regret this loss for a total of -5 utiles. Insomuch as I am a rational agent, I will not experience pangs of conscience, for I will have seen through the imposture of conventional morality. If then I am rational individual, I will steal the money. In these circumstances, when we can commit crime without getting caught, why-be-moral philosophers cannot demonstrate why it would be rational to refrain from immorality, for dissuasive factors in the utility model are no longer operative.[9] One might argue that criminals always get caught, but this seems unrealistic in the extreme. The best police forces cannot capture all of the criminals all of the time.

IS GOOD REBELLION IRRATIONAL?

Or consider the good rebel. Good rebels act morally in an evil society. They resolutely pursue a virtuous course of action in a society that harasses, oppresses, and severely punishes moral behavior. Uncooperative subjects in the Milgram experiment had to brook social disapproval, but the price for good rebellion may be much higher. Consider Jesus and Socrates, two figures who exemplify, for many people, the notion of good rebellion. Although these historical figures embody the moral impulse in its highest form, they rebelled against their respective societies. They championed, with heroic commitment, unpopular views. And what was their reward? They were summarily executed by their contemporaries.

On trial, with their lives at stake, Jesus and Socrates did not act in their own self-interest. A moral commitment to a higher ethical vision made each man embrace his own destruction. They both clearly recognized the danger they were in. And yet, for moral reasons, they refused to repudiate their moral commitment. They chose morality over self-preservation. Does this mean that they acted in an irrational manner?

The utility-maximization approach cannot demonstrate the rationality of good rebellion. Suppose you live in a Nazi society. What are you going to do with the frightened Jewish waif who bangs at your door in the middle of the night? If the authorities discover you assisting her, you will be tortured and killed. If you turn her in, you will be handsomely rewarded. (There is a bounty on "Jewish vermin.") What would the rational agent do? The arguments of the why-be-moral school are of little help here. The decision-matrix represented in table 7 depicts this particularly trying circumstance.

Table 7. Helping Jews in a Nazi Society

Possible Courses of Action	Expected Utility
Immorality Turn in the Jewish fugitive to the police: Conform to an evil society	$5 + 5 + 100 = +100$
Morality: Help her escape: Break with convention for a good cause	$-5 - 5 - 100 = -110$

If you act immorally, you will receive social approval (+5 utiles) , a substantial sum of money (+5 utiles) and, most importantly, you will not be molested by the Nazis (+100 utiles). If you act morally, you will suffer the loss of social approval (-5 utiles) and money (-5 utiles) but, most importantly, you will live in terror (-100 utiles). On this account, the rational agent will turn in the fugitive.

We could try to salvage the rationality of the moral course of action by arguing that any humane individual who did not help the fugitive would be plagued by a guilty conscience. If the disutility of living with a guilty conscience for the rest of your life is large enough, say -500 utiles, this would overshadow the positive aspects of such an immoral course of action (-500 utiles +110 utiles = -390 utiles) and make the moral choice (-110 utiles) the better of two bad options. But this approach is not available to authors in the why-be-moral school, for they address their arguments to amoral agents, agents without any conscience. The way they set up the problem, we must show that morality is rational by convincing agents who are not yet moral that it is in their self-interest to save the fugitive. This seems impossible. One only develops a guilty conscience if one embraces morality. So the amoral agent can eschew morality, derive the benefits of an immoral course of action, and avoid the immense pangs of regret a moral person would feel.

To argue that anyone who turns in the Jewish fugitive to the Nazis will inevitably feel guilty is to suggest that morality is an essential part of human nature, but this smacks of metaphysics. Philosophers in the why-be-moral school avoid any appeal to traditional notions of human nature or the natural law. They want to develop a contractarian rather than a metaphysical defense of morality. But the contractarian model, which derives from Hobbes, cannot provide an argument for heroic, self-sacrificing morality. On this account, morality is a social convention that only makes sense if you profit from the enterprise.[10]

The utility maximization model cannot secure the rationality of morality when it really counts. It can only show us that morality is rational when it is in our self-interest. If, however, we only act morally when it is profitable, when it is in our self-interest, we are acting on prudential rather than moral motives. Moral agents choose the moral course of action, not because it is in their self-interest, but because it is the moral course of action. If we hope to provide a watertight defense of morality, we must be able to show that even in these difficult cases, it is rational to act in a moral manner.

HEAVEN AND HELL

The contractarian model of moral choice is a secular reworking of earlier theological models of Heaven and Hell. Viewed from the perspective of a Heaven-and-Hell ethics, the decision to be moral or not to be moral can be represented by the decision-matrix in table 8.

Table 8. Heaven and Hell

Possible Course of Action	Expected Utility
Morality: Refrain from all immoral acts	End up in Heaven $0 - 13 + 4 + \infty = \infty$
Immorality: Do not refrain	End up in Hell $15 - 12 - \infty = -\infty$

On this account, the utility of Heaven and the disutility of Hell are infinite. This changes the decision-making process. If we refrain from doing immoral acts, we lose the pleasure of such acts (0 utiles); we suffer emotional discomfort at the loss of this pleasure (-13 utiles); we feel a sense of moral worth (+4 utiles); and, most importantly, we go to Heaven ($+\infty$ utiles) for a total expected utility of $+\infty$ utiles. If, on the other hand, we decide to perform an immoral act, we gain the resultant pleasure (+15 utiles); we may suffer from a sense of moral failure (-12 utiles); and most importantly, we go to Hell ($-\infty$ utiles), for a total expected utility of $-\infty$ utiles. But an outcome of $+\infty$ utiles is better than an outcome of $-\infty$. So the Heaven-and-Hell model secures the rationality of morality. On the religious model, a rational agent must always act in a moral manner.

Traditional arguments for religious belief were intended as a buttress to morality. Anselm proposes his ontological proof for the existence of

God as a rebuttal to the fool who says in his heart: "There is no God."[11] But the fool in question is not preoccupied with metaphysical questions. The issue is moral. As we read in Psalm 92:

> A senseless man knows not, nor does a fool understand this.
> Though the wicked flourish like grass and all evildoers thrive,
> They are destined for eternal destruction.[12]

The fool is not a fool because he asks metaphysical questions. He is a fool because, in focusing on the possibility of worldly gain, he ignores God's judgment and the possibility of eternal damnation. Although he acts in an evil manner so as to advance his own self-interest, he unwittingly plots his own destruction. In profiting from his own wickedness, he acts in an irrational manner.

If, however, the religious model provides a watertight defense of the rationality of morality, its success may be attributed to two different factors. In the first place, it reduces every serious moral decision to a choice between infinite pleasure and infinite pain. Faced with such unequal outcomes, rational agents must always decide on the side of infinite pleasure. They must always opt for Heaven over Hell.[13]

In the second place, cheating is not a viable option. God is a foolproof police agent who sees everything. One cannot commit a crime and get away with it. Everyone who does wrong will invariably get caught. Serious evil is necessarily linked to the infinite disutility of a never-ending punishment.[14]

The religious model successfully secures the rationality of all moral conduct. On the religious model, the rational agent will help the Jewish fugitive. Why? Because God will prepare a place in Heaven for those who help the unfortunate. The rational agent will not cooperate with the Nazis, even if it brings short-term gain, for those who cooperate with evil authorities will be eternally punished. Modern sentimentality aside, Jesus himself does not hesitate to give dire warnings about the eventual fate of evildoers. It would be better, he declares, if the sinner were to pluck out his sinful eye or cut off his sinful hand, than to persist in evil and have his entire body cast into Hell.[15] But this is to make the argument represented in table 8. It is to insist that the inevitable punishment of Hell undermines the rationality of any form of evil.

Even Socrates, who was not a Christian, appeals to similar beliefs. In the *Phaedo*, he assures his comrades that "there is something in store for those who have died . . . something much better for the good than the

wicked."[16] And again, he tells them "he who enters the next world uniniti-
ated and unenlightened shall lie in the mire, but he who arrives purified and
enlightened shall dwell among the gods."[17] Socrates also suggests that the
wicked go to Tartarus, a combination of both Hell and Purgatory, when
they die. The incurably evil languish there forever, whereas the less wicked,
having suffered for their sins, are eventually released.[18] This belief in ultimate punishment and reward secures, however, the rationality of morality.

When philosophers in the why-be-moral school rework the utility model
on a secular basis, they jettison the associated religious or metaphysical
beliefs. In the absence of these supporting beliefs, the utility model collapses. If, of course, one is a devout Christian or if one believes (like
Socrates) that the good must eternally prevail, this may be enough. But I
want to show that morality is a rational course of action using a different
approach. It is the nature of rational consciousness that makes morality a
rational endeavor. The problem with the why-be-moral account is that these
philosophers direct their argument toward amoral agents. This is unrealistic. Except for the very young, the mentally handicapped, the comatose, or
the insane, there are, within the human family, no such agents. Rational
agents are, in a manner that needs to be explained, inescapably moral.

2

A Different View of Morality

A Morality of Love

Here in the Western world, commonplace notions of morality derive, in large part, from the Judeo-Christian tradition. Christianity, in particular, proposes love as the only authentic source of moral aspiration. Charity, understood as love in action, is the moral act par excellence. This poses a problem, however, for philosophers in the why-be-moral tradition. It is hard to see how one can reconcile a morality based on the fundamentally selfless virtue of charity with a concept of rationality based on self-interest.

Charity necessitates an other-directed, disinterested giving. The notion can be traced back to the New Testament concept of *agape* (ἀγάπη). *Agape* is a love that is "not appetitive." It is not stimulated by any "need to satisfy that in oneself which is incomplete."[1] It represents a "seeking to confer good, rather than [to] obtain it."[2] In a theological context, this type of human love mirrors God's unmerited love for a corrupt humanity.

Medieval philosophers, early and late, such as Augustine and Aquinas, present charity in theological terms. In the contemporary period, however, it is usually defined in resolutely human terms. The *Random House College Dictionary* defines charity as "the performance of . . . benevolent actions for the needy with no expectation of material reward."[3] The *Oxford English Dictionary* refers to it as "almsgiving," and an older version of *Webster's* speaks of "free assistance of the poor, incapacitated, distressed." The *Catholic Encyclopedia* bemoans this "decayed usage,"[4] but even in a largely secular context, the term retains something of its theological origins. To act in a charitable manner is to imitate God. God, in his absolute generosity, does not love others so as to benefit himself. He loves others so that others can benefit. In the same way, people who perform works of charity act, not so as to benefit themselves, but to benefit others.

Authentic charity is an expression of an entirely selfless concern for the other. It is not, in any sense, self-seeking. A truly charitable person acts so as to improve the lot of the other. This is, for the truly charitable, enough. The accomplishment of this other-directed end is the only reward he or she is seeking.

OTHER TRADITIONS

We tend to identify the virtue of charity with Christianity, but charity plays a prominent role in other traditions as well. According to A. Cohen, one finds in the Talmud "numerous passages which demonstrate that charity was prized for its own sake as a supreme virtue."[5] Cohen lists precepts and dictums like "Greater is he who practices charity than all the sacrifices,"[6] "Charity is equal to all the other precepts put together,"[7] and "Whoever shuts his eye against charity is as though he worshiped idols."[8] This latter precept is a particularly stern warning about the necessity for charity, as idolatry was, in Judaism, the greatest sin.

The Talmud teaches that "True charity is practiced in secret."[9] Benefactors are not to know who receives their gifts, and beneficiaries are not to know who donated them.[10] This rabbinic insistence on secrecy ensures the purity of the benefactor's motivation. Charitable benefactors are prevented from extracting any benefit, any sense of prestige or social standing, from their acts. Individual agents are to practice charity purely out of a concern for other people's welfare, not for any personal benefit.

But again, charity is not, in any exclusive sense, a Judeo-Christian concept. In the Koran the Prophet declares that it is "excellent" to "manifest charity," telling believers to "hide" their donations "to the poor" because secret almsgiving is "good" for them.[11] Buddhism associates charity with enlightenment. According to the Buddha, "The charitable man has found the path of salvation."[12] "He is like an able warrior, a champion strong and wise in action."[13] And one finds similar sentiments expressed in other ancient religions.

Although we do not normally associate the concept of charity with Greek philosophers, ancient Athenian culture did emphasize, to some degree, the virtue of charity. Thucydides records a speech in which Pericles, the popular statesman, argues that Athenians are more virtuous than their neighbors because they "make friends by doing good to others, not by receiving good from them." Pericles extols the generosity of his fellow citizens, maintaining that they "do kindnesses to others," "not . . . out of any calculations of profit or loss," but "without afterthought, relying on [their] free liberality."[14] This is to assume, however, that one should do good to others, not because it is one's self-interest to do good to others, but freely, liberally, without afterthought, for the sake of charity itself.

Different traditions promote the concept of charity in another way. Consider the Golden Rule. This principle tells us that we are to treat others considerately, not because it is in our self-interest, but because they are human beings like ourselves. The command "Do onto others as you would have them do unto you" is categorical. It does not tell us to treat others like ourselves when it is in our self interest, when it increases our expected utility, when it maximizes preference satisfaction. We are to treat others like ourselves every time we interact with them. We are to be good without qualification.

Miller[15] lists versions of the Golden Rule from Buddhism,[16] Zoroastrianism,[17] Jainism,[18] Hinduism,[19] Sikhism,[20] Judaism,[21] Confucianism and Christianity. In China "The aspects of one's moral sense that received the strongest cultural support were duty and self-control; [whereas] those that received the weakest . . . were compassion and fairness."[22] But five hundred years before Christ, Confucius was able to elaborate his own version of the Golden Rule: "What you do not want done to yourself, do not do to others."[23] Although Confucius tended to limit his notion of reciprocity *(shu)* to the company of the good,[24] the Chinese Taoists went even further. Lao Tzu, reputed author of the *Tao Te Ching*, writes: "To those who are good to me I am good; and to those who are not good to me, I am also good."[25] Like Jesus, he stresses the categorical nature of the Golden Rule. It applies to everyone. We are to be good to others even when they are not good to us, when they take advantage of us, and even, presumably, when it is not in our self-interest.

Morris Ginsberg claims that "A list of virtues or duties drawn up by a Buddhist would not differ very greatly from one drawn up by a Christian, a Confucianist, a Muhammedan or a Jew."[26] C. S. Lewis, at the end of *The Abolition of Man*, pieces together a universal moral code from a wide variety of sources: ancient Egyptian, ancient Jewish, Babylonian, Hindu, ancient Chinese, Old Norse, and Roman.[27] All these traditions revere selfless qualities like self-discipline, self-sacrifice, and self-renunciation for the sake of some higher good. If, however, morality entails genuine selflessness, this subverts the why-be-moral project.

SELF-INTEREST RATHER THAN MORALITY

It is hard to see how philosophers in the why-be-moral school could secure the rationality of morality as it is commonly understood, for they cannot secure the rationality of charity. Seen from the perspective of a charity-based ethics, we cannot justify morality through an appeal to self-interest. Any such strategy is self-defeating. If agents practice charity in order to maximize utility, they do not act in a genuinely charitable manner. Anyone who chooses to act in a moral manner in order to further his or her own self-interest is a self-seeking rather than a selfless (or charitable) individual.

Appeals to the utility-maximization model make a business of moral-ity. The default position is not "Help other people in order to help them," but "Help others because it benefits yourself." An act of morality becomes a self-seeking act. It no longer counts, in any rigorous sense, as charity. It is the advantage of the self rather than the advantage of the other that is the central motivation and the rationale behind moral decision-making.

Philosophers in the why-be-moral tradition embrace a concept of ra-tionality which is at odds with traditional notions. On the traditional view, self-interested morality is only pretense; it is not the real thing. Consider the following analogy. Suppose some people were to collect fine art purely for investment purposes. They might get excited about painting. They might read books about art history. They might visit galleries and amass a sub-stantial collection. But purely financial collectors are not genuine lovers of art. When the activity of art collecting becomes financially unrewarding, they will stop collecting art. A genuine lover of art will collect art even if it is not financially profitable. In the same way, a person who acts morally for self-interested reasons is not a genuinely moral person. Self-interested agents will stop acting morally when morality is no longer in their self-interest. Genuinely moral people will act in a moral manner even when it is not in their self-interest. Just as the purely financial collector collects art for un-aesthetic reasons, the self-interested agent acts morally for reasons which are less than moral. In both cases we have pretense rather than reality.

People who have less than an absolute commitment to morality are less than moral. If self-interested reasons can prevail over moral reasons, cheating becomes, as we have seen, the most rational strategy. But a re-fusal to cheat is, if anything, the hallmark of genuine morality. Frank Murphy argues that the traditional thesis that moral reasons override other kinds of reasons should be rejected.[28] If, however, morality is conditional, if it does not apply universally, if it is open to compromise and exception, it is not, on the traditional view, authentic morality. If we are only moral when it is in our self-interest, we are not really moral.

We can now see how the previous utility calculations relating to Heaven and Hell go awry. These calculations do secure the rationality of morality. But if I care for others solely because I want to go to Heaven, this misses the Christian ideal by a wide margin. For the authentic Christian, morality is not rooted in utility calculations, but in an inexhaustible love that gratu- itously bestows value on others. Heaven is not simply a reward for a good life. It is the logical outgrowth of selfless love, just as Hell is the logical outgrowth of an exclusive self-centeredness.

Any attempt to found morality on self-interest is prey to a fundamental tension. Consider the Buddhist doctrine of nirvana, which situates salva- tion in the extinction or annihilation of individual existence. Selflessness leads to ultimate enlightenment. If, however, we have a self-interested rea- son for becoming selfless, we are no longer selfless. Likewise, if we have self-interested reasons for becoming charitable, we are no longer chari- table. We can secure the rationality of traditional notions of morality by appealing to some future, envisaged reward, but the genuinely moral per- son does not act morally as a means to a reward. Such behavior provides, at best, a modicum of morality. It is very far from moral perfection. The genu- inely moral individual does not act for any kind of reward, but in a genu- inely disinterested manner. If we want to provide a rational justification of traditional notions of morality, we must demonstrate that selfless action, *even without a reward*, is rational. We will not be able to do this if we conceive of rationality exclusively in terms of self-interest.

Charity is an indispensable ingredient of familiar notions of morality. We cannot replace a notion of "disinterested love" with a notion of "self- interested love" while retaining any recognizable account of moral behav- ior. Suppose you tell someone you are morally obliged to love—a parent, a spouse, or a child—that you love them because it is in your self-interest and that you will no longer love them when it is not in your self-interest. Even a simple child understands that this is not really love. Kant's formu- lation of the categorical imperative that people must be treated as ends rather than means is a philosophical restatement of this familiar principle. If you love other people *because it is in your self-interest*, you love them to further your own ends. You treat them as a means to the satisfaction of your own preferences, not as ends in themselves. You violate the categorical imperative.

It might be suggested that altruistic agents are really acting, on a sub- conscious level, in a self-interested manner. This seems ethnocentric. It seems implausible to suggest that all these diverse traditions are spiritually obtuse, that they all provide a superficial and deceptive account of the hu- man condition and of morality. If we adopt a purely economic view of human endeavor, we will be incapable of truly disinterested action. Moral- ity, as traditionally viewed, will be nothing but pretense, illusion. But this is to adopt a reductionist view of human life and nature.

Philosophers in the why-be-moral tradition try to provide a rational justification of morality. We can distinguish, however, between two models of rational justification. Those in the why-be-moral camp take a rationalistic, argumentative approach. On this model, belief follows justification. Informed agents will not believe in a particular morality until after securing a rational justification for it. They must first determine whether morality really is an advantageous proposition. When they have been rationally convinced that it is in their self-interest to act morally, they will go ahead and act morally.

If we hope to defend charity-based models of morality, we must invoke a different view, for the self-interested approach destroys the disinterested character of authentic morality. There is, however, another option, Early in the Christian tradition, Augustine argued that belief must *precede* justification. If we do not start with bare faith, we will never have rational understanding. In a famous sermon, Augustine declares; "If someone says to me: 'I would understand that I may believe,' I answer: 'Believe that you may understand. Unless you believe, you will not understand.'"[29]

Although Augustine applies this justificatory principle to the Christian faith, we can apply this same basic principle to the why-be-moral problem. If the amoral agent says, "I want to first understand why morality is in my self-interest, then I will be moral," we can answer by telling him or her: "First believe in morality, put it into practice, and you will come to understand why it is in your self-interest." On the traditional view, morality is rational, but it is only rational in hindsight. The movement of the will must precede understanding.

Morality is supposed to lead to happiness, but traditional wisdom insists on the paradoxical nature of happiness. We sacrifice ourselves for others and—paradoxically—find happiness for ourselves. We give everything away and—paradoxically—receive even more in return. We die to ourselves and are—paradoxically—reborn. It is this willingness to abandon one's own self-interest in favor of others that makes one moral. The inveterate immoralist, someone who is consumed by self-interest, cannot believe in the worth of selfless action. It follows that he or she will never know what morality is all about. Such individuals are imprisoned in a kind of ignorance, outside morality. On the traditional view, morality begins with conversion, some interior change of heart, some active commitment to others, not with mere argument. Perhaps this explains why sociopaths, people who have made a fundamental choice in favor of immorality, are often incurable.

Augustine writes: "We believe in order to know, we do not know in order to believe."[30] Philosophers in the why-be-moral school want to *know* that morality is in their self-interest so that they can *believe* in it. The process needs to be reversed. Philosophers like Aristotle and Aquinas suggest, at least indirectly, that we must *believe* in morality if we want to *know* what morality is all about. Both philosophers believe that only older people, people who are already moral, should study moral philosophy. Moral philosophy is not directed at the morally blind; it is directed at those who are already striving, however imperfectly, to do good and avoid evil.

In the next section, I will argue that human beings are, by nature, moral creatures. They *evaluate* their actions. Philosophers in the why-be-moral school direct their arguments at the amoral agent, but the amoral agent is an artificial construct.

MORALITY MEANS KNOWING-HOW

Philosophers in the why-be-moral school take an argumentative, rationalistic approach to morality. If, however, morality involves a certain kind of knowledge, the argumentative approach is inappropriate. In an introduction to phenomenology, Richard Schmitt distinguishes between two kinds of knowing: "knowing-how" and "knowing-that."[31] Schmitt argues that philosophers express in words the basic understanding that underlies human endeavor. They convert this general "knowing-how" into a corresponding "knowing-that." Consider a specific example.

Suppose I know how to recognize my brother Leo. To possess an adequate knowing-how in this regard is to be able to pick Leo out of a crowd or a police lineup. To convert this knowing-how into a knowing-that is to be able to describe his appearance in words, something I may or may not be able to do.

Life is regulated and maintained by innumerable kinds and instances of knowing-how. We know how to do many things: how to recognize specific objects, how to react in specific situations, how to think, judge, and make decisions. In short, we know how to live. According to Schmitt, philosophy raises to the level of a consistent commentary the understanding that regulates ordinary life. It "bring[s] to light what was previously anonymous or latent in our performances."[32] It identifies the necessary characteristics of everyday experience.

One may apply Schmitt's description of the philosophical craft to the problem of morality. There are moral heroes who know *how* to be moral. This does not mean, however, that they know how to express this moral knowledge in words. The task of moral philosophy is the conversion of this knowing-how into a corresponding knowing-that. On this kind of view, moral philosophers are not supposed to "invent" a theory of morality, but to arrive at an explanation that conforms to what is already known and experienced, on some pretheoretical level, in the give-and-take of everyday life.

Socrates identifies virtue with knowledge. More specifically, he identifies *aretê*, excellence or virtue, with *techne* or technique.[33] Knowledge of virtue is a specific kind of knowing-how. It is like knowledge of carpentry, medicine, or horse training. Just as the carpenter knows how to build cabinets, the doctor knows how to restore health, and the horse trainer knows how to train horses, so the virtuous man knows how to live a good life. But the virtuous may or may not be able to provide a detailed verbal description of what morality is all about. Individuals who are uneducated, unintelligent, or inexperienced may be able to act in a moral way, even though they are unable to express in words the moral ideals that motivate their actions.

On this view, moral knowledge is, first and foremost, a kind of knowing-how. If, however, moral knowledge involves a kind of knowing-how, it will follow that amoral judges are not competent judges of morality. Consider an example. Suppose I know how to ride a bicycle. I may not be able to provide an adequate verbal description of bike riding, an in-depth explanation of the mechanics of bicycles, or an exhaustive list of true propositions about this sport. This is not, however, what it means to know how to ride a bicycle. To know how to ride a bicycle is to be able to get on the bike and ride. And likewise for morality. I may not be able to provide an adequate verbal explanation of morality, an in-depth explanation of moral principles, or a complete list of true propositions about the moral life. But this is not, in the most fundamental sense, what it means to know how to be moral. To know how to be moral is to behave in a moral way in specific situations.

Knowing how to ride a bicycle places me in a particular position. Once I learn how to ride, I cannot unlearn to ride. Likewise, if I learn how to be moral, I cannot "unlearn" how to be moral. I may, of course, act immorally. But for someone who has learned morality, this will be an unpleasant experience. It will be like falling off the bicycle. It will involve serious emotional discomfort: shame, guilt, remorse, and so on.

Now suppose we have two agents: one can ride a bicycle and one cannot. Who is in a better position to judge whether bike-riding is a worthwhile endeavor? Surely, it is the bike rider, the person who has experience of bicycling. If an "a-bicycling" agent claims that bicycling is not a worthwhile endeavor, the bicycle rider will probably tell him that he does not know what he is talking about. In the same way, we might argue that amoral agents who discount the rationality of morality do not know what they are talking about.

It does not follow, as philosophers in the why-be-moral school suppose, that an amoral person with no experience of morality is in the best position to judge whether morality is a rational endeavor. An agent who has a never ridden a bicycle is not in a position to judge whether bicycle riding is a worthwhile activity. The a-bicycling agent is not objective but ignorant. Although the bicycle rider is already committed to bicycle riding, he or she is in a better position to judge the value of the sport.

In a similar way, the amoral agent, the agent in a before-morality stage, is not in a position to evaluate the rationality of morality. An amoral agent is not objective but ignorant. Although moral agents are, by definition, committed to morality, they have personal knowledge of morality and are in a better position to evaluate whether or not it is a rational endeavor. Even if they cannot rid themselves of moral beliefs, this does not detract from the fact that, unlike amoral agents, they have personal knowledge of whether morality provides some kind of fulfilling experience. If, as the Augustinian argument implies, a commitment to morality precedes understanding, the amoral agent cannot understand what morality is all about. And if they cannot understand what morality is all about, how can they judge whether the moral life is a worthwhile option?

Why-be-moral philosophers assume that only amoral agents can impartially judge the rationality of morality, but decent, moral human beings cannot judge morality in an amoral fashion. If Mary is a bicycle rider, she can pretend she does not know how to ride a bike, but she can never return to a precycling state; she can never be someone who has no experience of bicycle riding.[34] In a similar way, moral agents may *pretend* that they are amoral agents, that they have "unlearned" morality, but this seems to be a disingenuous strategy. In the next section, I will argue that human beings, because they are evaluators, cannot adopt a neutral stance toward morality.

Why, in any case, would anyone want to return, even hypothetically, to a premoral, amoral state? Suppose morality really is based on charity or love. Once I have loved and known love, I cannot "unlearn" the experience. But even if I could, why would I want to return to a state where I had no knowledge of love? Having experienced the value of charity, I am in a better position to judge whether love is a rational vocation or not.

Philosophers in the why-be-moral school seem to conceive of morality as a kind of knowing-that. It is textual, argumentative, philosophical. On the traditional view, morality is based on this mysterious, ineffable concept of love. Love is a kind of knowing-how that is difficult to express in words. Agents who have no knowledge of love have not only missed out on life. They are ignorant in a very basic way. Because they lack knowledge, they are not in a position to judge whether morality is a worthwhile endeavor.

HAPPINESS AS UTILITY? GEORGE ELIOT

Philosophers in the why-be-moral school sometimes argue that it is rational to be moral because (or when) morality makes us happy. These philosophers, following in the utilitarian tradition, define "happiness" in nonmoral terms, in terms of pleasurable feeling or agreeable sensation. On this account, an act is rational insomuch as it tends toward the production of happy feelings. But this is problematic, for most of us do not want bare utiles of agreeable sensation. We want a happiness that flows out of some legitimate sense of human accomplishment.

Robert Nozick proposes the following thought-experiment. Suppose there is an experience machine that will give you any experience you desire. "Neuropsychologists [will] stimulate your brain so that you [will] think and feel you [are] writing a great novel, making a friend, or reading an interesting book. All the time you [will] be floating in a tank with electrodes attached to your brain."[35] And suppose (as in the movie *The Matrix*) you are allowed to choose between the experience of being hooked up to the machine and *feeling* that you are writing a great novel and the authentic experience, in real life, of actually writing a great novel. Which would you prefer?

In the author's classroom experience, students invariably say that they would choose the real experience over the fictitious one. They recognize that the second option is intrinsically superior to the second. Their reasoning seems straightforward. They want a feeling of satisfaction or happiness that derives, not from an hallucination, but from some actual achievement. It is not dumb sensate pleasure they are after but a legitimate sense of personal worth. They do not hanker after bare feelings. They want feelings that flow from some sort of praiseworthy action.

The modern tendency to equate 'happiness" with "pleasant feelings" derives largely from Bentham and the utilitarians. Even a more sophisticated utilitarian like Henry Sidgwick contends that nothing is desirable other than feeling and that feeling is only desirable to the extent that it is pleasant.[36] If, however, it is only the experiential, the sensual component of the experience that counts, if the way in which pleasant feelings come into existence is inconsequential, if "feeling [is to be] valued merely as feeling

... without regard to the conditions and relations under which it arises,"[37] then someone who spends his or her entire life plugged into Nozick's experience machine might lead the "happiest" life of all.

Philosophers who use the decision-theory model of rationality speak of happiness in terms of utility maximization. We are happy when we satisfy our desires or our preferences. Every time we satisfy our desires, we are awarded a certain number of utiles. Each utile represents a unit of pleasure or happiness. The rational (self-interested) individual tries to procure as many utiles as possible. But to argue that we should be moral so that we can be awarded ever greater quantities of raw pleasure is not very compelling. Consider the following thought-experiment.

Suppose we lived in an advanced technological society peopled by brainy neurologists. Inspired by the utilitarian thought that one should maximize happiness, these neurologists create a "happy ward" filled with patients strapped into beds and plugged into computerized experience machines. These machines stimulate the pleasure centers in patients' brains, providing them with an endless supply of happy feelings. Without ever stirring from their beds, these patients are able to maximize their experience of pleasure. But would this be a happy fate? Should one give up an ordinary life of intermittent pain and struggle for a place in this happy ward? Most of us would not consider this to be a happy fate. This is not what we mean by happiness. We do not want to be plugged into a machine that makes us *feel* happy. We do not want pleasure or satisfaction per se. We want the pleasure or the satisfaction that derives from a legitimate sense of human accomplishment. Consider another example.

Suppose Jan is a great aficionado of classical music who slips into ecstasy every time he hears the polyphonic "Gloria" from Palestrina's *Mass for Pope Marcellus*. And suppose we could hook Jan up to Nozick's experience machine and make him experience the same feelings every time he hears the most mediocre, fatuous commercial jingle. "Sugar Pops! Sugar Pops! Sugar Pops! Sugar Pops! They're Tops! Tops! Tops!" (Each word, each note, so wonderfully expressed!) Surely, this would be a disaster. The commercial jingle Jan may experience more happiness than the polyphonic Jan. After all, fatuous commercial jingles abound. Superbly performed Renaissance music is much harder to come by. So would Jan agree to undergo the operation? Probably not. What Jan wants is not a pleasure that is associated with inane jingles but a pleasure that is associated with the polyphonic subtleties of Palestrina. Being able to appreciate and relish Palestrina is part of a worthwhile, meaningful life; appreciating and relishing fatuous popular jingles is not.

The connection between pleasurable consciousness and happiness is more oblique than authors in the why-be-moral tradition recognize. The *Oxford English Dictionary* defines "Happy" as: "Having good 'hap' or fortune; lucky, fortunate, favored by lot, position, or other external circumstance." To be happy is to experience, by what happens, by what comes to pass, an enviable fate. Early Christians, for example, thought of martyrdom as an enviable destiny. This was a blessed or a happy end. Obviously, martyrs did not experience pleasurable sensations. They suffered grievously. Nonetheless, they experienced by hap, by some turn of events, an enviable destiny. They had the good fortune to die for the truth and to win for themselves everlasting beatitude.

The early Christian martyrs were good rebels. They rebelled against society and they rebelled for the sake of the good. If, however, good rebels may suffer grievously, this is, in the traditional sense of the term, a happy fate. It is not that one should feel "pleasant feelings" on the gallows or the rack. The idea is that one should welcome with "supreme felicity" the thought of such a noble, virtuous end. Hence St. Francis of Assisi tells a traveling companion that if one bears innocent suffering without displaying anger or resentment, one experiences, not mere holiness, not mere sanctity, but "perfect joy."[38] It is not that we are to take masochistic pleasure in the brute fact of suffering. It is that we are to welcome with joy the fact that we have managed to remain virtuous.

One does not have to be religious or a Christian to draw a link between happiness and suffering. In a text on ethics, John Dewey approvingly quotes the Victorian novelist George Eliot, no orthodox Christian. Eliot insists that "We can only have the highest happiness, such as goes with being a great man, by having wide thought and . . . feeling for the rest of the world . . . and this sort of happiness often brings so much pain with it, that we can only tell it from pain by its being what we would choose before everything else, because our souls see it as good."[39] Eliot identifies happiness with compassion, with a sensitivity to all things great and small, with wide thought and feeling for the world. This kind of happiness brings, however, untold suffering. To speak of happiness as a quantity of bare sensation seems simplistic in comparison.

If we want to build up a system of ethics based on people's actual preferences, we cannot define happiness solely in terms of the pleasant feelings people experience. We must take into account how these feelings came into existence, the activity that produced them, the state of mind or character they exemplify or embody. Most of us believe that there are ways of producing or procuring pleasurable sensations that are illegitimate, base, or just plain wicked. To speak of "happiness" solely or principally in terms of utility, in terms of an action's ability to produce pleasurable sensation, is misleading.

Etymologically, the word "happy" is, as we have seen, akin to the word "blessed."[40] A "happy" individual derives pleasure "from [the] success or attainment of what is considered good."[41] In a religious context, for example, the blessed or happy in heaven do not only enjoy "pleasurable, joyful, blissful" feelings.[42] They enjoy these feelings because they have led good lives. This is an important aspect of the word's meaning. If a pedophile enjoys sexually abusing little boys, he is not a *happy* individual, for the pleasant sensations he experiences do not derive "from [the] success or attainment of what is considered good." A pedophile does not enjoy an enviable destiny. He is a pathetic individual. He experiences a despicable fate that should be condemned and abhorred.

Philosophers in the why-be-moral school correctly identify the link between happiness and morality. They misconstrue, however, the nature of happiness. To be happy is to experience an illustrious or an admirable fate. If, however, one is to experience a happy end, this entails more than experiencing pleasant sensations. It means, first and foremost, achieving what is praiseworthy or admirable.

The why-be-moral problem arises, in part, because philosophers in the why-be-moral tradition divorce happiness from morality. This is inconsistent with everyday experience. To speak of our wants or desires in terms of bare sensation is inexcusably ambiguous. At this level of generality, we cannot capture, in any interesting way, the content of our aims and aspirations. Morality is a means to happiness because happiness includes some sort of moral component.

SELF-LOVE: ARISTOTLE AND BUTLER

I have contrasted the self-interested morality of the utility-maximization model with charity-based models of ethics. But self-interest is only problematic when we consider happiness in amoral terms. In the *Nicomachean Ethics* Aristotle considers two opposing opinions: (1) that self-love is a character-defect and (2) that self-love is a characteristic of the virtuous man.

According to the first opinion, "a bad man [does] everything for his own sake, and the more so the more wicked he is."[43] According to the second opinion, a good man "is his own best friend and therefore ought to love himself best."[44] Aristotle claims that both opinions capture an aspect of truth. There are two different kinds of self-love: one base, one noble. Those who love themselves in an ignoble manner "assign to themselves the greater share of wealth, honors and bodily pleasures"[45] and "are grasping with regard to things which gratify . . . the irrational element of the soul."[46] Those who love themselves in a noble manner assign to themselves "the things that are noblest and best" and are desirous of those things which gratify "the most authoritative element" in the soul.[47]

Aristotle argues that insomuch as the virtuous love themselves, they select the best things for themselves—that is, they select morality! Aristotle includes in a list of those who love themselves: those who sacrifice "honour and office" for a friend,[48] those "who throw away wealth . . . on the condition that their friends will gain more,"[49] those who "strain every nerve to do the noblest deeds,"[50] those who "act justly and temperately, or in accordance with any other of the virtues,"[51] and even "those who die for others."[52] If these individuals act selflessly, if they sacrifice their own well-being for others, they also demonstrate the highest degree of self-love, for in acting in a virtuous manner, they secure for themselves "the goods that are the greatest, since virtue is the greatest of goods."[53]

Bishop Joseph Butler, the Anglican divine, mounts a vigorous defense of self-love from an explicitly Christian perspective. Butler defines self-love as a rational capacity, "a general desire [for our] own happiness . . . inseparable from all sensible creatures who can reflect upon themselves and their own interest[s]."[54] Self-love is a positive force that prevents us from engaging in "vagrant follies," "unruly vices," or "idle passions." It secures, in an orderly and prudent way, our own personal happiness. As Butler writes: "If the generality of mankind were to cultivate within themselves the principle of self-love . . . and if self-love were so strong and prevalent, as that they would uniformly pursue [their own happiness] . . . it would manifestly prevent numberless follies and vices."[55] In Butler's view, the problem is not that people have too much self-love; the problem is that they do not have enough.

While Augustine presents self-love and benevolence or other-love as opposing attitudes or emotions, Butler sees self-love as an emotion that facilitates and encourages benevolence.[56] He insists that "the greatest satisfactions to ourselves depend upon our having benevolence in a due degree,"[57] and that "there have been persons in all ages, who have . . . found satisfaction in the exercise of charity, in love of their neighbor, [and] in endeavoring to promote the happiness of all."[58] If we love ourselves and actively seek our own happiness, we will endeavor to love others, for we can only find true happiness in loving others.

Butler also claims, like Aristotle, that virtue is its own reward. It is not just that we go to Heaven when we die. Virtue is its own reward in this present life, for in endeavoring to help others, we will be gratified by our own awareness that we are involved in a virtuous pursuit. Indeed, Butler maintains that the consciousness of our own virtuousness is one of the greatest sources of happiness.[59] Although true charity requires that we love even without a reward, the practice of charity may be psychologically healthy.[60] It may lead to inner peace; it may render life meaningful, provide constant satisfactions, and, in general, make life worth living

Philosophers in the why-be-moral tradition work "from an initial presumption against morality."[61] They define happiness in amoral terms, in terms of pleasurable sensations. This is why the problem of self-interest arises. When we work from a moral perspective, self-love and morality coincide. The "self-interested" agent should act morally, for this is the only way he or she can achieve happiness, traditionally construed.

SOFT INSTRUMENTALISM

Authors such as David Schmidtz,[62] Miriam Thalos,[63] and Christine Chwaszcza[64] revamp the usual why-be-moral argument along more intuitive lines. These authors want to wed instrumentalism, the notion that the rational agent always maximizes utility, to a more altruistic notion of self-interest. Schmidtz, for example, embraces instrumentalism while rejecting *Homo oeconomicus*, the purely self-interested individual who cares about other people only insofar as this promotes their self-interest. Schmidtz proposes, in effect, a moral model of utility. Morality is rational *if* one already cares for others, *if* one has already accepted the importance "of fitting in with other people." He believes that immoral agents, agents who do not care about other people, may have no compelling reason to be moral.

David Gauthier suggests, like Schmidtz, that we may not be able to convince the utterly ruthless utility maximizer to care for other people.[65] If we are going to convince people to be moral, we need not just rational argument, but a change of heart. In Gauthier's own words, "We need exorcism as well as argument."[66] We need something akin to religious conversion, something that cannot be supplied by mere rationalistic philosophy. This is to provide, at best, a *partial* justification of morality. Soft instrumentalism may show that it is rational for people who already care for other people to act morally, but this is not enough. To provide a complete justification for morality, we need to show that morality is a rational venture for both moral and immoral (or amoral) agents, not simply for agents who are already moral.

In the next section on morality, I will argue that morality is a rational endeavor for all human agents. But though morality may be good even for immoral agents, it may be very hard to provide them with compelling reasons to act morally. We must distinguish between two very different questions: "Is it rational to act morally?" and "Can we convince an immoral agent that it is rational to act morally?" Even if we cannot convince an immoral agent to act in a moral manner, this does not mean that morality is an irrational venture, for immoral agents may, of course, be mistaken. They may have contradictory preferences, aims, or goals that are themselves irrational.

If we want to evaluate agents' actions, we must evaluate their ends as well as the means they choose to achieve those ends. Instrumentalism, which relies on the principle of utility maximization, only evaluates the latter. It should consider, not just whether agents satisfy their own preferences, but whether those preferences are worth having in the first place. Decision theory needs to be supplemented by value theory. We need an objective standard of human behavior that will allow us to evaluate an agent's preferences in light of what it is reasonable to believe about the world. Morality provides us with this standard. This is why morality is an essential aspect of happiness.

SOCIAL MORALITY

Philosophers in the why-be-moral school try to reconcile morality and rationality. More specifically, they try to reconcile a social interpretation of morality with an instrumentalist interpretation of rationality. Philosophers who adopt the social view of morality distinguish morality from ethics. P. F. Strawson writes that morality has to do with the "rule-requirements of social organization . . . [with] those systems . . . of recognized reciprocal claim that we have on one another as members of human communities."[67] Ethics has to do with "pictures of ideal forms of life, . . . with the vision that captures the ethical imagination."[68] Morality has minimal content and is universal in scope. Ethics is rich in content, private in scope. Morality is identified with public life, with that sphere of civic interaction that involves us as a community. Ethics is relegated to a sphere of personal, private interactions.

But we cannot divorce (social) morality from (personal) ethics. Morality must be understood as an extension, a consequence, a further development of ethics. It is precisely the estrangement of morality from ethics that precipitates the why-be-moral problem. Our social obligations to other people must be a continuation of a personal ethical commitment. If morality is a part of the personal ethical vision that gives meaning to my life and motivates my actions, then I have a very good reason for being moral. In acting morally, I am not submitting to a foreign constraint. Morality is a part of who I am and how I define myself. Why should I care about my next-door neighbor? Because—paradoxically—I must be true to myself. Social morality that is not supported by a serious commitment to personal ethics is at best perfunctory, at worst a fraud.

On the instrumentalist view, morality is something unnatural, something that goes against the grain, something we have to be badgered into. It is a concession to the interests of society. Hence the necessary appeal to self-interest. But this is to misunderstand the nature of the human predicament. We become, in the concrete details of our lives, the embodiment of the moral values we espouse. If we want to secure the rationality of morality, we need to demonstrate how our own ethical beliefs, consistently and carefully applied, lead to moral beliefs about how we should interact with other people. It is not a matter of waving a contractarian or a utilitarian wand over an ethical void and conjuring up some equitable system of social obligation. As the proponents of "soft instrumentalism" implicitly recognize, trying to jump-start morality from a position outside of ethics results in a moral Frankenstein. We are left, not with a paradigm of moral behavior, but with *Homo oeconomicus*, the purely self-interested man whose calculating concern for his own self-interest is a testament, not to the rule of reason and good sense, but to a fatal narcissism.

If we want to solve the why-be-moral problem, we need to demonstrate the ethical basis for morality. The moral philosopher ought to begin, not with a presumption against morality, but with a sensitivity toward personal ethics. Why be moral? Because the way I treat strangers, fellow citizens or the woman next door has a negative or a positive impact on my own sense of self-respect. It defines who and what I am. I cannot realize my own ethical aspirations if I am less than fully moral.

Ethical beliefs are pervasive. Not to understand the urgency of the *ethical* imperative is to be less than human. A few such individuals may exist, but as Aristotle intimates, there is little (if anything) that moral philosophy can do for them. Their problems are psychological and emotional rather than philosophical. The social model of morality provides a very narrow understanding of the moral dimension. If we are to successfully defend the rationality of morality, we must broaden our understanding of what it means to be a moral and rational being. I will pursue this project later in this text.

3

A Different View of Rationality

FORMALIST ACCOUNTS OF RATIONALITY

Philosophers in the why-be-moral tradition try to set out a rational account of morality. We have criticized their description of morality and its connection to happiness, and we can also contest their account of rationality.

Philosophers in the why-be-moral tradition propose an abstract, mathematical model of rationality. They adopt a game-theory approach. The goal of the game is the maximization of utility. Individual actions are awarded precise numbers of utiles with each utile representing a certain fixed quantity of pleasure or preference-satisfaction. Rational agents are, in effect, successful calculators. They are able to calculate the number of utiles associated with every possible outcome and to make choices that procure for themselves the largest number of utiles. Irrationality represents a departure from this maximization strategy.

Nel Noddings writes: "Ethical argumentation has frequently proceeded as if it were governed by the logical necessity characteristic of geometry."[1] "This emphasis gives ethics a contemporary, mathematical appearance."[2] Noddings, a feminist, argues that the introduction of mathematics into ethics derives from an overly masculine view of the world. The exaggerated and misguided concern for exactitude that characterizes contemporary ethics represents a repudiation of the feminine. It represents the triumph of the cerebral over the emotional, of science over aesthetics, of thought over feeling.

One way or another, this mathematical approach has been enormously influential, in large part, because of the epistemological prestige of mathematical science. We tend to associate reason and calculation. Decision theory provides us with a computational model of human reason, a physics or a mechanics of rational endeavor. It allows us to distinguish, in a quantitative way, between rational and irrational behavior. This is problematic, however, for one can seriously contest the applicability of such abstract formalism to human behavior.

Philosophers in the why-be-moral tradition use an artificial mathematical apparatus to identify and define rational behavior. If, however, decision-theory provides a set of rules and procedures that allows for some kind of rigorous calculation, rigor comes at the cost of enormous simplification. We cannot apply this formalism to actual life. There are too many variables. Each individual person is unique. Each individual circumstance is unique. Life is highly unpredictable. It does not occur in a controlled environment. One cannot *measure*, in any precise way, the contribution of a particular action to one's overall happiness. Indeed, one cannot *measure*, in any precise way, human happiness. The entire project of providing a quantitative analysis of human aspiration begs the question.

Analytic philosophy privileges symbolic logic, but the implementation of a symbolic or mathematical formalism cannot provide us with definitive answers to ultimate philosophical questions. As the American pragmatists argued, questions about rationality, truth, morality, or knowledge transcend mathematical analysis. In Hilary Putnam's words, "an algorithm which solves all of our epistemological problems is a philosopher's fantasy."[3]

The American pragmatist John Dewey was one of the leading figures in "a revolt against formalism" in twentieth-century American thought.[4] In contrast to fellow pragmatist Charles Sanders Peirce, Dewey detested formal logic, describing it as the *"fons et origo malorum"*—the fountain and origin of evil—in academic philosophy.[5] The vehemence of his views is a sore point with analytic philosophers, but Dewey makes a serious point. Dewey denigrates abstract academic speculation, criticizing the separation of theory from practice. He insists that practical, commonsense experience provides an appropriate starting point for all philosophy: "[Philosophy] has no call to create a world of 'reality' *de novo*, nor to delve into secrets of Being hidden from common sense and science. It has no stock of information or body of knowledge that is peculiarly its own. . . . [It] has no private store of knowledge or methods for attaining truth. . . . [I]t has no private access to good. . . . It has no Mosaic or Pauline authority of revelation."[6]

For the pragmatists, philosophy does not begin in abstract contemplation but in practical endeavor. It is not academic philosophy but life itself that brings us knowledge. Formal, mathematical accounts of rationality are a more specialized and simplified expression of a human aptitude that manifests itself, in a more fundamental way, in everyday life. The idea that philosophers can discover a mathematical or symbolic criterion of truth that is truer than ordinary truth, a formal criterion of certitude that is more certain than ordinary certainty, is nothing but an illusion. Symbolic logic restricts itself to questions of validity rather than addresses itself to questions of truth. It cannot, by itself, provide a complete proof of anything. As Pascal and Aristotle both observe, a perfect logical proof is, in principle, impossible, for the process of proving propositions and defining terms would have to go on to infinity.[7]

Philosophers in the why-be-moral school situate rationality, not in the practical everyday space where we act and live, but in an abstract theoretical space that is only accessible to professional thinkers. Dewey writes: "To frame a theory of knowledge which makes it necessary . . . to refer [moral ideas] to some other and separate kind of universe from that of common sense . . . is both provincial and arbitrary."[8] To be a rational agent is, first and foremost, to lead a successful life. But people who lead successful lives do not spend their time adding and subtracting utiles. Their actions are not motivated by some higher economic arithmetic, but by more complicated value systems, by considerations of friendship or love, by loyalties and commitments that transcend economic concerns about self-interest. The good rebel who selflessly dies for a cause is not motivated by economic concerns. One cannot translate the good rebel's motivation into the utility-maximization model without seriously misrepresenting his or her actions.

If we hope to account for the rationality of morality, we need to begin with an account of rationality that accurately reflects the way human beings really do act. We must, in James's words, turn away "from abstraction and insufficiency, from verbal solutions, from bad *a priori* reasons, from fixed principles, closed systems, and pretended absolutes and origins."[9] We must appeal to particulars, emphasize the practical aspects of problems, and refrain from useless questions and bald theoretical abstractions.[10] Even if philosophers in the why-be-moral school could show that morality is a rational endeavor, their account of rationality is less than compelling.

Dewey defines "pragmatism" as "the doctrine that reality possesses practical character."[11] James traces the origins of the movement to a particular insight of Peirce that "our beliefs are really rules for action" and that the meaning of a thought has to be cashed out in terms of the "conduct it is fitted to produce."[12] Truth must be defined in terms of the concrete, practical implications an idea or a belief has for our lives. Hence James's defense of religion as something that can be considered true, not because its dogmas can be logically demonstrated, but because believing in religion may have positive effects on our daily lives.

When traditional philosophers argue for the rationality of morality, they do not use the utility-maximization model. They argue, in line with pragmatism, that morality will have valuable practical effects on ordinary, everyday life. Morality is a means to the good life conceived, not in terms of bare utility-maximization, but in terms of practical human achievement.

PRAGMATISM

In his *Meditations* Descartes declares that epistemology "does not involve action but merely the acquisition of knowledge."[13] Pragmatists criticized, with a missionary zeal, this separation of theory from practice. They considered knowledge, not from a contemplative stance removed from the world, but from the viewpoint of the doer, the participant, the person leading an active life. On this view, philosophy is, at best, a critical extension of our own workaday selves. It is not a magic wand that allows us, with a little deductive flick of the wrist, to enter into new realms of existence that are more real or more true than ordinary reality.

On a familiar view, practical concerns interfere with knowledge. Thinking is separate from doing. Paul Feyerabend distinguishes between observer and participant questions: "An observer describes a life he does not lead (except accidentally), a participant wants to arrange his own life and [determine] what attitude to take towards the things that influence it."[14] In short, "Observers want to know what is going on, participants what to do."[15]

But surely, as the pragmatists suggest, this is an artificial distinction. In the world as we know it, every observer is a participant and every participant, an observer. Only dead people do not participate and they, of course, do not observe (except perhaps from Heaven). Those of us who remain below have to get on with the daily business of living. We cannot somehow step outside our position as participants and view the world from an exclusively observer point of view. It is, to borrow Neurath's image of the boat, as if we are already standing on the deck of a ship out at sea. We must participate in the business of sailing even as we observe.

Pragmatists identified truth with practical utility. James writes: "An idea is true so long as to believe it is profitable to our lives."[16] Prima facie this claim may seem suspect. In evaluating a particular idea, we may ask two apparently separate questions: (1) "Is this idea true?" and (2) "Does this idea have useful effects?" Even a false idea may, it seems, have useful effects. As Paul Carus, an early opponent of James, maintains, we can meaningfully speak of "the useful lie"[17] or "a lie that works satisfactorily."[18] Carus points to financier Baron Rothschild's practice of spreading false rumors about the stock market in order to drive stock prices up or down, a practice that was profitable or useful for him, but clearly devious. This is, however, to misrepresent the pragmatist position.

The pragmatists did not argue that the purpose of life is financial gain. If the goal of life is happiness, spiritual fulfillment, moral accomplishment or personal integrity, we may plausibly argue that dishonesty—or, more broadly, serious vice—is highly unprofitable. At the very least, this is not an absurd position. If then we roll moral, scientific, empirical, aesthetic, spiritual, and religious aspirations into one and regard the world, not as detached observers, but as active participants, we can argue, with some plausibility, that the apparent utility produced by false beliefs has, in the long term, negative consequences and that, given appropriate circumstances, true beliefs are always useful. We can make sense of the epistemological claim that "usefulness" and "truthfulness" eventually come together, that that which is useful leads to the truth and that that which is truthful is, in the final analysis, useful. At the same time, we can understand why other philosophers prefer to treat utility and truthfulness as separate categories of evaluation. In either case, pragmatism provides an important service. It brings philosophy down to earth, importing into academic practice the same criteria for knowledge that we use in ordinary life. This apparent "de-sophistication" of philosophy is philosophically sophisticated, for it allows us to elaborate an objective view of knowledge without running into the epistemological problems that have plagued modern philosophy.

The pragmatists argued against any notion of perfect proof or absolute certitude. They argued for fallibilism, but they did not argue for skepticism.[19] Authors like Dewey, James, and Peirce wed a vigorous belief in human fallibility to an equally vigorous belief in the reality of a commonly perceived and shared world. Unless we are seriously ill, dysfunctional, or neurotic, we are not obsessed with metaphysical worries about whether we can know the real world. We do not doubt, in nonacademic situations, the reality of cement trucks and sunshine and roses and moral principles and other people. Every time we act we overcome skepticism, for skepticism is, in a bad sense, just another metaphysical argument, separated from the world of action.

Pragmatism overcomes the kind of paralyzing moral skepticism that motivates authors in the why-be-moral school. We do not have to convince people to adopt moral convictions. We all have moral ideas. We all make value judgments. We all feel guilt and shame. We all admire certain types of actions. We all distinguish, in some way or another, between success and failure. On the pragmatist view, the why-be-moral issue is a pseudoproblem. We do not have to argue our way to morality, for we are already there. Rational agents inevitably operate on some kind of moral understanding.

The pragmatists argued that the separation of knowledge from action was misguided. If we have enough knowledge to act, then we have enough knowledge to know. In our daily lives, we do not hesitate to judge, to condemn, to praise, and to act. We all make decisions based on some conception of the good. Though we cannot prove, in any absolutely certain way, that moral knowledge is possible, the unavailability of any absolute proof need not incite any hasty descent into moral skepticism. Practical experience teaches us that there are better and worse ways of fixing a bicycle tire, of building a house, of calculating one's income tax, of training for football, of succeeding at marriage, of successfully raising children, of keeping friends, and so on. Likewise, there are better and worse strategies for human living. All views about human achievement, all theories of knowledge, all moral opinions, are not equally sound or equally plausible. If we want to be happy, if we want peace of mind, if we do not want to be racked by guilt and shame, some approaches will work better than others. Through the careful examination of ordinary experience we can develop standards that will allow us to distinguish between moral beliefs and worldviews that are more or less reasonable, more or less truthful.

Pragmatism changes the focus of moral philosophy. We do not need to convince people to be moral. What we need to do is improve the moral notions people already have. We need to critically examine the ideas that underlie our actions. We need to scrutinize our beliefs for inconsistencies, contradictions, and discrepancies. We may never have absolute knowledge, but we can distinguish, in a more modest sense, between inconsistency and consistency, between truth and falsehood, between morality and immorality. If we cannot provide an absolute proof for specific moral assertions, there is compelling evidence that points in definite directions.

THE FACT-VALUE DISTINCTION

The pragmatist view of rationality takes moral knowledge seriously. It situates epistemological discourse in the world of action where moral ideas predominate. There is, however, a further obstacle to rational discourse about morality: the modern tendency to sharply distinguish facts from values. Call this view, which historically derives from Hume, epistemological dualism.[20]

Epistemological dualism distinguishes between two types of claims. Facts tell us what *is*. Evaluations tell us what *ought* to be. Facts describe the world. Evaluations describe our inner feelings or dispositions. Facts possess objective validity. Evaluations are, in Ayer's words, "pure expressions of feeling," "ejaculations or commands" that have "no objective validity whatsoever."[21] On this view, facts are epistemologically strong. Evaluations are epistemologically weak. Facts provide us with universal truths; evaluations are a matter of taste or individual perspective. Facts are subject to empirical verification; evaluations are not subject to empirical verification. Facts can be proved or disproved; evaluations cannot be proved or disproved. Science deals with facts; moral philosophy deals with values.

The dualist view undermines the epistemological status of morality. Moral evaluations are subjective, soft, neither true or false. We cannot derive an evaluation from a description, an "ought" from an "is," for evaluation does not originate in the objective world but in some kind of subjective feeling.[22] On the dualist view, morality is, fundamentally, a matter of pure feeling. It has little to do with reason.

Alasdair MacIntyre criticizes dualism.[23] On the dualist account, factual propositions tell us what is true about the world. On the other hand, it is the case that "when anyone says 'this is right' or 'this is good,' he is only expressing his own feeling; . . . he is not asserting or judging at all; he is really making an exclamation that expresses a favorable feeling."[24] It follows that moral agreement cannot "be secured by any rational method."[25] The term "moral philosophy" becomes a misnomer. Morality becomes a matter of emotion, not of clear-thinking.

Philosophers in the why-be-moral school accept the fact-value distinction, and this renders the rationality of moral decision-making inherently problematic. These philosophers circumvent the problem by appealing to a contractarian model of utility-maximization. As we have seen, this approach is problematic. There are, however, other ways we can solve this problem. If we can show that moral statements, like factual statements, are, in the strongest possible sense, true, it will be rational to believe in them. If, moreover, moral statements are "literally" true, then the fact-value distinction collapses.

Even a more mitigated proponent of the fact-value distinction like Anthony Flew insists that there is "a differentiation" between facts and values that "has to be made and insisted upon."[26] I will argue, on the other hand, that the fact-value distinction, rigorously understood, is a fallacy. Close examination reveals that facts and values are interdependent. We cannot disentangle the two. Every meaningful factual statement has ethical or normative bearing and every meaningful normative statement has a factual basis.

On the dualist view, language has two mutually exclusive functions. To describe the world is to do one thing; to recommend action is another. These are two entirely separate perspectives. But truthful discourse does not function in such a single-minded manner. Suppose we are arguing about police brutality and I say to you: "Six police officers were murdered in

Manhattan last week. *That is a fact.*" What am I trying to tell you? I am trying to tell you that six police officers *really* were murdered in Manhattan last week. I am informing you that you *ought* to believe this. But this is to engage in normative discourse. It is to recommend a course of action. So the distinction between descriptive and normative statements quickly dissolves. When I say, "Six police officers were murdered in Manhattan last week" I am telling you (1) this *is* what happened, and (2) this is what you should do, you *ought* to believe this. The is-statement encloses an ought-statement within its meaning.

Suppose Mary, the chemistry teacher, tells the class: "The benzene ring *is* made up of six carbon atoms." What is Mary doing? She is telling the class members that they *ought* to believe that the benzene ring is made up of six carbon atoms. She is saying, "If you want to be a knowledgeable person: Believe in this!" She is, *at the same time,* describing the way the world is *and* recommending a particular course of action. The assertion "The benzene ring has six carbon atoms" means (1) this is the way the world *is* and (2) this is what you should do, you *ought* to believe this. The is-statement and the ought-statement go together.

Language is a complex endeavor. Suppose I go to the theater. An actor shouts: "The king is dead!" This is a fiction. No king is really dead. Nonetheless, the character on the stage is saying: "You *ought* to believe the king is dead." The meaning of the statement is qualified by the context of the utterance. What the actor is really saying is: "For the duration of the play, in order to understand the author's intention, to participate in this game of make-believe, you *ought* to believe that the king is dead." Still, this is an ought-statement. The actor is telling you what to do. He is recommending a course of action.

Hume's law tells us that we cannot derive an "ought" from an "is."[27] But we can derive an "ought" from an "is." Every claim that "this is the case" includes the claim that we ought to believe that "this is the case." On the dualist model, language either describes the world or it recommends a course of action. This is, however, a false dichotomy. To insist on a fact is to recommend belief in that fact. The very notion of description would lose its meaning in a universe of discourse where truth is irrelevant.

If, however, every is-statement contains within itself an ought-statement, we can also argue that every intelligible ought-statement presupposes an is-statement. Ought implies can. I cannot logically maintain that you *ought* to do something unless I also maintain that it *is* the case that you are able to do it. This is not so controversial. Suppose your track coach asks you to run the one-hundred-yard dash at the speed of light. This is not a meaningful statement. We cannot consistently claim that you *ought* to run the one-hundred-yard dash at the speed of light without maintaining an absolute absurdity—that it *is* a real possibility that you can run at the speed of light. An ought-statement that is not conjoined with the appropriate is-statement is only nonsense. Contrary to what proponents of the naturalistic fallacy suggest, evaluative and descriptive statements come together.

How we describe the world depends on how we evaluate the world, and how we evaluate the world depends on how we describe the world. Suppose that in reading the New Testament, I am so taken with the morality of Jesus' preaching that I am converted to a belief in Christianity and, subsequently, to a belief in the physical fact of Jesus' miracles. In this case, my belief in an ethical ideal leads to a belief in alleged facts. For early Christians, the process was reversed. Jesus' miracles are presented, in the Gospels, as a sign of divine authority. The general sense of the text might be paraphrased: "Look! You must believe what Jesus said. He performed miracles. He rose from the dead!" In this latter case, a belief in the physical fact of Jesus' miracles secured belief in the ethical ideal of Christianity.[28] Just as a particular evaluation of the world may lead to a particular description of the world, a particular description of the world may lead to a particular evaluation.

The is-ought distinction derives its authority, in part, from a lingering positivism. Positivists argue that facts must be empirically verifiable. Because values are not empirically verifiable, they are not, in any sense, descriptive or factual. But there are at least two different meanings of the word "fact." A fact is that which is empirically verifiable. And again, a fact is that which is, in the strongest possible sense, true. Suppose I declare: "There is a God. That is a fact." I clearly do not mean that the existence of God is empirically verifiable, that one can somehow perform a scientific test and prove that He exists.[29] I mean, more simply, that we should believe that the proposition "There is a God" is true. Positivists conflate these two different meanings of the word "fact." To assume that whatever is in the strongest possible sense true must be an empirical fact is, at the very least, to beg the question.

As Copleston observes, the fact-value distinction is not itself a fact.[30] It is an assertion, not an argument. Scientific verifiability, narrowly interpreted, is not the only standard of truth. We cannot simply assume, because of an uncritical enthusiasm for science, that other standards of truth are not valid or useful. There is something inconsistent or even hypocritical about a philosophical stance that recommends one standard of truth for ordinary life and a different standard of truth for academic philosophy. If we want a consistent epistemology, we must critically elaborate, in philosophy, the standards of truth we use in ordinary life.

Description and evaluation overlap. As thinking, affective human beings, we are motivated and oriented by worldviews that incorporate both facts and values. These ways of understanding are not exclusively factual, nor are they value-free. Positivists and neopositivists, in brandishing the is-ought distinction, champion the epistemological preeminence of science, but this seems contradictory. To presuppose that an is-statement made by science is something we *ought* to believe in is, in a single stroke, to derive an "ought" from every scientific "is." Such a move can only be justified if we assume that "ought-ness"—normative import—is *inalienably* associated with the is-statements made by science. It will follow that there is no great divide between normative and descriptive discourse *within the realm of science.* As it turns out then, the operating assumption of positivism is not that one cannot derive an "ought" from an "is," but that one can *only* derive an "ought" from an "is" within science. But this is a much less radical claim. Even if science is the only methodology for producing truthful propositions, this does not show that "ought-ness" is not an inextricable aspect of "is-ness." It only shows that "is-ness" is a much more restricted feature of reality than is usually supposed.

Modern scientific culture self-consciously separates facts from values, but there are other possibilities. Seen from a premodern religious perspective, the statement "Murder is evil" describes the objective nature of an act and, at the same time, recommends a specific course of action. The prescriptive is contained within the descriptive and vice versa. Seen from this perspective, a purely empirical description of the world is, if not completely wrong, at the very least, incomplete. The universe encloses a moral reality. Murder really is evil in as strong a sense as snow is white. This religious worldview has been largely set aside in academic circles, because there has been a radical shift toward a secular set of values.

Christianity, Buddhism, Marxism, secular humanism: all worldviews involve an interchange between facts and values. The positivists believed that science was somehow different. Scientists could somehow sheer off all interpretation and look at the bare facts of nature under the cold, clear light of reason. They could produce an isolated set of truths that was entirely factual and value-free. But as proponents of the sociology of knowledge point out (at times with undisguised glee), no one has been able to discover conspicuous criteria that distinguish science from nonscience.[31] We cannot, in any simple and straightforward way, distinguish the scientific pursuit of knowledge from the nonscientific. Science itself is a value-laden enterprise.

Authors like Thomas Kuhn and Paul Feyerabend have written critical accounts that emphasize the role of the historical and the irrational in the institutional world of science. Andrew Pickering, in a largely technical book on the history of high energy particle physics, writes that the bosons and quarks that constitute the fundamental facts of contemporary physics are not bare facts but "artifacts," constructions of a social institution, a particular methodology, a specific value-system and a unique historical development. We tend to embrace uncritically the theories and discoveries of modern science. But Pickering makes a startling claim. He insists that there is "no obligation on anyone framing a view of the world to take account of what twentieth-century science has to say. . . . [Scientific] world-views are cultural products; there is no need to be intimidated by them."[32]

An Older View of Reason

The modern distinction between morality and reason may gain plausibility from a disturbing fact. Experience shows that psychopaths, serial killers, Nazi war criminals, perpetrators of atrocities, and sociopaths may be able reasoners.[33] These horrendously immoral agents can count; they can calculate; they can perform highly complex technical tasks; they can choose the means needed to accomplish their ends; they can draw conclusions from evidence, make arguments, defend themselves, rationalize their actions, and so on. And yet they cannot comprehend the simplest moral truths. This might be taken as evidence in support of a modern view that identifies reason and morality as two separate abilities or faculties. What follows from this fact is, however, open to interpretation.

Ancient thinkers devised a very different account of reason. To begin with, they believed that reason included, among other things, the ability to tell the difference between right and wrong. What separated humans from animals was the capacity for moral insight. On this account, psychopaths and such like have left the human community. They are brutes, monsters, Yahoos, beasts. Their lack of moral blindness is, however, a failure of reason. They no longer qualify as rational animals. They are not just morally ill. They are defective reasoners.

But the ancient view does not stop here. Even if we divest rationality of any trace of moral content, we will still have, on the ancient view, two distinctly different faculties or abilities associated with rationality. As Joseph Novak explains, ancient writers, in general, distinguished between two types of logical insight or illumination.[34] Reason, on this account, can "link premises to conclusions and thereby display a properly discursive side," or it can "intuit simply apprehended truths or even simple essences in a sort of indivisible non-propositional knowing."[35] Later medieval authors such as Boethius and Aquinas called the first kind of reason *ratio* and the second kind of reason *intelligentia*.[36] *Ratio* involves a stepwise progression toward the truth from one understood proposition to another, whereas *intelligentia* provides an immediate, indivisible grasp of simply apprehended truths.[37] These authors generally considered *intelligentia* (the thought pattern of angels) to be the highest form of reason. *Ratio* is a laborious process, while *intelligentia* provides immediate, instantaneous enlightenment.

We must be careful not to misconstrue the meaning of these earlier authors. The *ratio-intelligentia* distinction does not correspond to the familiar analytic-synthetic distinction introduced into modern logic by authors like Hume and Kant. Synthetic propositions record the results of empirical observation. Analytic propositions, on the other hand, are purely linguistic, tautologous, and devoid of real content. The *ratio-intelligentia* distinction, in contrast, does not signal any difference in empirical or nonempirical content. The difference between the propositions apprehended by *intelligentia* and those apprehended by *ratio* has to do with the way in which they were discovered. The propositions intuitively grasped by *intelligentia* are not purely linguistic. They are better classified as "self-evident" than "analytic." They are not tautologous. They may provide real insight into the nature of reality.

This older account of reason explains a basic fact about logic. The process of argument has to start somewhere. If apparently human agents are unable to grasp a basic logical truth like the principle of noncontradiction, we cannot make them accept the point through some ingenious process of argumentation, for one needs the principle of noncontradiction to get the process of logical reasoning underway. Without it, *logical* deliberation simply is not possible. What this shows is that reason, understood in a discursive sense, depends upon a prior ability, namely *intelligentia*. As C. S. Lewis explains, "A life of unmitigated [argument] where nothing was simply 'seen' and all had to be proved, would . . . be impossible; for nothing can be proved if nothing is self-evident."[38]

This twofold model of reason may now be adapted to the case of the morally inert psychopath. Those who champion the reason-morality distinction may claim that these kinds of example show that reason must exist distinct from morality. If, however, the morally inert are able to argue, this only shows that they can reason in a discursive manner. This is not enough to secure fully rational status. These agents do not lack *ratio,* but *intelligentia.* They lack the first principles on which (moral) reasoning depends.

This is the sense in which they are defective reasoners. They may be able to talk and argue with understanding, but they do not possess the moral starting points secured by a fully rational nature.

Medieval thinkers developed this ancient view of reason in an explicitly moral manner. In a discussion of moral psychology, Aquinas refers to a faculty of *synderesis,* which Timothy Potts describes as the "natural disposition of the human mind by which we apprehend the basic principles of behavior . . . without inquiry."[39] *Synderesis* is like moral *intelligentia.* It is the ability to grasp, in an immediate, nondiscursive way, basic moral truths. If someone cannot understand, for example, the glaring inconsistency that arises when we treat other people in ways in which we do not want to be treated, there may be little we can do for them. The problem is not merely, as on the modern view, a lack of feeling. They suffer from a mental handicap that has, in one way or another, undermined their reasoning faculty. Although, on Aquinas's account, we can achieve moral knowledge through a stepwise process of argumentation, there are also self-evident moral truths that we must apprehend directly.

The modern separation of morality from reason gains plausibility from a unilateral focus on the discursive side of reasoning. To assume that the morally inert can reason because they can make discursive arguments is, however, contentious. As these earlier authors indicate, serious moral ignorance may be understood as a rational as well as a moral failing. People who lack all moral insight will then lose their status as moral reasoners. I will argue that the morally inert cannot be free in the way in which rational agents are free. They cannot achieve autonomy.

COHERENTISM AND THE WORLD

If we want to defend the rationality of morality, we must be able to demonstrate that a robust sense of morality is philosophically legitimate, even astute. This means doing epistemology. A layperson may cringe at the thought. Epistemologists wonder (like Russell) why it does not make sense to say that the nonexistent king of France is bald, or study, in unpardonable detail, strange metaphysical theories such as Meinong's belief that golden mountains and unicorns exist as conceptual objects. But this kind of close study is not what the present circumstances require. If we want to shore up the intellectual and academic status of moral discourse, we need to sketch out some general view of the place and legitimacy of moral knowledge.

If moral statements are true or even valid, it is rational to believe in them. Although philosophers in the why-be-moral school identify rationality and self-interest, the practice of rationality does not originate in a notion of self-interest, but in a notion of true belief. The whole point of believing is not having beliefs per se, but having beliefs that are true. To be a rational agent is to have true beliefs and act accordingly.

The pragmatists argued for a coherentist theory of truth. This does not mean, as is often supposed, that they repudiated any notion of correspondence. Peirce, for example, contends that the converging opinions of a scientific community provide the best account of reality.[40] He suggests that metaphysical statements are not true because we believe that they are true, but because they *correspond* to experimental results, to empirical data, to a "real world" that, in some important sense, exists outside ourselves.

Again, James argues that moral beliefs are true because they *correspond* to ideas in the mind of God. In James's words: "Actualized in [God's] thought already must be that ethical philosophy which [is] the pattern . . . our own [ethical philosophy] must evermore approach."[41] In both cases, truth involves a kind of correspondence with ultimate reality.

The notion that knowledge can "mirror" reality has been largely denigrated in modern philosophy. Nonetheless, the idea that a true proposition represents, mirrors, or corresponds to an objective reality retains a certain basic usefulness. Bertrand Russell, at the end of his career, was to write: "I think that we can, however imperfectly, mirror the world like Leibniz's monads; and I think it is the duty of the philosopher to make himself as undistorting a mirror as he can be."[42]

Richard Rorty, who presents himself as a modern pragmatist, defends an influential form of coherentism. Rorty is heavily influenced by Kant and Wittgenstein.[43] He argues, in line with Wittgenstein, that all human discourse takes place within a particular language game, and that although there may be better or worse ways of using words in a particular language game, there is no such thing as a better or worse game. No game gives a truer or a more accurate description of reality than any other. As Kant insists, we have no access to "things-in-themselves," to the noumena, to reality as it independently is. We cannot move beyond a particular cultural description to the unmediated reality of a preconceptual given.

Rorty reduces metaphysics to the Great Conversation. Truthful concepts do not correspond to the nature of the real world. They cohere with other concepts in the same language game. They refer to linguistic categories rather than reality categories. But this leaves us in a quandary. We are left with a self-referential language, with nothing but words, symbols that refer to other symbols. We cannot go beyond language and touch the bare bodkin of reality itself. Language is no longer a tool that refers to something outside itself. It is a kind of Chinese puzzle made up of interlocking pieces that floats in its own self-contained bubble, unattached to anything existent, to anything real. On Rorty's view, we have perhaps gained a Great Conversation but we have lost the world.

Pragmatism has been criticized because of this kind of exclusive coherentism, but Rorty is less than faithful to his pragmatist roots. The original pragmatists argued that we should begin philosophy in the everyday world. Rorty paints himself into a corner, because he begins his philosophy in the wrong place—not in the world of action, but in the world of philosophical speculation. Once we have divorced language from reality, we cannot open the door and let reality come back in. We cannot bring reality back into existence through some sort of transcendental argument. If we want a philosophy that deals with reality, we must begin our speculation in a different place, in the everyday existent world of work and action.

The pragmatists conceived of philosophy as the critical extension of beliefs we already have. But we already have existential commitments about the nature of the world. When I say: "Please move that refrigerator," the existence of the refrigerator is not at issue. It is something that is built into the very meaning of the sentence. Existential assumptions are not something that have to be argued into the system after the fact. They are part and parcel of the original meaning of language. We do not have to import the "real world" into the meaning of ordinary sentences and utterances. Language is not just commentary on language. It is a commentary on the only world we know, the real world in which we live.

Rorty, true to the pragmatist tradition, wants to define truth in terms of coherence, but the coherence that characterizes a justified belief system is a coherence between sentences that already carry within themselves commitments about what really exists. These existential assumptions do not arise in any arbitrary fashion. Even in ordinary life, we make careful distinctions between reality and illusion. We distinguish reliable forms of perception from optical illusions, dreams, or hallucinations. We distinguish real people from characters in novels; real landscapes from the landscapes we see in paintings; plastic fruit from real fruit; children in pirate costumes from real pirates; and so on. Basic metaphysical distinctions between what is and what is not can be said to originate, not in philosophy, but in the practical realm of ordinary, everyday endeavor.[44]

Pragmatism grounds philosophy in practical endeavor. Epistemological concepts like "truth," "justification," "objectivity," "proof," and "correspondence" must be defined, not in relation to some noumena, but in relation to the world we inhabit. To be alarmed at the epistemological inaccessibility of a made-up category of things-in-themselves, to argue that all possibility of knowledge is lost because we cannot know a phantom world of things-in-themselves, is a simple case of overstatement.

One can try to tie the coherentist and correspondence accounts of truth together. We ought to believe that particular propositions are true because we have evidence. But coherence is the best evidence we have for truth. When we are faced with inconsistency, discrepancy, contradiction, this is a sign that there is something awry, that the world view we have internalized does not *correspond* to the world we actually live in.

FALLIBILISM

This wedding of coherence with realism will not satisfy the professional skeptic. There will always be the lingering doubt: Do our perceptions and beliefs correspond to the real world, the noumenal world, the world as it independently is? Modern philosophy cultivated this kind of metaphysical doubt which gave rise to an impressive speculative tradition. The pragmatists, however, rejected this academic tradition as a deluded "quest for certainty." There is no point laboring over questions we cannot answer. We must act on the evidence we are presented with. We are human beings, not gods. If we have been tricked by Descartes's evil demon, this is just too bad.

Pragmatism includes an admission of a basic fallibilism. As human beings, we are, first and foremost, fallible creatures. We cannot see the world from a God's-eye point of view. We cannot erect any transcendental architecture of knowledge and truth, any foolproof metaphysical or scientific system immune to all doubt and skepticism. As Laurence Bonjour points out, philosophical pretensions to infallible, indubitable, or incorrigible knowledge constitute "philosophical overkill."[45]

Philosophers, down through history, have proposed various sources of knowledge: *epagôgé*, induction, intuition, *Offenbarung*, revelation, divine recollection, the "Interior Teacher," common sense, *bon sens, finesse*, the principle of noncontradiction, empirical verification, formal considerations, practical considerations, coherence, and so on. But whatever means we use to establish knowledge, we must accept certain claims as true, not because we can *prove* in any absolute sense that they are true, but because, in some less than perfectly certain manner, they conform to the evidence. We all believe in the existence of other people, in the relationship of cause and effect, in the veracity of sense perception, in logical principles, in the laws of probability, in common sense, in intuition, in various types of moral judgment, and so on. In light of these necessary beliefs, knowledge, argument, and even proof become possible. If human knowledge is imperfect, this does not mean that all claims to knowledge are equally valid. If we cannot know the world from a God's-eye point of view, this does not mean that we cannot know the world. If we cannot have an incorrigible epistemology, we can, in a more modest sense, do epistemology.

The pragmatists themselves were suspicious of the philosophical tradition, and Rorty amplifies and expands on this tradition of mistrust. He claims that the Kantian view undermines the foundation of speculative metaphysics, but Kant's notion of the noumena is itself a speculative metaphysical construction that distracts us from the real world we inhabit. And Kant's views are not entirely novel nor unprecedented. The noumenal world is, roughly speaking, in the language of earlier debates, the world as God sees it. Boethius reminds us that only God, "looking down from above. . . comprehends the form itself which could not be known to any other."[46] Only God sees the thing as it is in itself. Human beings cannot transcend the severe limitations of an earthly perspective.

We cannot, as the pragmatists argued, see the world from "a God's-eye point of view."[47] This is, no doubt, an important insight. Contrary to what Rorty implies, however, it is hardly breaking news. Earlier philosophers, working within a religious framework, did not aspire to "a God's-eye point of view." This would have been blasphemous as well as unthinkable. For the orthodox Christian, Jew, or Muslim, "The greatness of God exceeds our knowledge" (Job. 36:26). It is "impossible to penetrate [God's] motives or understand his methods" (Rom. 11:33) "As high as the heavens are above the earth, so [God's] thoughts are above [our] thoughts." (Isa. 55:9)

Western science, not traditional religion, proposes—as a completable project—the elaboration of a God's-eye view of things. In the Old Testament, the Psalmist proclaims:

> [God's] knowledge is beyond my understanding,
> A height to which my mind cannot attain.
>
> (Ps. 139:6)

According to the author of Ecclesiasticus:

> It is impossible to fathom the marvels of the Lord. . .
> When a man finishes [considering them] he is only beginning,
> And when he stops he is as puzzled as ever.
>
> (Sir. 18:3–7)

In Christian and Jewish Scripture, human wisdom is often ridiculed. St. Paul quotes the Old Testament: "God is not convinced by the arguments of the wise" (1 Cor. 3:20). And again: "[God] shall destroy the wisdom of the wise and bring to nothing all the learning of the learned" (1:20). When Zophar asks Job,

> Where does wisdom come from?
> Where is understanding to be found?
> (Job 28:20)

Job responds

> It is outside the knowledge of every living thing . . .
> God alone has traced its path
> and found out where it lives.
> For [only] He sees to the end of the earth,
> and observes all that lies under heaven.
>
> (Job 28:21–24)

Western philosophy is not a monolithic edifice of worn-out, single-minded, absolutist, foundationalist discourse. Bernstein laments: "Why does Rorty think that philosophy (or 'Philosophy') amounts to little more than the worn-out vocabulary of 'bad' foundational discourse? So much of his recent writing falls into the genre of the 'God that failed' discourse. There seems to be something almost oedipal—a form of patricide—in Rorty's obsessive attacks on the father figures of philosophy and metaphysics."[48] Traditional authors who preceded Descartes and Kant were not all "raving Platonists"[49] blindly pursuing absolute knowledge. Their views are highly detailed and complex. They themselves comment, in various ways, on the problematic nature of knowledge. MacIntyre cites Aristotle: "It is difficult to discern whether one knows or not."[50] And Aquinas: "It is difficult to discern whether we know from appropriate principles, which alone is genuinely scientific knowing."[51]

Popular caricature notwithstanding, earlier historical authors were not naively optimistic about the possibility of human knowledge. In a commentary on the Apostles' Creed, Aquinas states that even philosophical "knowledge is so imperfect that no philosopher has ever been able to discover perfectly the nature of a single fly."[52] Aquinas insists on the limitations of human intelligence. Just as the uneducated person knows far less than the expert, so too "the intelligence of an angel surpasses that of the greatest philosopher far more than the intelligence of the philosopher surpasses that of an ignoramus."[53] The man who thinks he knows as much as the angel or, worse yet, as much as God is an utter fool. He is, according to Aquinas, condemned by the words of Job: "Behold, God is great, exceeding our knowledge" (Job 36:26). And again, by the words of Ecclesiasticus: "What is too sublime for you, seek not; into things beyond your strength search not. Meddle not, when shown things beyond human understanding" (Sir. 3:20–22).[54]

There are other traditional authors who emphasize the imperfection and the limits of mere human knowledge. Boethius writes that "it is not allowed to man to comprehend in thought all the ways of the divine work or expound them in speech."[55] If God governs the world according to providence or fate, "men are in no position to contemplate this order."[56] Nicholas of Cusa speaks of human knowledge as "learned ignorance," *docta ignorantia*. According to Nicholas, "Our intellect which is not truth, never comprehends the truth so precisely that truth cannot be comprehended infinitely more precisely."[57] Leibniz argues that knowledge of why God permits sin "passes the capacity of the finite mind,"[58] that "most knowledge is only confused or indeed assumed,"[59] and that there are "many things which surpass the powers of our natures and indeed all limited natures."[60] According to Thomas à Kempis: "Human reason is weak and easily mistaken."[61] Pierre Nicole writes: "The most solid philosophy is only the science of human ignorance; it is better fitted to unmask those who pride themselves in their knowledge than to instruct those who desire to learn something certain."[62] Cardinal Henry Newman quips: "What do I know of substance or matter? Just as much as the greatest philosophers, and that is nothing at all."[63] And so on.

The pragmatists, like the best philosophers in the Western tradition, recognize the limitations of human fallibility. We may be rational creatures, but we are not infallible. We cannot devise a model for rationality that eliminates all possibility of error. On the other hand, human knowledge, properly understood, is possible. If the pragmatists embrace fallibilism, they did not embrace skepticism. We can be reasonably certain that the world corresponds to certain parameters, descriptions, rules, or principles. Skepticism is a kind of philosophical luxury. Even skeptics believe in reality when they cross a busy street. But a philosopher who believes one thing while doing philosophy and another thing while crossing the street participates in a glaring inconsistency, one that is philosophically (and even morally) suspect. It is this theoretical two-facedness, the reliance on one knowledge criterion for philosophy and another knowledge criterion for ordinary life, that the original pragmatists contested.

COHERENTISM AND RATIONALITY

We have argued against a narrow formalist conception of reason, eradicated a false dichotomy between facts and values, proposed two modes of rational illumination, situated philosophy within the real world, and embraced fallibilism. We are now in a position to briefly investigate the practice of rationality.

Pragmatists like Dewey and James propose a coherentist theory of truth. In line with this coherentist view, we might identify consistency or coherence as the root notion of rationality. Rational agents act in a consistent manner; irrational agents lose themselves in incoherence and inconsistency. One can, however, define consistency in many different manners. Philosophers in the why-be-moral school, for example, define consistency in terms of the utility-maximization principle. Rational agents act in ways that are consistent with the goal of maximizing utility. Irrational agents violate the principle. These philosophers do not dispute the consistency account of rationality. Rather, they introduce a more specialized account of consistency.

Philosophers in the why-be-moral school generally take this instrumentalist account of reason for granted. If they were to defend the utility-maximization model, they would have to appeal to some metacriterion of consistency. They would have to demonstrate that action in accordance with the utility-maximization principle is, in a more fundamental sense, consistent. This would be a difficult undertaking, for we can show that action in conformity with this principle may be, in a more fundamental sense, inconsistent.

Telling lies may be, in specific circumstances, a good way of maximizing utility. Likewise, on the instrumentalist model, it may be considered rational behavior. But what do we do when we tell a lie? We act in an inconsistent manner. To tell a lie is to say that something we know to be false is true. This kind of claim is, however, embedded in inconsistencies. It is inconsistent with the nature of the world, with our own beliefs and knowledge, with its apparent purpose. When we tell a lie, we suffer a kind of psychic disintegration. We live on two incompatible levels—on a public and a private plane—which are inconsistent with one another. Telling lies may be consistent with the utility-maximization principle. But lying is, in the most fundamental sense, an incoherent act. It follows that certain ways of maximizing utility are, in fact, irrational.

We can define rationality as the operation of a fundamental consistency. The actions of a rational agent must be consistent, not merely with the utility-maximization principle but with the world, with human nature, with higher aspirations, with the principles of success in practical endeavor. To privilege a purely economic, utility-maximization account of rationality is to adopt a very narrow view of human achievement.

Philosophers in the why-be-moral school wonder about the rationality of morality. If, however, rationality is consistency *simpliciter*, morality is the practice of a particular type of consistency. Normative accounts of morality invariably impose some kind of consistency on human behavior: Treat your neighbor as yourself; obey the categorical imperative; obey the Lord thy God; *always* act so as to procure happiness for the greatest number; *always* do your duty; *never* break your promises, repudiate sin; and so on. When we examine different moral theories, we observe an underlying modus operandi. Do you want to know how to behave? Here is a principle, a method, a way of understanding the world. Act *consistently* with this principle and you will be moral. Insomuch as morality signifies a particular kind of consistency, however, rationality and morality come together.

One might argue that the practice of rationality does not originate in a notion of self-interest but in a notion of true belief. Coherence and truth go together. Worldviews that are consistent are, in all likelihood, true. Their coherence or consistency is evidence for their truth.[64] If, however, rationality originates in a notion of true belief, so does morality. Moralists inevitably appeal to some criterion of truth.

The arguments moralists propose proceed in two logical steps: (1) "This is true belief" and (2) "If you want to act morally, act in accordance with this belief." Ethical relativists, for example, argue that none of us can discern objective standards for belief or action within the world. If, however, this is true, we ought to resist absolute judgments. Divine Command theorists argue that there is a benevolent, all-knowing God who promulgated laws to regulate our actions. If, however, this is true, we ought to submit to His laws. Egalitarians argue that all human beings share equal dignity. If, however, this is true, we ought to grant human beings equality. Utilitarians argue that only happiness has intrinsic value. If, however, this is true, we ought to produce as much happiness as possible. And so on.

Authors in the why-be-moral school also base their moral reasoning on a notion of true belief. Contractarians like Gauthier and Narveson argue that we should be moral so that we can escape Hobbes's state of nature. Does Hobbes's frightful depiction of a lawless state of nature provide us with a true picture of the world? Stoics like Posidonius and anarchists like Kropotkin argue that the state of nature is the state of grace.[65] It is the establishment of law and order that spawns immoral action. Government corrupts. In a pregovernment state, neighbors would live in peace and harmony.

We will not resolve this dispute here. The point is that contractarians appeal, like everyone else, to some picture of the world that is assumed to be true. Their accounts of morality and rationality do not provide any privileged account of reality, but depend on presumptions and beliefs that are assumed to be true. The debate between contractarians, stoics, and anarchists is not about whether a rational agent should act in accordance with true belief. The debate is inevitably about which of these belief systems is really true.

Philosophers in the why-be-moral tradition separate morality and rationality. But these are not separate aspirations. Agents who deliberately act in a moral manner order their actions in line with beliefs that they believe to be true. They may, of course, be mistaken. Nonetheless, their moral striving entails a striving toward conduct that is consistent with truth. But action that is consistent with the truth, very broadly construed, is what we mean by the term "rationality."

THE ZEALOUS NAZI

I have argued that rationality may be identified with the practice of consistency. Some moral views are more consistent—that is, more rational—than others. This is not, however, a widespread view. A relativist like Rorty argues that moral and immoral practices are equally consistent. He tells a story about the development of his position:

> Like a lot of other people who wind up teaching philosophy, I, too, got into the business because, having read some Plato, I thought I could use my budding dialectical talents to *demonstrate* that the bad guys were bad and the good guys good—to do to contemporary bad guys (for example, the bullies who used to beat me up in high school) what Socrates thought he was doing to Thrasymachus, Gorgias, and others. But, some twenty years back, I finally decided that this project was not going to pan out—that "demonstration" was just not available in this area and that a theoretically sophisticated bully and I would always reach an argumentative standoff.[66]

Rorty subscribes to Hare's view that "there is no way to 'refute' a sophisticated, consistent, passionate psychopath—for example a Nazi who would favor his own elimination if he turned out to be Jewish."[67] But Hare's famous example is an ingenuous red herring. On one level, the zealous Nazi is consistent, for he treats all Jews in the very same manner. But on another level, he is radically inconsistent, for he does not treat all human

beings in the very same manner. But humanness is a much more fundamental trait than Jewishness. If the zealous Nazi is, on a superficial level,
consistent, he is, on a more fundamental level, radically inconsistent. He
acts in an irrational manner.

Treating Jews as if they were not human beings is an inconsistent—
that is, an irrational—action. The zealous Nazi displays a single-minded
allegiance to his cause, but he is not, in any deeper sense, a rational agent.
Those who helped fugitive Jews in World War II, on the other hand, were
often motivated by some deeper, underlying sense of moral consistency.
Norman Geras, in a text that takes issue with Rorty, tells the true story of a
February 1945 escape by Russian officers from Mauthausen, one of the
most brutal Nazi concentration camps in Poland.[68] Many local families,
afraid of lethal reprisals, refused to shelter or hide the men and even joined
in a search for them organized by the SS. Captured prisoners were summarily executed. There were, however, a small number of families that
helped escapees.

Geras reports on the motivation of Maria and Johann Langthaler, who
hid two men in their house for the rest of the war. The Langthalers felt
obligated, as Christians, to help someone in need. Asked why she was moved
to save the fugitives, Maria responded: "The Lord God is for the whole
world, not only the Germans . . . I did not ask to which party they belong, I
asked nothing at all, that made no difference to me. Only because they
were human beings."[69]

Geras uses this incident (along with other evidence) to contest Rorty's
assertion that those who helped the Jews during the war were not influenced by any universal morality. If the Langthalers' actions were unusual
and heroic, they were utterly consistent. It is clear that subjecting prisoners
to cruel and unusual punishment (in Mauthausen twenty to thirty prisoners
died each day), ignoring the runaways' desperate pleas for help, and summarily executing them is inconsistent with the very rudiments of civil conduct that we ourselves expect and take for granted as human beings.
Insomuch as rationality is a pursuit of consistency, this kind of selective
barbarity is not only immoral, but irrational.

The problem faced by families such as the Langthalers was not
epistemic. In this kind of perilous circumstance, the logical conclusion was
not obscure, ambiguous, or difficult to discern. It was not a difficult matter
to figure out what was right. The real problem was summoning up the courage and the resolve to act. Maria's simple logic, with its perhaps fatal consequences, is entirely cogent and blindingly obvious. Human beings ought
to be treated as human beings. This may be a momentous conclusion, but it
is hardly an extravagant or unfamiliar one. In Nazi-occupied Poland, it was

a fear of reprisals, not some deep-seated uncertainty, that obscured this logic.

The Langthalers' motivation is a model of logical clarity as well as of moral compassion. The Nazis treated some human beings—Jews, the mentally retarded, these Russian prisoners—as if they were less than human. They overlooked the most fundamental trait of all, our basic humanness. This is inconsistent and thereby irrational. If zealous Nazis would willingly die for their faulty belief system, this does not make the belief system true. The intensity of their partisan commitment carries no logical merit. It only aggravates—it does not repair—the underlying epistemic fault.

NAZI ARGUMENTS AGAINST THE JEWS

Authors like Rorty and Hare insist that the zealous Nazi is a rational being. If, however, the zealous Nazi is consistent in his hatred of Jews, the Nazi worldview he embraces is inconsistent, unscientific, uncritically emotional, delusional, rabid, anything but rational. Can anyone come up with a sound argument in favor of Nazism? We can point to three complaints the Nazis historically marshaled against the Jews: (1) the Jews killed Jesus Christ, (2) the Jews controlled world finances, and (3) the Jews were racially impure. The truth is that none of these charges forms the basis for any kind of sound argument. Consider them briefly.

Overlook the fact that Jesus was himself a Jew and that his original followers were Jewish. Overlook the fact that it was the *Roman* Legion which put him to death. How can one argue that *all* Jews should be indiscriminately killed because some Jews crucified Jesus two thousand years ago? If Jesus really was the Son of God, one should presumably put his teachings into practice. But Jesus told Christians to love their enemies, to turn the other cheek, not to judge, to pardon without limit, and so on.[70] The indiscriminate killing of Jews cannot be vindicated on Christian grounds.

The Nazis were able to kill Jews because they controlled the forces of law and order, not because they applied consistent standards of justice to them. Even if the Jews committed an outrage killing Jesus, it was not twentieth-century German Jews who murdered Jesus. Suppose the courts were to sentence me to death because a great-great-great-great-grand-uncle of a third cousin to the half-brother of distant relative of mine committed a murder two thousand years ago in Ireland. Would this be just? Hardly. Any consistent system of law reposes on a simple principle of identity. The people to be punished for a particular crime are the people who committed the crime. One does not punish innocent relatives. Surely, the Nazis would not have sentenced ethnic Germans to death on a similar basis. What motivated the legal persecution of the Jews was, once again, not some ideal of ethical consistency, but the unspoken belief that one could bypass the requirements of justice in dealings with the Jews.

A second argument that fueled German anti-Semitism was that hostile Jewish interests were taking over the financial world. The evidence for these beliefs was, in large part, built on rumors, prejudice, propaganda, and ethnic jealousy.[71] Even supposing there were rich Jews, does it logically follow that the Nazis were justified in killing them? The forced redistribution of wealth is one thing, killing is another. And, of course, the zealous Nazi wants to kill not just rich Jews but also middle-class Jews, Jewish laborers, poor Jews, Jewish children, Jews who have absolutely no connection to high finance, Jews who are not friends with other Jews, Jews who have converted to Christianity, Jews who do not even know that they are Jewish, and so on. How could this be consistent with the idea of justice?

Finally, consider the racial argument. It is hard to imagine the stridency of Nazi anti-Semitism. Lord Edward Russell writes that German children, "from the moment they started going to school, were taught to loathe and despise all Jews as revolting and disgusting."[72] One textbook for school-children that discussed the Jewish question was entitled *Der Giftpilz* (The poisonous fungus). In one lesson, students learned how to recognize the Jew by the shape of "his crooked nose" which was said to look like "the figure six" and was hence called the "Jewish Six." The Jew could also be "recognized by his lips" which were "usually thick." The lower lip hung down, the eyelids were "thicker and more fleshy," and the look on his face was "more cunning and sinister." At the end of the lesson: "The children would . . . chant a little rhyming chorus to the effect that the Devil looked out from every Jew, and they would only remain free if they struggled to subdue the Jewish Devil."[73]

Nazi anti-Semitism was fueled, in part, by ideas of ethnic pollution, eugenics, and racial superiority. In an article appearing in the "semi-medical journal" entitled *The German People's Health through Body and Soul*, Julius Streicher, German "Jew-Baiter Number One" as he liked to call himself, assures the reader that interracial intercourse would be fatal to the German race. Streicher declares: "One simple cohabitation of a Jew with an Aryan woman is sufficient to poison her blood forever. Together with [his] alien albumen she has absorbed an alien soul. Never again will she be able to bear Aryan children. . . . They will all be bastards. . . . She is never again to bear German children!"[74] Streicher goes on to describe, in lascivious terms, the predatory nature of Jewish men.

It was this absolutely irrational hodgepodge of nationalism, eugenics, quackery, *Volk*-spiritualism, and ethnic chauvinism that was behind the Final Solution. Nazi anti-Semitism is based on the most shoddy reasoning, on the kind of elementary logical fallacies one warns students about in beginning courses in critical thinking.

The Final Solution is a paradigm case of immorality, but it is also a paradigm case of irrationality. We cannot, within the bonds of reason, describe the genocide of the Jews in a way that makes it right. Contemporary neo-Nazi arguments bear this out. Neo-Nazi apologists like Jim Keegstra and Ernst Zundel do not, in general, question the immorality of genocide. They argue that the genocide of the Jews did not really happen. In their own tortured way, they bear witness to the universal claims of morality.

MORAL OBJECTIVITY

Rorty claims that because the zealous Nazi acts consistently with his own beliefs, he acts in a consistent manner. But the Nazi's beliefs are themselves inconsistent. The zealous Nazi may be a consistent Nazi, but a consistent Nazi is by definition an inconsistent human being.

Rationality is not a matter of subjective self-approval. If my actions are consistent with my beliefs, this is not enough for me to qualify as a rational agent. My beliefs must be consistent with some criterion of knowledge that exists outside myself. They must be, in a phrase, objectively true. If, however, rational beliefs must correspond to some objective criterion of truth, one can also argue that there are objective moral truths. We do not experience morality as a subjective whim or fancy, as something impulsive or arbitrary, as something we can change at will. We are confronted with a moral imperative that *forces* us to act in certain ways. Morality, in some important sense, comes from outside ourselves.

George Moore's analogy between goodness and color elucidates, at the very least, this aspect of morality. Moore conceived of goodness as a simple, nonnatural quality that transcends the natural features of things. On Moore's theory, goodness is like the color yellow. It can be pointed to (defined ostensively), but it cannot be analyzed (divided into simpler concepts). If Moore's theory sins against common sense, it rescues morality from a rampant subjectivism. Consider: When I look at the world, I do not decide what colors I am going to see. The fire truck is red even if I wish it were green. I cannot, by a simple mental act, turn blue into orange. Specific colors present themselves to me independent of my willing. In a similar way, I cannot conjure up moral predicates and attach them to objects at will. A shameless act of treason is a shameless act of treason. I cannot see it otherwise. Likewise, if my roommate is a coward, there is no use pretending he is brave. Our moral perceptions may change over time but not through a summary act of will. Any genuine shift in moral perception requires some in-depth revision of the way we perceive and understand the world.

Moore conceives of goodness as an ontological feature of reality. This is, however, to elaborate a very nonintuitive picture of reality. We do not have to go to such extremes if we want to think of morality in objective terms. Charles Taylor, who identifies himself as a moral realist, has recently argued for an objective view of morality based not on an a priori metaphysical account of existence, but on a "best account" principle of human experience.[75] Taylor, who dismisses popular epistemological views based exclusively on the natural sciences, maintains that we cannot make sense of that "domain of human affairs" where we assess one another's feelings, reactions, characters, and actions without recourse to moral concepts and intuitions. According to Taylor, nonmoral language "is of no use to the agent in making sense of his own thinking, feeling, and acting."[76] If, however, moral concepts "prove ineradicable,"[77] and "if we cannot deliberate effectively, or understand and explain people's actions illuminatingly, without such terms, . . . then these [terms must represent] real features of our world."[78]

Taylor equates what is real with what is indispensable. "What is real is what you have to deal with, what won't go away just because it doesn't fit your prejudices."[79] If we cannot make sense of our own lives without having recourse to necessary moral fact, this moral fact "is real, or as near to reality as you can get a grasp of at present."[80] On Taylor's view, "Virtue terms like courage or generosity" are like the properties "red" or "square."[81] They are not imaginary, not merely emotional, not mere emanations of whim or fancy. If the existence of human beings makes moral properties possible, these properties "are no less real features of [a] world which does contain humans than any 'neutral' properties are."[82]

Taylor evinces a concern for moral ontology that pertains to a more analytic British tradition that includes authors like G. E. Moore, Ludwig Wittgenstein, and Iris Murdoch. But to subsume debate about the reality of moral predicates within ontology seems to betray a Platonizing tendency that Taylor himself condemns. Pragmatism provides more effective support for this kind of insight. On the pragmatist model, everyday life is the ultimate criterion for reality. The beliefs that guide our everyday actions depict the fundamental constituents of reality. If moral beliefs guide our everyday actions (and they do), they must be factored in as one important aspect of reality.

WHAT IS OBJECTIVITY?

Some authors contend that objective notions of morality are intellectually disreputable. J. L. Mackie states categorically: "There are no objective values."[83] As Mackie explains: "If there were objective values, then they would be entities or qualities or relations of a very strange sort, utterly different from anything else in the universe. Correspondingly, if we were aware of them, it would have to be by some special faculty of perception or moral intuition, utterly different from our ordinary ways of knowing anything else."[84] The idea of a separate category of immaterial moral objects grasped by a faculty of moral apprehension seems remarkably unintuitive. As Jan Narveson remarks, in a modern scientific age, any appeal to "what seem to be mysterious entities and faculties is likely to elicit impatience, and perhaps a certain amount of irritation."[85] It may seem then that any notion of objective values must be mistaken.

Mackie's "argument from queerness" provides an effective riposte to Moore's moral philosophy, because Moore supplies a straw man of objectivity, one that can be easily knocked down by opponents. Moore's theories notwithstanding, morality is not in the business of adding a new class of immaterial objects onto reality. To speak of objective moral truth is to comment on the independent nature of moral knowledge. Moral truth is true independent of our opinions. We do not judge it. It judges us.

In an overview of Western philosophy, Bertrand Russell takes a personal stab at Dewey's alleged subjectivism. Russell complains of "Dewey's . . . refusal to admit 'facts' into his metaphysics in the sense in which 'facts' are stubborn and cannot be manipulated."[86] If, however, facts are truths that "are stubborn and cannot be manipulated," then there are surely moral facts. Consider the proposition: "Torturing your three-year-old for the fun of it is wicked sport." Surely, this must be a moral *fact* in the sense "in which facts are stubborn and cannot be manipulated." This is a necessary belief. We do not have a choice! We *must* submit to this moral principle. To act otherwise would be inconceivable.

Wittgenstein writes: "Ethics must be a condition of the world, like logic."[87] Moral propositions are objective in the same way that factual propositions are objective. Let us assume that the proposition "Torturing your three-year-old is wicked sport" is an objective moral truth. To say that this proposition is an objective moral truth is to say that it is a true moral proposition regardless of what you or I or anyone else says about the matter. If someone or a whole society believed that torturing babies was a moral act, this would not make torturing babies a moral act. It would make them a wicked person or society. Moral standards remain true even if we, as individuals or as a society, refuse to consent to them.

Modern logicians invoke the concept of possible worlds when explaining the notion of necessary truth, and the same analysis applies to moral propositions. The proposition "Torturing your three-year-old is wicked sport" is true in every possible world. One can perhaps conceive of a world in which babies are tortured for the fun of it. If, however, this is a metaphysical, logical or empirical possibility, one cannot conceive of a world where this would be a morally good thing to do. A world inhabited by people who torture babies for the fun of it would be a world inhabited by savages and barbarians. It would be an evil world, a world that needs to be condemned in the strongest possible terms. If, however, this moral truth must hold true for every possible world, it must, in the strongest possible sense, be true.

Philosophers who disapprove of any notion of an "objective moral truth" might try to argue that one can describe a world in which torturing babies would be a good thing to do. One could perhaps (?) imagine a world in which babies love to be tortured, a world in which babies are tortured by accident, a world in which parents are forced to torture babies to prepare them for the rigors of a harsh environment. But this is to misconstrue the meaning of the original proposition. Torture is by definition an act that babies find extremely unpleasant. If adults are doing this for sport, for their own fun, this suggests that they are not doing it for the child's welfare. It also suggests that they are doing it, not by accident, but freely and deliberately. Imagine the scene: the adults laughing as they rip out fingernails while the baby writhes and screams in agony. Could this be a moral act in any possible world? Surely, it must be condemned in any and all possible worlds. It seems, then, that the proposition "Torturing your three-year-old is wicked sport" is not a contingent but a necessary truth.

We cannot prove that torturing babies is wrong in any way that will satisfy the determined skeptic, but neither can we prove that two plus two equals four in any way that will satisfy the determined skeptic. To speak of objective truth is not to claim certain or infallible knowledge. It is to claim that particular propositions are true, not because we believe they are true, but because they correspond to some independent criterion of validity.

To believe in moral objectivity is to disavow solipsism. Our own beliefs, opinions, or attitudes do not determine whether or not particular moral propositions are true. If moral beliefs do not lend themselves to the justificatory apparatus of science, there are standards of compassion and fairness, duty and decency, that stand outside ourselves and offer an independent criterion by which our own acts can be evaluated. As Taylor puts it: "The standard subjectivist model . . . is false to the most salient features of our moral phenomenology."[88] We experience morality as an independent authoritative voice that obliges us to act in certain ways. We experience it, not as a subjective whim, but as an objective constraint on human action. Moral judgments, in Taylor's words, "involve discriminations of right or wrong, better or worse, higher or lower, which are not rendered valid by our own desires, inclinations, or choices, but rather stand independent of these and offer standards by which they can be judged."[89]

A belief in the ultimate subjectivity of moral discourse is often motivated by moral pluralism, but claims about the extent of moral pluralism may be exaggerated. Montaigne tells us that what is truth on this side of the mountains is falsehood on the other side,[90] but he also suggests that local mores, laws, and customs diverge because we do not pay sufficient attention to the universal laws of human nature.[91] As we have already seen, Wilson argues that this older view of human nature is the more correct one, that modern findings in biology and the social sciences support the idea that human beings share a common moral sensibility, a certain capacity for sympathy, a sense of duty, a desire to please, a belief in fairness, and a faculty of disinterested reflection. According to Wilson, we cannot contrive an abbreviated set of moral absolutes because of varying cultural, historical, geographical, and religious situations. In one culture, an exaggerated display of courtesy may be a sign of disrespect; in another, an obligatory sign of veneration. In one society, remarking on an elderly person's age may be a compliment; in another society, it may be an insult. In one geographical location, taking your neighbor's canoe without permission may be expected practice; in another, it may be brazen theft. One society may cherish the virtues of a great warrior, another may prize meticulous intellectual endeavor. There are labyrinthine customs that change the import and the meaning of particular human acts. If, however, moral feelings are expressed in different ways in myriad circumstances, it does not follow that human beings always disagree about morality.

The very same moral impetus may be expressed in vastly different ways. Consider A, B, and C. Suppose A believes that Mohammed, the Prophet, is God Incarnate; B believes that Jesus Christ is God Incarnate; and C believes that God does not exist. A, B, and C will act in very different ways. A will pray to Mohammed, B will pray to Jesus, and C will not pray at all. A, B, and C may disagree most vehemently. But the actions of these three individuals all obey a similar moral impetus. They all believe that one is morally obliged to act in a manner that is consistent with the truth. The problem is that they disagree about what the truth is. The disagreement here is as much philosophical as it is moral.

Moral diversity does not, in any case, undermine the objectivity of moral discourse. Objective notions of moral truth are entirely compatible with the fact of human disagreement. Human beings may disagree, in part, because they misunderstand one another and, in part, because they miscon- strue the truth. Richard Rorty attacks objectivity as a misguided belief in philosophical certainty.[92] But Rorty conflates two separate questions: "Can we know with certainty?" and "Is truth objective?" To argue for objective truth is not to argue for human infallibility. If we are fallible creatures, our moral beliefs cannot be true merely because we believe in them. They can only be true if and when they correspond to some independent standard of evidence situated outside our individual selves. A belief in objectivity does not presuppose infallibility. Quite to the contrary, it provides opportunity for error.

SOLIPSISM

Rorty champions a consensus view of objectivity. He insists that "The ap- plication of such honorifics as 'objective' or 'cognitive' is never anything more than an expression of the presence of, or hope for, agreement among inquirers."[93] "The only usable notion of 'objectivity' is 'agreement' rather than mirroring."[94] A proposition is not true because it corresponds to the way the world is. It is true because we all believe in it.

As David LeBoeuf remarks, Rorty confuses persuasion and truth. On his consensus theory of objectivity, "Convincing one's peers is all there is to the game of truth."[95] But truth entails more than mere persuasion. It does not matter what we believe as a community. This does not determine what is true. Human belief is eminently fallible. Davidson supplies us with a platitude: "Believing in something does not in general make it true."[96] Leiter supplies us with its corollary: "The community's believing in something doesn't make it so either."[97]

Suppose Vincent breaks a window. Even if everyone in the community believes Philippe did it, even if Philippe himself has been brainwashed into thinking that he did it, even if historians until the end of time contend that Philippe did it, the fact is: Vincent did it. The proposition "Philippe broke the window" is false. It is false because it does not *correspond* to what actually happened.

Kent Peacock objects to "a certain kind of solipsism that seems to be very popular these days."[98] To identify objectivity with consensus is to fall into solipsism. Subjective theories of truth enshrine the collectivity or the individual in the place of God or reality and make them the arbiter of what is true. But we are fallible creatures. Our beliefs cannot stand as the ultimate criterion for truth. As Peacock observes, "we cannot doubt that there is something 'out there,' something other than us, something that we have no choice but to respond to in terms not entirely of our own choosing."[99] Reality is not a projection of our subjective selves. "The world, universe, matrix or whatever we choose to call it . . . never ceases to proclaim to us, by its constant confounding of our wishes and plans, by the obstinate demands it presses on us, that it is most emphatically *other* than something determined purely by human whim."[100] Peacock focuses on empirical claims, while I have argued, along with Taylor, that our relationship to the world has an inescapable moral dimension.

If our knowledge of the world has an objective component, solipsism is an error. Scholars traditionally distinguish between ethical, metaphysical, and epistemological solipsism. Rollins, for example, speaks of moral solipsism (egoism), reality-solipsism, and knowledge-solipsism.[101] Egoism denotes purely self-interested action, a relentless self-seeking.[102] Reality-solipsism is the metaphysical doctrine that nothing beyond the self exists, and knowledge-solipsism is the idealistic doctrine that knowledge originates, in some exclusive sense, in the self and its mental states. In solipsism, we have a philosophical attitude that privileges the desires, the existence, or the ideas of the self. In the case of moral solipsism, the desires of the self determine the way one should act. In the case of metaphysical solipsism, the existence of the self constitutes the sum total of reality. And in the case of epistemological solipsism, the beliefs or opinions of the self determine what counts as knowledge, as true justified belief.

Webster's New International Dictionary tells us that "solipsism represents only a hypothetical position,"[103] an extreme form of subjectivism that thinkers rarely and perhaps never adopt.[104] And yet in the practical dealings of everyday life, we regularly encounter individuals who seem, as a matter of principle, to accept little or no criticism of their own opinions. The underlying mode of reasoning seems to be: *This is my opinion, therefore it must be right.* Anyone who adopts this kind of attitude is espousing an implicit solipsism. The real claim underlying their arguments is that their beliefs are true, not because they conform to external evidence, but merely because they themselves believe them.

This kind of epistemological solipsism is so inane as to be intellectually disreputable. But one occasionally encounters more overt expressions of such solipsism in modern intellectual discourse. Consider the recovery movement, a psychological self-help group initiated by ex-seminarian John Bradshaw and psychiatrist M. Scott Peck. As Michael Miller explains, "recovery experts" have replaced "the idea of original sin or sexual repression or faulty neurotransmitters" with the idea of the "dysfunctional" family. They contend that the American family "is a stricken institution that churns out nothing but emotionally crippled individuals." It is "the first cause of all our ills."[105] If, however, the supporters of the movement argue that psychological problems can be traced to childhood abuse, how can one determine whether one was abused as a child? David Rieff quotes recovery expert Steven Farmer: "No matter how abuse is defined or what other people think, you are the ultimate judge: If you think you were abused, you were."[106] *If you think you were abused you were.* This is a simple case of unabashed solipsism. It is your subjective convictions about the event that determine what really happened. There is no need to consult the objective evidence. In Rieff's sardonic phrase, "to imagine is to make it so."[107]

We might distinguish between two types of solipsism. Solipsists may adamantly insist that the beliefs of a particular individual or of a particular group form the ultimate criterion of truth. Argumentation theorists identify various fallacies that are, on closer inspection, solipsistic: fallacious appeal to authority, appeal to common opinion, bandwagon fallacy, *consensus gentium*, authority of the select few, and so on. In these kinds of arguments, one is asked to believe that a proposition is true because groups of people believe that it is true.

Our own beliefs, even as a collectivity, do not define truth. As S. Morris Engel observes: "The fact that many people agree with [something] does not make it true."[108] Engel criticizes an argument advanced by Italian philosopher Benedetto Croce. Croce apparently justifies the Spanish Inquisition, arguing that if it was disastrously wicked, widespread opinion and the judgment of leading intellectuals would not have supported it. In Croce's words: "The Inquisition must have been justified and beneficial, if whole peoples invoked and defended it, if men of the loftiest souls founded and created it severally and impartially, and its very adversaries applied it on their own account, answering pyre to pyre."[109] But mere consensus does not provide any guarantee of truth. As Engel points out, "the fact that many people endorsed the Inquisition did not make it right."[110] People are eminently (woefully) fallible. One cannot argue that the Inquisition was justified because many people supported it. The beliefs of any human collectivity do not provide the ultimate criterion for truth. To insinuate that they do is to adopt a kind of collective solipsism.

To identify objectivity with consensus is, like Rorty, to lapse into solipsism. Solipsism inevitably inverts the epistemological process. We should not think that public religion is civic virtue because this is what we believe. We should believe that it is a civic virtue because we can identify some independent reason why it is virtuous. There are, no doubt, truthful worldviews, accurate beliefs, authoritative opinions. But a worldview is not true, in any objective sense, because a certain group believes that it is true. It is *objectively* true because it corresponds to or coheres with the evidence.

History is filled with good rebels, moral and intellectual heroes, who revolt against consensus for the sake of the truth or the good. Rorty's epistemology does away with this kind of good rebellion. If we identify consensus with objectivity, we eliminate the possibility for error. There is little room in Rorty's philosophy for the little child in Anderson's famous story who cried out that the emperor was entirely naked. In the fairy tale, there was a definite consensus: "The emperor is dressed in the finest clothes." And there was an objective truth: "The emperor is stark naked." The little child played the part of the good rebel, alerting society to an objective truth that had been obscured or overlooked. We need a place in our philosophy for those who defy consensus and condemn collective untruth.

Rorty subscribes to a basic fallibilism, but his fallibilism is self-defeating. It initiates a kind of slippery slope. We move from the skeptical realization that "We cannot really know the world" to the relativist assumption that "All positions are equally true," and finally to the solipsistic conclusion that "What we believe, individually or collectively, is as good as true." If we do make mistakes, there must be something independent of human opinions that secures truth. Whatever this is—ideas in the mind of God, the final theory science is heading toward, the present state of the universe, or some philosophical interpretation of nature—it lies outside ourselves and provides a privileged perspective from which our own actions and beliefs must be judged. We will never have full or absolute knowledge of the world, but we do have good evidence that can demonstrate that it is more one way than another.

Perspectivism

Philosophical perspectivists have argued that objectivity is impossible. The view can be traced to Nietzsche who, in the Third Essay in the *Genealogy of Morals*, argues that concepts such as "pure reason," "absolute spirituality," and "knowledge in itself" are absurd, for such concepts "always demand that we should think of an eye that is completely unthinkable, an eye turned in no particular direction."[111] There is, according to Nietzsche, "only a perspective seeing, only a perspective knowing."[112] Any assertion, truthful or otherwise, must always be identified with a specific human perspective.

Karl Mannheim, in *Ideology and Utopia* (1926), rejects "the older static ideal of eternal unperspectivistic truths independent of the subjective experience of the observer,"[113] replacing it with the notion of a "perspectivist truth" that "contains the traces of the position of the knower."[114] Contemporary authors such as Arthur Danto, Paul de Man, Jacques Derrida, Alexander Nehemas, Sarah Kofman, Ruedigger Grimm, Alan Schrift, Jeremy Davey, Bernd Magnus, Daniel Conway, and Mary Warnock argue for a similar perspectivism.[115] These authors dispute the possibility of objectivity. We can never, no matter how hard we try, shed our own cultural, social, and historical perspective and view reality in any neutral fashion. We cannot get outside ourselves. We can only see what we are programmed to see or, more insidiously, what we want to see. We are, in a sense, trapped inside our own subjectivity.

The perspectivist argues that objectivity is impossible, for it would have to entail "a nonperspectival seeing," "a view from nowhere."[116] On this account, there is no objective right or wrong, no better or worse view, no objective truth or falsehood. In Leiter's words: "No [perspective] gives a better picture of the world as it really is than any other."[117]

Leiter brings up the example of a chair: "viewed from a distance of five feet, viewed while sitting on it, viewed closely so as to reveal its texture, viewed from underneath, viewed with a magnifying glass, viewed from a third-floor window and so on."[118] These different perspectives give us radically different images of the chair and yet each perspective gives us as true an image of the chair as any other. Perspectivists argue, in the same way, that competing descriptions of the world are equally valid. It is not that one is right and one is wrong. They just represent different but equally valid interpretations of reality.

Perspectivists misconstrue, however, the meaning of objectivity. To argue for objectivity is not to argue that we must all look at Leiter's chair from the same perspective. Nor is it to argue that the chair looks the same from every angle. To argue for objectivity is to argue that there is something independent of our beliefs about the chair,—the physical chair itself (whatever that is)—that determines what we see. It is the nature of the chair, not the nature of our beliefs about the chair, that shapes and controls the content of perceptions. Every person who looks at the chair from the same perspective will see the same chair. It is not the person but something objective, something outside the person—namely, the thing that comprises the chair (and its surroundings)—that determines the resultant image. Except perhaps in dreams or hallucinations, we do not see what we want to see. We see what is out there.

If we can view the world from radically different perspectives, we still have to distinguish between accurate and inaccurate descriptions of reality. There can be false descriptions of Leiter's chair. Suppose I say that the chair has zebra stripes when the pattern is in fact paisley. Suppose I say that the chair legs are made of gilded wood when they are really made of stainless steel. Suppose I say that the chair is Louis Quatorze when it is really American Frontier. In each instance, I supply a false description of the chair. Likewise, one can provide false descriptions of the world. There are ethical, political, scientific, or philosophical views that are not only false but devious, vacuous, or stupid. If perspectivists are going to elaborate an adequate epistemology, they must show us how to distinguish legitimate perspectives, bona fide perspectives, insightful perspectives, from lies, falsehoods, rationalizations, and misconceptions.

There are descriptions of the world that entail blatant falsehoods, but even true description may be more or less adequate. Images of Leiter's chair may be more or less revealing, more or less insightful, more or less pertinent to our present purposes. A photograph of the chair with one leg is showing may be less revealing, in a specified sense, than a photograph of the chair with all four legs showing. The "four-legged picture" may provide us with more information, even though both pictures are, in some absolute sense, equally true. Within a particular context and for different purposes, one perspective may be more revealing than another.

The perspectivist insists that we have no access to the real world outside ourselves, but we cannot speak of the perspective from which the blind view a painting. They do not see the painting at all. If we had no knowledge about the world, we could not meaningfully talk about perspective. Perspectivism should logically foster, not the radical skepticism of "We cannot know the world;" but a hopeful realism: "There are many routes to knowledge."

There may be different perspectives on the world, but as the pragmatists suggest, these perspectives, insofar as they are true, must add up to one coherent object. Leiter lists a number of viewpoints from which we can view his chair, but the choice is between different perspectives, not between incoherent or contradictory images. Taken together, these individual perspectives on the chair provide us with a coherent overall view. We can see the *same* chair from different distances or angles, and objectivity is possible.

RATIONALITY AND MORALITY

We have defined rationality, in pragmatist terms, as the operation of a fallible consistency that satisfies some kind of objective criterion. Rationality looks at the world from different perspectives. It critically evaluates facts *and* values. It describes the world and recommends action. It supplies the first principles of logic and morality. It realizes itself not solely in philosophical or mathematical speculation but, first and foremost, in everyday life. It is not purely theoretical. It is not overwhelmingly skeptical. It embraces existential commitments. It provides the impetus for action. It does not supply absolute knowledge but it does supply good reasons for belief. Considered from a God's-eye point of view, human reason is eminently fallible. Considered from a human point of view, it provides evidence that is entirely compelling.

This account of reason is not a case of special pleading. It is in line with what is best in the Western philosophical tradition. If philosophers in the why-be-moral school attempt to demonstrate the rationality of morality, they overlook this traditional account and provide an impoverished account of reason. They assume, from the outset, a resolutely theoretical perspective. They erect a reductionist scheme that informs us: this is the way the world is; this is what human beings are; this is how we calculate rationality. Pragmatists suggest a different approach. We begin in the world of action. We do not have to introduce morality into human decision-making. Morality is already there. We must test the moral views we already have to see if they are consistent. This is the job of moral philosophy.

Stanley Fish has argued that the pragmatists had no use for philosophy.[119] But while the pragmatists may have disputed the transcendental turn of modern speculative philosophy, they do not denigrate philosophy. They reinvent modern philosophy in line with an earlier realist tradition. We begin with a particular moral view. Although this view may be defective, we can, through a process of clarification and correction, struggle to a more consistent worldview. This is what happens in moral thinking. As Taylor suggests, moral reasoning "is a reasoning in transitions."[120] Suppose we begin by believing A and later come to believe B. We might move from A to B by resolving a contradiction in A, by eliminating a confusion that A relied on, or by acknowledging some unseen factor that A screened out. Insomuch as the move from A to B is a "error-reducing move," it represents a legitimate epistemological gain. We can, in this manner, improve our moral knowledge without claiming any kind of absolute knowledge about the world or morality.

If rationality is consistency per se, morality is the practice of a specialized consistency. Morality provides an answer to ultimate questions: What is a good human life? What is worthwhile endeavor? What is shameful, reprehensible, disgusting? These are enormous questions. Moral agents do not, however, answer them in an arbitrary manner. Morality insists on consistency. Hence the golden rule: My behavior toward other people must be *consistent* with the way I would like to be treated. Promise keeping is a form of consistency, but promise keeping is also a form of morality. Telling the truth is a form of consistency. Avoiding cruelty to animals is a form of consistency. Animals are not inert. They have highly developed nervous systems. They feel pain. When we treat them in ways that avoid unnecessary suffering, we act consistently with their nature. And so on. Morality does not entail a lack of consistency. It is consistency itself. It is the practice of reason applied to ultimate, evaluative questions about human life.

Against Internalism

Rationality and morality go together. There is no problem reconciling the two. But what about the relationship between autonomy and rationality? Autonomy means successful self-government, and successful self-government presupposes rationality; that is, it presupposes a basic consistency in act and belief. As Lindley argues, rationality is a necessary precondition for autonomy.[121]

Susan Dimock, in a review of recent literature, distinguishes between internalist and externalist theories of autonomy.[122] Simply put, the internalist argues that autonomous agents must act in a manner that satisfies their own expectations and desires. The externalist argues that autonomous agents must act in a manner that satisfies an objective criterion of rationality or morality that exists independently of the agent herself. Dimock associates internalism with the authors Harry Frankfurt and Gary Watson, and externalism with the authors Thomas Hill and Susan Wolf. She herself, in a largely technical discourse, argues for externalism.

As we shall see, internalism is a popular position today. Even those authors who argue for an externalism of rationality usually adopt an internalist point of view when it comes to morality. If autonomous agents must be, in an objective sense, rational, they do not have to be, in an objective sense, moral. They do not have to satisfy any moral standards other than their own. As Dimock writes: "The individual's own attitude is the final arbiter of autonomy."[123]

This emphasis on the subjective aspects of autonomy is characteristic of contemporary academic literature. In 1972 Joel Feinberg defined personal autonomy in one succinct and intrepid phrase: "I am autonomous if I rule me, and no one else rules I."[124] That very same year Thomas Scanlon defined an autonomous person as someone who "see[s] himself as sovereign in deciding what to believe."[125] Robert Paul Wolff, two years earlier, had defined moral autonomy as "a submission to laws that one has made for oneself."[126] These philosophers, in individual but analogous ways, jettison the existentialist-phenomenological baggage of earlier discussion and define autonomy as the rule of the self by the self.

Diana Meyers writes: "Autonomous people must be disposed to consult their selves and be equipped to do so. They must be able to pose and answer the question 'What do I really want, need, care about, believe, value, etcetera?'; they must be able to act on the answer; and they must be able to correct themselves when they get the answer wrong."[127] On this internalist view, autonomy is a kind of self-expression. To be autonomous is to be in touch with one's "true self."[128] To get it wrong is not to act immorally. To get it wrong is to act on a desire that does not coincide with that which is really me. The cardinal sin is inauthenticity, not immorality.

Of course, autonomy must entail some kind of robust *self*-government. Autonomous agents must be ruled by some strong, internal "I," by some kind of internal consistency, by an internalized allegiance to a coherent, structured belief system. As Feinberg points out, "A person who [has] no hierarchical structure of wants, aims, and ideals . . . would fail of autonomy . . . because [he or she] lack[s] internal order and structure."[129] The self cannot rule the self if there is no self to begin with. We need some kind of identifiable commitment, some kind of characteristic consistency that defines who we are. As a feminist, Meyers is perhaps arguing that women need to embrace some kind of strong belief-system. If, however, autonomous agents must internalize strong beliefs, they must also act in a manner that is, in a much larger sense, consistent with the world.

John Locke differentiates between idiots and madmen. Madmen practice an internal consistency. "Thus [we] find [that] a distracted man fancying himself a king . . . require[s] suitable attendance, respect, and obedience; [while] others who have thought themselves made of glass have used the necessary caution to preserve such brittle bodies."[130] The lunatic-king who requires submissive behavior from others acts in a manner that is consistent with his own beliefs. So does the "glass man" who walks on tiptoe so as not to shatter himself. Nevertheless, these internally-consistent madmen do not constitute examples of successful self-government. To be autonomous is to act in a manner that is consistent not only with our own beliefs and expectations but also with the objective nature of the world. It is to act in a manner that is internally *and* externally consistent.

Autonomy is the practice of an overall consistency. That is, it is the practice of rationality. My friend Gloria, the mathematician, may act in a rational manner when she is solving math problems, but she might also lead an unsuccessful, unfulfilling life. Autonomy is not rationality applied to technical problems. It is rationality applied to the way we live our lives. If we are to be truly autonomous, we must act in ways that are consistent with our own personal beliefs (which have a inescapable moral dimension). But we must also act in a way that is consistent with the world. Neurosis, insanity, poor judgment, and false beliefs do not empower an individual. They detract from autonomy.

Internalists argue that self-approval is the only measure of successful self-government. If we approve of our actions—that is, if we believe that we have successfully governed ourselves—then, ipso facto, we have successfully governed ourselves. But we cannot assume that our actions are commendable or praiseworthy or shrewd or successful because we believe that our actions are commendable or praiseworthy or shrewd or successful. We are fallible creatures. We may be mistaken.

Internalism reduces to solipsism. We cannot assume that agents have successfully governed themselves because they believe that they have successfully governed themselves. There is an objective as well as a subjective component to personal autonomy. If autonomous agents must act in a manner that satisfies their own expectations and desires, they must also act in a manner that satisfies external criteria of excellence or worthiness. If we hope to provide a sound theory of individual achievement, we must reject internalism and propose a double "externalism," one that appeals to objective standards of both morality and rationality.

Social critics decry a cultural preoccupation with the self. Tom Wolfe has complained about the Me-Generation.[131] Daniel Bell worries about a contemporary "idolatry of the self."[132] Christopher Lasch attacks a "culture of narcissism."[133] Gilles Lipovetsky presents the figure of the new Narcissus.[134] Richard Sennett criticizes the popularity of introspective psychological techniques of "self-absorption."[135] Sociologist Robert Bellah and his associates describe an American society that has been balkanized, divided and fragmented by "an isolating preoccupation with the self."[136] They make an unsurprising prediction: "American individualism seems more than ever determined to press ahead with the task of letting go of all criteria other than a radical private validation."[137] This is what internalism does. It provides an entirely subjective account of autonomy. One looks to private self-satisfaction or self-approval as the sole barometer of genuine achievement and healthful living.

We must elaborate a view of individual autonomy that avoids the excesses of a contemporary narcissism. According to Kernberg, people who suffer from narcissistic personality disorder exhibit "an unusual degree of self-reference in their interactions."[138] On an internalist theory, autonomy is defined solely in terms of self-awareness. It is the attitude I take toward my actions that determines whether or not I have successfully governed myself. The most fundamental question is not "Is this a good or a rational act?" but "How do I feel about the act?" "Do I approve of myself?" "Am I still pleased with the direction my life is going?" Or even, "Do I still like myself?"

Autonomy is the practice of rationality. If I argue against internalism, it is that rationality, broadly construed, must be a part of any successful life. Locke's glass man is not, in any successful sense, self-governed. He fails at self-government because he is irrational. He does not understand the nature of the external world. This is why he is a "madman." I will argue that someone who does not understand the significance of moral imperatives fails, in a similar way, at autonomy. The self-approving rapist or the self-approving serial killer does not succeed at self-government, no matter how fervently he approves of his actions.

The Rational Hockey Player: Haworth

If we want to identify autonomy and rationality, we need an account of reason that takes into consideration individual circumstances, an agent's feelings, and the importance of practical endeavor. Kant, perhaps more than any other Western philosopher, has elucidated the connection between autonomy and rationality, but Kant provides a very narrow view of reason. As Richard Lindley explains, Kant's rational agent is "motivated by purely rational principles . . . untainted by particular inclinations or principles."[139] These idealized agents do not focus particulars. They are not swayed by feeling. They act in accordance with strict duty. Their behavior provides a universal law for all humanity.

Rationality does have a transcendental aspect. If, however, autonomy is the practice of rationality, we need a broader account of reason, one that can embrace all aspects of a successful life. Lawrence Haworth provides such an account. Haworth distinguishes between Cartesian and Deweyan deliberation. Cartesian deliberation is rationality, traditionally conceived. One abstracts from the world and mentally wrestles with the problem at hand. Deweyan deliberation is rationality in a practical mode. If Cartesian deliberation is contemplative, speculative, transcendental, propositional, and systematic, Deweyan deliberation is a kind of thoughtfulness that is expressed in the heat of action. The person who engages in Deweyan deliberation participates, nonetheless, in ordered, coherent, goal-seeking endeavor.

Consider, for example, a professional hockey player.[140] The hockey player does not spend his ice time in one corner of the rink, thinking. He does not engage in Cartesian deliberation. He is not, in any traditional sense, engaged in thoughtful endeavor. But the hockey player does not act in a purely impulsive or a random manner. He is conscientious, alert, creative; he moves in strategic ways; he is sensitive to feedback. He thinks with his body. He anticipates and outmaneuvers his opponents. Despite the apparent lack of intellection, his behavior represents a form of rational decision-making. His playmaking represents a form of Deweyan deliberation.

Kant thinks of rationality in terms of rule-obeying behavior. There are rules in hockey. One cannot move across the opponent's blue line ahead of the puck. One cannot elbow or cross-check. One cannot carry the puck in one's glove. One cannot kick in a goal. One cannot have more than six team-members on the ice. And so on. If, however, we wish to excel at hockey playing, we cannot be satisfied with rule-obeying behavior. We would never say, "Claude was an excellent hockey player! He never scored any goals; he wasn't very good on defense; he was a slow skater and a poor stick-handler, but he really played by the rules! Wow! What an outstanding athlete!"

We might write a book on how to play a good game of hockey and fill it with rules of thumb. When you have a penalty, play the zone, not the man. When you cannot stop shots on goal, prevent rebounds. When you are inside your own blue-line, emphasize forechecking. These rules might help the beginner. But anyone who tried to play hockey by mechanically following any set of rules would be a poor player indeed. One cannot depict good playmaking in terms of strict obedience to a set of universal hockey imperatives. A good hockey player does not play by routine, by regulation, by dictate, or by formula. And so it is with ordinary life. If successful self-government is to be equated with rationality, rationality is a creative endeavor. It is, in part, a matter of shrewd observation, changing perspectives and new insights. It entails more than a mechanical kind of rule-obeying behavior. It might, more aptly be described, in Aristotelian terms as a kind of *phronesis*, a highly developed form of judgment.

On the Deweyan model, the exercise of rationality entails concentration, enthusiasm, strategy, intuition, a creative response to problematic situations, a sensitivity to concrete detail and circumstance. Haworth does not argue, of course, that Deweyan deliberation is the only form of rational deliberation. Cartesian and Deweyan deliberation form an important part of the rational life, but Haworth's two-fold model provides a much fuller account of rationality.

Kant provides us with a very narrow account of human nature. We are, in part, beings that recognize and obey universal precepts, but we are also beings that feel empathy, cultivate habits, display character, make judgments, and experience emotions. We are able to approximate, extrapolate and summarize. We understand not only the universal but also the particular and the specific. Individuals who excel at successful self-government do not only obey rules. They solve difficult problems in some creative and uniquely individual way. This is, in some wider sense, the meaning of rationality.

The Good Rebel Revisited

I will present the good rebel as the model par excellence of autonomy. But if we restrict the practice of rationality to the maximization of utility, engaging in good rebellion will, in all likelihood, be an irrational venture. On the why-be-moral model, rational agents adopt a strategy of "constrained maximization." They will only act morally when they are reasonably certain that they are dealing with agents who act morally. But good rebels act morally even when they know they are dealing with immoral agents. They choose morality even when morality may result in severe and perhaps fatal penalties.[141] On the utility-maximization model, the good rebel is an irrational agent but, as we have seen, the utility-maximization model presents an impoverished account of rationality.

We have examined two models of rationality:

1. Rationality is the practice of an (internal and external) consistency.
2. Rationality is the maximization of utility.

Although good rebels may not maximize their own utility (definition 2), they are rational agents in a more fundamental sense (definition 1). In an evil society, the best way to maximize utility is perhaps to act in an evil manner, but society may be mistaken in what it believes. It is, at best, a fallible source of moral authority. It is not the approval of society, but the consistency of one's acts that guarantees one's status as a rational agent.

Human societies, like individual human beings, are eminently fallible. Social conformism may be a good strategy for the maximization of utility, but human societies do not provide us with any ultimate criterion of what is good or what is true. In an irrational society, a society gone wrong, acting in a rational manner may jeopardize my well-being. But rational acts are still rational acts even when they do not maximize utility. Because acts of good rebellion are performed under conditions of extreme duress, they stand out as models of rational behavior.

Authors in the why-be-moral tradition argue that we should be moral so that we can maximize utility. But surely, I should be moral because, more simply, I should be moral. Morality is an end in itself. I should act morally, not as a means to something else, but because moral acts are, in some intrinsic sense, valuable or worthwhile. If, however, this is what morality is all about, it makes sense to argue that we should act morally when other people act immorally. If other agents fail to achieve the good, why should this motivate a corresponding failure in me? Why should their inability to apprehend or secure something valuable convince me to do the same? If morality is a valuable end in itself, it would be irrational to follow suit.

Part II:
Morality

4

The Immoral Autonomous Agent?

THE PRESENT CONSENSUS

Susan Babbit, in an anthology of recent philosophy, suggests that cold-blooded murder may be, in certain circumstances, a liberating act. Babbit describes the plot of the film *A Question of Silence:* "Three women—a secretary, a waitress, and a housewife . . . come together in a dress-shop and (gruesomely) murder the dress-shop owner, a man they have never seen before. . . . Nothing material is gained by the act. . . . Yet the women show no remorse and it appears that each is to some extent liberated by the performance of the act, that while she ends up losing her liberty in one sense, she gains it in another sense."[1]

The three women lose liberty in that they are eventually incarcerated, but they gain liberty in that they are, to use a ubiquitous slogan, "true to themselves." Although Babbit accepts that this murder is "obviously immoral," she insists that "for these women being true to themselves [may be] the committing of murder."[2] In a misogynist society that oppresses women, their random act of aggression may be understood as a repudiation of societal values and an exercise of willful self-assertion. "Their choice liberates them, at least conceptually, from a system that precludes even the [possibility] of their being really true to themselves."[3] If the store-owner dies (gruesomely) in the process, this is just too bad. His death is perhaps a distressing but a necessary byproduct of someone else's liberation.

In contrast to Babbit, key figures in Western philosophy all contend that morality is a necessary precondition for freedom. Plato, Aristotle, Augustine, Cicero, Aquinas, and Kant may all be variously interpreted as arguing that immorality is the worst form of subjection and that only a moral agent can truly be free. Among contemporary philosophers, this is not a widespread position. Contemporary philosophers tend to view morality and autonomy as distinctly separate aspirations. Meyers assures us that "personal autonomy. . . can be identified and explored quite apart from" morality;[4] Thomas Hill writes: "It is hard to see why [autonomy] should be regarded as a moral goal";[5] John Christman argues that one may "specify morally *neutral* conditions for [autonomy]";[6] Lindley does not count morality among the essential ingredients of autonomy[7]; John Keykes writes that "autonomy is often put to evil uses";[8] and David Cooper and Joel Feinberg present theories of personal autonomy that are explicitly amoral.[9] Even Joseph Raz, who comes closest to elaborating a moral theory of autonomy, insists that "personal autonomy" is "only very indirectly related" to moral notions.[10]

These and other philosophers all assert, reluctantly or otherwise, that an agent who fails to be moral may achieve autonomy. Raz speaks of "the autonomous wrongdoer";[11] Gerald Dworkin insists that an "autonomous person can be a tyrant or a slave, a saint or a sinner";[12] Robert Young argues that tyrants and the wantonly cruel may be autonomous and that we can exercise autonomy "for both good and ill";[13] Keykes maintains that there are "moral monsters" who act autonomously;[14] S. I. Benn asserts that there is nothing to suggest that an autonomous individual cannot be immoral;[15] and even Haworth suggests that "an extremely autonomous person" may be "highly immoral."[16]

On this popular view, autonomy does not mean acting morally. It means, more or less, doing what we want to do. Alan Rosenbaum posits a basic polarity. We may be subject to the will of others, or we may follow our own inclinations. Autonomous agents follow their own inclinations. They do what they themselves want to do. They are "socially free"; they escape "control relations"; and "they exercise their self-chosen pursuits."[17] Autonomy, in this context, is akin to some kind of rugged individualism.

According to Young, "The fundamental idea of autonomy is that of authoring one's own world without being subject to the will of others."[18] The emphasis here is on *not* being subject to the will of others. Freedom is defined, in negative terms, as an absence of external coercion. There are, however, at least two problems with this definition. Firstly, it obscures the complex relation between external coercion and human welfare. Coercion is not invariably evil, nor can it be totally eliminated from human lives. As David Stove points out, "A new-born human is so helpless . . . that it could never survive for one day if hands which are both *coercive and loving* did not guide it to the nipple which it would never find on its own."[19] Human life entails, to some extent, dependence on others. We would not be here today if we had not been supervised and protected by systems of social control that were both beneficial and coercive.

Secondly, this negative definition of autonomy has no substantive content. It provides an impoverished account of the human good. We can escape from the influences of others and satisfy our own desires in ways that are demeaning, destructive and futile. Freedom means more than the mere satisfaction of subjective preferences. If I want to be autonomous, it is not enough that I act according to a criterion of worthwhile behavior I posit for myself. I must also act in accordance with some objective criterion of worthwhile behavior. Before exploring this alternative view, however, we need to take a critical look at some of the more influential theories of personal autonomy advanced in the literature.

Brave New World: Gary Watson

In discussing the meaning of autonomy, contemporary philosophers engage with earlier views. Gary Watson invokes the Platonic division of appetite and reason; Robert Paul Wolff reinterprets the Kantian conception of autonomy; Harry Frankfurt, Gerald Dworkin, and Irving Thalberg revisit a traditional, hierarchical view of the self, and David Gauthier and Donald Davidson, in effect, rework the traditional notion of man as the rational animal. After considering these separate views, we will conclude our review of contemporary positions with a more general account of the "liberal" view of autonomy as summarized and enumerated by John Keykes.

Watson argues in favor of the view that "a person is free to the extent that he is able to do or get what he wants."[20] Freedom is, in short, a psychological state. To say that I am free is to say that I feel good about myself; I am satisfied with the way my life is going; I approve of my actions. Freedom here means freedom from guilt, freedom from any sense of self-alienation, freedom from psychological discomfort or disintegration.[21]

Watson distinguishes between the "evaluational" and "motivational" systems of an individual agent. Free or autonomous agents are characterized by internal harmony. They are what they want to be; they do what they want to do; they are not beset by inner tension or feelings of guilt; they are at peace with their prospects; they sleep soundly at night. Their "evaluational" and "motivational" systems are in perfect sync. But though Watson brings a much needed psychological richness into contemporary discussions of autonomy, psychological harmony is no substitute for freedom. Freedom means, in some important sense, choosing for oneself. But agents who are coerced, agents who are fundamentally mistaken, who suffer from false consciousness, may be, to all appearances, happy and well-adjusted.

In Aldous Huxley's famous novel *Brave New World*, the all-powerful state uses a sophisticated process of genetic engineering and environmental conditioning to determine the temperaments, intellectual abilities, and bodily characteristics of individual citizens. The Epsilons, Alphas, Gammas, and Deltas that inhabit this world do not, in any fundamental sense, decide for themselves. Yet they enjoy psychological harmony. Their appetites are ordered in line with their mental capacities; they are not troubled by their consciences; they identify with and approve of their actions; they do what they want to do. And yet *Brave New World* is a paradigm of nonfreedom. Why? Because its inhabitants exert no real control over their own lives. It does not matter how much internal harmony one experiences. One cannot be truly free in an environment that makes choosing for oneself, for all intents and purposes, impossible.

To equate psychological harmony with autonomy seems unrealistic and even sentimental. Even the most successful life may be characterized by bitter and scarring psychological conflict. Suppose Margaret experiences reprehensible desires but does not allow her behavior to be controlled by them. In resisting her reprehensible desires, Margaret gains a great victory over herself. She is, to some extent, autonomous. Even if the motivational and evaluational systems of an agent are at war with one another, this does not preclude all achievement of autonomy.

Watson presents his own view as a variation on Plato. Freedom is a harmonious relationship between the reason (the evaluative system) and the appetite (the motivational system) *of a single agent.* This corresponds to Plato's account of the just man as someone who regulates his desires in accordance with reason. But there is an important difference. On the Platonic view, there is something outside the individual agent that determines the good. Plato does not identify Reason with the subjective beliefs of a single agent, but with an objective criterion located in the world of forms. Successful agents do not only approve of their own actions. They conform to a higher criterion of goodness expressed in universal ideas that are objectively true.

Plato's concerns are epistemological and moral, whereas Watson's concerns are primarily psychological. Watson's interpretation of the relationship between Reason and Appetite represents a radical subjectification of the Platonic doctrine. On Plato's model, to be free is to conform to a truth that is greater than oneself. On Watson's model, to be free is to conform to our own expectations. But agents who approve of their own behavior may be less than moral.

In Plato's parable of the cave, the philosopher tries to liberate the slaves who rise up and murder him. In remaining in the cave, the slaves act so as to avoid the psychological discomfort and disintegration that would accompany

any explicit recognition of their own ignorance. They remain in the comfort zone; they refuse to question their own beliefs; they embrace self-satisfaction rather than self-criticism; they preserve, at all costs, their sense of dogmatic certainty and internal harmony. This is, however, folly, error, unrepentant ignorance. It does not represent any kind of successful self-government.

In Plato's system, the goal is not psychological comfort. The goal is truth or moral enlightenment. Agents who successfully govern themselves perceive an objective truth that directs and orients their own striving. Their behavior corresponds, in some fundamental sense, to the nature of reality. One cannot reduce a Platonic account of successful self-government to a doctrine of purely psychological harmony.

Anarchism and Kant: Robert Paul Wolff

While Watson reinterprets Plato in line with a relatively subjective account of human achievement, the political philosopher Robert Paul Wolff provides a similar reinterpretation of Kant.[22] Wolff is both an anarchist and a self-proclaimed Kantian. (An interesting marriage.) Anarchy is a means to personal autonomy. The elimination of government provides for the liberation of the individual. If autonomy is a "refusal to be ruled,"[23] it necessitates, in a political sphere, a radical absence of official government. Governments are collective, independent powers that exert control over the lives of individual citizens. They are inevitably oppressive. If individuals are to exist as self-legislating or fully autonomous units, they must eliminate government and institute a state of anarchy.

But Wolff misconstrues Kant's original intentions. Firstly, Kant explicates autonomy in moral rather than political terms. Secondly, Wolff's reconstruction of Kant represents a radical subjectivization of the German philosopher's doctrines. Wolff situates the criterion of successful self-government squarely inside the agent: I successfully govern myself because I make my own decisions, because I refuse to be ruled by other people. But Kant situates the criterion of successful self-government in a universal law of nature that transcends the individual human agent. Autonomy does not only mean making decisions for yourself. It means conforming to a universal standard of right and wrong. It means *obeying* the categorical imperative. Like Plato, Kant defines individual human achievement in objective terms. The fact that you make your own decisions, the fact that there is no government control, does not, in itself, constitute self-government.

Kant does not, in any case, define autonomy as "a refusal to be ruled."

Autonomous agents are ruled by something larger than themselves, by the moral law, by the dictates of impersonal reason. Wolff defends political liberty; Kant is more concerned with the submission of the recalcitrant will to universal law. Wolff contests the submission of individuals to other people, whereas Kant condemns heteronomy, a relinquishing of self-control that leads to a dereliction of duty. Kant believes in freedom, but freedom is first and foremost an internal, moral issue. One may perhaps elaborate a Kantian defense of anarchy, but anarchy is at best a precondition or a requirement for autonomy.

DESIRE-BASED THEORIES: FRANKFURT AND DWORKIN

Philosophers since Aristotle (and before) have, in various manners, divided the human self into a higher and a lower part.[24] The higher part possesses the ability to think, to reason, to discern right from wrong. The lower part is made up of appetites, desires, emotions, sense impressions, bodily functions, even physical acts. Autonomy is traditionally construed as the rule of the higher over the lower, the rational over the irrational, the spiritual over the carnal, the distinctly human over the merely animal. In developing separate theories, Harry Frankfurt[25] and Gerald Dworkin[26] revisit this older view of autonomy.

Frankfurt and Dworkin define autonomy as action in accordance with the highest part of the self. Unlike Aristotle, however, they do not identify that which is uniquely human with any special faculty of objective moral judgment.[27] Human beings are unique, not because they have access to objective knowledge about right and wrong, but because they can experience higher-level desires, second-order desires, desires about desires.[28] Suppose I desire to smoke a cigarette. This is a first-order desire. And suppose I desire to stop smoking. That is, suppose I desire not to feel a desire for an after-dinner cigarette. This is a second-order desire. If I act autonomously, I will act in accordance with my second-order desires; that is, I will, in this case, refrain from smoking.

Frankfurt and Dworkin define autonomy as action in accordance with second-order desires. If I desire to desire to stop smoking, autonomy means not smoking. If I desire to desire to continue smoking, autonomy means smoking. It is my second-order preferences, and these preferences alone, that supply the ultimate criterion of successful self-government. But this represents, once again, a radical subjectification of the traditional view. On the traditional model, the actions of autonomous agents conform to an *objective* morality. They satisfy some independent criterion of the good. On the Frankfurt-Dworkin model, there is nothing outside the higher-order desires of the agent that legitimizes an act. If I desire in a second-order sense to perform an act, this legitimizes it and renders it autonomous.

There are at least four conspicuous problems with these second-order, desire-based models of personal autonomy. Call them (1) the problem of human nature, (2) the problem of infinite regress, (3) the problem of self-centeredness, and (4) the problem of solipsism. Let us consider these problems in order.

Contemporary philosophers are leery of metaphysics, but Frankfurt and Dworkin both provide an implicit account of human nature. Frankfurt writes: "It seems to be peculiarly characteristic of humans . . . that they are able to form what I shall call second-order desires or desires of the second order. . . . No animal other than man . . . appears to have [this] capacity."[29] But is the capacity for higher-order desires, for desires about desires, the essential feature of humanity? I may, qua human being, desire many things that animals cannot desire. I may desire a winning lottery ticket. I may desire to go to the computer store. I may desire *not* to go into the woman's rest room. I may desire to understand Aristotle, to go to Heaven, to be a good American, to drink a glass of green beer because it is St. Patrick's Day, to wear a Republican pin, and so on. All these desires presuppose a level of intelligence or critical reflection that only characterizes *Homo sapiens*. It is the ability to engage in critical reflection, not the specific ability to desire desires, that constitutes the uniqueness of humans.

The second problem with desire-based models of autonomy is that they seem to lead to an infinite regress. If first-order desires must be legitimized by an appeal to second-order desires, should it not follow, on the same grounds, that second-order desires must be legitimized by an appeal to third-order desires, that third-order desires must be legitimized by an appeal to fourth-order desires, that fourth-order desires must be legitimized by an appeal to fifth-order desires, and so on ad infinitum? If desires can only be ratified by an appeal to a higher-order desires, the legitimization of desire becomes a Sisyphean task that can never be completed. To stop the process of legitimization at any particular order of desires seems arbitrary.

Thalberg writes: "Both Frankfurt and Dworkin assume that when you ascend to the second level [of desires], you discover the real person and what she or he really wants."[30] But how can we be certain that these second-level desires represent the "real person"? Perhaps the "real person" is situated at the third, the fourth, the twenty-sixth, or the one-hundred-and-sixteenth level of desires. To identify the real person with any particular level seems again capricious.

The third problem with desire-based notions of autonomy is their inherent self-centeredness. To describe human agency, primarily or exclusively, in terms of higher-order desires is to promote a crippling self-consciousness. The focus is not outward: "Is this a worthwhile thing to do?" The focus is inward: "Is this, in a second-, third-, fourth- or higher-order sense, what I desire to do?" One fixes one's gaze, not on others' needs, but on the deepest, highest, most interior levels of the self. Suppose I want to perform an act of charity. The primary concern is not "Is the welfare of the needy being served?" but "Am I acting on the desire I desire to act on?" Instead of focusing on the needs of the other person, I end up focusing on myself. On a desire-based model, a disinterested concern for others may be transformed into a self-absorbed preoccupation with my own desires and motivations. Trying to be autonomous entails a narcissistic dwelling on the hidden, higher-level self rather than an outward concern for other people.

The fourth problem with desire-based models of autonomy is their inevitable solipsism. If I am to achieve autonomy, it is not enough that I act in accordance with my second-order desires. My secondhand desires must be properly ordered with respect to reality. Internal consistency is not enough. If I have erroneous beliefs and unhealthy attitudes, I may fail at self-government even when I do act in accordance with my higher-order desires. The desires of a fallible agent do not provide us with an infallible criterion of successful self-government.

One cannot explain human agency solely in terms of desire. Multiplying the levels of desire, creating a second, or even a third, or a fourth level of desire, will not solve the problem. What we need is not more desire, but something different, an epistemological faculty of moral and rational judgment. On the traditional Aristotelian model, the higher self supplies the agent with objective knowledge that corresponds to the nature of the world as it can be known. Autonomy does not only mean acting in accordance with one's desires. It means, first and foremost, acting in accordance with true belief. It is not the agent's feelings but the objective nature of the world that provides the ultimate standard of successful self-government.

CLEVER ANIMALS: GAUTHIER & COMPANY

According to the ancient and medieval formula, a human being is "a rational animal." David Gauthier and other authors in the why-be-moral tradition also conceive of human agency as a rational venture. They radically redefine, however, the traditional conception of rationality. According to Gauthier, "One chooses *rationally* in endeavoring to maximize the fulfilment of . . . preferences . . . in the choice situation."[31] In less technical language, we act rationally when we act so as to satisfy our own desires to the utmost degree. Human agents are *rational* creatures in that they are able to satisfy their own desires much more efficiently than animals.

Historical authors like Aristotle (and Plato) distinguish between reason and appetite. Rational agents order their actions according to reason rather than appetite. In deciding what to do, they make their desires conform to a higher, moral point of view. One might, however, imagine a very intelligent being who, ignorant of moral considerations, cleverly plans its decisions so as to satisfy its appetites to the utmost. This is, in effect, Gauthier's rational agent. Seen from the viewpoint of traditional philosophy, however, this kind of being is only a very clever animal.

Gauthier equates thoughtfulness with rationality, but mere thoughtfulness is not enough.[32] To be truly rational, thoughtfulness has to embrace a moral dimension. On the traditional view, a reflective libertine who thoughtfully plans his life so as to maximize the gratification of his appetites forfeits his humanity. It does not matter how efficiently he satisfies his desires. In overlooking the moral dimension, he behaves like an animal. Gauthier bases his theory of *rational* decision-making on a calculus of preference-satisfaction. This is, in Aristotelian terms, self-defeating. It is to generate an account of rationality based on appetite rather than reason.

Gauthier's account of reason is purely instrumental. Rationality selects the means, whereas appetite supplies the end. On Aristotle's account, rationality evaluates ends as well as means. It provides a new perspective, orienting the individual towards principles, duties, ideas, and causes that are larger than the self. On Gauthier's model, humans do more efficiently what animals do less efficiently. On Aristotle's model, humans do something entirely new, something genuinely incommensurable. The ultimate goal is not the satisfaction of desires but virtue.[33] Animals cannot live a virtuous life, for they lack reason, the ability to distinguish right from wrong.[34]

Gauthier's account represents, once again, the subjectification of an earlier doctrine. Gauthier does not propose an objective account of the good. It is our preferences that define what the good is. The gauge or measure of successful endeavor is no longer located in the objective nature of reality. It is situated inside the will of the individual agent. But human beings are, after all, fallible creatures. If my desires are mistaken—if they are unsound, insane, immoral, demeaning, impractical, or imprudent—I err in satisfying them. Even if I do what I want to do, this does not prove that I successfully govern myself.

As John Dewey observes: "The fact that something is desired only raises the *question* of its desirability; it does not settle it."[35] If we want to evaluate human conduct, we need something objective, something higher or more primary than our own desires, something that provides a standard by which these desires can be evaluated. If I am passionately attached to particular aims, this does not necessarily mean that these aims are legitimate, commendable, or valuable. As Michael Sandel writes: "Values and ends must have a sanction independent of the mere fact that I happen to hold them with a certain intensity."[36] As a fallible creature, I may be passionately attached to the wrong values or the wrong ends. Values and ends are legitimate or worthwhile, not because they are my values or my ends, but because they satisfy some independent criterion of reason and good judgment.

DAVIDSON: CONFUSING JUDGMENT AND DESIRE

Authors like Watson, Frankfurt, Dworkin, and Gauthier seem to conflate notions of judgment and desire. According to Gauthier, "To suppose one preference superior to another is simply to prefer one to the other."[37] On this view, desire and judgment are fundamentally the same. Judgment is, at best, a higher level of desire.

Donald Davidson, in a parallel development, claims that judgment *is* the same thing as desire. Davidson constructs a so-called tautology: "If an agent *judges* that it would be better to do *x* than to do *y*, then he *wants* to do x more than he wants to do y."[38] In other words, if I *judge* that *x* is better than *y*, then I *desire x* more than *y*. But this is demonstrably not the case. Suppose I am a reluctant smoker. I want to stop. At the same time, on a sensual, psychological, physical level, I desire this cigarette. If I judge that not-smoking is better than smoking, I may still desire to smoke. Tension often arises between mere desire and a faculty of moral and rational judgment. So Davidson's tautology is not a tautology. We cannot equate, in any unqualified way, judgment, and desire.

Robert Young has contested the truth of Davidson's "tautology" by raising the possibility of a conflict between moral and prudential principles.[39] In the case of the reluctant smoker, however, there is no compelling moral reason that pushes the smoker to smoke. The conflict here is not between morality and prudence, but between judgment and desire. Young also suggests that conflicts between desire and judgment may be attributed to faulty judgment. Our reluctant smoker does not, however, suffer from faulty judgment. He or she suffers from the wrong desires.

Frankfurt and Dworkin try to deal with the problem of internal dissonance by introducing the notion of second-order desires. This is, at least, to recognize the problem. But we need to appeal to something more than mere desire. On the traditional model, the higher-level self sits at a distance, directing, regulating, and evaluating the agent's comportment from a perspective outside the immediate interests of the self. Moral judgments derive from some higher process of critical reflection. Because there is some distance between the reflective judgments of the self and the self's own desires, autonomy does not reduce to subjectivity or mere selfishness. Rational behavior incorporates a striving toward objectivity.

Davidson, in equating judgment and desire, reduces judgment to a feeling. This leaves us, once again, with a subjective account of successful self-government. Successful self-government means more than acting in accordance with our feelings. It means having the right feelings, feelings that are, in some objective sense, admirable. Judgment, traditionally understood, is a form of epistemological insight that allows us to evaluate our feelings in light of objective principles. To reduce judgment to mere sensation—a feeling or craving or yearning for something—is to confuse appetite and reason. It is, on the traditional view, to confound the man of appetite with the man of reason.

THALBERG: JETTISONING CONSCIENCE?

Frankfurt and Dworkin invoke a hierarchical view of the self that emphasizes higher-level desires. Ian Thalberg has criticized this model. Thalberg asks a rhetorical question: "Why should we agree, in effect, that our conscience is our real self, and that our moral principles specify what we really, or 'most' want?"[40] In contrast to Frankfurt and Dworkin, Thalberg argues that our *lower-level* desires constitute the real self. We may be more genuinely ourselves when we act on our first-order desires, when we act spontaneously and *un*reflectively, when we ignore the voice of moral judgment. On this view, the kind of higher-level critical reflection we engage in when evaluating higher-order desires is often a mask, something that stops us from being what we really are.

It is, of course, true that we can overintellectualize our moral choices. We cannot spend every waking moment analyzing and evaluating our first-order desires. There are, however, serious problems with Thalberg's account. In the first place, Thalberg himself subscribes to an overly intellectual view of morality or judgment. Moral principles are not purely intellectual. As Aristotle suggests, we act morally from habit. We develop a habit of being courteous or kind or generous. We do not have to reevaluate the importance of courtesy or kindness or generosity every time we act. The habit of courtesy, kindness, or generosity comes to constitute who we are. We can be moral, then, without overintellectualization.

Secondly, Thalberg provides an extremely limited account of human nature. Other accounts of personal autonomy situate the ultimate standard of right or wrong inside the judgment of the agent, but Thalberg goes one step further. He eliminates judgment altogether. We are not what we think; we are what we crave, what we, in a genuinely unreflective sense, desire. The *unexamined* life is the only life worth living. If, however, we are creatures of impulsion and intuition, we are also rational agents. To ignore the rational element in human decision-making is to deny our own humanity. We think about our decisions. We reflect on our choices. This is what it means to be human.

Thirdly, Thalberg's strategy for successful self-government is incoherent. Agents who were obliged to act contrary to conscience so as to be true to themselves would be seriously dysfunctional. Disregarding moral judgment—literally, acting like an animal—is not a recipe for human happiness. If we disobey the moral code we sincerely believe in, we will come to despise ourselves. If our moral understanding is mistaken, the solution is to correct it. It is not to act contrary to our own consciences.

Thalberg provides another subjective treatment of human agency. To eliminate judgment altogether is to precipitate a slip into our own unexamined feelings. This has the effect of driving us down into ourselves, out of the reach of claims that are larger than our own unmediated desires. We are no longer forced to consider our own behavior from the perspective of a larger consistency. What matters is only our own attitudes, impressions, feelings. So the search for authenticity leads, not to self-fulfillment, but to an isolating subjectivity.

KEYKES'S ACCOUNT OF LIBERAL AUTONOMY

Contemporary authors elaborate individualized accounts of personal autonomy. John Keykes has summarized, in more general form, the liberal view. Although Keykes is a conservative arguing against liberalism, he pieces together a fair account of the liberal position from a vast array of primary sources.[41] His retelling of the liberal position is both telling and comprehensive.

Liberal authors argue that an autonomous agent must satisfy, in general, five requirements: (1) the performance condition, (2) the choice condition, (3) the unforced choice condition, (4) the evaluation condition, and (5) the understanding condition. What does it mean to be an autonomous agent? Firstly, autonomous agents must perform actions. Secondly, they must choose "from a number of alternatives they reasonably believe are available."[42] Thirdly, they must choose "between alternatives that are not forced on agents."[43] Fourthly, they must have "favorably evaluated the actions they choose to perform."[44] And fifthly, their "favorable evaluation of their chosen actions must be based on sufficient understanding of these actions."[45]

The liberal view emphasizes the process of choice. Autonomous agents possess a number of options; they understand these options; they are able to evaluate them, and they are allowed to make a choice between them. This leaves open the possibility that autonomous agents may choose to act in ways that are not, in any objective sense, illustrious or praiseworthy. As long as agents choose for themselves, this kind of failure need not detract from their autonomy. As Keykes explains: "Agents . . . may fail to be objective because of self-deception, inattention, delusions, self-centeredness, fanaticisms, fantasy, stupidity, and so forth. These ways of failing in objectivity are themselves chosen, unchosen or somewhere inbetween. The extent to which they are unchosen is the extent to which the agent's lack of objectivity renders their actions non-autonomous."[46] On the liberal view, to be autonomous is to choose for oneself. If one chooses to be self-centered, or stupid, or inattentive, one is autonomous to the extent to which one is self-centered, stupid or inattentive. Immorality, or even irrationality, need not entail a failure of autonomy.

On the liberal view, an autonomous agent must be aware of the moral status of his or her actions (condition five), but autonomy does not entail morality. In Keykes's words: "The requirement is not that the agents' actions be morally praiseworthy, for morally blameworthy actions can also be autonomous."[47] Liberalism (as described by Keykes) provides an entirely subjective criterion for successful self-government. The issue is: "Who is in control?" Or, more pointedly: "Is the self controlling the self?"[48] If I choose to deceive myself, to be stupid, to be self-centered, or to be a fanatic, then, in deceiving myself, in being stupid, self-centered, or fanatical, I do what I want to do. I successfully govern myself. As long as I act in accordance with my own aspirations, I am an autonomous individual.

The liberal authors Keykes discusses measure human achievement in terms of the subjective wants and aspirations of the individual agent. Authors like Thalberg, Davidson, Gauthier, Frankfurt, Dworkin, Wolf, and Watson follow suit. But the views of an individual agent do not provide an infallible measure of human achievement. Even if agents satisfy their aims and desires, they may not successfully govern themselves. To equate agent self-satisfaction with autonomy is to lapse into solipsism.

In this section I will argue that autonomous agents must be moral. Morality provides a measuring stick that allows us to evaluate the achievement of individual agents. We may disagree about the normative content of morality. Morality may be thought of as a rampart against human weaknesses, but it is also proof against human fallibility. To argue that agents have embraced the right aims and values because they have chosen these aims and values for themselves is not enough. It is not enough that we satisfy ourselves. Morality supplies a criterion of reasonableness and good judgment that transcends our foibles and our prejudices. It provides a vantage point from which we can be judged, whether we assent to it or not.

Discourse about autonomy, about liberation, and about personal freedom must touch upon the moral dimension. It does not make sense to argue, like Babbit, that someone who commits a heinous murder liberates himself. It is only because we conceive of freedom solely from the viewpoint of the beliefs and aspirations of the individual agent that this is even conceivable. I want to argue that morality is an essential aspect of autonomy. The same agent cannot be both immoral and autonomous. As we shall see, the very narrow view of morality prevalent in present-day philosophy has served to obscure the moral aspects of autonomous action.

5

Comprehensive Morality

Charles Taylor has complained of the "cramped and truncated view of morality"[1] proposed by contemporary analytic philosophy. MacIntyre expresses similar sentiments. In focusing on normative issues, academic authors tend to limit morality to a very restricted domain of human endeavor. If we want to understand the nature of moral practice, we need to look beyond these received distinctions and examine what people are trying to do when they act morally. This will lead to a much wider view of moral practice than is current in academic philosophy.

St. Augustine, in the *City of God*, considers whether certain monstrous races of men are descended from Adam's seed. There follows a fanciful inventory of the human race. Augustine writes:

> It is reported that some have one eye in the middle of the forehead; some feet turned backwards from the heel; some, a double-sex, the right breast like a man, the left like a woman, and that they alternatively beget and bring forth [children]: others are said to have no mouth and to breathe only through the nostrils; others are but a cubit high, and are therefore called by the Greeks Pigmies: they say that in some places the women conceive in their fifth year and do not live beyond their eighth. So too they tell of a race who have two feet but only one leg, and are of marvelous swiftness though they do not bend the knee. They are called Skiopodes, because in hot weather they lie down on their backs and shade themselves with their feet. Others are said to have no head, and their eyes in their shoulders; and other human or quasi-human races are depicted.[2]

Augustine is cautious. "We are not bound to believe all we hear of these monstrosities." Nonetheless, he concludes that these peculiar species, insomuch as they are rational and mortal, are descended from Adam.

Augustine's fanciful human genealogy can stand as a striking meta-
phor for human diversity. I want to argue, in less flamboyant fashion, that
all human endeavor, however peculiar or distinctive, encapsulates a moral
element. This is not to deny the great disparity and apparent incongruity of
human behavior. The actions of particular human beings may be extreme,
outlandish, bizarre, even monstrous. Nonetheless, human beings are motivated by moral considerations. That is, they are able to investigate and
appreciate the nature of their own and other people's acts and to use this
knowledge as a guide and as the impetus for their own behavior. This is an
activity all but the extremely dysfunctional, the very young, or the comatose engage in continually.

What characterizes humanity is not the peculiarly modern attempt to
prove the logical cogency of morality. To be a human being is to "know
how" to evaluate other human beings, their beliefs and their actions.
Noddings writes: "We can present a coherent and enlightening picture [of
morality] without *proving* anything and, indeed, without claiming to present
or seek moral *knowledge* or moral *truth*. The hand that steadied us as we
learned to ride our first bicycle did not provide propositional knowledge,
but it guided and supported us all the same, and we finished up 'knowing-
how.'"[3]

Human beings are evaluators. They evaluate means and ends. They
recognize virtue. They know what it means to care. They can engage in
self-examination. They are able to apply moral laws and principles. They
have an aesthetic sense. They can appreciate intent. They are able to approve and disapprove. They often strive toward objectivity. If we tend to
overlook the moral aspects of human endeavor, however outlandish or bizarre, this is because we do not always investigate very deeply or thoroughly the values that underlie our real-life decisions.

What is morality, in the broadest sense, about? In discussing virtue
ethics, Frankena quotes Leslie Stephen: "The moral law . . . has to be expressed in the form, 'be this,' not in the form, 'do this.'"[4] This sounds
about right. Morality is not just about doing (or not doing) certain kinds of
acts. It is, first and foremost, about *being* a particular kind of person. The
only reason we have for following moral rules or principles is that they
turn us into the kind of person we ought to be. In this sense at least, morality is a personalist endeavor.

If, however, morality is about being a certain kind of person, it includes a much wider field of activity than is often acknowledged. What
kind of person should I be? I may believe that I ought to be the kind of
person who goes to mass on Sundays. Or the kind of person who gives
generously to charity. Or the kind of person who always tells the truth.

Then again, I may believe that I ought to be the kind of person who wears designer clothes, who owns a luxury car, who travels to Europe, who climbs mountains, who skateboards, who bench-presses 350 pounds, who is attractive to women, who has a college degree, and so on. These latter notions are not usually dignified with the appellation "moral." Nonetheless, they motivate, to a very large degree, human behavior. Insomuch as they contribute to our ideas about the kind of person we ought to be, they function as moral beliefs.

Rational agents embrace ideals of life or character. Morality means living up to these ideals. Dan Lyons and Jan Benson have recently argued that people in contemporary America regulate their lives according to notions of worth or excellence that have very little to do with morality narrowly construed. As they insist, "Not all standards people wish to uphold are strictly moral."[5] On the negative side, "Shame is far more feared than guilt, and it often occurs over a failure that has nothing to do with morality."[6] On the positive side, individuals are often motivated by a feeling of personal accomplishment: "Individuals find it important to accomplish feats that others admire—to be promoted in their jobs, to create, to discover, to feel that something got done in their lives. People often plan an action with a desire to achieve, not because it is required by morality."[7]

Lyons and Benson elaborate an "honor code" that is recognizably different from the "moral code." If, however, morality is about being the kind of person one ought to be, then notions about honor form an integral part of morality. Lyons and Benson speak of honor, Rawls and Kohlberg of justice, Gilligan and Noddings of care. Ross speaks of duty, Royce of loyalty, Hutcheson of benevolence, Augustine of faith, the Stoics of equanimity, Tillich of courage, Jesus of love. But these ideals all serve a similar function. They indicate the kind of person we ought to be. When I act honorably or courageously, when I treat other people fairly, when I do my duty, when I am loyal, when I show compassion, when I believe, when I endure suffering patiently, when I love my neighbor as myself, I become the kind of person I ought to be. These different ideals all represent different (but similar) ways of construing the good. They each provide a unique perspective on morality.

Morality, as it exists out in the world and not just in philosophers' heads, entails an allegiance to a heterogenous array of value judgments. Many of these attitudes and judgments are not usually classified as moral. Philosophers provide a rather exalted view of morality, but it behooves us to develop a less exalted and more realistic view, one that describes the kinds of ideals, both noble and petty, that ordinary people, in whatever peculiar or outlandish ways, strive toward. Popular culture may be motivated by a morality that is shallow, contradictory, misleading, maudlin, and clichéd, but it is a morality just the same. It is a morality because it provides us with an image of who and what we should be.

Consider the oral tradition, a repository of thought and reflection often overlooked in academic writing. Proverbs, clichés, well-known aphorisms, favorite sayings, political slogans, and personal mottoes continually advise, enjoin, admonish, supplicate, or command us to behave in various ways. The examples are endless:

1. Speak softly and carry a big stick.
2. Spare the rod, spoil the child.
3. Don't be a crybaby.
4. Waste not, want not.
5. Mind your manners.
6. Make love, not war.
7. An idle mind is the devil's playground.
8. He who plays with fire gets burned.
9. Cleanliness is next to godliness.
10. Winning is not everything—it's the only thing.
11. *Qui donne aux pauvres prête à Dieu.* (Who gives to the poor, lends to God.)
12. Early to bed, early to rise, makes a man healthy, wealthy, and wise.
13. Don't count your chickens before they're hatched. Or, in the French version: *Ne pas vendre la peau de l'ours avant de l'avoir tué.* (Don't sell the bear's skin before killing it.)
14. Say no to racism.
15. The early bird gets the worm.
16. Keep a stiff upper lip.
17. A stitch in time saves nine.
18. *La patience est amère, mais son fruit est doux.* (Patience is bitter but its fruit is sweet.)
19. *Pauvreté n'est pas vice.* (Poverty is not vice.)
20. When the going gets tough, the tough get going.
21. "Ours is not to question why; ours is but to do and die."[8]
22. *Qui vole un œuf, vole un bœuf.* (Who steals an egg steals a chicken [literally, a cow].)

23. No pain, no gain.
24. Think positive!

These are all moral injunctions. They all tell us, in one manner or another, the kind of person one ought to be. One ought to be a winner (10), a pacifist (6), an optimist (24), a stoic (3, 16, 23), courteous (5), clean (9), patient (18), industrious (7, 12, 15, 20), frugal (4), prudent (8, 17), tough (3, 16, 20, 23), charitable (11), someone who does not discriminate (14), who keeps good company (8), who is honest in the smallest matters (22), who follows orders (21), who keeps emotions in check (3, 16), who does not exaggerate the importance of money (19), who disciplines children (2), who protects oneself (1), who does not jump to conclusions (13), and so on. In short, one ought to be the kind of person that abides by the axiom in question.

Philosophers divide up morality in diverse and sundry ways. Aristotle points out that there are many goods: physical beauty, material wealth, a happy domestic situation, education, health, honor, friendship, pleasure, contemplation. In living out an allegiance to specific goods, we carve out a picture of the kind of person we ought to be. In real life, agents often embrace divergent moral ideals, ideals that are often overlooked in the philosophical literature. Bernard Williams suggests that the "amoralist," the person who repudiates all moral commitments, might have a very peculiar and limited morality after all.[9] I want to suggest, in a more robust way, that the amoralist does not even exist. A notion of values or ideals, an awareness of merit, a sense of ought, of conscious but perhaps erroneous obligation, is an inescapable part of the human condition.

This broader view of morality provides a more complete account of human striving. It also provides a better explanation of immorality. Agents are often immoral, sometimes egregiously so. But they may be immoral in two different ways. Agents may fail to put into practice widely accepted moral norms through some fault of character. They may be unable to live up to the moral ideal they believe in. But they may also be immoral, not because they lack the requisite strength of character, but because they believe in values that are at odds with genuine morality. That is to say, agents may be immoral because they subscribe—surreptitiously perhaps—to the wrong moral values, the wrong moral system. In the former case, agents fail at morality because of *akrasia* or weakness of will. In the latter case, agents fail at morality because of moral ignorance. Contemporary moral philosophy does not sufficiently recognize the latter kind of failure. To say that agents are morally ignorant is not to say (in most cases) that the moral impetus is totally extinguished. It is rather that moral passion is perverted and comes to serve the wrong ends. Later in the text, we will identify both types of moral failure as failures of autonomy.

Morality supplies an objective measure of human achievement. Moral agents measure up to a criterion of excellence that transcends the individual agent. They obey a higher law. They recognize an external authority. They devote themselves to some transcendent, objective ideal. This is why many liberal authors regard moral accounts of autonomy with suspicion. Submission to a higher law is interpreted as submission to a foreign power and, in the case of the unwilling agent, as a form of bondage rather than freedom.

For most mainstream authors, morality remains an option. Autonomous agents may be moral. There are, however, thinkers who go so far as to argue that morality is incompatible with freedom. Antimoralists like Thrasymachus, Callicles, Machiavelli, Sade, Nietzsche, and Rand can be variously construed as saying that morality is equivalent to slavery and that free agents will not submit to restrictions posed by the moral perspective. Some of these authors posit immoral behavior as a kind of liberation. Sade, for example, goes so far as to claim that a free agent *must* actively practice evil.[10] This "Extreme Argument," however implausible, is useful, for it expresses in bold, uncompromising terms—in capital letters, so to speak— the usual objection brought against moral accounts of freedom.

There are at least two problems with the Extreme Argument that one must be immoral to be free. Firstly, antimoralists portray morality as an external constraint, something completely outside ourselves that demands our complete subservience, but this is misleading. Morality is as much an internal as an external constraint. If morality possesses objective validity—it tells us what we ought to do—it is also part of who and what we are. Human beings are by nature creatures equipped with a moral sense, with compassionate feelings, with a capacity for empathy, with conscience, with a sense of respect, with a hunger for the truth, and so on. When we ignore the moral perspective, we ignore a part of ourselves. As we shall see, even flagrantly immoral agents may adhere to an implicit moral code in the most scrupulous manner.

Morality is ever present, in all walks of life and in all strata of society. Leave aside philosophy for a moment and consider a true incident. A friend is a criminal lawyer. One of her clients, a member of a motorcycle gang, was killed in a private settling of accounts. When the police arrived, he was lying in a pool of blood. He had been stabbed thirty-three times. The police repeatedly asked for the names of his assailants. But no matter how much they pleaded, he refused to give any information. His dying words to the police: "F—— off!"

What is happening here? The biker is not, by conventional standards, a moral person. He deals in drugs, drinks to excess, takes risks, participates in loose sex, acts aggressively, steals, swears, and refuses to cooperate with legitimate authority. Still, the biker is not an *amoral* person. When he tells the police, in rough language, to mind their own business, he is living up to an outlaw ideal. This is what a biker should do. Bikers are supposed to be unconventional, tough, independent, fierce, stoic, crude, cool, full of bluster. Most of all, they are *never* supposed to cooperate with the police. They settle accounts outside the law. They do not stool on fellow gang members. The behavior of the dying gang member fits the image to a T. In refusing to tell the police the names of his assailants, he embraces a moral ideal. It is perhaps a specious ideal. But it is a moral ideal nonetheless. The biker is just as much a member of the human species as any one else.

Proponents of the Extreme Argument do not, in the first place, recognize the pervasive, internal nature of morality. In the second place, their claims are contradictory. An author like Sade claims that submission to anything other than the self is subservience, not freedom. If, however, we *must* be immoral in order to be free, immorality becomes something we must submit to—whether we like it or not—in order to be free. We are not ridding ourselves of all subservience. We are only changing one form of subservience for another. As Ortega y Gasset observes, to argue that one *ought* to be immoral is to impose another normative standard on human behavior.[11] That is, it is to propose another morality

Antimoralists like Callicles, Machiavelli, Sade, Nietzsche, and Rand may appear to champion immorality, but these are all moralists in disguise. Their writings are didactic. For all their pious blasphemy, they propose a picture of the kind of person one ought to be. The ideal type is physically and mentally tough, ruthlessly honest, yea-saying, life-affirming, virile, sensual, intelligent, proud, a giant among men who scoffs at convention, exploits the weak, and does whatever he wants. The result is a moral argument that effectively says: "Be the Übermensch!" "Be the Prince!" "Be a libertine!" "Be such a person!"

The antimoralist is not an amoralist, someone who has no moral beliefs. If anything, philosophers like Nietzsche and colleagues are intent on proselytizing. Their rhetoric partakes of the peculiar emotional urgency that characterizes the moral crusader. The ideal they present is not calmly and dispassionately argued for. As readers, we are badgered by hyperbole and battered by invective. We are placed before an urgent choice. Either become the ideal type or remain a member of the herd, a contemptible worm, a dupe, a slave, a nonentity, a Milquetoast, a lackey!

If antimoralists are able to write or speak with such passion and vigor, this only serves to show how meaningful, how vital, and how intensely important the normative content of morality is. An amoral individual, an individual without values, would not argue that we *ought* to oppose conventional morality. He or she would be indifferent to such issues. He or she would not care one way or the other. In preaching—with great passion—the gospel of immorality, antimoralists are, in spite of themselves, obeying a moral impetus. This is how their arguments must be understood: not as a denial of all morality but as the zealous presentation of a renegade morality with a different normative content.

If antimoralists are construed as repudiating all morality, this is only because we tend to conflate normative and descriptive accounts of morality. To say, in a descriptive sense, that someone like Ayn Rand is a moral agent is not to say that her actions are inspired by the proper understanding of morality. It is only to say that she does subscribe to some kind of value system. We can make sense of her actions. They are not random or haphazard. They originate in some identifiable system of values. Whether Ayn Rand has the right value system is a separate issue. Antimoralists are, at best, people who have embraced true moral beliefs that conflict with conventional society or, at worst, people who have embraced the wrong moral beliefs. Either way, they propose a moral criterion of successful self-government.

LIBERALISM

The Extreme Argument does not provide us with any fatal objection to moral theories of autonomy. Of course, most mainstream authors do not subscribe to the Extreme Argument. They do not argue that morality is incompatible with autonomy but that there is no necessary connection between morality and autonomy. Morality may be a legitimate goal, but there are equally important goals outside of morality. Autonomous individuals do not have to focus on morality. They can achieve other kinds of goals and be equally autonomous.

Call this more qualified position the Mitigated Argument. Proponents of the Mitigated Argument assume that there are fields of endeavor outside morality. They argue that moral conceptions of autonomy repose on a very restricted account of human achievement. I will argue, in response, that there are, on closer inspection, no serious nonmoral aspirations. Any belief or attitude that contributes to our idea about the kind of person we ought to be has definite moral content. Although we may act in flagrantly immoral ways, we cannot escape the moral impetus. Purposeful, value-driven striving is always based on notions of value. We inevitably strive to fulfill some sort of moral aspiration, and when we fail at morality we fail at self-government.

If the constricted view of morality presupposed by the Mitigated Argument strikes moderns as eminently credible, there are historical factors at work. The extreme narrowness of the contemporary views of morality may be attributed to (1) liberal views of morality, to (2) the general influence of Christianity, and to (3) a latent Puritanism. Although the historical phenomenon of Puritanism provides important clues as to why and how autonomy was first divorced from ideas about morality, consider first how liberalism and Christianity have served to narrow the moral focus.

Classical liberalism derives from authors like Hobbes, Locke, Kant, and Mill. This political doctrine defends and protects individual liberty. Mill's "no-harm" principle provides a negative restriction on action: "Do not interfere with the liberty of others."[12] Though this is a necessary restriction, it does not tell us enough about the content of praiseworthy action to serve as a full-bodied measure of morality. If society tells me that I ought to refrain from interfering with other people's liberty, this does not, in any comprehensive sense, tell me what kind of person I ought to be. The liberal no-harm principle may leave us the space to do what we want with our lives, but it is too weak to provide us with any definitive moral guidance. It does not provide us with an ethical insight that can adequately orient our striving.

Liberalism restricts morality to the public realm. In our private lives, we are free to fulfill our own dreams, hopes, beliefs, or aspirations as we wish. These private aspirations exist, for the most part, outside the moral domain. If we want to judge whether someone has successfully governed himself, we must look to these extramoral aspirations. Morality has such a restricted, public focus that it comes to be perceived as extraneous to successful self-government. I may be moral and not autonomous. Or again, I may be autonomous and not moral.

Liberalism may be associated with certain virtues such as tolerance, individuality, and impartiality. These virtues do not, however, comprehend the whole of morality. In a liberal society, individuals strive after personal accomplishment or self-fulfillment in ways that are not officially moral. If I climb mountains, if I play first violin, if I go to church on Sunday, these are not matters of official public obligation. The moral impetus is too restricted to motivate or orient much personal striving, so we come to conceive of personal accomplishment as separate from morality. This explains, in part, the popularity of amoral notions of personal achievement.

The liberal ideal of tolerance (construed positively) or indifference (construed negatively) does not provide us with an adequate measure of morality. But while liberalism perceives morality as a minimalist endeavor, Christianity moves in the opposite direction. Liberalism restricts morality to the public sphere, leaving us free to do whatever we want with our private lives. Christianity, on the other hand, proposes a spiritual understanding that is supposed to transform our every thought and action. Whereas liberalism tells us not to interfere with our neighbor, Christianity tells us to actively help our neighbor. Whereas liberalism emphasizes neutrality between divergent descriptions of the good, Christianity proposes a definitive account of good and evil. Whereas liberalism views morality as primarily public or legal, Christianity views morality as primarily personal and spiritual.

Popular misconceptions notwithstanding, Christianity imposes a harsher, more rigorous moral law. It does this in various ways. Firstly, it enlarges the scope of immorality, of actions one must avoid. Jesus tells his Jewish disciples: "You have heard the commandments imposed on your forefathers, 'You shall not commit murder, every murderer shall be liable to punishment.' What I say to you is: everyone who grows angry with his brother shall be liable to judgement; any man who uses abusive language towards his brother shall be answerable to the Sanhedrin; and if he holds him in contempt, he risks the fires of Gehenna."[13] Again, he warns them: "You have heard that it was said, 'Do not commit adultery.' But I tell you that anyone who looks at a woman lustfully has already committed adultery with her in his heart."[14]

Secondly, Christianity emphasizes moral commitment. Jesus declares: "You must be Perfect as your Father in Heaven is Perfect."[15] On the Christian model, the whole person, the motivation and the thought behind the act, must be, to the utmost degree, moral. There is no limit to the required degree of moral perfection. In Revelation, the Spirit tells the damned: "Because you are lukewarm—neither hot nor cold—I am about to spit you out of my mouth."[16] Christianity does not propose a morality of perfunctory compliance but a morality of absolute commitment.

Thirdly, Christianity tells us that the consequences of immorality are utterly disastrous. Sentimentalized versions of Christianity abound, but the

Gospels are full of dire warnings about the wages of sin. Those who do evil perish. If anyone causes another to sin, "it would be better for him to have a large millstone hung around his neck and to be drowned in the depths of the sea."[17] Jesus tells of a final time when "everything that causes sin and all who do evil" will be "thrown into the fiery furnace, where there will be weeping and gnashing of teeth."[18] He admonishes the wrongdoer: "If your hand or your foot causes you to sin cut it off and throw it away. It is better for you to enter life maimed or crippled than to have two hands or two feet and be thrown into eternal fire. And if your eye causes you to sin, gouge it out and throw it away. It is better for you to enter life with one eye than to have two eyes and be thrown into the fire of hell."[19]

Fourthly, Christianity preaches an ideal of servitude and disinterested selflessness. Jesus teaches his apostles that they are not to strive for positions of influence and status like the Scribes and the Pharisees. "If anyone wants to be first, he must be the very last, and the servant of all."[20] On the Christian model, you are to love your neighbor as yourself.[21] Behavior must be wholly, enthusiastically other-directed or benevolent. Jesus is adamant. If someone wants your shirt, you must give him your coat. If someone asks you to walk one mile, you must walk two. If someone strikes you on the right cheek, you must offer your left cheek as well.[22] If liberal views of morality are too narrow, the Christian account is so full, so comprehensive, so demanding, it tends to obscure the wider scope of morality as it is actually practiced in the world.

If we want to provide a descriptive account of morality, one that captures the values that really spur people to action, we must devise an accurate account the way people really live. There is a fundamental duplicity that characterizes Western society. Many individuals pay lip service to the Christian ideal but order their lives according to divergent value systems. We are left with an official morality that describes how people are supposed to act and an unofficial morality that is implicit in their actions. Philosophy is party to this split between practice and theory. It has not adequately exposed this incoherence.

Christian values have so profoundly influenced the West that morality has come to be identified with a concern for the welfare of others. We call belief systems that highlight altruistic, other-oriented notions of value "morality." We do not dignify other value systems with the appellation moral, but there are many ways of evaluating the world; that is, many moralities. If, on an authentically Christian view, uncharitable behavior is, in a most crucial sense, a bad thing, we also think that other kinds of failures are a bad thing. Many people believe that it is a bad thing to be fat, ugly, stupid, effeminate, a financial failure, a boor, an underachiever, a frumpy dresser, a physical weakling, a sucker, and so on. Individuals experience feelings of shame, humiliation, regret, and guilt over these things. They believe that such failures are bad, not just for practical reasons, but because they are intrinsically unattractive.

Although Christianity emphasizes solidarity between individuals, morality does not have to revolve around this kind of altruistic insight. Rigorously speaking, I may embrace, not a morality of love, but a morality of wealth, of fame, of physical beauty, of personal popularity, of political power. If it sounds odd to speak of "a morality of political power," it is because the normative content of Christianity is so powerful, it seems so right, that we intuitively disqualify the other value systems that motivate human agency. But there are individuals who devote their entire lives to power politics, not out of any Christian sense of service to others, but because they value the power and prestige of political rank. Even if these individuals profess an allegiance to an ostensibly Christian morality, it may be an ethics of power that orients their lives.

To equate Christianity with all morality is to obscure the breadth, the width, and the depth of moral striving. Christianity may provide us with the right ethical beliefs, but people often organize their lives according to the wrong ethical beliefs. One does not have to sanction popular values to recognize their force and their influence. I may not think much of a woman who spends hours grooming her physical appearance, but this woman would not spend these hours at the mirror unless she believed, rightly or wrongly, that her physical appearance had an important value.

Morality is the sense that certain things have value, that certain kinds of achievements are the worthy end of striving, that there are rules, habits, or activities that transform us into the kinds of people we ought to be. Properly understood, it is the force that underlies all human striving. I may value material wealth, physical beauty, fame, corporeal pleasure, a new sports car, hunting rifles, vacations in the Caribbean, whatever. If these are the real values that orient my life, this is my morality. Even in these cases, I organize my life in accordance with some identifiable system of values.

Proponents of the Mitigated Argument want to restrict morality to a very narrow domain of endeavor. Christianity has driven competing value systems underground, but there are many other moralities that motivate human striving. The official altruistic morality of our Judeo-Christian heritage is only one alternative among many. To identify one particular kind of value system as the only possible source of morality is to misrepresent the human dilemma. We are not faced with a choice between adhering to Christian morality or not adhering to any morality. We are faced with a choice between competing moralities. It is never a question of deciding to have or not to have values. It is always a question of which values. If nothing had value, we would wither up and die from apathy. Morality is the rationale we use to evaluate ourselves and other people. It is the motor of rational, goal-seeking endeavor. A truly amoral agent who did not subscribe to any value system would have no reason to do anything whatsoever.

Considered from a normative perspective, rational agents do not always act morally. Considered from a metaethical perspective, on the other hand, rational agents cannot opt out of morality. It is at least possible that we only act morally—in a normative sense—when we act on Christian or on liberal principles. Nonetheless, agents do espouse values that are at odds with liberalism and Christianity. I may believe that might makes right; I may be a libertine, an egoist, a committed neo-Nazi, a nihilist, whatever. In this sense, at least, neither liberalism nor Christianity supplies us with a complete descriptive account of morality. In a liberal Christian society, agents may not admit their allegiance to the true values that motivate their actions. Nonetheless, this allegiance is there and it is the cause of their striving.

PURITANISM

If liberalism and Christianity tend to restrict the moral focus, one particular form of Christianity, historical Puritanism, is largely responsible for the origins of the liberal view. Understanding Puritanism can help us to understand why amoral theories of autonomy have grown so popular. And it can help us understand what is wrong with these theories.

Ethics has shed its religious orientation, but one can still discern the remnants of a historical link between the mainstream ethical thought and the social, political beliefs of the original Pilgrim Fathers who, fleeing from oppression in England, emigrated to America in the 1600s.[23] Both Puritans and liberals propose strikingly similar philosophical treatments of the problem of freedom. The Puritans, for theological reasons, emphasize negative liberty in a way that diminishes, if it does not eliminate altogether, the moral dimension of personal freedom.

Like other Calvinists, the Puritans believed in predestination. This belief was so extreme, it may strike some as incredible. Consider the TULIP formula, the so-called Five Points of Calvinism adopted by assembled theologians and church leaders at the Synod of Dort (1618–19). According to this declaration of faith, the true Christian had to assent to five different doctrines. As one authority explains, this entailed a belief in (1) the "*total depravity*" of man—that "man in his natural state is so totally corrupt and helpless that he is incapable of even desiring salvation"; in (2) "limited atonement"—that "Christ dies for the elect alone, not for all mankind"; in (3) the condition of "irresistible grace"—that man "is helpless to resist" God's grace; in (4) the "perseverance of the saints"—that "God so assists his elect . . . that it is impossible for them to fall from grace"; and in (5) a notion of "unconditional election"—that "God's predestinating decrees derive solely from his decisions, and do not in any way depend on the beliefs or behaviour of individuals."[24]

The TULIP formulation attributes all power to God and makes humanity entirely dependent on His will. If, however, one subscribes to this five-point program, it will follow that a human individual cannot be, in any serious sense, "self-determining." Salvation—the major event of one's religious life—is not something the individual has any control over. Everything, literally everything, is controlled and accomplished and predestined by God. Autonomy, "self-mastery," governing oneself is not an option.

Calvinism eliminates the possibility of moral autonomy. In other Christian theologies, the agent can choose to accept or reject grace, an infusion of heavenly aid. This leaves room for the free exercise of will.[25] Radical Calvinism is more extreme. If I am a member of the elect, I cannot resist the action of grace. If I am not a member of the elect, I will not receive any grace at all. Either way the individual's moral status derives from the totally free choice of God. It does not depend in any way upon the agent's beliefs or behavior.

Seen from the radical Calvinist perspective, an individual agent does not, properly speaking, choose to be moral or immoral. Everything depends on grace. Everything is predestined by God. The notion that one can author one's own moral destiny, no longer has any relevance. Taking charge of one's life is, in a metaphysical and a moral sense, an impossibility. Self-mastery is, in a deeply philosophical sense, a contradiction in terms. God is the Only Master in charge of everything.

The Puritans piously accepted this Calvinist dogma. Their theology undermined, however, the traditional concept of human freedom. So Puritan thinkers such as Jonathan Edwards devised, in its place, a new, more restricted concept of freedom. They argued that although human beings cannot be free in religious or moral terms, they can be free in a secular, worldly sense. Although they are not free to choose salvation, they can be free to do as they will, to do as they like. This is to formulate a negative account of human liberty.[26] As Armand Maurer explains: "Although Edwards denied that the human will has freedom of self-determination, he granted that in a sense man is free. Like Hobbes and Locke, he defined human liberty as the ability to carry out what the will inclines man to do. Liberty [was merely] the absence of impediments to action."[27]

This Puritan understanding of freedom as negative liberty is the historical source of liberalism. It is also represents the advent of modern amoral notions of autonomy. The Puritans had a religious reason for defining freedom in amoral terms. Morality was not a human achievement but a gratuitous gift of God. Some Puritans went so far as to preach that it did not matter what the sanctified did. As Passmore comments: "In 1650 the English House of Commons found it necessary to pass a bill laying down penalties for those who argued that the spiritual elite could without sin freely engage in 'Whoredom, Adultery, Drunkenness or like open Wickedness.'"[28]

On this almost schizophrenic account, personal choice is so insulated from eternal reward and punishment as to be morally irrelevant. Human conduct, achieving our own goals, making choices between alternatives, becomes a perfectly amoral activity. Success or failure within the human domain does not affect our moral standing. It is a different kind of success or failure that pertains to personal accomplishment as opposed to morality.

Morality provides an objective standard for human success. For Puritans, the ultimate moral standard was the inscrutable will of God. Because we cannot, as humans, know the mind of God, we must judge individual conduct by some other standard. In line with an influential Protestant tradition that gave rise to utilitarianism, the Puritans suggested a decidedly secular, amoral criterion of human success. To ask: "Did Mary successfully govern herself?" is to ask: "Did Mary do what she wanted to do?" "Did Mary satisfy her desires?" In this way, desire-satisfaction, self-satisfaction, pleasure in the utilitarian sense, becomes the criterion for successful self-government.

In modern society, the religious rationale has withered away but the idea of a realm of personal success or failure untouched by moral standards persists. Contemporary philosophers, in discussing personal autonomy, focus on human achievement understood in secular terms. It is not the will of God but the will of the individual that provides the ultimate criterion for personal achievement. Successful agents do as they will. That is all. Morality is a separate issue.

In divesting ordinary endeavor of decisive moral import, Puritanism paved the way for an amoral understanding of human agency. But the Puritans provided a one-sided interpretation of Christianity. Seen from a Christian perspective, natural goodness and supernatural goodness are not distinctly separate things. Larmore, in an attack on Alasdair MacIntyre, champions an Enlightenment conception of a morality that exists "independently of a religious world view."[29] Larmore complains that Christian theology posits morality as means to something outside itself, namely salvation. Virtue becomes a means for lifting up human nature to some supernatural telos. Virtue has little to do with living the good life in the here and now. But Larmore misconstrues MacIntyre.

MacIntyre himself rejects any sharp separation of natural morality from religious morality. In his words: "The law which God utters to us is entirely congruent with the nature that he created in us and with the ends that nature pursues. . . . The divine law . . . enable[s] us to move towards both our natural and our supernatural *telos*."[30] Seen from an authentically Christian perspective, the religious and the natural ends of man do not diverge. It is not as if we have two separate aims: doing what God commands and doing what is naturally good. Understood from a traditional Christian standpoint, these are one and the same thing. Christians historically thought of morality in terms of a *natural* law, a law that is not imposed from the outside but that derives from our innermost nature.

Puritanism leaves us with a bifurcated image of human striving. People can achieve moral success; that is, they can be a member of the elect. Then again, they can be autonomous in an amoral sense; that is, they can successfully use their negative liberty to get what they like or what they want. Neither achievement depends upon the other. If we call the first kind of success "morality" and the second kind of success "autonomy," we are left with a reasonable facsimile of the contemporary view.

Margaret Moore complains that modern liberalism has produced "a series of unbridgeable dualisms."[31] These unresolvable dichotomies are a direct heritage of the Puritan tradition. If we separate personal achievement from moral and spiritual standards of success, we generate a standard of successful living that is divorced from our most profound aspirations. We are left with a divided individual who has very little reason to be moral, for the sphere of personal achievement does not include morality.[32] In proposing a moral theory of autonomy, I want to reintegrate moral considerations into the domain of personal achievement.

The Puritans had theological reasons for proposing an amoral account of human achievement. Contemporary authors lack this theological commitment. They do not believe in predestination, in morality by divine appointment. Once this very strict view of predestination goes, however, we must achieve the good on our own—with the help of God perhaps, but as the outcome of an autonomous process of decision-making. Morality is brought back down to earth and becomes an inalienable part of everyday striving. It follows that we can no longer separate morality from personal achievement.

MORALITY: IMPOSED FROM THE OUTSIDE

The staunchly supernatural bias of the Puritan account of morality has fallen out of favor, but there are ways in which the Puritan influence lingers on. Much contemporary ethical thought reiterates, in secular guise, two seemingly contradictory and much misunderstood strands of Puritan thought: (1) the idea that gratification of our worldly desires is after all a positive good and (2) the idea that morality is something that has to be imposed from the outside on a recalcitrant human nature.

Authors like Nathaniel Hawthorne and H. L. Mencken successfully stereotyped the Puritans as an extremely austere, scrupulous, and morbidly religious people, but the Puritans had a more worldly side.[33] They rejected the Roman Catholic notion of *contemptus mundi* and a long Christian tradition of "monkish" asceticism. In a Puritan metaphysics, the split occurs, not between the world and the saved, but between the saved (who, as Brinton explains, "were few") and "the damned [who] were many."[34] The saved were to enjoy—in moderation but with relish—the fruits of God's creation.[35] As one Puritan divine was able to proclaim: "God hath given us Temporals to enjoy . . . we should therefore suck the sweet of them."[36]

Instrumentalist accounts of reason and an influential utilitarianism have amplified this rejection of asceticism. If earlier religious models stressed otherworldly self-denial, the Puritan account stressed involvement in the world and in earthly occupations. Everyday activity took place in a secular arena that lacked decisive religious import. The saved were already saved. Human freedom had a different meaning. Freedom meant doing what one wants, what one likes to do. On this new model of human achievement, however, asceticism becomes irrational, if not immoral. Self-denial is prima facie pointless. In the modern period, this Puritan view takes over with a vengeance. With the secularization of thought, the satisfaction of human desire comes to be seen as the only good, and doctrines of self-mortification and self-denial come to be seen as a perversion.

Though the original Puritans did not spurn earthly pleasures, they did believe in "universal human depravity." True to their Calvinist roots, they adopt an extremely negative view of human nature. As Taylor explains, they conceived of morality as a form of external constraint, as something that curbs a depraved nature and hinders natural human development. In this Puritan account, "God's law is *doubly* external to us fallen creatures. First, we cannot identify the good with the bent of our own natures; . . . and second, [morality] runs against the grain of our depraved wills. It has to be imposed on an unwilling nature."[37] Hobbes and Kant, two important philosophical precursors of modern liberalism, inherit this negative view of human nature.

Hobbes presents a sordid picture of the human animal. Human beings are naturally belligerent, uncooperative, egotistical, jealous, covetous, perfidious, aggressive. The citizen needs to be saved from the earthly hell of a natural state, not by the grace of God, but by the authority of government.[38] Kant, on the other hand, conceives of morality as a kind of muscular Christianity. "Brought up in the spirit of the pietist movement," he conceives of morality as something imposed by universal reason upon our wayward wills.[39] Morality does not issue out of natural feelings or inclinations. One becomes a moral person, not by grace or by natural inclination, but by dint of hard work and sheer willpower.

Kant's moral philosophy represents, according to MacIntyre, "a precisely defined stage in the secularization of Protestant Christianity."[40] It is not faith in a personal savior but faith in reason that triumphs. Moral agents act out of a sense of duty. They do the right thing, not because they want to do it, but because they are obliged to do it. Morality is not motivated by feelings of compassion, brotherhood, altruism, affection, or love. Reason triumphs over desire; intelligence triumphs over inclination; willpower triumphs over human nature.

Contemporary moral philosophy is, in large part, still committed to a curious mixture of two ideas: (1) that the satisfaction of desires is the ultimate good and (2) that morality is something that has to be imposed from the outside on a deficient nature. This leads to an inevitable conflict. Morality instructs us to curb those very desires, the satisfaction of which is the only good! Morality becomes an onerous practice—in Kurt Baier's words, "a necessary evil."[41] This is why it needs to be defended or justified by ingenious philosophical argument. Hence the elaborate rationalizations of philosophers in the why-be-moral tradition.

MORAL RULES

If we hope to understand the importance of morality to autonomy, we need to elaborate, not a morality of external constraint, but a morality of self-realization. In an age of moral controversy, rules may seem to provide an attractive alternative to a substantive moral philosophy. Jan Narveson has recently argued that morality consists of rules "—of 'thou shalts' and 'thou shalt nots'— with the 'thou shall nots' predominating."[42] The Puritans,[43] Kant,[44] and Hobbes[45] conceived of morality in terms of rule-obeying behavior. This is, however, to adopt an impoverished view of morality. Moral rules represent one useful way of identifying some universal standard of human behavior. They provide us with a neat pedagogical device that allows us to compress large amounts of knowing-how into very small amounts of knowing-that. If, however, moral rules have their place and function, they do not represent, in and of themselves, the sum total of morality.

Narveson proposes a set of moral rules that are alleged to be neutral between competing conceptions of the good. Morality is then coercive, minimalistic, and nonpartisan. This view of moral rules as sufficient unto themselves is, however, contentious. Inherent in any proposed moral law, there is a moral philosophy, a conception of the good, that may not be explicitly stated but is implicitly argued for. MacIntyre comments, "The idea of a set of rules adequate to secure cooperation as such, independently of what it is cooperation towards or for and neutral between rival conceptions of the good is a chimera."[46] Liberal authors propose a bare-bones morality made up of rules that are not based on any moral, metaphysical, or religious viewpoint, but in MacIntyre's judgment "There are no such rules."[47] Moral rules are always an expression of some previous moral understanding. They are like the tip of an iceberg—hard-edged and conspicuous, but resting on a submerged understanding.

Larmore joins forces with MacIntyre, criticizing the idea "that what is morally right can be fully specified by rules."[48] Larmore rejects this "desiccated view of virtue," appealing instead to an Aristotelian notion of practical wisdom or *phronesis*.[49] In Aristotle's theory, morality does not originate in a set of hard-and-fast rules, but first and foremost, in the capacity for individualized practical judgment. Even if we were able to come up with a complete and comprehensive set of moral rules to cover every human circumstance, these rules could not stand on their own. In the first place, we would have to rely on a prior faculty of moral intelligence when devising these rules. In the second place, we would have to rely on the same faculty when applying these rules to individual circumstances.

Moral law, in general, cannot exist on its own. It needs to be interpreted in light of changing circumstance. Consider what happens in a legal context. As the Canadian neo-Thomist Charles de Koninck observes: "Even the most specific law . . . will always be characterized by a certain confused generality . . . which is the reason why judges, who apply it to specific cases and respect its nuances, are indispensable for a just order."[50] Judges must oversee the application of criminal law because the individual circumstances that surround individual human acts are too complex and variable to be fully specified or catalogued in a mechanical set of rules.[51] In and of themselves, the laws do not suffice. In the same way, moral law cannot function on its own. It must be interpreted and applied to specific cases and examples. Ordinary human beings must use their best judgment in adapting moral rules to everyday circumstance.

If we conceive of morality as law, as an extraneous force imposed by authority from the outside, it will be perceived as a form of repression. Hence the eternal protests of Sade or Nietzsche or Rand. But morality is better understood as an aid rather than as a hindrance to human flourishing, as something that perfects human nature rather than stunts it. If we want to develop a moral concept of autonomy, a morality of external constraint must give way to a morality of self-realization or authenticity.

MILL: THE BEGINNINGS OF AUTHENTICITY

If the Puritan tradition was immensely influential, John Stuart Mill, the father of liberalism, elaborates a view of human nature that lends itself to a very different interpretation of morality. Mill's philosophical views are complex. He proposes a "qualitative" sort of utilitarianism as an ethical view,[52] subscribes to liberalism as a political view, and endorses a highly romantic view of human nature. Most importantly for our purposes, he rejects the Puritan view of morality, belittling the Calvinist doctrine "that all the good of which humanity is capable is comprised in obedience"[53] and "that the one great offence of man is self-will."[54]

Mill compares human nature to a living organism that, if it is to be healthy and flourish, must be allowed to grow and develop in all directions according to some interior principle. As Mill observes: "Human nature is not a machine . . . but a tree, which requires to grow and develop itself on all sides according to the tendency of the inward forces which make it a living thing."[55] Every person possesses a potential for individual genius that needs to be nurtured, affirmed, even gloried in. In Mill's words: "It is not a mechanical adherence to rules but the active cultivation of individual genius that makes human beings become a noble and beautiful object of contemplation."[56]

An author such as Narveson proposes an external, rule-based morality that derives historically from earlier Puritan thought. One may, however, in line with Mill's romantic view of human nature, conceive of moral behavior in terms of self-realization or individual flourishing, as the amplification, the continuation, the development or the flowering of the good that is already within us.[57] This is to propose a morality of authenticity. On the authenticity model, morality is not a matter of external coercion. Moral behavior means realizing our true nature, fulfilling our innermost desires, living up to that which is best in ourselves.

The Puritans thought of morality as rule-oriented and repressive. In Narveson's phrase: "The shalt-nots predominate." This conflicts with a liberal optimism about human nature. Because human beings are naturally bad (or at least amoral), we have to force them to be good.[58] The authenticity model sketches out a more positive picture. Moral behavior is an expression of a deep reservoir of natural virtue and good feelings. There are many routes to morality. We may act morally on good-hearted impulses, out of sheer kindness, according to sentiment, in conformity with accumulated experience, from habit, in pursuit of ideals, from pure "thoughtless" love, for the sake of honor, in accordance with temperament, from entrenched attitudes, in loyalty to various principles, and so on. All these emotional and intellectual resources may play a role in helping us be the kind of people we ought to be. Morality cannot be confined to rule-obeying behavior.

To argue for a morality of authenticity is not to dispute the importance of moral rules. Nor is it to deny the necessity of self-denial. Rules must be obeyed; appetites curbed; sacrifices made, and unpleasant duties performed. Even when we do obey moral rules, however, we may act authentically, in accordance with our innermost inclinations and nature. When we deny ourselves, these acts of self-denial can be construed as part of a larger process of self-affirmation. If, for example, trained athletes deny themselves in order to achieve a goal, the achievement of this goal is often thought of as the epitome of self-affirmation. Denying ourselves for the sake of a greater good is then a necessary part of goal-oriented endeavor.

CHRISTIANITY AS SELF-REALIZATION

If the Puritans were self-consciously Christian, Christianity also lends itself to a morality of authenticity. As Augustine explains the Christian view, immorality is a foreign intrusion, an absence, something that goes against the grain of Creation, something that hinders the natural development of the world. Immorality is negative, unnatural, anomalous, counterfeit, external to what we really are. It is a perversion.[59] It separates us from God and ourselves. Adam's first sin frustrated or thwarted God's plan, but moral behavior restores the original goodness of Creation,

Theologically, Puritanism breaks with traditional natural law Christianity. St. Paul argues that even "pagans who never heard the [Divine] law . . . can point to the substance of the law engraved in their hearts."[60] Historical formulations of the natural law doctrine situate morality squarely inside each individual human nature. Human beings possess some deepseated moral capacity. They are not "totally depraved" but "gone astray." They stand in need of grace, but they are not irreducibly evil. If Adam's

first disobedience introduced sin into the world, it could not transform something fundamentally good into something fundamentally evil.

On the traditional Christian view, successful self-government cannot
be separated from morality. Being an authentic person and a moral person
are not separate aspirations. In obeying the will of God, one obeys one's
original nature. Morality is an aid to self-realization. The Puritans placed
moral and religious achievement beyond the purview of individual aspiration. In stressing the self-sufficient glory and grandeur of God, they transformed morality into an arbitrary reward gratuitously bestowed by an inscrutable God. This led to the marginalization of both morality and religion and to the inevitable secularization of modern society. Fervent Christians though they were, their influential worldview betrayed their original
intentions.

TAYLOR: THE AUTHENTICITY TRADITION

Charles Taylor has explored the philosophical currents that, in modern times,
gave rise to a morality of self-realization. Taylor identifies four eighteenth-
century traditions that combined to produce the modern concept of personal authenticity.[61] These include: Hutcheson's theory (associated with
Shaftesbury and the Cambridge Neoplatonists) that morality derives from
deep feelings of benevolence inside the individual; Rousseau's idea that
intimate contact with nature is a source of well-being and morality; Herder's
notion that each one of us possesses "an individual way of being human";
and Rousseau's and Hegel's concept of positive freedom.

Authors in this authenticity tradition attribute evil to the artificiality
and prejudice of conventional society. Immorality results when we are es-
tranged from our deepest, most natural selves. As Taylor expresses this
Rousseauian thought: "The original impulse of nature is right, but the effect of a depraved culture is that we lose contact with it. . . . We no longer
depend on ourselves and this inner impulse, but rather on others and on
what they think of us, expect from us, admire or despise in us, reward or
punish in us. We are separated from nature by the dense web of opinion . . .
and can no longer recover contact with it."[62]

When morality is described in such terms, there is a noticeable shift in
moral thinking. The source of morality is removed from a locus outside the
individual and comes to reside inside the self. Morality does not mean
killing off the self. Moral behavior is a form of self-affirmation or self-
expression. It is a kind of liberation from the stereotypes and prejudices of
society that enslave and restrain the self. Morality is no longer an infringe-

ment on individual freedom. It means cultivating what is best within the self.

To say that morality dwells within the self is not to say that morality is subjective. As Taylor argues, morality is an objective perspective that compels consent. I am not a moral human being because I do anything I feel like doing. I am a moral human being because I measure up to some objective standard of worthwhile achievement. This objective standard exists, however, inside the individual. It is part of one's innermost nature, of one's deepest, most personal identity.

Authors in the authenticity tradition claim that morality has an internal component. It is not something extra added on to our actions, something imposed from the outside. There is an authenticity gone bad, an authenticity that is no longer able to focus outwards on the world and on other people, an authenticity that leads to a self-absorbed narcissism. But this is an aberration. I will argue that morality has an objective and a subjective component. It is both the satisfaction of an objective standard of success and the realization of our innermost desires and aspirations. It represents, at the same time, an objective constraint and an opportunity for personal liberation.

DISCONNECTING THE CONNECTION: NAGEL

This view of morality, as the union of the subjective and objective, is seriously at odds with the prevailing view. Consider the influential discussion of "objectivity" that appears Thomas Nagel's celebrated book *The View from Nowhere.*[63]

Nagel proposes, in line with the Puritan tradition, a philosophy of disconnection. On his model, objectivity and subjectivity represent two radically different ways of looking at the world. An agent may consider the world from a personal, subjective viewpoint. Or he or she may consider the world from an objective perspective, from the viewpoint of "nowhere in particular." To consider the world from a personal perspective is to adopt the perspective of autonomy; to consider the world from an objective perspective is to adopt the perspective of morality. If these contrasting viewpoints are equally valid, the relationship between them is *in principle* problematic. There is an "internal-external tension [that] pervades human life."[64] The moral and the personal cannot be reconciled except in some very partial and unsatisfactory manner.

Nagel proposes a world that has been neatly cleaved in two. Experience is fundamentally and irreparably fractured. To one side, there is subjective experience. To the other side, there is objective experience. However we strain and fret, we cannot bridge the gap between them. In Nagel's words: "When we juxtapose the . . . subjective and objective views at full strength, . . . instead of a unified world view, we get the interplay of these two uneasily related types of conception, [resulting in an] essentially incompletable effort to reconcile them."[65] On Nagel's account, moral values and personal values are ultimately irreconcilable. Subjectivity is eternally, inevitably, necessarily at odds with objectivity.

Nagel posits, on many different levels, a glaring dichotomy between subjective and objective perspectives. Like Hume, he elaborates a compatibilist account of human freedom. Seen from an internal, subjective point of view, we are free. Our acts seem to arise out of some personal volition. Seen from an objective, external, scientific point of view, however, we must believe that every event has a cause; all our acts are, consequently, predetermined.[66] Nagel insists that both views of human action are equally valid. They can never, however, be reconciled with one another.

Nagel approaches morality in a similar manner, juxtaposing a subjective realm of personal, nonmoral values with an objective realm of universal, moral values. Subjectively, individual agents eschew morality to seek their own private good. They maximize their own preferences. They strive toward personal success. Objectively, they embrace morality and seek the common good. They maximize the preferences of society as a whole. They strive toward justice.

Nagel views the split between morality and self-interest as symptomatic of an inevitable collision between subjective and objective points of view. Either we act from an internal, subjective perspective—we advance our own interests, or we act from an objective, external perspective—we obey the commands of morality. We can "live well" and/or "live right." Living well is having personal success; living right is acting morally. We have different reasons for living well and living right.[67] "Doing the right thing, is part of living well," but "it is not the whole of it, nor even the dominant part."[68] The impersonal, otherworldly standpoint of morality is only one ingredient of any healthy, normal life.[69]

Nagel views the subjective-objective dichotomy in almost metaphysical terms. He does not present this alleged tension between objective and subjective worldviews as what it is—one ramification of a cramped and truncated worldview that can be traced back to the Puritan tradition. Understood as a comment on the human condition, however, this worldview is deeply problematic. Consider five problems with Nagel's argument.

In the first place, Nagel successfully separates personal autonomy from morality only because he artificially limits morality to a very narrow range of endeavor. As I have already demonstrated, individual agents strive to be moral in divergent ways that are not officially designated as moral. Nagel and his colleagues do not recognize the length and breadth and depth of moral striving. They do not see that morality, the sense that things have value, is ultimately the engine of all human striving. Consider a specific example.

Suppose I am interested in mountain climbing. And suppose I decide to climb Mt. Everest. On the standard view, which Nagel supports, mountain climbing is a hobby, a sport, a pastime, a game, an idiosyncrasy. People climb mountains for purely personal satisfaction, because they entertain some private vision of the good. Like drinking fine wine or raising thoroughbreds, mountain climbing may be a fulfilling occupation, but it does not constitute serious moral endeavor. There is no moral commandment: "Thou must climb mountains." The moral law is something else altogether.

This official view does not correspond, however, to the way in which people in the real world organize and orient their lives. To begin with, people who climb mountains do not think of it as a frivolous occupation. Conquering this or that mountain is at the center, not at the periphery, of their aspirations. Between 1922 and the year 2000, 155 climbers died trying to scale Mt. Everest. There were thirteen recorded deaths before the first successful assent. Many climbers—rightly or wrongly—are willing to risk everything in pursuit of the summit. But one does not risk one's life for something frivolous and unimportant. In the minds of these people, conquering Mt. Everest is an endeavor of momentous importance.

On Nagel's account, morality proposes an objective criterion of accomplishment. Personal achievement is irredeemably subjective. Mountain climbing is not, on this account, a moral endeavor. But mountain climbers scale high mountains precisely because they provide an *objective* criterion of achievement. A successful ascent is an objective fact that places the achievement beyond the vagaries of opinion and interpretation. In the end, one reaches the summit or one does not. Mountain climbing is not like daydreaming. One does not, in any unqualified sense, do what one wants to do. One does not retreat inside oneself. One has to make one's actions conform to objective necessity in order to survive. One interacts in a demanding and meticulous way with physical reality.

Morality is alleged to involve a series of imperatives. One could formulate any number of mountain-climbing imperatives: "Focus." "Watch your footing." "Plan properly." "Always climb with a buddy." "Know your limits." Obviously, there is no moral imperative that commands everyone to become a mountain climber. But then again, there is no moral imperative that commands everyone to become a doctor, a bush pilot, a missionary, and so on. Yet these are all, in some essential sense, moral occupations.

They all enclose and shape some form of moral striving. In each case, there is some kind of interior imperative that may drive people onward through all sorts of lethal dangers to the extremes of self-sacrifice and heroism.

Nagel separates moral aspiration from personal achievement, but real-life mountain climbers often describe their mountaineering exploits in explicitly moral terms. Sir John Hunt, who participated in the first ascent of Everest, explains the meaning of the achievement in the following way: "The story of the ascent of Everest is one of teamwork. If there is a deeper and more lasting message behind our venture than the mere ephemeral sensation of a physical feat, I feel this to be the value of comradeship and the many virtues which combine to create it. Comradeship, regardless of race or creed, is forged among high mountains, through the difficulties and dangers to which they expose those who aspire to climb them, the need to combine their efforts to attain their goal, the thrills of a great adventure shared together."[70] Mountain climbing is not, for Hunt, an amoral or a self-centered activity. Quite the contrary. The inevitable battle with an inhospitable environment forces individuals to transcend their petty, selfish, egotistical selves. It fosters a mutual concern, an other-directedness, a sense of self-sacrifice and community. But concern for others is, according to Nagel, what *morality* is all about. So even on Nagel's system, a *personal* pastime like mountain climbing takes on a distinctly *moral* color.

Mountain climbers often invoke moral concepts when explaining the purpose of their exploits. One climber describes mountaineering as "a venue and a vehicle" for the discovery of "courage, or bravery, or commitment or clarification of ideals."[71] Another describes it as a "pilgrimage."[72] Another explains that her ascent of Everest was motivated by the belief that "it was important to do something with one's life."[73] Still another argues that mountaineering is a form of protest, an act of rebellion against consumer society, "against an existence full of distorted values, against an existence where a man is judged by the size of his living room, by the amount of chromium on his car."[74] But these are all value judgments. They reveal a moral impetus behind this allegedly amoral endeavor.

At its worst, mountain-climbing is about breaking records, conceit, and vaingloriousness. At its best, it is about discipline, abnegation, perseverance, courage, humility, selflessness. One might argue that mountaineering is not an adequate instrument for moral aspiration. Although the normative status of mountaineering can be contested, this does not alter the fact that it is a way of life for some human beings. As I have already argued, we need to base an account of human behavior on a descriptive morality that identifies the diverse value systems and the codes of behavior that real individuals actually live up to. An author like Nagel is able to restrict morality to a very narrow range of human endeavor only because he ignores the moral content of diverse human activity. But this is to overlook the moral impetus that permeates human striving.

The second major problem with Nagel's account is that it removes the motivation for genuine morality. Nagel's ethics are almost Kantian in tone. It is as if we have desires and reason pulling us opposite ways. Desires are subjective; they demand limitless satisfaction. Reason is objective; it demands that we curtail our desires. In this uncomfortable tug of war, the truly rational agent sides with reason. But there is something seriously wrong with this picture. Morality is not opposed to (subjective) notions of desiring, for moral agents *desire* to be moral. If morality was not included in our desires, our subjective hopes and aspirations, what could move us to be moral? We might be forced to act morally by a punitive society, but truly moral agents act morally of their own free will. Although our moral inclinations may be at war with other, less reflective inclinations, we must desire to be moral or we could not be moral on our own.

Good rebels provide a conspicuous example of moral desire. These figures champion some kind of moral and political cause. They do not view morality as an aloof imperative but as their very raison d'être. In many cases, they risk their lives for their conception of the good. Ordinary citizens may be less successful defending their own commitments. Nonetheless, we all identify with whatever we value. These allegiances and loyalties make us who we are. They constitute an important part of our self-identity. Moral agents are not moral because they are forced to be moral. They are moral out of some kind of urgent personal commitment.

Nagel's account of moral motivation is reminiscent of Aristotle's account of the "continent man." The continent man manages to act morally in spite of bad inclinations. He struggles against himself in order to accomplish the good.[75] Nagel conceives of the continent man as the epitome of morality, but for an author like Aristotle the continent man is a failure. It is, of course, better to be continent than immoral. But the continent man is not *fully* moral. Fully moral agents do not have to strain and strive against personal inclination in order to be moral. They have the right inclinations, the right habits, thoughts, and attitudes. They are naturally, habitually moral.

Thirdly, Nagel does not recognize the intensely personal character of moral experience. A modern personalist like Lawrence Blum goes so far as to argue that a theoretical concern for universal ethical principles should be replaced by a concern for particular individuals.[76] Nel Noddings presents a similar argument. Even if we do, however, accept the notion of universal moral rules, moral knowledge may come to us in intensely personal ways.

Consider the work of the American journalist John Howard Griffin. In the late 1950s Griffin, a white man, darkened his skin with medication and traveled through the American South disguised as a colored person. His book *Black Like Me* is a plea for racial equality. That all men (and women) should be treated equally is a universal moral principle. Griffin makes a statement in favor of this universal principle, but he does not appeal to impersonal, objective philosophical arguments. He takes a radically different approach. He tells a story, chronicling in detail his own often painful experiences. Griffin communicates the injustice of racial discrimination by describing the *subjective* experiences of an oppressed person. When we read the book, we identify with the narrator. We make his experience our own. Reliving the details of his life as a Negro—sitting at the back of the bus, being refused service in a white restaurant, meeting with distrust, rudeness, condescension—it is the particularity of such experiences that reinforces the universal claim that all human beings *ought* to be treated equally.

Nagel believes that moral, objective considerations pull us violently in one direction, whereas our personal inclinations pull us violently in the opposite direction. Griffin's book provides a different picture of moral endeavor. Morality obliges us to treat all human beings in an equal manner, but this objective requirement is not at odds with personal experience. If anything, it is an insensitivity to the individual elements of the oppressed person's plight which leads to immorality. It is an inattention to particular circumstances that allows one to overlook or reject the universal.

Fourthly, Nagel presents a one-sided view of morality. He identifies morality with impartiality, but morality may sometimes *require* partiality. For example, morality informs us that we should have a special, privileged concern for the weak, the poor, the disadvantaged. Or consider what it means to be a good parent. A good father does not treat all children impartially. He has a special regard for his *own* children.

Nagel tells us that moral agents "act on the world from outside [their own] particular personal place in it," but our particular place within the world is an important reference.[77] It carries with it specific duties and obligations. If, for example, I am a father, I am obliged to love my own children in a peculiarly intense and immediate way. Any so-called morality that does not take into account my station in life is, at best, a caricature. There will, no doubt, be situations in which agents experience genuine conflicts of interest. In these cases impartiality takes on singular importance. These special circumstances cannot, however, provide a model for all morality. However we resolve particular cases, the standards of goodness we invoke must be sensitive, not just to universal imperatives, but to individual needs and circumstances.

Fifthly, Nagel does not sufficiently recognize the importance of community. If we believe in human solidarity, we cannot separate our own private good from the good of others. Martin Luther King Jr. writes: "We are caught in a network of mutuality, tied in a single garment of destiny. Whatever affects one individual, affects all indirectly."[78] Nagel claims that agents must choose between an objective good for others and a subjective good for themselves. If, however, human beings are social—or even altruistic—animals, if there are bonds of concern and care that cut across individual lines, then what is good for you is also good for me and what is bad for you is also bad for me. The liberal paradigm of the isolated, self-interested individual distorts the human predicament. Social awareness and concern contribute to and place a limit on individual well-being.

POLITE SUPPORT FOR NAGEL: SPARKES

There are other problems with Nagel's account. His view gains, however, some support from a commonsense distinction between moral and nonmoral goods. A. W. Sparkes, in a discussion of the meaning of the word "morality," argues that there are evaluations, judgments, and recommendations that are distinctly non-moral.[79] In Sparkes's view, "Moral rightness or wrongness, goodness or badness [is] a special type of rightness [or] wrongness, goodness [or] badness."[80] Morality is concerned with a particular type of right or wrong. It is not "concerned with right or wrong ways of using a shovel or a soup-spoon, or with good and bad omelettes or poems."[81]

Sparkes lumps together within the category of nonmoral values: rules of etiquette ("you must say please"), technical imperatives ("you *ought* to use a different-size wrench"), grammatical rules ("a pronoun is not to be used without prior identification of the noun to which it refers") and aesthetic judgments ("that is a beautiful picture"). Some of these usages may be distinctly nonmoral, but Sparkes does not explain the difference between moral and nonmoral evaluations. To say that this diamond, limerick, birthday cake, baseball card, or sunset committed an immoral act would, of course, be just plain silly.[82] Moral evaluations are directed at rational agents. Only people can act morally or immorally. Does it follow that rules of etiquette, technical imperatives, grammatical rules, or aesthetic judgments never play a significant role in our evaluation of other people? Surely not. To say that these are *nonmoral* forms of evaluation is to say that they play (or should play) a relatively minor role in our evaluation of other people. "Nonmoral" in this context means something like "lacking in *decisive* moral significance." In actual fact, however, we do employ these kinds of standards when we judge and evaluate other people.

Sparkes suggests that social etiquette is a nonmoral issue. Although Mark Kingwell wants to base the idea of morality on a notion of social courtesy or politeness,[83] etiquette is, for most of us, a trivial issue. It is, at best, a kind of dwarf morality, a morality of pettiness, providing us with polite conventions and imperatives that play a minor role in defining the kind of people we ought to be. If I murder my next-door neighbor with an ax, this is a serious breech of morality. If I hold my soup spoon in the "wrong" manner, this social faux-pas seems, in comparison, insignificant. To say that social etiquette is a nonmoral issue is, however, only to say that it possesses little normative content.

There are personality traits, inclinations, abilities, or actions that lack decisive moral significance. Tom, for example, does not have to be a good hammer-thrower in order to be a good person. Mary may be moral individual even though she does not speak proper French. I am not a corrupt human being because I cannot cook a delicious omelette. Nonetheless, trivial factors play a much larger role in our evaluations of other people than we are often willing to admit. If I despise you because you do not hold your soup spoon in the proper way—I whisper to my wife that you are insufferably common—this sounds like a moral judgment. It may be distressing to think that we judge other people on such superficial grounds, but in point of fact we often do. If we want to provide a descriptive account of morality, we must pay attention to the way in which people really act. Insomuch as our evaluations about other people are based on ideas about the kind of people they ought to be, they have a moral content. They contribute to some sort of morality.

Morality is a larger aspiration than authors like Sparkes and Nagel are willing to accept. People take great pride in their accomplishments. They are intensely proud of the fact that they play chess well, run marathons, climb mountains, make large sums of money, catch the biggest fish, and so on. These activities do have an ethical component. They may be understood as particular expressions of human values. If I say that Tom is a poor marathon runner, this may seem to be anything but a moral judgment. But perhaps Tom is a poor runner because he is too lazy to practice. He may lack the "guts," the courage, the strength of character to run hard when it hurts. He may be too proud, too self-centered to listen to his coach. He may lack humility and chronically·injure himself because he over-trains. He may lack a certain capacity for self-sacrifice. And so on. Morality pervades evaluative discourse in ways that authors like Sparkes neglect to acknowledge.

AGAINST MORAL SAINTS: SUSAN WOLF

In *The View from Nowhere* Nagel approvingly refers to a well-known article by Susan Wolf on moral saints.[84] Wolf argues *against* moral saintliness. According to Wolf, "Moral perfection, in the sense of moral saintliness, does not constitute a model of personal well-being toward which it would be particularly rational or good or desirable for a human being to strive."[85]

Wolf elaborates a "beauty spot" theory of moral virtue. The occasional beauty-spot looks attractive, but when beauty-spots cover the whole body, they become an ugly disease. Saintliness is then an "unattractive" option.[86] We must be careful not to be too moral, for when "moral virtues . . . [are] all present in the same individual . . . to an extreme degree, [they] are apt to crowd out the nonmoral virtues, as well as many of the interests and personal characteristics that we generally think contribute to a healthy, well rounded, richly developed character."[87]

In her paper, Wolf recognizes her debt to Nagel.[88] Like Nagel, she presents morality as an impersonal, impartial, objective perspective insensitive to individual difference. "The moral point of view . . . is the point of view . . . that one is just one person among others equally real and deserving of the good things in life."[89] Wolf contrasts this moral viewpoint with "the point of view of individual perfection." The perfectionist viewpoint is, in contrast, sensitive and attentive to individual peculiarity. It focuses on issues of self-realization and personal accomplishment. The distinction Wolf makes between the perfectionist and the moral viewpoint parallels Nagel's distinction between subjective and objective goods.

Wolf seems to view morality as an exotic and exceptional activity separated from personal achievement. Because it is too narrow an ideal to provide us with an adequate conception of the good life, she feels compelled to create a second set of values so as to regulate and evaluate the domain of personal achievement.[90] This new perfectionist viewpoint provides us with a way of "comprehensively" and "objectively" evaluating our personal selves. It allows us to determine "what kinds of lives are good lives, and what kinds of persons it would be good for ourselves and others to be."[91] To introduce a separate, individualistic "way of perfection" is only, however, to create a second morality in disguise. Wolf does not show that morality has nothing to do with personal accomplishment. Rather she elaborates a second, surreptitious morality of self-realization that is richer than the impoverished, Puritan notion of morality she inherits from Nagel.

Wolf argues that a person should not "wholly rule and direct his life by [such] abstract and impersonal consideration[s]" as the idea that his life must be "morally good."[92] But her reliance on a Kantian or a utilitarian point of view seems partisan; the moral psychology underlying her view is flawed, and the concept of economic self-interest central to her view can be contested. Rather than accepting her attack on morality, one might devote one's energies to presenting a more generous conception of morality, one that realistically describes the moral ideals that actually move people to act.

Wolf's account gains plausibility, in part, because she provides a caricature of moral sainthood that is divorced from the way in which real people—even supremely good people—live their lives. Her account, which borrows from the Humean stereotype of the fanatic, morose, hair-shirted ascetic, is unrealistic in the extreme. Wolf suggests, among other things, that moral saints can never rest, that they are inevitably unhappy, that they must be "very very nice," that they cannot express their individuality, that they can never have particular friendships, and so on. These stereotypical claims are at odds, however, with the lives of reported saints.

For example, Wolf argues that moral saints can never rest. They must spend *all* their time working for other people. But there are limits to human endurance. Even saints understand this. Consider the Desert Fathers, those ancient Christian monks who practiced a rigorous religious asceticism many moderns would find horrendous. Even they recognized that human beings need to rest. Thomas Merton retells a familiar story:

> Once Abbot Anthony was conversing with some brethren, and a hunter who was after game in the wilderness saw them. He saw Abbot Anthony and his brothers enjoying themselves, and disapproved. Abbot Anthony said: Put an arrow in your bow and shoot it. This he did. Now shoot another, said the elder. And another, and another. The hunter said: If I bend my bow all the time it will break. Abbot Anthony replied: So it is also in the work of God. If we push ourselves beyond measure, the brethren will soon collapse. It is right, therefore, from time to time, to relax their efforts.[93]

Again, Wolf argues that moral saints must spend all their time promoting the happiness of others. They can only experience their own happiness "by accident." But traditional philosophers tell us that morality is the road to happiness. We must be moral *in order to* be happy.[94] The goals of being moral and being happy converge. Saint Theresa of Avila is reported to have quipped, "God save us from sullen saints." Erasmus describes Saint Thomas More as the most happy of individuals. In Erasmus's words:

His countenance is . . . expressive of an amiable joyousness, and even an incipient laughter. . . . In human affairs there is nothing from which he does not extract enjoyment, even from things that are most serious. If he converses with the learned and judicious, he delights in their talent, if with the ignorant and foolish, he enjoys their stupidity. He is not even offended by professional jesters. With a wonderful dexterity he accommodates himself to every disposition. As a rule, in talking with women, even with his own wife, he is full of jokes and banter.[95]

Again Wolf writes: "A moral saint will have to be very, very nice. It is important not to be offensive."[96] And the moral saint "will be very reluctant to make negative judgements of other people."[97] But niceness is not morality. Moral behavior is often disruptive. Consider the good rebel. There are saints, holy men and women, who are good rebels. A prophet like Isaiah in the Old Testament did not gain a reputation for saintliness because he was agreeable, courteous, and bland. He was a firebrand, an agitator, a gadfly, someone who spent his time pointing out, in a very blunt and untactful manner, the moral failings of Israel.

Wolf states that a saint cannot have "a cynical or sarcastic wit," but Saint Jerome was a recognized master of insult and invective.[98] He was known for his irascible temperament and sarcastic wit. And yet, he was widely considered to be a saint, in spite of his prickly personality.

Wolf deals in exaggerations and stereotypes. People are not regarded as saints because they have nice, pleasant, inoffensive personalities, but because they are militant activists, because they accomplish astounding feats, because they epitomize, to an extraordinary degree, particular virtues, because they make ordinary lives seem so petty and ignoble in comparison to theirs.

Faced with an excessively narrow conception of morality, Wolf introduces a second set of values and standards that tell us what we ought to do and what kind of people we ought to be. This is to propose another account of morality. What Wolf seems to be arguing is that the traditional ideal of moral saintliness is too cold, too stiff, too Stoic, too inhuman, too impersonal an option to emulate. She seems to be saying that there is something seriously amiss with the traditional ideal. Rather than offering frank criticism of this ideal, she offers a competing, nonmoral value system. This seems, at best, remarkably indirect.

In her attack on moral saintliness, Wolf misconstrues the purpose of moral discourse. Moral discourse is, in large part, an attempt to motivate people to be better. There are two ways of encouraging moral behavior. We may institute a law. This is to place a lower bound on morality. This is to say: "You must be at least this moral or you will be punished." Or we may posit a moral ideal. This is to say, "Here is a higher degree of perfection toward which you should strive." Morality is not just about satisfying some minimal requirement. It is not just about obeying the law. It is also about striving to be better. To exist without ideals is a moral fault. It is to be apathetic, complacent, smug, self-satisfied. Hence the need for an ideal of moral saintliness. To rid morality of the notion of an exemplar or an ideal would be to impoverish it.

Wolf wants to place some "kind of upper bound on moral worthiness."[99] In the case of a moral law, we draw a line in the sand and exclaim: "Do not be *less* moral than this!" Wolf wants to draw another line and exclaim: "Do not be *more* moral than this!" But why should we propose an upper limit for morality? We do not, in general, motivate people to be better by telling them that they should be less moral. People need, not limits, but goals they can continuously strive towards.

A self-conscious preoccupation with moral perfection may be a serious obstacle to morality. If, however, there are serious risks associated with moral scruples and fanaticism, an agent cannot be "too moral." Fanatics are not too moral; they are not moral enough. Fanaticism is not a moral virtue but a moral failing. The moral saint is not someone who is an extremist in a bad sense, for someone who is extreme in a bad sense is by definition less than moral.

Morality may not be, in every circumstance, an attractive option. In oppressive societies, good rebels are incarcerated, tortured, even killed because they refuse to abandon morality. It makes perfect sense not to desire this kind of suffering. But this does not mean that we do not desire moral excellence. It only means that we do not desire to be placed in such a painful predicament. Good rebellion remains a worthy ideal even if we cannot desire the suffering it entails and even if, when the opportunity arises, we are ourselves unable to live up to such heroic standards.

If we cannot live the life of a moral saint, the solution is not to repudiate the ideal but, within our opportunities and capacities, to try to be better. Moral saints serve a particular function. They ward off smugness and self-satisfaction. They remind us that we should be humble, that we are not nearly as good as we could be, that we have to strive to be better. The last thing we need is a philosophical argument that will rid us of all sense of moral discomfort. Exaggerated guilt may be counterproductive, but we need to feel a little queasy about our pleasant bourgeois lives. This uneasiness is, in part, what motivates moral striving.

In Walter Savage Landor's poem "Dying Speech of an Old Philosopher," the old sage declares:

> I have warmed both hands before the fire of Life;
> It stinks, I am ready to depart.

If Landor thinks of the world as a rank and fetid place, this is only because individual human beings are again and again selfish, inconsiderate, vain, boastful, vindictive, greedy, cruel, brutal, and so on. Most of us are not so close to being moral saints that we have to worry about being *less* moral! The problem is that we are not moral enough.

6

Morality and Autonomy

DEWEY: MORE THAN VIRTUE ETHICS

In this section of the book I will argue that morality is an essential component of autonomy and that agents who successfully govern themselves must
satisfy objective moral criteria, criteria that possess validity independent
of their own expectations, beliefs, or desires. Human agents are inevitably,
ineluctably fallible. They are not rational, moral, or autonomous because
they believe they are rational, moral, or autonomous. They are rational *and*
moral *and* autonomous when they succeed, in some objective sense, at
human achievement.

John Dewey provides a descriptive account of morality that elucidates
the relationship between morality and autonomy.[1] Dewey conceives of
morality as a process of self-formation. We may invoke various moral standards, but whatever normative standard we invoke, "the real moral question is what kind of a self is being furthered and formed."[2] Ordinary, workaday decisions are momentous not simply because they affect other people
but, just as importantly, because they change and alter the self. In Dewey's
words: "[Moral] choice . . . reveals the existing self and it forms the future
self. . . . In choosing this object rather than that, one is in reality choosing
what kind of . . . self one is going to be."[3] On Dewey's account, morality is,
most fundamentally, a process of self-realization.

Commentators associate Dewey's emphasis on character building with
virtue ethics, but this may be misleading. Dewey himself insists that the
"emphasis upon character is not peculiar to any type of moral theory."[4]
Morality, any kind of morality, has to do with becoming, in some ultimate
sense, the right kind of person. To use the phrase already employed, one
has to become "the kind of person one ought to be." Perhaps I ought to be
the kind of person who possesses specific character traits (virtue ethics).
But then again, perhaps I ought to be the kind of person who fulfills certain

154

duties (deontology), who obeys the will of God (Divine Command ethics), who submits to the natural law (Thomism), who increases the amount of happiness in the world (utilitarianism), who keeps promises and honors contracts (contractarianism), who follows conscience (intuitionism), who conforms to the laws and customs of a particular time and place (social relativism), who treats people as subjects rather than as objects (personalism), who obeys the universal law (Kant), who respects property rights (Narveson), who is "loyal to loyalty" (Josiah Royce), and so on. Even if we define morality in terms of *being* a certain kind of person, it does not follow that we must subscribe to some narrowly defined notion of virtue. Virtue ethics, the idea that particular character traits are the most important or conspicuous measure of morality, is one alternative among many.

Frankena divides moral philosophers into two camps: those who define morality in terms of "being," and those who define morality in terms of "doing."[5] Philosophers who emphasize "being" study the nature of the moral self. Those who emphasize "doing" study the nature of moral acts. But "being" is more fundamental than "doing." If we wish to investigate an agent's moral status, we must focus, not on an agent's acts, but on the kind of self that stands behind these acts. It is not enough to inquire into what an agent is doing. We must also answer the question: what kind of self is this? As Dewey explains, "The essence of reflective morals is that it is conscious of [this] persistent self" and how it is responsible for "what is externally done."[6]

Dewey's account has two basic consequences. Firstly, it leads to a much broader understanding of morality. Dewey insists that "There is no act, since it is a part of conduct, which *may* not have definitive moral significance. . . . For all acts are so tied together that any one of them may have to be judged as an expression of character."[7] Because a person's life must be construed as "a serial whole" with individual actions leading "forward . . . , *conducting*, leading up, to further acts and to a final fulfilment or consummation,"[8] even seemingly trivial actions like opening a window or taking a walk may, in the appropriate setting, have serious moral ramifications.

Secondly, in contrast to some modern pragmatists, Dewey secures an objective basis for morals. Dewey does not argue that morality is relative. Morality tells us that we *ought* to adopt an attitude of benevolent cooperation toward other people. This is an objective moral truth; that is, it is a moral truth whether we assent to it or not. Those who do not accept this insight are simply mistaken. As we shall see, Dewey views moral practice in objective terms. Moral agents cannot presume the truth of their own personal opinions. They must strive to make their views and actions conform to some higher standard.

Dewey is, in present-day language, a communitarian.[9] He emphasizes the relationship between the individual and the community. Individuals can never separate themselves totally from their origins in society: "When a person is alone he thinks with language which is derived from association with others, and thinks about questions and issues that have been born in [social] intercourse."[10] Even the cultivation of healthy individuality does not occur in isolation. "The human being is an individual because of and in relations with others."[11] Someone who exists apart from others "is an individual only as a stick of wood is."[12] They do not possess, in any interesting sense, individuality. They are only "spatially and numerically separate."[13] If "independence of character and judgement is to be prized," independence "does not signify separateness; it is something [that is only] displayed in relation to others."[14]

Dewey's philosophy may seem characteristically American. Being moral means turning outwards, engaging with the world, focusing on practical, everyday problems that need to be solved. The emphasis is on efficiency, on action, on participation in practical endeavor. This explains Dewey's instrumentalism. Knowledge does not entail a correspondence between the meaning of sentences and some noumenal reality. Knowledge is a tool, an instrument that facilitates our interaction with the environment. An idea is true if it gets the job done. To say that moral ideas are true is to say that they help us lead happy and healthy lives. The emphasis is not on speculation, not on abstract thinking, but on the practical give-and-take of day-to-day living.

Dewey distinguishes between three types of moral theory: theories of the good, theories of justice, and virtue theories.[15] Theories of the good enjoy a certain theoretical preeminence, but Dewey argues that morality can be viewed from any one of these perspectives. Each different theory is, in its own way, able to contribute to the clarification and direction of moral practice. Pursuing the good, fulfilling one's duty, and acting in a virtuous manner are different ways of understanding moral success.

Dewey's account of morality picks out three noticeable facts about moral phenomena. Firstly, there is the fact that we desire certain things. Reflective agents will not act blindly, impulsively. They will ask themselves: "What are the good things to desire?" How can we discriminate "between specious, deceptive goods, and lasting true goods?"[16] They will look for principles that will help them distinguish between "ends that deceptively promise satisfaction" and "ends which truly constitute it."[17] Philosophers who articulate theories of the good try to answer these kinds of questions.

Secondly, there is the fact that human beings struggle to control desire and appetite. Desire is seen "to be the source of temptation, . . . the cause which leads men to deviate from the lawful course of action."[18] Prominent in different moral systems are "commands, prohibitions and [many] devices that regulate the play of passions and desires."[19] This is the role of moral law. Reflective agents will elaborate specific formulations of the law. They will ask questions about the content of law. What are the rights and duties that pertain to each individual person? What are our duties and obligations to society? Philosophers who develop theories of justice try to answer these kinds of questions.

Finally, there is the fact that people praise and blame one another. Human life is characterized "by facts of approbation and condemnation, praise and blame, reward and punishment."[20] One finds "in human nature a spontaneous tendency to favor some lines of conduct, and to censure and penalize other modes of action."[21] Reflective agents will try to investigate the rationale behind these practices. What kind of behavior should we encourage? What kind of behavior should we censure? How can we establish notions of praise and blame on a comprehensive, uniform basis? Philosophers who espouse virtue ethics try to answer these kinds of questions.

Dewey's threefold account of morality rests on an implicit appeal to some notion of objectivity. In each case, Dewey argues for an objective morality. In discussing notions of the good, for example, Dewey distinguishes between "desiring" and "the desirable," between "prizing" and "appraising," between that which we are merely attracted to and that which is good in an objective sense. The very purpose of a theory of the good is "to determine the *real* good as distinct from things that merely *seem* to be so."[22] An entity is not good because we happen to believe that it is good. It is good because it satisfies an objective criterion of goodness.[23]

Theories of justice determine rights and obligations: what we are free to do, what is right to do, and what we are obliged to do. But a notion of rights or obligations presupposes a standard of proportionality that exists beyond our feelings and beliefs. In Dewey's words: "The right is that which asserts that we *ought* to be drawn by some object whether we are naturally attracted to it or not."[24] In Dewey's system, rights and obligations do not derive from some arbitrary formal convention.[25] "There is nothing arbitrary or forced in the existence of right and obligation."[26] Rules and regulations possess moral authority, not because we believe that they possess moral authority, but because they conform to the reality of a specific situation.[27]

Dewey's account of virtue ethics also appeals to an objective standard of right and wrong. Dewey distinguishes between two levels of virtue ethics. On the most primitive level, virtue ethics unthinkingly reflects "prevailing habits of valuation."[28] "Traits of character are not approved because they are virtuous, [they] are virtuous because they are approved."[29] "What is generally censured is, *ipso facto*, regarded as vicious."[30] On a more sophisticated level, virtue-ethics introduces an objective standard of evaluation that is removed from the subjective biases of any particular individual. "An *ideal* spectator is projected and the doer of the act looks at his proposed act through the eyes of this impartial and far-seeing objective judge."[31] In the latter case, moral evaluations are correct or true because they conform to the views of this "objective judge." Agents are obliged to evaluate their acts from an impartial perspective, from a perspective that is, in the appropriate sense, external to the self.

Dewey argues that morality must be "reflective" rather than customary or conventional.[32] Moral individuals will not submit uncritically to the standards of time and place. They will think deeply about issues and personally inquire into the basis of morality. If necessary, they will rebel against errors prevalent in society. Dewey himself brings up the possibility of the good rebel. He writes: "A choice and deed are not wrong *merely* because they fail to conform with current laws and the customary code of duties. . . . Some persons persecuted as moral rebels in one period have been hailed as moral heroes at a later time; children build monuments to those whom their fathers stoned."[33]

Dewey recognizes that a particular moral consensus may be wrong. Even if we all happen to believe in a particular moral claim, this will not guarantee its truth. Moral truth cannot be associated with collective or individual whim. Some positions are more coherent, more practical, more efficient, more truthful than others. I will argue that Dewey presents a moral account that is in line with the autonomy ideal. The good rebel who opposes the going consensus for the sake of the good is both highly moral and highly autonomous.

THE AUTONOMOUS GUNMAN?

My argument that morality and autonomy are necessarily connected contradicts a prevailing view that an immoral agent may be autonomous. H. L. A. Hart, in a famous example in *The Concept of Law*, discusses the "gunman," the holdup artist who robs other people under threat of violence.[34] The gunman is obviously an immoral agent. Nonetheless, the contemporary view is that the gunman, however immoral, may be an autonomous agent.

I want to suggest that the idea of an autonomous gunman is a contradiction in terms, that the concept only has plausibility because we have come to embrace an impoverished view of morality. To be moral is, on the reigning liberal view, to conform to some onerous social system of reciprocal obligation. Authors who maintain that one can be simultaneously autonomous and immoral would argue that an autonomous gunman may do the wrong thing in a public, social sense, while achieving his goals in a personal, private sense.[35] On this account, the successful gunman is immoral in that he is not respecting the rights of others. On the other hand, he may be doing what, in a critical, calculating sense, he wants to do. He may be advancing his own interest. This argument presupposes the dichotomy between personal self-interest and moral achievement one finds expressed in authors like Nagel and Wolf.

Just as Dewey refers to three types of moral theory, we can advance three parallel arguments in favor of a necessary connection between morality and autonomy. Call these the argument from authenticity, the argument from virtue, and what I have already called the argument from the good. These arguments invoke, in turn, notions of justice, of virtue and of the good. Consider first, the argument from authenticity.

If contemporary authors are able to separate the pursuit of personal autonomy from the fulfillment of the social requirements of morality, this is because they tend to conceive of human agents as isolated atoms of individuality. The standard view supplies two criteria for successful choosing: (1) autonomous agents choose for themselves; and (2) autonomous agents choose authentically and are, in their choosing, true to themselves. To argue that autonomous agents choose for themselves is to impose a procedural criterion for successful choice, one that refers to the way in which the choosing is be carried out. To argue that autonomous agents are true to themselves is to impose a substantive criterion for successful choice, one that refers to the content of the agent's actions. I will argue that an immoral agent may fulfill the first, but not the second, criterion of successful choice.

Autonomous agents choose authentically. But how can agents who are at war with the rest of humanity be true to themselves? We are not disembodied, nontuistic sources of self-maximization. As Dewey points out, our relationships to other people are an important part of who we are. Treating other people equitably, fairly, compassionately, even generously is a part of being true to ourselves. Classical authors tell us that if we repudiate the rest of the world, if we treat other people unfairly, this will seriously affect our own sense of self-worth, our psychological health, our emotional and spiritual well-being.

On the standard modern view, we can conceive of an "autonomous gunman." But what is a gunman? A thug who robs innocent victims of

hard-earned savings by threatening to kill them. Standard models of autonomy would have us believe that the gunman can continue merrily on,
pursuing his criminal vocation, all the while remaining psychologically
well-adjusted, at home in society, on good terms with his family, spiritually at peace, full of self-esteem, a paragon of sensitivity, efficiency, dedication, intelligence and optimistic feelings. Such suggestions seem psychologically uninformed and hardly credible. It can be argued that serious
immorality is inevitably self-destructive, that it makes the individual emotionally dysfunctional, compulsive, fraught with psychological trauma, disingenuous, unfulfilled, and so on. We certainly cannot assume that one can
compartmentalize serious evil, that serious criminals can do wicked things
at work and lead idyllic, happy lives away from work.

<h2 style="text-align:center">MACBETH: "OUR NAKED FRAILTIES"</h2>

Literature supplies us with truths about experience. Consider Shakespeare's
Macbeth, the story of a man who commits a serious crime and gets away
with it. Macbeth murders his king while he is a visitor to his castle (a double
crime) and accedes to the throne. If, however, Macbeth successfully seizes
the throne, what happens in the aftermath? Does goodness spring out of
wickedness? Does he live happily ever after? Not by any means.

The success of Macbeth's conspiracy is his own undoing. Crowned as
king, he is slowly but inexorably pulled into a dark, murky web of unhappiness, guilt, physical illness, and spiritual restlessness. His wife sleepwalks at night, trying to wash the blood from her hands. Macbeth himself
becomes a brooding, lonely figure, eating his meals "in fear," and sleeping
"in the affliction of these terrible dreams that shake [him] nightly."[36] His
mind "full of scorpions,"[37] he is hounded by a bitter conscience and driven
to further crimes. As the embattled king declares, shortly before his death:
"I have supp'd full with horrors."[38]

Does serious crime pay? The Bard certainly does not think so. Shakespeare pitilessly chronicles Macbeth's psychological disintegration. When
his mad wife finally commits suicide, the anguished king responds with a
famous soliloquy, reflecting on how the very passage of time has come to
seem so utterly meaningless and trivial:

> To-morrow, and to-morrow, and to-morrow,
> Creeps in this petty pace from day to day,
> To the last syllable of recorded time;
> And all our yesterdays have lighted fools

> The way to dusty death. Out, out, brief candle,
> Life's but a walking shadow, a poor player
> That struts and frets his hour upon the stage,
> And then is heard no more. It is a tale
> Told by an idiot, full of sound and fury,
> Signifying nothing.[39]

The passage may reflect a rather bleak and even cynical worldview, but Macbeth's words are not a comment on how life appears to the virtuous but on how life appears to the damned. The message is not: Life is petty and meaningless. The message is: Participate in serious evil like Macbeth and life will become petty and meaningless. It is Macbeth's own treachery which sucks the meaning out of life, like juice out of a fruit, leaving nothing but a hollow, empty rind. It is his own misdeeds that lead inexorably to his spiritual and political downfall.

Shakespeare's *Macbeth* illustrates a simple moral principle: serious immorality can exact a terrible psychological and spiritual price. For unrepentant agents, agents who continue to profit from their crimes, there may be no escape from the resultant sickness. Lady Macbeth exclaims, while busily trying to wipe away the imaginary bloodstains: "All the perfumes of Arabia will not sweeten this little hand."[40] Why does she sleepwalks at night, muttering incoherently? The doctor explains: "Unnatural deeds do breed unnatural troubles; infected minds to their deaf pillows will discharge their secrets."[41] But in this nightmarish confession, there is no absolution. The pillow is deaf. It cannot listen. Lady Macbeth is not only physically but morally sick. As the doctor observes: "More needs she the divine than the physician."[42]

Amoral accounts of autonomy seem spiritually obtuse. They glibly skate over what Banquo calls our "naked frailties."[43] Human beings are vulnerable creatures. They are prey to unhappiness, depression, insanity. Why should one avoid immorality even if one can get away with it? Because one cannot freely engage in deceit, brutality, unfairness, debauchery, and treachery without entangling oneself in some web of darkness. Macbeth and his wife are not pious, God-fearing people. It is not a sincere, heartfelt concern for the good that drags them down into their guilt-ridden neurosis. They do not want to feel guilty. They are consumed by psychic forces much larger than themselves. Shakespeare presents their mental and physical disintegration as the working through of an implacable law of nature. Do evil and you will soon be dragged down into despair and wretchedness. Such is the nature of human tragedy.

Contemporary authors want to separate personal fulfillment from morality. They seem to believe that it is possible to restrict or isolate immorality to one part of our lives—say, our relations with strangers—without having it affect the other parts of our lives. Shakespeare, on the other hand, portrays evil as a malignant cancer. One cannot unleash the forces of evil in one area of life without having them spill over into other areas. The infection spreads whether we like it or not. Rot consumes the entire limb. Containment simply is not possible. Looked at from a Shakespearean perspective, philosophers who speak of serious immorality as an innocuous option and even an aid to human flourishing misconstrue the nature of evil.

Shakespeare believes, like Plato, like Aristotle, that wicked acts lead to further wickedness. Macbeth is possessed by the evil he has initiated. It becomes something larger than himself, pulling him ever further into a maelstrom of iniquity, turpitude, and meaninglessness. The first crime leads to other crimes, to a general corruption of the people around him, and eventually to the downfall of the entire political state.[44]

Contemporary thought separates the private from the public, the personal from the moral, but Shakespeare views the personal and the public as intimately related. Macbeth is guilty of a political crime: he assassinates a head of state. But this political crime has personal, private ramifications. The worm that consumes Macbeth's conscience eats away at any sense of self-respect, turning his personal life into an empty shell. Macbeth is hardly a happy king. The consciousness of what he has done to gain the throne eternally oppresses him. As Angus reports, he feels "his title / Hang loose about him, like a giant's robe / Upon a dwarfish thief."[45] Macbeth's evil machinations poison his self-esteem and bring him to the edge of psychic disintegration.

As Dewey insists, the opinions and good will of others contribute to our happiness. By the end of the play, Macbeth has effectively alienated himself from those around him. As one Scottish nobleman reports: "Those he commands move only in command, / Nothing in love."[46] Macbeth himself laments: "That which should accompany old age, / As honor, love, obedience, troops of friends, I must not look to have."[47] Serious evil alters irrevocably our relationships to other people and thus compounds our unhappiness.[48]

Macbeth has been referred to as a "morality play." But Shakespeare does not adopt the role of the moralist spinning a didactic tale. Rather he adopts the role of the psychologist. He takes the position of a detached observer and simply observes what unfolds. His message is less a call to sanctity than a resigned comment on some inevitable law of human nature. The play, which is still timely today, throws harsh but probing light onto the human condition. It puts into question amoral concepts of autonomy.

Shakespeare's character Macbeth is ultimately a failure, and there is no reason to suspect that the violent and the treacherous will fare much better in the twenty-First century. In a popular short story about World War II Germany entitled "The Head and the Feet," C. S. Forester chronicles the demise of a Nazi SS doctor who descends into madness and hangs himself after the head of a decapitated prisoner accidentally strikes his foot.[49] Georg Schmidt, the reluctant SS officer, is expected to supervise Nazi atrocities at a local death camp while carrying on a life of exemplary civility, attending birthday parties and consorting with polite society. But the strain is too much to bear. Schmidt loses his grip on reality and in one final, pathetic gesture commits suicide.

Literary figures like Forester's SS doctor and Shakespeare's Macbeth illustrate the disastrous consequences of serious evil. They discredit the idea of the autonomous gunman, the gunman who participates in serious crime while leading a happy, healthy life. The picture strains the imagination. We are to imagine a self-confident holdup artist, physically robust, intellectually tranquil, psychologically whole, trustful about the future, loved and respected by all, guilt-free, sans neurosis, unmoved by depression, addiction, jealously, anger, frustration, etc. This gallant figure seems more a bit of idealistic reverie than a realistic comment on life.

Let me summarize the argument from authenticity. Contemporary authors associate autonomy with authenticity. If, however, authenticity, psychic wholeness, is destroyed by serious immorality, it will follow that autonomous agents cannot be seriously immoral. This is not an analytic but an existential argument. It tells us that if we look at the empirical evidence, if we cultivate a knowledge of human beings and embrace a wide experience of life and human affairs, we will be forced to conclude, like Shakespeare, that serious immorality hampers successful self-government.

Macbeth is an immoral agent, someone who rebels against the good. The propagandist, journalist, or philosopher may try to rescue the immoral agent from ignominy by turning him into a moral hero. A Hitler may be transformed into the *Übermensch*; de Sade into a freethinker; the holdup artist into another Robin Hood. This is a common dodge, a way of gaining respect and saving conscience, but it does not prove that immoral agents can be autonomous. What this additional piece of information does is transform the gunman's so-called crime into an admirable, moral occupation or, at the very least, into an occupation that is not morally offensive. It only shows us that we were wrong to think that our "gunman" was an immoral agent in the first place.

THE VIRTUOUS GUNMAN?

Two other arguments can be made in favor of an explicitly moral account of personal autonomy. Next consider what I will call "the argument from virtue." This argument needs to be elaborated within the framework of virtue ethics. Though Dewey is widely identified as a virtue ethicist, the first philosopher one thinks about in this connection is Aristotle.[50] In the Aristotelian system, the virtuous person is someone who has built up, through habit and experience, a disposition to act in a morally appropriate way. Does it follow that autonomous agents, agents who successfully govern themselves, must be, in the language of Aristotle, virtuous people?

Aristotle writes: "We become just by doing just actions, temperate by doing temperate actions and brave by doing brave actions."[51] In Aristotle's theory, the relationship between good deeds and a good character is, in a benign sense, circular. Good deeds form a good character and a good character prompts good deeds. But the same circular relation also holds between evil deeds and an evil character. Engaging in evil deeds forms an evil character, and possessing an evil character makes us engage in evil deeds. For the sake of brevity, let us define immoral acts, from the standpoint of virtue ethics, as expressions of bad character.

Consider then our "autonomous gunman." Amoralists argue that the successful holdup artist can be both immoral and autonomous. On the social contract account, armed robbery is an immoral kind of act because of its deleterious effect on other people. On the virtue ethics account, armed robbery is an immoral act because it is an expression of a bad character. We can imagine various scenarios. Perhaps gunmen rob other people because they are violent and treacherous. Perhaps they are greedy. Perhaps they are too lazy to work. Perhaps they are self-absorbed and inconsiderate. Perhaps they lack discipline and are addicted to drugs. Whatever is the correct explanation, what is important is that, viewed from a virtue perspective, the immorality of the gunman's activities must be linked to some important character flaw. To say that the gunman is an immoral person is to say that there is something seriously wrong with his character. If the gunman had a good character, he would not be acting in an immoral way.

The amoralist wants to argue that the gunman can be both immoral and autonomous, but this involves a contradiction in terms. Aristotle argues that virtuous agents are able to control their appetites in accordance with reason. Agents who lack virtue are unable to control themselves. They lack this ability. To be autonomous is, however, to be able to *govern* oneself. But the gunman is not well-governed. Indeed, he is unable to govern himself. He is motivated by laziness, greed, lack of discipline, selfishness, whatever. And these character flaws all indicate, as Aristotle observes, a serious lack of self-control.

Virtue ethics does not define successful self-government in terms of doing what you want to do. Even if the gunman wants to be a gunman, he does not successfully govern himself in pursuing his chosen vocation. An analogy may help. Suppose Naomi has to drive her car from point A to point B. And suppose Naomi lets go of the steering wheel, closes her eyes, and lets the car drive itself. It might happen, by complete coincidence, that the car arrives at point B. But this is not because Naomi is a good driver. Being a good driver means, first and foremost, driving. It means conscientiously directing the car toward the intended goal. Even if the car arrives, by sheer coincidence, at point B, it would be a contradiction in terms to say that someone who does not drive is a good driver.

The gunman does, in a certain sense, have an intended goal. He wants to rob strangers. He wants to turn a profit as quickly and as easily as possible. All his actions are directed toward this goal. But this apparent decisiveness is misleading. What the gunman really wants is to give in to his animal appetites and give up governing altogether. He wants to let go of the steering wheel and let the car do the driving. He may have many different strategies for doing this. If, however, his criminal involvement is motivated by a lack of virtue, the end result is always the same—a lack of self-control.

Suppose, for example, that the gunman is too lazy to get a job. Laziness is a lack of discipline or self-control. Or suppose that the gunman is a greedy person. To be greedy is to "give in" to an inordinate desire for money. It is to lack self-control. Or suppose the gunman steals to support a drug habit. To be addicted to drugs is to lack, in a decisive way, self-control. Or suppose the gunman is an angry, violent, bitter person. To give in to negative, abusive emotions is to lack self-control. And so on. If, however, our gunman is unable to control himself, he does not govern himself; that is, he is, by definition, nonautonomous.

The gunman is not someone who successfully governs himself. He is someone who has given up on self-government. He may have many strategies and projects for criminal employment, but underneath all this goal-driven endeavor, he is out of control. Underneath it all, he is a creature of unreflective emotion and compulsion, someone who has let his animal nature overrun and control his rational nature. It is no use arguing that the gunman could control himself if he wanted. As Aristotle argues, if you do not control yourself now, you will be unable to control yourself later. You simply harden into your vices.

For Dewey, all moral questions ultimately resolve into questions about character. To ask "Is armed robbery a moral endeavor?" is to ask "Will armed robbery help me become the kind of person I ought to be?" In the case of the gunman, there is an obvious answer. Accumulating *stolen* money cannot help the gunman become the kind of person he ought to be, for the act of stealing demeans and corrupts his own character. This is why stolen money is a bad thing, an apparent good that is somehow sullied or tainted. If self-control is an essential aspect of successful self-government, then an immoral agent cannot be autonomous.

Viewed from the perspective of virtue ethics, morality is a necessary condition for autonomy, but autonomy could also be considered a necessary condition for morality. Autonomy is the organizing "principle" of virtuousness. It is a way of regulating, of governing and directing, all character traits. Prima facie we regard autonomy as a virtue, as an admirable trait of character. Autonomy can be understood not merely as one virtue among many but, more properly, as the virtue par excellence, as the most important virtue of all. We will discuss the importance of autonomy to morality below.

AUTONOMY AND THE GOOD

In discussing theories of the good, justice theories, and virtue theories, Dewey wants to preserve the differences in these three moral approaches. Moral theory should not be collapsed into a single unified structure. At the same time, it could be argued that our understanding of the good is, in a logical sense, prior to our understanding of justice or of virtue. Theories of justice and virtue must be organized around an idea of the good if they are to be established on a "reflective," rational basis.[52]

Thomas Aquinas maintains that to be a moral person is "to know the good and follow after it."[53] Charles Taylor writes that "one of the most basic aspirations of human beings [is] the need to be connected to or in contact with what they see as good."[54] The idea of the good is the motor of human striving. As Dewey explains: "Men have desires: immediately and apart from reflection they want this and that thing, food, a companion, money, fame and repute, health, distinction from their fellows, power, the love of friends, the admiration of rivals, etc. But why do they want these things? Because value is attributed to them; because they are thought to be good. As the Scholastics said, we desire *sub specie boni;* beneath all the special ends striven for is the common idea of the Good, the Satisfying."[55]

Morality, viewed as the pursuit of the good, is a matter of right knowledge. It helps us differentiate between true and false goods. Out of a vast selection of competing goods, it identifies "the real good," "the permanent good," "the lasting true good," "the only good that satisfies," "the good that leads to true happiness," and so on.

Some liberal theorists propose a theory of justice that is alleged to be neutral on questions of the good.[56] Even if we accept this kind of procedural account, however, the goal of liberalism is, in the final analysis, the achievement of the good. What motivates the liberal commitment to negative liberty is not the idea that there is no good, but the idea that individuals are best equipped to judge what is good for themselves. The only reason procedural goods are valuable on a liberal scheme is that they allow individual citizens to *privately* (and successfully) pursue the good. On a liberal scheme, society must be organized so as to facilitate this pursuit.

Considered from the viewpoint of the good, however, an immoral autonomous agent is an impossibility. As Dewey argues, every rational or reflective creature pursues or desires the good. A moral individual achieves an authentic good. An immoral agent achieves a false good, a good that is not really a good. If, however, agents fail to achieve the good, then, judged by their own aspirations (they were, after all, pursuing the good), they do not achieve what they want, they do not accomplish what they intended to do. Judged even in light of their own goals, they do not successfully govern themselves. They are not autonomous.

A theory of the good provides a higher perspective from which to judge outstanding human achievements. Someone who subscribes to a theory of the good may not believe in a single exclusive good. There may be a plurality of goods, a hierarchy of goods, even competing goods. Seen from the viewpoint of the good, a successful act obtains a true good. Why then do people climb mountains? In order to achieve a true good. Why do people play the piano? In order to achieve a true good. Why do people conduct scientific experiments? In order to achieve a true good. Why do people write poetry? In order to achieve a true good. We may argue about the ways in which these activities are alleged to embody or promote the good, but that is a different debate. Suffice it to say that authentic good—whatever the authentic good may be—is the goal of human striving. If agents fail to achieve an authentic good, they fail at their chosen endeavor.

Different schools of philosophy try, in turn, to elucidate the origin and nature of the good. Debate about the substantive content of morality does not impugn, however, the argument from the good. Only absolute nihilism, the belief that nothing has value, could defeat the argument from the good, but absolute nihilism is inconsistent with human striving. If nothing has value, why prefer pleasure to pain, health to sickness, happiness to misery? Why strive toward aims or goals? Why not just lie down and die? Human

exertion defeats nihilism. We all make judgments about the good, judgments that are susceptible to more rigorous scrutiny. Agents who subscribe
to a particular theory of the good will judge human endeavor on that basis.
Insomuch as there are right or wrong ways of assigning values, some agents
will succeed and some will fail at human achievement.

Contemporary authors tend to define autonomy in terms of agent self-
approval, but to argue that agents have achieved the good because they
believe they have achieved the good would be solipsism. To say, for example, that Andrea has achieved the good is not simply to say that Andrea
is a self-approving agent. It is to say that her attitude can be substantiated.
It can be argued for. There is corroborating evidence. It is to say that an
attitude of approval corresponds to or coheres with what we know about
the nature of Andrea, about the nature of her actions, and about the nature
of the world. One cannot make judgments about the good without appealing to objective norms, standards of achievement that are, in the appropriate epistemological sense, independent from or external to the agent.

The argument from the good rules out any possibility of an autonomous gunman. What is the gunman doing when he performs an armed
robbery? Dewey would argue that he is striving after the good. If, however,
ill-gotten material wealth does not constitute an authentic good, if the gunman only amasses a false good, a good that is not really good, then he does
not achieve what he sets out to achieve. Judged even by his own aspirations, he is less than successful. He is not autonomous.

MEANS AND ENDS

Seen from the perspective of the good, rational subjects are able to distinguish between good and bad ends. Their aspirations are well-ordered. They
choose the right goals. Note, however, that the way one achieves one's
ends affects the value of those ends. Suppose there is a rule that says I must
dip my hands in red paint before picking up a white dish. The means I use
to procure the dish will detract from the value of the plate. I will end up
with a dish that has been smeared with red stains. In a similar way, the
moral value of particular ends may be diminished by the means we use to
achieve them.

The gunman has an obvious end. He desires material wealth. Now,
material wealth may be a moral end. If, however, I am so concerned about
material wealth that I murder other human beings to obtain it, material
wealth is no longer a worthy end. It is only a good end when it is procured
in a just and equitable manner.

Seen from the perspective of the good, the gunman is an ignorant agent. He is unable to tell the difference between right and wrong and does not understand what the good consists of. Wealth is not *at any price* a good. It depends on how you obtain it. Although the gunman can steal physical money, he cannot steal the good the money represents, for the act of stealing negates or cancels out any goodness associated with material wealth.

Any definitive distinction between reasoning about ends and reasoning about means ultimately breaks down. Choosing the wrong end may entail choosing the wrong means, and choosing the wrong means may entail choosing the wrong end. Popular myth had it that Paganini sold his soul to the devil in order to become a virtuoso violinist. Seen from one perspective, Paganini resorted to evil means in order to achieve good ends. He did something evil (bargained with the devil) in order to achieve a noble end (musical virtuosity). Seen from another perspective, however, it could be said that Paganini chose the wrong end, virtuosity, over the right end, virtue. In such a case, mistaking means is tantamount to mistaking ends. The two mistakes include one another.

This analysis could be applied to our gunman. Construed one way, the gunman chooses the wrong means, violence, to attain a legitimate good, money. But it could also be said that he chooses the wrong end, "money at any price," over the right end, "money as an award for legitimate effort." As it turns out, then, the gunman is an ignorant agent twice over. His means-reasoning is faulty, but his ends-reasoning is also faulty. There are cases where one way of construing an agent's conduct will make more sense than the other, but that will depend on individual circumstance.

OBJECTIONS TO THE ARGUMENT FROM THE GOOD

An adequate theory of the good will supply right knowledge about what has or does not have value. Seen from the perspective of such a theory, immoral agents lack knowledge of the good. They pursue illusory goods, goods that lack any true, lasting value. They do not govern themselves successfully. One might try to contest the argument from the good in three different ways.

To begin with, an antimoralist who believes in material wealth might try to salvage the autonomy of the gunman by redefining his moral status. Perhaps the gunman comes to possess a true good. But a gunman who achieves a true good no longer qualifies as an immoral agent. This kind of argument only serves to show that conventional ideas about morality are wrong. It cannot be used to show that an *immoral* agent can be autonomous.

The second way in which one might contest this argument is by restricting the scope of moral endeavor. One might imagine an amoral gunman, a gunman who operates without any moral aspirations, without any idea of the good. But a gunman who lacked any idea of the good would have nothing to strive for. He would not be attracted toward or repulsed by anything. He would be like a zombie or a machine. His actions would not derive from any internal sense of value. They would have to originate in unconscious instinct or in external forces. Such a person could hardly be called a "self-governing" agent.

In any case, the gunman is clearly not an amoral agent. It is not that he has no convictions about the good. It is that he will do almost anything to procure the good as he sees it. The problem here is not a lack of conviction but a misunderstanding of what the good consists of. The problem is moral ignorance, not lack of motivation. Individuals who lacked motivation would not go to the trouble of breaking the law.

The third way in which one can dispute the connection between autonomy and morality is through some kind of appeal to solipsism. One may tenaciously insist that *because* the gunman believes he successfully governs himself, he does successfully govern himself. But why should we accept the gunman's opinions about himself as an infallible source of truth? The gunman is, like the rest of us, a fallible creature. He may be mistaken. If he believes he has achieved the good, it does not necessarily mean he has achieved the good. He may be just a very ignorant creature.

Agent self-satisfaction is not a secure criterion for autonomy. Suppose our gunman, in a heated battle with police, comes to the realization that his ill-gotten gains were a false good. He has just begun to regret his past actions when a bullet passes through his heart, killing him instantly. On the self-approval model, this agent has failed at autonomy. Suppose, however, that our gunman is shot one minute before he comes to this realization. If self-approval is the ultimate criterion for autonomy, the gunman who dies before realizing the error of his ways is an autonomous agent. But this seems absurd. Both agents have led the very same life. The only difference is that the gunman in the second scenario dies before he sees the truth. He dies locked in the illusion that he has led a successful life. But an agent who is too stupid to realize his own mistakes is not an autonomous agent, *because he is stupid.* Successful self-government includes a truthful appraisal of our failures and our achievements. Self-deception may lead to self-approval, but it does not lead to autonomy.

Autonomous agents must satisfy two separate criteria: (1) they must choose for themselves, and (2) they must be true to themselves. Obviously, if agents cannot choose for themselves, autonomy is not possible. But freedom of choice is not enough. If one is to be true to oneself, one must avoid evil (the argument from authenticity), one must choose the good (the argument from good), and one must be a virtuous person (the argument from virtue). Human striving is inescapably moral. If we fail at morality, we fail at self-government.

THREE LEVELS OF ACHIEVEMENT

Autonomous agents, agents who successfully govern themselves, must be both moral and rational. We may distinguish three levels of human achievement:

1. Agents may do whatever they want to do.
2. Agents may freely do what they believe they ought to do.
3. Agents may freely do what, *in some objective sense*, they ought to do.

Agents who exist at the first level of achievement engage in the uncritical satisfaction of desire. At this level of achievement, desires do not have to meet with the approval of judgment. Agents do not try to govern themselves in accordance with any coherent system of values. They simply do whatever they want to do. They give in to every whim and impulse. They do not strive toward self-control, toward autonomy. To live on this level is to relinquish one's status as a rational, reflective, critical agent.

At the second level of achievement, agents act in accordance with judgment. They do not indiscriminately satisfy desire. They strive toward some conception of the good. They discipline themselves in accordance with specific goals and aspirations. This represents a move toward autonomy, but individual judgment is a fallible capacity. Even a well-intentioned agent may be mistaken. To be an autonomous individual, to succeed—in the highest possible sense—at self-government, is not simply to act in accordance with one's own judgment. It also means acting in accordance with some objective standard of true belief or sound judgment. This brings us to the third level of achievement.

On the third level of achievement, agents willingly do what they ought to do. Simply put, they do the right thing. They do not do it accidentally, because they are forced to do it, for the wrong reasons, or because they *misunderstand* the situation. They do it by design and of their own accord. They willingly do the right thing because they correctly perceive that it is the right thing to do. They not only satisfy their own desires or wants. At the same time, they measure up to some objective norm of excellence. Only the third level of achievement represents true autonomy.

Theories of rationality and morality supply objective criteria that we can use to measure the success or failure of individual attempts at self-government. To say that agents act in a rational manner is to say that their behavior satisfies objective norms of consistency and reasonableness. Likewise, to say that agents act in a moral manner is to say that their behavior satisfies objective norms of merit or excellence—it adheres to the mean, it demonstrates respect for other human beings, it obeys the categorical imperative, it promotes human flourishing, it conforms to God's commandments, whatever. To exist at the third level of achievement is to be a moral and a rational agent. The third level of achievement represents the height of human accomplishment.

THE "ANYTHING-I-WANT-TO-DO" DEFINITION OF FREEDOM

Contemporary authors generally identify autonomy with the second level of achievement. In philosophical debate, the first level is not a serious contender. The word "autonomy" means successful self-*government*. It means governing, controlling our impulses, our attitudes, our desires, our actions. Agents who operate at the first level of achievement would be impulsive choosers, anomic individuals. They would do whatever they feel like doing. They would not direct their actions in accordance with any rational conception of the good. They could not be said to "govern" themselves.

If autonomy means self-mastery, agents who exist at the first level of achievement do not even try to master themselves. This is a premoral, prerational state. It is unreflective, blind, instinctive, entirely animal. The question of autonomy does not even arise.

Living only on the first level of achievement—even if it were possible—would be a recipe for disaster. If we were to follow all our impulses, we would be unable to complete even the simplest tasks. We would change our minds. We would be imprudent. We would be indiscreet. We would contradict ourselves. We would not do what we are obliged to do. We would not do what external circumstances require. We would take unnecessary risks. We might even end up killing ourselves. Louis de Bernières writes of his experience on the edge of an English cliff.[57] Peering down into the abyss, he felt an almost irresistible urge to jump. It was as if the emptiness was pulling him down, drawing him over the edge. Successful self-government cannot mean, in this particular instance, "doing-whatever-you-want-to-do." Jumping off English cliffs does not constitute a successful strategy for living.

Successful living requires supervision by some higher, intelligent self. It does not mean acting on every whim and fancy. Children may live at the first level of achievement, but even they must learn the importance of self-control. Recent literature on emotional intelligence (EQ) bears this out.[58] In the Stanford "marshmallow test," psychologists told individual four-year-olds that if they could refrain from eating one marshmallow until a lab worker came back from a fifteen-minute errand, they would be rewarded with two marshmallows. Children who were disciplined enough to wait for the second marshmallow came up with various strategies for coping with the situation. Some talked or sang to themselves. Some closed their eyes. Some tried to go to sleep. In one manner or another, they were able to master themselves and delay gratification. A follow-up survey of parents and teachers found that those children who were able to exert self-control generally grew up to be better adjusted, more confident, and more dependable teenagers. When students in the two groups took the SATs, children who were able to restrain themselves and wait for the second marshmallow scored an average of 210 points higher.

What the marshmallow test demonstrates is that prolonged existence at the first level of achievement is problematic, unhealthy and inefficient. There is already something underdeveloped or ill-formed about a four-year-old child who exists solely or primarily on the first level of achievement. Being able to exercise restraint is an important ingredient of successful self-government. Children who flourish need to be able to discipline their behavior according to some higher plan of action.

Older children and adults do not usually remain, except perhaps for brief periods of time, at the first level of achievement. Nonetheless, there are pathological and even permanent examples of this kind of condition. Consider the genetic disorder known as Praeder-Willi Syndrome, a mild to moderate form of mental retardation that is accompanied by a persistent hyperphagia, a preoccupation with food that tends to very severe overeating. Patients with this syndrome are so obsessed with food that if they are left unsupervised, they will literally eat themselves to death. For whatever reason, they are unable to resist the impulse to eat. It is as if there is no inner capacity for supervision, no internal regulating physiological or psychological mechanism that curbs action. Unable to rationally regulate their desires, such individuals are caught eternally at the first level of achievement, a condition that can have tragic consequences.

Health-care professionals have complained that a liberal emphasis on individual autonomy presents grave health risks for patients with Praeder-Willi syndrome.[59] Policies and legislation that grant these patients greater freedom to decide for themselves have the inevitable side-effect of removing external controls that are, at times, necessary for their survival. Some liberal authors may confuse autonomy with negative liberty, but autonomy cannot be equated with mere nonrestraint. Although patients with Praeder-Willi syndrome may be left to their own devices in other domains, taking away needed restrictions on food intake cannot be construed as an aid to successful self-government. Agents who are incapable of rising above the first level of achievement are incapable of autonomy.

AUTONOMY AS SELF-SATISFACTION

One cannot identify autonomy with the first level of achievement, but many contemporary philosophers identify autonomy with the second level of achievement. They present the self-approving agent as the model par excellence of autonomy, but this is to fall into solipsism. It does not follow that because an agent believes he is free, he is free. Our beliefs about ourselves may be mistaken. Imagine the following (heated) conversation:

> *Successful Businessman*: I've lead a good life . . .
> *'60s Radical*: You're a poor excuse for a human being!
> *Successful Businessman* At least I don't live off the government! I don't depend on other people. I'm autonomous! I take care of myself . . .
> *'60s Radical*: You don't run your business. Your business runs you. You wouldn't know what freedom was if it hit you in the face . . .
> *Successful Businessman*: Listen, I make my own decisions. No one forced me to do this. This is the way I want to live . . .
> *'60s Radical*: You've never had an independent thought in your life. You're just another cog in a mindless machine. You don't know what freedom is . . .

Is our businessman free? There is no agreement here. The businessman believes he is free; the 1960s radical certainly does not think so. Both have their reasons. Whatever we might personally feel about the issue, the whole point is that there is room for argument. It does not follow that the businessman must be free because he believes he is free. Certainly, the businessman acts in accordance with his own beliefs, but his beliefs may be mistaken.

Believing that one is free does not make one free. Suppose I were to make my sister my slave. If believing that one is free is tantamount to really being free, I could "liberate" her by brainwashing her into thinking that she really is free. But even if I could manage to convince her that she is free, this would not be a form of liberation. If anything, it would be a more pernicious form of oppression. In a case like this, freedom means rejecting one's erroneous beliefs. It means, in Marxist terms, repudiating false consciousness. It does not mean willingly embracing enslavement.

Agents who act in accordance with their own beliefs exist at the second level of achievement. If, however, it is good to act in accordance with our own beliefs, it is not good enough. Successful agents do not merely do what they believe is right. They do what is *objectively and substantively and materially* right. They attain the third level of achievement. Reflective endeavor aims at the third level of achievement. It is not enough to do what I believe is right; I want to do what is really right. Reflective agents who do not reach the third level of achievement do not do what they intend to do. They do not successfully govern themselves. They are not autonomous agents.

HEROES AND HEROINES

Agents who reach the third level of achievement are bona fide heroes and heroines. Michelangelo, for example, wanted to be a great artist. And Michelangelo produced great works of art, works that display technical expertise, works that are spiritually deep and emotionally powerful, works that capture the human condition, works that make people more human, more compassionate, more thoughtful. In this sense at least, we can claim that Michelangelo successfully governed himself, that he was an autonomous agent, that he reached the third level of achievement.

To exist at the third level of achievement is to satisfy an objective standard of excellence, one that can be rationally defended. There is, of course, disagreement about who is or is not an authentic hero. Still, there are obvious examples: Mother Teresa, Florence Nightingale, Benjamin Franklin, Louis Pasteur, Jesus, Socrates, the Virgin Mary, Einstein, Lord Byron at the end of his life, someone who rescues a child from drowning, the first violin at the symphony orchestra, brave soldiers, political dissidents, or even, in Iris Murdoch's phrase, "some quiet unpretentious worker, a schoolteacher or a mother, or better still an aunt."[60] Of course, the process of evaluating human achievement is very complicated. This is not an easy task for several reasons.

Firstly, autonomy is something we never fully achieve but something we continually strive towards. At different times and in different situations we may be more or less autonomous, we may successfully govern ourselves to a greater or a lesser degree, but we can never think of ourselves as perfect paradigms of autonomy. As a general rule, agents do not, in any penultimate sense, reach the third level of achievement.

Secondly, judging a person's actions is a very difficult task. In most cases, we lack intimate knowledge of someone's deepest aspirations, inner struggles, failures and successes. As Murdoch asks: "What . . . do we really know about the detailed lives of famous holy men?"[61] Even when we try to evaluate our own actions, we often overlook the real motivations behind specific actions. If, however, we do not understand why someone has acted in a particular way, we may not be able to properly judge their actions. Hence the biblical injunction that only God should judge, for only God can see into the human heart.[62]

Thirdly, as Dewey insists, human achievement must be evaluated in terms of a person's character. But if we want to judge a person's character, it is not enough to consider isolated acts. We must consider a person's conduct, the general disposition of a series of acts, and ultimately, a particular agent's life as a whole, but this complicates the problem. It is not just that we usually have limited knowledge of an entire life. Our lives are often filled with tension, with contradictory inclinations, with competing goals and contrasting actions. Individuals may achieve great things in one field of endeavor but fail miserably in others. How we should balance different failures and successes against one another and come up with an accurate overall evaluation of a whole life is not an easy question.

Despite these difficulties, we do evaluate other people, at times with surprising accuracy. We do have authentic role models and heroes, people we look up to and, conversely, people we detest. In a skeptical age, moral pluralism may make agreement about these issues problematic. People who have different moral views will subscribe to different models of autonomy. Even if there is serious disagreement about human achievement, however, it does not follow that all views are equally sound or rational. As I have demonstrated, a careful overview of competing moral views reveals more moral consensus than we sometimes suspect.

SOCRATES, PLATO, AND ARISTOTLE

Christine Swanton has elaborated a defeasibility theory of freedom.[63] She defines freedom as the absence of certain flaws or failures in the decision-making procedure. Autonomous agents are able to avoid the kinds of errors that typically characterize unsuccessful lives. Using our three-level schema, we can identify three different ways in which free agents fail to be autonomous:

1. Agents who function solely at the first level of achievement are, to use Watson's term, "wantons." They do not achieve autonomy. They do not even aspire to autonomy. They simply do what they want to do.

2. Agents who attempt to move beyond the first level of achievement may fail to attain the second level of achievement. These agents have convictions about what they should or should not do, but through some fault of character, they are unable to make their behavior conform to their own convictions. They are guilty of *akrasia* or weakness of will.

3. Finally, agents who attempt to move beyond the second level of achievement may fail to reach the third level of achievement. Although these agents may act in a manner that is consistent with their own beliefs, their beliefs may be mistaken. They may do what is wrong thinking that it is right. These agents are guilty of ignorance.

This three-tier view of autonomy or personal achievement is in line with the Western philosophical tradition. Ancient Greek philosophers believed that we may fail at human achievement in at least three different ways. Although Socrates, Plato and Aristotle do not set out their views in the same systematic way, they each condemn, as a serious moral error, one of the failures outlined above. We can combine their separate analyses within a single model of achievement that explains and accounts for the full range of human achievement.

Greek philosophers conceived of human beings as rational animals. In the eyes of these philosophers, wantons, agents who exist at the first level of existence, are hardly human. They repudiate their rational nature and thus forfeit their humanity. In Plato's *Republic* the unjust man who is dragged this way and that by his appetites is just such a wanton.[64] He relinquishes control, allowing himself to be pulled this way and that by unreflective desire. He does not even try to govern himself. He lives like an animal. He is not autonomous.

Plato equates moral and spiritual failure with unrestrained action, while Aristotle argues that evil is often the result of *akrasia* or weakness of will.[65] The morally weak man *(akratês)* has the right beliefs and values, but he is unable to put them into practice. He perceives the good, but he is too weak-willed to pursue it. We can use Aristotle's account of *akrasia* to explain why agents who exist at the first level of achievement fail to reach the second level of achievement. These agents are unable to live up to their own ideals. They lack the necessary discipline. They fail at self-government because of a weak character.

Socrates had earlier argued that evil is invariably the result of ignorance. Evil agents do evil things because they misconstrue the good.[66] They pursue a false good. We can use Socrates' account of moral ignorance to explain why agents who exist at the second level of achievement fail to reach the third level of achievement. These agents live up to their own ideals, but they have the wrong ideals. They possess the necessary discipline, but they achieve disreputable goals. They fail at self-government because of ignorance.

In the *Nicomachean Ethics* Aristotle distinguishes between the "incontinent" and the "self-indulgent" man. The incontinent man suffers from *akrasia*. He knows that he is acting wrongly but lacks self-control. He fails to reach the second level of achievement. The self-indulgent man, on the other hand, suffers from ignorance.[67] He acts wrongly while thinking he is acting rightly. He fails to reach the third level of achievement. Neither the incontinent nor the self-indulgent man successfully governs himself. They both fail, for different reasons, at autonomy.

Contemporary theorists tend to define personal autonomy in terms of the second level of achievement. Seen from this perspective, nonautonomous agents suffer from *akrasia* or weakness of will. Ignorance is, however, an equally serious defect that can subvert personal achievement. We all make mistakes in choosing. Even if we manage to live up to those critical standards we set for ourselves, we may select the wrong standards. Ignorance counts, then, as an infringement on autonomy. Any theory of autonomy that does not recognize that fallible agents sometimes pursue the wrong goals would be seriously inadequate.

CULPABLE MORAL IGNORANCE: EICHMANN

Consider next the way in which ignorance, and in particular moral ignorance, prevents the achievement of autonomy. On the theory I have proposed, ignorant agents misconstrue the good. They choose the wrong ends. This is a common enough occurrence. In our daily lives we say things like: "Linda thought what she was doing was right, but she should have known better." That is to say, Linda was well-intentioned but ignorant. And what is more, she must be held responsible for her ignorance.

We can begin by distinguishing between two kinds of ignorance. An agent may, through ignorance, choose the wrong means or the wrong ends. Agents who are ignorant about means are unable to muster the means needed to achieve their goals. Agents who suffer from an ignorance of ends do not know what the good is. Within the general system of nomenclature in this text, the term "ignorance" will mean "ignorance of ends." Ignorance of means may be, in special cases, a form of *akrasia* or weakness of will.

I have argued that all serious human striving has a moral component. Agents who choose the wrong ends make a moral mistake. Consider then a conspicuous example of a culpable moral mistake: the case of Nazi war criminal Adolf Eichmann. Hannah Arendt describes Eichmann as a bland little man with "a horrible taste for clichés" who selflessly dedicated himself to the hygienic extermination of Jews.[68] Judged by any moral or human standard, Eichmann did not successfully govern himself. Why? Eichmann was certainly not weak-willed. He was not incontinent, self-indulgent, careless. He was not a shirker, a hanger-on. He was a model bureaucrat. He worked very hard. He devoted himself diligently to his cause. If Eichmann did not successfully govern himself, it was not because he was weak-willed. It was because he was ignorant of the good. Either he was wicked or insane. If he was really insane, he cannot be held responsible for the Nazi atrocities he supervised. If, of course, he was wicked, he must be held responsible for crimes against humanity.

The psychiatrists that examined Eichmann concluded that he was not insane.[69] Papadatos reports that one professional went so far as to declare: "'This man is entirely normal.'"[70] If, however, Eichmann was in full possession of his faculties, how can we explain his participation in the Holocaust? How could this bland little bureaucrat, this shuffler of paper, this wearer of starched collars with the squeamish stomach, become a key perpetrator of the genocide of millions of Jews? How was this possible? Eichmann was an evil man, but he was not the bloodthirsty maniac he was later made out to be. If Eichmann failed—and failed horrendously—at morality, his failure must be traced to a disturbing lack of personal autonomy.

Eichmann presents a perfect foil to the figure of the good rebel. If the good rebel stands as the paradigm case of autonomy, Eichmann was an evil conformist. He failed at human decency because he was not a *self*-governing individual. He was an unoriginal man who unquestioningly accepted the imperatives and prejudices of a malevolent society. As Arendt explains: "[His] conscience was . . . set at rest when he saw the zeal and eagerness with which 'good society' everywhere reacted as he did. He did not have to 'close his ears to the voice of conscience,' . . . not because he had none, but because his conscience spoke with a 'respectable voice,' with the voice of respectable society around him."[71] Eichmann was too lazy, too cowardly, too complacent, too smug, too ambitious, to think in an independent manner. He went along with respectable German society. It was the easy thing to do. It gave him a sense of importance, of purpose and respectability. Like the cooperative subjects in the Milgram experiment, Eichmann blindly followed orders. He was unwilling to think things through for himself and act on his own. The risks were too great. His uncritical submission to an evil authority accounts for his lack of autonomy.

Contemporary theorists equate autonomy with agent self-approval. To the bitter end, Eichmann approved of and defended his actions, but to suggest that he successfully governed himself would be an aberration. Even if Eichmann achieved the goals he set for himself, he failed, in the most elementary sense, as a human being. He was culpably ignorant of the good. He should have known that what he was doing was wrong. *Through his own fault,* he became impervious to the claims of his victims.

Aquinas distinguishes between direct and indirect voluntary moral ignorance. In his theory, we may choose to be morally ignorant "directly, as when a man wishes of set purpose to be ignorant of certain things so that he may sin more freely."[72] Or we may choose to be morally ignorant "indirectly, as when a man through stress of work or other occupations, neglects to acquire the knowledge which would restrain [him] from sin."[73] Eichmann was guilty on both accounts. He deliberately refused to inquire into the moral character of his military orders and developed a strategy of immersing himself totally in the details of his work. Hence his famous phrase: "Ich sass am Schreibtisch und machte meine Sachen" [I sat at my desk and did my work].[74] Facing up to the immorality of the "final solution" would have had devastating professional consequences for Eichmann. Instead, he deliberately and successfully averted his gaze from moral truths we are all obliged to know. He was voluntarily ignorant, and, as Aquinas argues, voluntary ignorance compounds the sin.

Eichmann reached the second level of achievement. If, however, Eichmann approved of his actions, if he did what he believed he ought to do, he did not successfully govern himself. Why? Because autonomy must entail, not a complacent self-satisfaction with the second level of achievement, but a striving toward the third level of achievement. It is not enough that we do what we believe we ought to do. We must continually reexamine our beliefs to see if they are true. We must be critical, attentive, and alive to discrepancy, rigorous and honest in self-scrutiny. Eichmann was none of these things. There is no indication that he had an *active* moral conscience. He acquiesced in his moral blindness.

And yet Eichmann was not an amoral man. He had a very definite moral view. In his trial, he insisted that he was morally *obliged* to carry out his duties as the head of section Iv B-4 of the Gestapo. Papadatos explains: "Eichmann . . . declared that during the whole of his life he had tried to follow the precepts of Kant and particularly the 'categorical imperative' of the great philosopher, according to which the principle of his will and that of his life should be such that they could at any moment be transformed into one general . . . principle."[75] Kant's original principle is: "Act only according to that maxim by which you can at the same time will that it should become a universal law of nature."[76] This became, to borrow Arendt's formulation, "Act as if the principle of your actions were the same as that of the legislator or the law of the land."[77] And then, in Hans Franck's formulation: "Act in such a way that the Führer, if he knew your action, would approve it."[78]

Eichmann's moral outlook was premised on a cult of blind obedience that left no room for autonomous decision-making. He carried out his superiors' orders instead of making decisions himself. It was his refusal to be autonomous, his unwillingness to govern himself, that led to his participation in the Jewish genocide. This is not to suggest that Eichmann cannot be held morally and legally responsible. Eichmann was guilty of cowardice. He did what all cowards do: he refused to do what was morally necessary.

Eichmann presents a disturbing foil to the good rebel. The good rebel exemplifies, in a conspicuous way, both freedom and morality. In the case of Eichmann, we have an agent who is immoral because he is not autonomous and not autonomous because he is immoral. Autonomy means choosing for oneself. And it means making the right choices. Eichmann, the reprehensible conformist, failed on both counts.

A PRAGMATIC ACCOUNT OF HUMAN IGNORANCE

Ignorance is a barrier to autonomy. Understood as a human fault, however, ignorance cannot be measured in absolute terms. There are definite limits to human knowledge. The achievement of autonomy requires intelligence and insight, but we cannot set our standards unrealistically high. Human beings cannot be expected to make their decisions from a God's-eye point of view. They cannot be expected to know everything.

Consider a true incident. A juvenile was brought before a Canadian provincial court judge on a charge of attempted murder. Bail was requested. The psychiatrists consulted all agreed that there was no chance that the youth would reoffend. The judge granted bail. Upon release, however, the youth immediately went out and murdered the original victim. In this particular case, the judge made the wrong decision. The youth should not have been released. Can we say that the judge acted in the right manner? In coming to his decision, did he successfully govern himself? Did he do what he ought to have done?

If the judge released the youth because he was incompetent, because he was a neighborhood friend, because he was too lazy to read the psychiatrist's report, this would constitute a serious breach of conduct. But in this particular case the judge carefully examined the psychiatric evidence and made, on the basis of the available evidence, the best possible decision. We can then say that the judge acted in a moral manner, that he successfully governed himself. He did, within the limits of human fallibility, what he ought to have done.

We cannot be held accountable for the unpredictable consequences of our acts. The judge in the previous example did the best he could. Viewed from the perspective of omniscience, he made the wrong decision. Viewed from the perspective of human fallibility, he successfully governed himself.

One way of dealing with the problem of "inevitable human ignorance" is to distinguish between "procedures" and "outcomes." Dewey argues that ideas are instruments. Roughly put, true ideas help us get things done. In an unpredictable world, however, good procedures occasionally result in bad outcomes. The judge in the previous example may have followed the proper decision-making procedure, but in this unfortunate instance, the proper procedure brought about the wrong outcome. When a bad outcome does not result from bad decision-making procedures but from factors beyond the agents' control, it is only right to absolve them of responsibility.[79]

A fallibilist approach to epistemology will solve, in a more general way, the problem of human ignorance. If there is an objective basis for values, objectivity must be defined, not in terms of perfect knowledge or absolute certitude, but in terms of reasonableness. The judge in the previous example did what was objectively right. In light of the information he had access to, he acted in a most reasonable manner. We cannot fault his decision-making process. In an imperfect world, successful self-government does not mean getting everything right. It means doing the best we can.

THE STORY OF HUCK FINN

Autonomy is not an ideal of simple permissiveness ("Anything goes"), nor an ideal of smug self-satisfaction ("I did what I thought I should do"), but an ideal of objective accomplishment ("I did, of my own accord, what I was required to do"). Autonomous agents must satisfy a subjective and an objective criterion of achievement. They must do what they approve of (the second level of achievement), and they must approve of the right things (the third level of achievement). To divorce autonomy from any objective notion of value is to trivialize the ideal. It is not enough that we realize our aspirations. We must have the right aspirations. We must do what is objectively right. We must do this, not accidentally, not because we are coerced, but because we are insightful enough to perceive the difference between right and wrong.

We have identified three distinct levels of achievement. On the first level, agents do not even aspire toward autonomy. They satisfy, in an uncritical manner, appetite. On the second level, they act in accordance with their own beliefs about the good. And on the third level, they, knowingly and willingly, achieve an objective good. Agents who fail to reach the second level suffer from *akrasia* or weakness of will. Agents who fail to reach the third level suffer from ignorance. We can represent this model as in table 9.

Table 9. A Three-Tiered Account of Autonomy

Levels of Achievement	Qualifications
First Level	uncritical behavior
Second Level	not weak-willed
Third Level	not weak-willed, not ignorant

On this model, there are two basic errors reflective agents can make: (1) they may be weak-willed or (2) they may be ignorant. We may ask ourselves: Which is the worse fault? Is it better to be weak-willed or ignorant? Aristotle[80] and Aquinas[81] both argue that it is better to be weak-willed. Ignorant agents are in a worse situation than weak-willed agents, because they identify with their wicked choice. Weak-willed agents, in contrast, distance themselves from their choices.[82] Moreover, ignorant agents do not know that they have done anything wrong and cannot regret their actions. At the very least, weak-willed agents regret their actions.[83]

Aristotle goes on to argue that ignorance is a permanent disease and that weakness of will is an intermittent condition.[84] The weak-willed agent is curable, whereas the ignorant agent is incurable.[85] It might be argued, however, that ignorance is a transitory condition, since the ignorant may be educated. A weak-willed agent, on the other hand, has a deformed character, a chronic condition that cannot be easily surmounted.[86] Aristotle and Aquinas both seem to assume that an ignorant agent will behave in an evil manner, but agents may be ignorant through no fault of their own. In exceptional cases, they may even act in an exemplary manner. Let us consult an illustrious example.

Huck Finn, the hero of Mark Twain's classic story, confronts a terrible predicament. The King, a petty criminal, has sold Jim, a runaway slave, for forty dollars. Huck decides that he will help Jim escape to freedom, but he has scruples. Freeing a captured slave is a seriously immoral act. It is, in his mind, akin to stealing another person's property. As Huck describes his troubled train of thought:

> The more I studied this the more my conscience went to grinding me, and the more wicked and low-down and ornery I got to feeling. And at last . . . it hit me all of a sudden that here was the plain hand of Providence slapping me in the face and letting me know . . . that people that acts as I'd been acting about that nigger goes to everlasting fire.[87]

Wrestling with his conscience, Huck decides to send Jim back into slavery. He begins to write a letter to Jim's original owner to inform her of his whereabouts when he has a sudden change of heart: "I studied a minute, sort of holding my breadth, and then says to myself: All right then, 'I'll go to hell'—and tore it up." Huck concludes with a painful meditation:

> It was awful thoughts and awful words but they was said. And I let them stay said: and never thought no more about reforming. I shoved the whole thing out of my head and said I would take up wickedness again, which was in my line, being brung up to it, and the other warn't. And for a starter I would go to work and steal Jim out of slavery again; and if I could think up anything worse, I would do that, too; because as long as I was in it for good, I might as well go the whole hog.[88]

What is happening here? Huck is unwittingly an ignorant agent. He does not see through the smoke screen of social convention. He wants to do the right thing, but the value system he has inherited tells him that the right thing is the wrong thing. So he decides to do the right thing, all the time thinking that it is the height of wickedness.

Huck is not a weak-willed agent. He does not do evil hesitantly. Once he makes up his mind to do evil, he decides to "go whole hog." Huck's problem is that he misconstrues the good. As a white resident of the American South in the pre–Civil War era, he has been inculcated with the wrong values. He is able to help Jim escape, but intellectually he is unable to escape the weight of social opinion.

Huck Finn is an ignorant agent, but he is an exemplary moral character. He is a compassionate individual. He has a good heart. It would be better if he came to understand the evil of slavery, but we forgive him for his ignorance, for he is only a boy. In this case, at least, ignorance seems a lesser fault than weakness of will. Suppose Huck felt he had to rescue Jim but was unable to do so because of a chronic weakness of character. He would, in this instance, be less than sympathetic. An ignorant agent who does good is surely better than a weak-willed agent who does evil.

Philosophers traditionally consider moral ignorance a more grievous fault than *akrasia*. This is entirely understandable. Philosophy emphasizes our capacity to know. To be unable to know is, from a philosopher's standpoint, to be annihilated as a rational being. To focus exclusively on ignorance or weakness of will is, in any case, misleading. One condition may lead to the other and vice versa. Neither is to be recommended. One does not want to be either ignorant or weak-willed. One wants to be autonomous.

Our conclusions can be represented as in table 10.

Table 10. The Two Faults that Prevent Autonomy

	W	not W
I	(1) nonautonomous	(2) nonautonomous
not I	(3) nonautonomous	(4) autonomous

W=weakness of will (*akrasia*, incontinence).
I=ignorance

The goal is square (4). One wants to exist in a state of "double negation." One wants to be neither ignorant nor weak-willed. This is true autonomy.

THE BUNDY CASE: COOPER AND FEINBERG

I have argued that an immoral agent cannot achieve autonomy. David Cooper and Joel Feinberg provide a more conventional account of the autonomy ideal. Though these authors are, in effect, moralists, they conceive of morality as something that exists separate and apart from autonomy. They do not view immorality as an obstacle to autonomy. Let us consider their individual views in some detail.

Cooper claims that morality is personal autonomy plus something else.[89] Autonomous agents gain "independent control of life."[90] Moral agents go further and control themselves in line with moral restrictions. If morality is an admirable goal, even an immoral agent can be autonomous. Cooper points to Ted Bundy, the convicted mass murderer and sexual deviant, as a possible example of an immoral autonomous individual. For Cooper, the fact that Bundy's activities were grossly immoral is beside the point. "By itself, personal autonomy is morally neutral; it is consistent with choosing good or bad, moral or immoral options."[91] Bundy was in control of his own life.[92] He was therefore autonomous. If Bundy is not an appropriate role model, this is because he was an immoral agent, not because he failed to be autonomous.

Cooper proposes two requirements for personal autonomy: (1) the autonomous agent must possess "a stable internal I"; (2) this "stable internal I" must be in "charge of decision-making."[93] This definition need not exclude sociopaths, for, as Cooper explains, "sociopaths . . . are controlled for the most part by their own internal beliefs . . . and do not act on whim or impulse any more than the rest of us."[94] If anything, a sociopath has an easier time conforming to his chosen value system and intended life plan. "Because a sociopath is not bothered by social emotions such as remorse or guilt, his life choices are simpler than the norm."[95] The sociopath's acts "can be consistently stable, under his own will and according to his belief system."[96] In other words, even he can be autonomous.

Joel Feinberg elaborates a very similar view. Feinberg insists, like Cooper, that an autonomous agent may be immoral. According to Feinberg, "No further analysis can be expected to rule out as impossible a selfish but autonomous person, a cold, mean, unloving but autonomous person, or a ruthless, or cruel autonomous person. After all, a self-governing person is no less self-governed if he governs himself badly, no less authentic for having evil principles, no less autonomous if he uses his autonomy to commit aggression against another autonomous person. The aggressor is morally deficient, but what he is deficient in is not necessarily autonomy. He may have more than enough of that."[97]

Authors like Cooper and Feinberg present a subjective account of autonomy. Autonomous agents satisfy their own private criteria for successful self-government. A sexual deviant like Bundy had, it seems, the wherewithal to achieve the goals he set for himself. If personal autonomy means living the life one wants to live, he achieved autonomy. In brutalizing unsuspecting young women, Bundy successfully governed himself. But this conclusion is not only morally repugnant. It presupposes a solipsistic view of personal achievement. Even if it turns out that Bundy thought he led a successful life, why should we accept Bundy's view of the situation?[98] If we want to determine whether a particular agent is autonomous, we must appeal to objective standards, not to the perhaps fallacious views of that individual agent. The standards Bundy applied to his own life are so outrageous, we cannot possibly use them ourselves.

On the theory I propose, Ted Bundy was not an autonomous individual. Consider a parallel example. Suppose Gerard is an alcoholic. Gerard mindlessly submerges himself in drink. What does it mean to say that Gerard is not autonomous? It means that Gerard is unable to take control of his life and make himself do what he ought to do. He is unable to master himself. And what about Bundy? Surely, it is precisely the same kind of situation. Bundy is a sexual fiend, someone who mindlessly submerges himself in the wrong kind of sex. What does it mean to say that Bundy is not autonomous? It means that Bundy is unable to take control of his life and force himself to do what he ought to do. He is unable to master himself. Even if Bundy mistakenly believes that he has mastered himself, why should we grant his opinions any credence? If Bundy approves of himself, this is further proof of his neurosis. It is not a legitimate gauge of successful self-government.

Gerard, the alcoholic, and Bundy, the sexual pervert, both lack autonomy. Imagine a social worker talking to Gerard: "This alcoholic thing is way out of line. If you're not able to control yourself, we'll have to put you under some sort of tutelage or in a private institution." This is perfectly intelligible discourse. The fact is that people like Gerard are sent to the local detox or the rehab center. And we put people like Bundy in prison. We institutionalize them because they are unable to govern themselves. In both cases, we take it upon ourselves to govern those who are, criminally or otherwise, incapable of self-government.

Feinberg writes: "[A] self-governing person is no less self-governed if he governs himself badly." It depends, of course, what we mean by "self-governed." Bundy may be held responsible for his actions. He was not legally insane. In this sense, he was self-governing. But this is not enough for autonomy. There are two aspects of successful self-government. In the first place, autonomous agents *govern* themselves. According to the *Random House College Dictionary*, to govern is "to exercise a directing or restraining influence over; guide; to hold in check; control."[99] Bundy did not exercise a directing or restraining influence over himself. He did not hold himself in check. He was unable to control his appetites in any appropriate fashion. He was not, in the relevant sense, self-*governed*.

In the second place, Bundy was not *self*-governed. To be *self*-governed is to be governed by the higher, human self, by a principle of intelligence, by a moral, spiritual, critical, and rational self. In Bundy's case, the human *self* did not govern. It did not, in the words of the *Oxford English Dictionary*, "sway, rule, influence, regulate, determine; be the predominating influence [for]."[100] Bundy may have done what he wanted to do, but he was not, in the appropriate sense, *self*-governed. This is why he was not autonomous.

Did Bundy, in any objective sense, lead a satisfactory life? Although the precise nature of his motivation is a matter for psychiatric investigation, we may envisage three possibilities. Bundy may have been a wanton, someone who did whatever he wanted to do. He may have been weak-willed. Or he may have been ignorant. Consider these three possibilities in order.

If Bundy was a wanton, then he did not even strive toward self-government. He uncritically satisfied his appetites like an animal or a nonrational being. He did not rise above the first level of achievement. He was not autonomous.

Perhaps then Bundy was weak-willed. Perhaps he realized his sexual desires were evil but could not control them. If, however, Bundy was weak-willed, he knew what the good was but he was unable to achieve it. Judged by his own aspirations, he failed horrendously. He was not autonomous. He did not reach the second level of achievement.

Perhaps then Bundy was ignorant. But such serious ignorance would be a definitive barrier to autonomy. If Bundy sincerely believed he was leading an acceptable kind of life, he was wildly mistaken. In pursuing the good, he was distracted by a false good. For one reason or another, he choose the wrong goals, the wrong aspirations. Judged by his own aspirations,—he wanted to achieve the good—he failed at self-government. He was not autonomous. He did not reach the third level of achievement.

Whether Bundy was a wanton, a weak-willed, or an ignorant agent, the conclusion remains the same. He was not an autonomous agent. In a case like Bundy's, we have an example of a monstrously-misguided individual who is incapable of personal merit or human excellence. Bundy was not just morally but psychologically dysfunctional. His failure at common decency was so extreme, he was hardly human.

Feinberg tells us that autonomous agents may be selfish, cold, mean, unloving, ruthless, cruel, and so on. There are two ways to interpret his claim. Feinberg may be arguing that we can call agents autonomous *because* they are selfish, cold, mean, and so on. Or he may be arguing that we can call agent autonomous *in spite of the fact* that they are selfish, cold, mean, etc. Although the second claim is easier to defend, it is a much weaker claim. Consider these two interpretations of Feinberg's argument.

Does it make sense to argue that agents are autonomous *because* they are selfish, cold, mean, unloving, ruthless, or cruel, and so on? To link negative character traits to the concept of self-mastery seems dubious. Consider, for instance, selfishness. How could we argue that Germaine is autonomous *because* she is selfish? This could only mean that Germaine wants, in some critical sense, to be selfish; that in being selfish, she realizes her aspiration toward selfishness. But selfishness is not a personal ideal. A Nietzsche or an Ayn Rand might contend—with telltale exaggeration or even hysteria—that selfishness is a virtue. But this is to play with words. Nietzsche and Rand bend the meaning of language to a rhetorical purpose. Nietzsche's Zarathustra blesses "the wholesome, healthy selfishness that wells from a powerful soul,"[101] and Rand goes so far as to entitle one of her books *The Virtue of Selfishness*.[102] But even these authors do not believe that we should display an *excessive* amount of self-concern. What they believe is that we should display more self-concern than conventional *bourgeois* society considers proper. But this is just another way of saying that what society considers to be excessive is not really excessive.

The term "selfishness" denotes an *excessive* amount of self-concern. This is what the word literally means. To argue that Germaine is autonomous *because* she is selfish is to say that she has successfully governed herself because she displays an *excessive* amount of self-concern. This is a contradiction in terms.

Negative character traits like selfishness are self-admitted failures, character faults, shortcomings, deficiencies, sins. They are not the goals of self-realization. They are not the things we strive toward. To suggest that a negative character trait like selfishness may be a manifestation of autonomy is to change the original meaning of the term. One could perhaps argue that no amount of self-concern can be considered excessive, but this would be to argue that there is no such thing as "excessive self-concern," that is, there is no such thing as selfishness.

Negative character traits do not provide evidence of successful self-government. To say that I am selfish, cold, mean, unloving, ruthless, cruel, and so on, is to enounce a negative opinion about my behavior. It is to disapprove of my acts. But to say that I act in the wrong way and that I successfully govern myself would be inconsistent. To the degree that I exhibit negative character traits, I must be either weak-willed or ignorant. I do not do what I ought to do. I am not autonomous.

The first reading of Feinberg fails. What about the second? If agents cannot be autonomous *because* they are selfish, cold, mean, unloving, ruthless, cruel, and so on, can they be autonomous *in spite of the fact* that they are selfish, cold, mean, unloving, ruthless, cruel, and so on? Here two points must be made. On the one hand, an agent may have minor failings and still be autonomous. On the other hand, an agent cannot be seriously immoral and autonomous. Autonomous agents may have conspicuous imperfections, but they cannot be egregiously immoral.

Consider first the case of minor imperfections. Autonomy is an ideal that is never perfectly realized. Minor flaws are an inevitable aspect of any human life. I may say that although George was a coward, he was such a kindhearted and generous person, one would have to consider his life a success. The important thing is that imperfections like George's cowardice do not add to the agent's autonomy. They detract from it. But perhaps they do not detract enough to destroy any claim to successful self-government. Just where one draws the line between minor imperfections and serious immorality—between mortal and venial sins—is difficult to answer in the abstract, but in point of fact we do make these distinctions. We say that certain people led good but imperfect lives and that other people led lives that cannot, in any sense, be condoned.

Consider, second, the case of serious immorality. Some moral lapses are so extreme, they eliminate all possibility of successful self-government. Suppose that Professor Bob is a extremely kind and considerate university professor who happens to be a serial killer. It does not matter how wonderful the rest of Professor Bob's life seems to be. Being a serial killer is such a categorical evil, it is absolutely incompatible with successful self-government. Feinberg and Cooper argue that an agent who is a complete moral failure may be autonomous. This seems incredible. Serious immorality is a definitive barrier to autonomy. A successful human agent must (1) be true to some interior sense of morality (the argument from authenticity), (2) choose the good (the argument from good), and 3) be a virtuous person (the argument from virtue). One cannot be a serious moral failure and, at the same time, successfully govern oneself.

Authors like Feinberg and Cooper compartmentalize life. One can be seriously immoral—that is, fail completely in the moral department—and still achieve personal self-fulfillment. I have argued against this artificial restriction of the moral perspective, providing a much broader definition of morality. To successfully govern oneself is to do something excellent, good, worthwhile, noble, or meritorious. But to do something excellent, good, worthwhile, noble, meritorious is what it means to be moral. Autonomy presupposes morality. A morality of authenticity posits self-realization as the end of all human achievement and bridges the gap between morality and autonomy.

Cooper expresses an admiration for Kant, but to define morality as personal autonomy plus something else is to miss a central point of Kant's analysis. For Kant, morality is not something added on to freedom. *It is freedom itself.* For Kant, there are not two different freedoms—a rational freedom and a moral freedom, a freedom that involves matters of bare fact and a freedom that involves values. For Kant true freedom involves rationality *and* morality. The free agent, the agent who masters himself, is, by necessity, autonomous, rational, and moral.

7

Normative Accounts of Freedom

OBJECTIVE THEORIES OF FREEDOM

One may distinguish between "internalist" and normative theories of personal autonomy. On an "internalist" theory, autonomous agents realize their own aspirations. On a normative theory, autonomous agents realize their own aspirations, but they also satisfy some objective criterion of excellence. They must act in a manner that coheres, not only with their own personal views, but with what is reasonable to believe about the world.

Although autonomy is often portrayed as the satisfaction of those criteria for success one sets for oneself, there are other alternatives. Classical authors such as Socrates, Aristotle, the Stoics, Aquinas, Kant, and Mill define personal autonomy in objective terms. Contemporary authors such as Moore, Taylor, Haworth, Swanton, Barry, Murdoch, Naess, and Noddings implicitly or explicitly follow suit. We have already explained how moral insights from Socrates and Aristotle can contribute to an objective theory of autonomy. Consider next the notion of natural law that surfaces most forcefully in the Stoics, in Cicero, and in Aquinas.[1]

NATURAL LAW: AQUINAS

I have proposed the good rebel as the model of the autonomous agent. Natural law theorists do not employ the word autonomy. They do, however, recognize the importance of good rebellion. Aquinas is most forthright on this point. Agents who find themselves in an evil state must ignore the dictates of government and obey those objective moral standards they somehow discover within themselves. Unjust laws "do not oblige the court of conscience,"[2] and in the case of laws contrary to God, "to observe them is in no wise permissible."[3]

Natural law theory avoids the extremes of subjectivism and social relativism. Good rebels do not, in any simple sense, do whatever they want to do. Nor do they, in any simple sense, do what society wants them to do. The criterion for successful self-government is not self-approval nor the approval of society. In searching inward, agents discover an *objective* criterion of the good. In so much as their actions conform to this objective standard, they successfully govern themselves.

The Stoics, Cicero, and Aquinas equate morality with reason. The Stoics identify the natural law with the *logos*, the divine order or pattern that pervades the cosmos. According to Cicero: "[Natural] law is the highest reason, implanted in Nature, which commands what ought to be done and forbids the opposite."[4] For Aquinas, the natural law is a participation in the Divine Reason.[5] In each case, to obey the natural law is to obey something beyond oneself. The moral laws agents discover inside themselves have an independent, objective reality. They are valid moral laws, not simply because the agent simply believes in them, but because they conform, at the very deepest level, to nature itself.

In natural law theory we have, long before Kant, a moral theory that identifies freedom, morality, and rationality. In obeying the prescriptions of the natural law, moral agents obey themselves, for the natural law is incorporated within human nature. As Cicero insists: "Whoever is disobedient [to the natural law] is fleeing from himself and denying his human nature."[6] Natural law theory could serve as the basis for an objective theory of autonomy.

KANT AND NIETZSCHE

Kant elaborates, in the most explicit terms, an objective account of autonomy. To be autonomous is to obey the categorical imperative. Agents who obey the categorical imperative are free, for in obeying the imperative they obey themselves. Immoral agents like Bundy are not self-governed, for, in repudiating morality, they repudiate their own nature.

Kant argues for the conjunction of morality, rationality and autonomy. Autonomous agents are free, not because they do what they want to do, but because they obey the moral law. The principle moral fault for Kant is weakness of will. Rational agents, by definition, know the moral law. They cannot be accused of ignorance. They must, however, strive against inclination in order to do their duty. This is, at times, an arduous task. Those who fail lack the necessary will. They lack strength of character. They perceive the good but, for self-interested reasons, they are unable to accomplish it.

Kant's theory is problematic, for he adopts a very narrow view of both rationality and morality. In submitting to the categorical imperative, moral agents are not motivated by enthusiasm, natural temperament, love, indignant righteousness, inspiration, a sense of the beautiful, or moral intuition, but by an almost mechanical obedience to a moral law that is insensitive to individual circumstances or concrete particulars.

Among his many critics, Nietzsche in particular attacks Kant's moral philosophy with a vengeance, dismissing it as a corrosive, dehumanizing force that grinds men down, turning them into machines, making them dull, stupid, and herdlike. In *Twilight of the Idols*, Nietzsche imagines an exchange between an oral examiner and a Ph.D. candidate. In this biting piece of satire, the candidate gives all the right answers:

> What is the task of higher education?
> To turn men into machines.
> What are the means?
> Man must learn to be bored.
> How is that accomplished?
> By means of the concept of duty.
> Who serves as the model?
> The philologist: he teaches grinding.
> Who is the perfect man?
> The civil servant.
> Which philosophy offers the highest formula for the civil servant?
> Kant's: the civil servant as a thing-in-itself raised up to be judge over the civil servant as phenomenon.[7]

Kant's morality is, for Nietzsche, a morality of bookworms, philologists, bureaucrats, and civil servants. Yet Nietzsche, who despises Kant, still manages to display a parallel preoccupation with autonomy. Nietzsche disdains conformity and glorifies conspicuous, radical, uncompromising individuality. There is one all-important duty: great men must be true to themselves. Over and over again, Nietzsche stresses the importance of authenticity. Human beings exist as individuals. Each individual is unique, this uniqueness imposes a duty, and the rare individual who understands and fulfills this duty is transfigured in a quasi-supernatural way. In a panegyric to Schopenhauer, Nietzsche writes: "Each of us bears a productive uniqueness within him at the core of his being: and when he becomes aware of it, there appears around him a strange penumbra which is the mark of his singularity. Most find this something unendurable because they are . . . lazy, and because a chain of toil and burdens is suspended from this uniqueness."[8] Uniqueness, individuality, self-identity, is, for Nietzsche, the source of all value. Being true to oneself is an arduous, almost impossible task, but it is the only thing that has merit or worth. Self-realization is the epitome of human achievement.

Nietzsche jettisons what he sees as a morality of repression in favor of a morality of self-realization. His thought is complex and perhaps paradoxical. Although he appears to reject objective notions of truth in favor of an unrestrained subjectivism, he formulates objective standards for human achievement when he discusses themes like eternal recurrence, the master-slave morality, the overman, the last man, the herd. In *Ecce Homo* then Nietzsche discloses his "formula for greatness in a human being . . . that one wants nothing to be different, not forward, not backward, not in all eternity. Not merely bear what is necessary . . . but love it."[9] On Nietzsche's account, great men affirm life, its pains as well as joys. They do not regret, complain, feel self-pity. They *embrace* eternal recurrence. Herd-members, the last men, those who embrace the slave morality, those who cultivate ressentiment represent all that is contemptible in human endeavor.

Although Nietzsche is less than systematic, he proposes in unequivocal terms an *objective* standard of excellence or merit, a moral ideal, that we can use to measure human achievement. Those who repudiate this standard only demonstrate their own inadequacies. Their refusal to subscribe to this value system does not, in the least, detract from the validity of the value system itself. It only contributes to their own mediocrity.

Nietzsche articulates a renegade morality that allows us to distinguish between those who do and do not successfully govern themselves. One could use the normative criteria he supplies, in a more systematic way, to provide an objective account of autonomy. Authors like Kierkegaard and Heidegger are engaged in a similar endeavor. In Kierkegaard's case, the so-called Knight of Faith is the personification of a value system that could be used to measure and evaluate individual endeavor.

Although Kant is astute enough to perceive a connection between autonomy, morality, and rationality, his view needs to be supplemented by a more expansive view of morality, one that is sensitive to the importance of individual character. Nietzsche fills in the picture with a fervent plea for individuality. A liberal author like John Stuart Mill elaborates, in more measured tones, a similar view, one that privileges values of individuality, authenticity, and nonconformity.

HEROIC INDIVIDUALISM: JOHN STUART MILL

John Stuart Mill's *On Liberty* represents a watershed in philosophical literature on individual freedom.[10] Mill is not only a utilitarian and a political liberal. He is also a romantic. In John Rees's words: "What is said to make for the special quality of *On Liberty* . . . lie[s] in [Mill's] affirmation of a romantic notion of individuality."[11]

Mill's account of individuality provides us with an objective account of autonomy. We can distinguish between a utilitarian Mill and a romantic Mill. For Mill the utilitarian, the aim of a civilized society is the production of the greatest possible happiness. For Mill the romantic, the aim of a civilized society is the creation of heroic individuals. The utilitarian Mill articulates a liberal morality of social obligation; the romantic Mill subscribes to a kind of virtue ethics.[12] This second Mill is more concerned with character formation than with any hedonist calculus. As he himself maintains: "It really is of importance, not only what men do, but also what manner of men they are that do it."[13] For the romantic Mill, the goal of life is not primarily the building of beautiful houses, poems, machines, hospitals, whatever. It is, more properly, the building up of man. As Mill himself insists: "Among the works of man, which human life is rightly employed in perfecting and beautifying, the first surely in importance is man himself."[14]

Although Mill recognizes the importance of individual flourishing, he never develops this, in any explicit, systematic sense, as a *moral* view. But Mill's account of human nature encloses a moral ideal. As Lancaster explains: "When [Mill] insists that the character of a man is of equal importance with his acts; and when he speaks wistfully of the kinds of men and women that 'nature can and will produce,' he is voicing moral aspirations."[15] The romantic Mill elaborates an objective ideal of heroic individuality, prizing values such as mental vigor, strength of character, moral courage, individual genius, tolerance, self-reliance, reasonableness, conscientiousness,[16] eccentricity,[17] and nonconformism.[18] These are, on Mill's account, moral attributes. To possess strength of character is to overcome weakness of will. To possess individual genius is to further knowledge and overcome ignorance. Tolerance is a moral attitude. Moral courage, conscientiousness, and self-reliance are virtues. And so on. One could use these criteria to elaborate a normative account of successful self-government.

If I present the good rebel as a model par excellence for personal autonomy, this is in keeping with Mill's creed of heroic individualism. We will discuss the problem of negative liberty below, but Mill's no-harm principle is, in any case, a political principle. We may not have the right to interfere with someone else's behavior, but this does not mean that we have to admire him or her. The whole point of negative liberty is not negative liberty but personal autonomy. In Mill's words, citizens must be allowed to express "all that is individual in themselves" so that they can become "noble and beautiful object[s] of contemplation."[19] To make one-self into a noble and beautiful object of contemplation is, in modern termi-nology, to achieve autonomy.

OBJECTIVE VALUE: CHARLES TAYLOR

The philosophers we have discussed provide normative accounts of free-dom. The contemporary Canadian philosopher Charles Taylor does not provide any overt evaluation of human achievement. He is interested in metaethics rather than normative ethics. Though Taylor's project is de-scriptive rather than normative, he elaborates the most influential defense of objectivity in modern philosophy. Taylor defends the rationality of value discourse. In a wide-ranging opus, he critiques the rise of a modern subjec-tivism, openly acknowledges the connection between freedom and moral-ity, and reasserts the importance of objective values that transcend the self. Let us consider only briefly Taylor's understanding of individual freedom.

Taylor speaks of "authenticity" as *the* modern ideal. At the same time, he vigorously criticizes a modern preoccupation with self that neglects our connections to outside reality, to community, to history, to religious truth—in short, to anything that transcends the self. Taylor calls this "descent into subjectivity" the "malaise of modernity."[20] He argues that the authenticity ideal—that we should be true to ourselves—does not have to be jettisoned. It needs instead to be rescued from a facile subjectivism that has overrun modern culture. In Taylor's words: "The struggle ought not to be *over* au-thenticity, for or against, but *about* it, defining its proper meaning. We ought to be trying to lift the culture back up, closer to its motivating ideal."[21]

Taylor situates the authenticity-ideal within an "objective" theory of value. Value must not be rooted in arbitrary choice, but in an encounter with an objective world, a world that provides a criterion for belief inde-pendent of our own preferences and ideals. Taylor presents four arguments in favor of objectivity: developing a doctrine of self-referentiality, offering a critique of radical choice, pointing to the presence of a "preexisting hori-zon of significance," and formulating a theory of strong and weak evalua-tion. Let's examine these themes in order.

Taylor's doctrine of self-referentiality rests on a distinction between the manner and content of action. To inquire about the *manner* in which the agent acts is to ask whether agents act freely.[22] To inquire about the content of an action is to ask about the values the action embodies, the intellectual considerations that prompted it, the goal toward which it is directed. Taylor argues that modern discourse conflates these aspects of human agency. If the actions of an autonomous agent must originate in an individual will, they must, at the same time, connect up to a larger sphere of values and issues that transcend the self. If the *manner* of action must be self-referential, the *content* of an action must connect with something outside the self. Taylor argues, then, for a self-referentiality of will but not for a self-referentiality of content.

When self-referentiality of will is confused with self-referentiality of content, the call to authenticity degenerates into a narrow egoism. But egoism is self-defeating. As Taylor points out, a meaningful existence cannot be based on values that are centered exclusively on self.[23] Self-fulfillment comes about not through a self-centered concern for private well-being, but through an enlightened submission to ends, causes, groups, and issues that transcend the self. Truly human action must be self-motivated, but it must also link up to objective values that are larger than the self. Properly understood, autonomous human endeavor should not be a means of isolating individuals but a way of integrating them into a larger web of social, cultural, and moral concerns.

Taylor's criticism of a self-referentiality of content is motivated by a moral and a psychological concern. In his critique of "radical choice" he turns to epistemological matters. The idea of a radical moral choice has been identified with Nietzsche.[24] On such a theory, moral values "issue ultimately from a radical choice, . . . a choice which is not grounded in reasons."[25] The individual wills into existence—through a completely arbitrary act of will—a value system. All subsequent value judgments derive their authority from this initial choice.[26] We are left with a system of morality that is grounded, not on an objective notion of reality or moral belief, but on a gratuitous and purely subjective act of will.

Jean-Paul Sartre brings up the example of a young man who, at the time of the German occupation of France, "is torn between remaining with his ailing mother and going off to join the Resistance."[27] Sartre argues that there is no rational way of adjudicating between these competing moral claims. The young man must choose, through a raw exercise of will, between incommensurable alternatives. He must simply throw himself one way or the other. There is no room here for objectivity, for reasoning, for philosophy. All he is left with is pure choice.

Sartre points to the young man's moral dilemma as an example of a radical moral choice. But, as Taylor observes, the salient feature of the circumstance is the forced nature of the predicament. The young man is caught between two contradictory moral imperatives. He *must* care for his ailing mother and he *must* defend his country. It is not a question of doing one or the other. He *must* do both but he cannot. Hence his predicament. If, however, morality was a matter of radical choice, the young man "could do away with the dilemma at any moment by simply declaring one of the rival claims as dead and inoperative."[28] In point of fact, he cannot will either moral claim away. These moral claims are forced upon him by the nature of the world, the human condition, and the nature of the reasoning process.

As Taylor demonstrates, moral dilemmas are a potent reminder, not of the arbitrary nature of morals, but of the objective content of morality. We do not choose. Morality is forced upon us. If morality was ultimately arbitrary, moral dilemmas could, in principle, be willed into existence. The young man in Sartre's example might have a moral dilemma, not just about staying with his mother or going off to war, but about whether he should buy strawberry or chocolate ice cream.[29] He could will into existence a strawberry morality and a chocolate morality and be caught between them. But morality does not work that way. For all but the mentally ill, selecting different flavors of ice cream is not a moral issue. It cannot be, for we cannot invent morals through an arbitrary act of will.

Taylor argues that ethical decision-making is never, in any healthy, normal sense, a question of creating values ex nihilo. One may modify already existing values so as to gain a new value perspective, but the process of ethical choice never begins with a state of absolute noncommitment. There is no such thing as a valueless prechoice state. Values are not an option. To possess a personal identity is to have values. We cannot remove our values and commitments the way we remove our clothes and stand there completely undressed. As Taylor explains: "The agent of radical choice would be . . . utterly without identity . . . a kind of extensionless point, a pure leap into the void. But such a thing is an impossibility, or rather could only be the description of the most terrible mental alienation."[30] Even if one could begin from zero and make a radical choice of values, one would have to destroy oneself in order to do this.

On the Nietzschean model of radical choice, an object possesses value because we have decided to attribute value to it. On Taylor's model, personal choice does not bestow value. Personal choice is a way of moving toward that which possesses value apart from our own desires and volitions. What we choose is not valuable *because* we choose it. Rather, we are called on to choose that which is, in some independent sense, already valuable.[31]

In elaborating an account of moral choice, Taylor, à la Heidegger, situates the agent within "a pre-existing horizon of significance."[32] What determines whether a particular fact possesses moral significance for an agent is the place it occupies with respect to this horizon of significance. It is this preexisting structure of meaning, not the will of the agent, that determines the content of our moral judgments. As Taylor observes, there is an inalienable connection between what the world is and what morality is. We cannot arbitrarily decide that a particular fact is going to have moral significance. Insomuch as the world possesses a certain nature, we will be compelled to apportion value in specific ways.

Suppose, for example, I were to claim that I am a moral person because I have exactly 3,732 hairs on my head.[33] The suggestion that personal merit is related to the number of hairs on my head cannot be taken seriously. It is a ludicrous idea. Suppose, however, that the quantity of hair on one's head could be linked, in some important way, to a larger explanation of the world. Perhaps I belong to a religious sect that believes that the Messiah will have exactly 3,732 hairs on his head. Within the parameters of this (admittedly crazy) belief system, a claim about the number of hairs on my head would carry authentic moral force. The argument that I am a good person because I have exactly 3,732 hairs on my head would suddenly be rendered intelligible. It would still be a ridiculous claim, but it would, at least, be intelligible. And it would be intelligible because it ties up with an explanation of the way the world is. Moral discourse is then anything but arbitrary. It must have an objective foundation in a reasonable explanation of the world.

Finally, Taylor distinguishes between two methods of ethical judgment. Weak evaluation is about satisfying preferences. One chooses the course of action that satisfies one's desires to the utmost. Strong evaluation is about becoming the right kind of person. One refrains from acting on a particular desire, not because it produces a smaller quantity of pleasurable sensations, but because the desire is "bad, base, ignoble, trivial, superficial, unworthy, and so on."[34]

Taylor is a vigorous proponent of strong evaluation. Weak evaluation reduces rational decision-making to a quantitative tabulation. It is the sum total of satisfying sensations that counts. Strong evaluation eschews the numerical. One articulates judgments about right or wrong in a qualitative language that escapes quantification. Actions are characterized by their "contrastive" qualities. They are noble or base, integrating or fragmenting, clairvoyant or blind, courageous or cowardly, generous or niggardly. Taylor insists that these "contrastive" terms should not be understood as covert references to different degrees of pleasure but as the names of different kinds of things. Strong evaluations identify the properties of different kinds of acts. They do more than measure different degrees of desirability.

Taylor contends that the modern emphasis on quantitative distinctions has led to an impoverishment of moral discourse. Weak evaluation is an ethics of inarticulateness. In overlooking the descriptive, nonquantitative character of human motivation, the weak evaluator misses out on a crucial aspect of human agency. Strong evaluation, on the other hand, provides us with a moral vocabulary that can be used to express sophisticated attitudes of approval or disapproval.[35]

A pronounced shift from strong to weak evaluation in modern moral discourse represents a movement towards solipsism. Weak evaluation is a self-centered value system. An object is good because I desire it. The more I desire this object, the more valuable it becomes. In strong evaluation, an object is not good because I desire it. To say that an object is good is to say that I *ought* to desire it. Strong evaluations "involve discriminations of right or wrong . . . which are not rendered valid by our own desires, inclinations, or choices, but rather stand independent of those and offer standards by which they can be judged."[36] In the case of strong evaluation, value does not attach to objects, people, or actions because of our idiosyncratic desires or opinions. Value attaches to objects because of what they objectively are. Value does not arise out of the agent's act of evaluation. It is an inherent feature of the world.

Taylor presents an objective account of values. Values connect up with something larger than the self; they are forced upon us by our understanding of the world; they are necessary rather than arbitrary, and they cannot be reduced to mere preference satisfaction. It follows, on this view, that self-approval is not enough. To make ourselves the center of the moral universe is to buy into a degenerate culture of authenticity. Praiseworthy endeavor has to meet objective norms, norms that can be discovered through some rigorous reasoning process.

Taylor provides the framework for an objective account of personal autonomy. Agents who do not engage in strong evaluation are ignorant. Agents who master a legitimate moral vocabulary but are unable to live by the corresponding values are weak-willed. Both kinds of agents fail at successful self-government. They are not autonomous.

INTRINSIC VALUE: MOORE

Taylor's theory of strong evaluation has a historical precedent. Early in this century, American and British philosophers such as G. E. Moore, William Ross, and Ralph Perry[37] discussed the question of "whether or not a good thing has its value as a result of . . . the desire someone has for it."[38] As Christine Korsgaard reports, Moore and Ross proposed an "intrinsic" theory of the good, arguing that the value of an object "has nothing to do with mental attitudes shown towards things at all."[39] These philosophers believed, like Taylor, that an object has value, not because agents take an interest in it, but because of the inherent goodness of its nature.

Moore argues for an objective notion of value. It is not the attitude we take toward a particular object that determines its value. Value is not something we project onto an object. It is an intrinsic property of the object itself. According to this theory, agents who successfully govern themselves would be neither weak-willed nor ignorant. They would know the true value of objects and act accordingly.

There are, however, problems with Moore's theory. He claims, for example, that the value of a particular object must be the same for everyone. "So long as the thing remains what it is, it has the same value: the value is the same . . . for everyone."[40] But surely, value changes according to the circumstances. A glass of water will possess a different value in the desert or in a flood. Although there may be transcendental objects, objects that possess the same value for all agents in all circumstances, the value of ordinary objects may change according to circumstance. Value might be compared to a physical property like weight. A bowling ball weighs less on the moon than on the earth. Nonetheless, the weight of the bowling ball is an inherent feature of its existence. It is not something we project onto the bowling ball according to our will and fancy.

To say that there is an objective criterion for value is not to say that an object must have the same value for everyone. It is only to say that the degree to which a particular agent or group of agents values an object does not determine the degree to which it *ought* be valued. Agents may value an object to the right extent; then again they may not. To ask "How much is an object worth?" and "How much do these people value it?" is to ask two different questions. We are all fallible. We may be guilty, not just of *akrasia*, but of ignorance. As Moore intimates, the evaluations of fallible agents may be seriously mistaken.

Moore and Taylor propose an objective theory of value. What determines the extent to which we should value a particular object is not the degree to which we actually do value it but the nature of the object and the circumstance, the way things really are. Seen from the vantage point of this kind of theory, human achievement is not a matter of self-approval but of objective success.

SUBJECTIVE AND OBJECTIVE VALUE: RORTY AND TAYLOR

Compare Taylor's views to those of Richard Rorty. Taylor situates his view of individual freedom within an objective theory of values. Good rebellion becomes an epistemological endeavor, a way of directing attention toward or recuperating objective moral values. Good rebels rediscover or discern objective standards of the good that exist apart from our own opinions and offer criteria by which our own opinions are to be judged. They champion these values in the face of corruption, apathy, or social ignorance. They reach through the fog of prejudice and consensus and grapple, in some more immediate and intimate way, with the world as it really is.

Rorty dismisses the notion of objective value. He defines objectivity in terms of consensus. But this subverts the notion of good rebellion. To strive toward objectivity is to move toward consensus, to try and act in accordance with the opinions of most people. But this is a definition of conformism, not of individual freedom. So Rorty reduces rebellion to an entirely subjective response devoid of objective validity. This is to trivialize the notion of good rebellion.

Contemporary philosophical discussions of autonomy grew out of a 1960s preoccupation with the moral ideal of nonconformity, but this kind of heroic nonconformism means more than being different from other people. Jeffrey Dahlmer, the Milwaukee murderer who cannibalized his victims, was different from other people, but he was not, in any praiseworthy sense, a nonconformist. Nonconformism, of any praiseworthy sort, brings together uniqueness *and* goodness. The ideal nonconformist is a good rebel who breaks with the conventions of society for the sake of an objective good.

Rorty and Taylor propose different views of individual freedom, because they adopt different epistemologies. Rorty thinks of freedom in negative terms. In his words: "My own hunch, or at least hope, is that our culture is gradually coming to be structured around the idea of freedom—of leaving people alone to dream and think and live as they please, so long as they do not hurt other people."[41] On Rorty's theory, free agents do as they please. But some ways of pleasing ourselves are vicious, dishonorable, mediocre, base, cowardly, self-indulgent, and so on. Freedom cannot be defined solely in terms of agent self-approval.

Taylor criticizes postmodernist authors like Derrida, Lyotard, and Foucault because they present individual freedom as an unconstrained, utterly self-sufficient idea, unregulated by any idea of the good.[42] Rorty maintains that "freedom can stand on its own two feet."[43] But the idea of freedom needs to be supported by a robust conception of the good. Negative freedom, the freedom to do as we please, needs to be complemented by a parallel notion of moral responsibility. One cannot be free unless one is, in the broadest sense, a rational and a moral agent.

In a book on personal autonomy, Lawrence Haworth defines autonomy as a form of "sensitivity to feedback."[44] Some contemporary authors define autonomy in terms of self-approval, but Haworth emphasizes the relationship between the self and the outside world of which the self forms a part. Critical reflection is not uniquely centered on the self. There is something outside the agent—the environment—that provides a criterion for successful action. Every individual agent is radically situated within a culture, a time period, a natural order, a political order, and perhaps within a spiritual order. Self-mastery manifests itself not solely through bouts of introspection but also through an outward focus on other agents, institutions, circumstances, and things. Successfully choosing a way of life does not mean dwelling on one's own internal desires and volitions. It means turning one's attention to and interacting with the outside world.

Haworth is an avid student of Dewey, who distinguishes between "two modes of freedom, namely, intelligent choice and power in action."[45] Agents who make intelligent choices do not suffer from ignorance, whereas agents who put those choices into action do not suffer from weakness of will. Haworth, in line with this tradition, stresses the interaction between agents and their environment. He defines autonomy as the adoption of a successful strategy for living. Successful agents respond to their environments in appropriate ways. Unsuccessful agents ignore important warning signals and court self-destruction.

Haworth's explanation supplies an analytic tool that can be applied to difficult cases. It repairs deficiencies in other contemporary accounts of personal autonomy. Consider the case of Harold Parker, a mental patient who suffered from an obsessive compulsive personality disorder. As the authors of one psychology textbook explain:

> A business manager, Harold Parker, developed an intricate system of rituals that he used to ward off bad luck, bad thoughts, or bad feelings. When his plant manager, Edgar, first told him his company was failing, Parker started chanting to himself, "Edgar will have his health, Harold will have his wealth," and he would touch something solid twice, once with his right foot and once with his left. Over the years he developed more and more such magical rituals, to the point where he spent most of his time thinking about the rituals and little time thinking about his real problems.[46]

Obviously, Harold is not a successful human being. Something has gone wrong. There is something disastrously amiss in his life. There is something about the decision-making process he participates in that undermines his ability to govern himself. Harold is a dysfunctional agent; he needs psychiatric help; he is not autonomous. And yet some contemporary theories cannot account for his lack of autonomy.

Gerald Dworkin, in an influential series of texts, proposes two criteria for personal autonomy.[47] Firstly, he argues that autonomous agents must act in an authentic manner. They must identify with their actions. But Harold identifies with his actions. When he recites his magic spells, this is precisely what Harold, in his heart of hearts, wants to do. These are his real desires. This is authentically Harold. If, however, Harold identifies with his magic rituals, this does not make him autonomous.[48]

Secondly, Dworkin argues that the actions of the autonomous individual must be procedurally independent, that the agent must not be forced or coerced by other agents into doing whatever he is doing. But Harold is acting freely, without external constraint. No one has forced Harold to perform magic rituals. He has chosen, of his own accord, this unhealthy course of action. Although Harold acts in a manner that is procedurally independent, this does not make him autonomous.

Harold satisfies both of Dworkin's criteria. Nonetheless, he lacks autonomy. The problem is that Dworkin's criteria are entirely subjective. We need to invoke objective standards of achievement if we want to understand what is wrong with Harold's actions. Why is Harold not autonomous? Because autonomy presupposes, in Haworth's phrase, a successful strategy for living. Self-will is not the sole criterion of individual achievement. An agent is situated in a surrounding world, and the reality of that world—the way it acts upon the agent—provides an objective criterion of success.

Harold lacks autonomy because he is, to use Haworth's formula, insensitive to feedback. Harold's magic rituals do not solve his personal problems, yet Harold goes on acting as if they did. Harold is too self-absorbed to notice the way in which his environment thwarts his efforts. He continues to persist in a course of action that brings him no positive results. Tapping something solid with the right foot and left foot does not produce wealth. Harold's byzantine rituals have had no appreciable effect on his financial life. If anything, they have been a fatal, time-consuming distraction. Harold has not learned from his mistakes, from his failures. This is why he does not successfully govern himself.

Haworth, like Taylor, supplies an objective criterion of autonomy. Harold is a strong-willed agent. He is persistent and thorough in his projects. The problem is that he is interacting with his environment in an uninsightful and entirely fruitless manner. In the real, nonmagical world in which we live, Harold's actions are impractical, a distraction, a recipe for failure. Harold is an ignorant agent. This is why he lacks autonomy.

WOLF'S SANITY REQUIREMENT

I have already criticized the narrowness of Susan Wolf's view of morality. In her discussion of autonomy, however, Wolf does provide an objective account of human achievement.[49] Wolf posits sanity as a necessary condition for autonomy. In order to qualify as an autonomous individual, an agent must satisfy some objective requirement of psychological health or epistemic reasonableness. It will follow that a neurotic agent like Harold cannot be autonomous.

Mental illness may be considered from a psychological or an epistemic point of view. Considered from the psychological viewpoint, the insane suffer from weakness of will. The seriously neurotic are prey to a kind of psychic disintegration. They are, in Wolf's words, cut off from their "deep selves." "Their wills are governed . . . by forces external to and independent from them. . . . [They] exemplify individuals whose selves are alienated from their actions."[50] To successfully act, a certain psychological machinery must operate properly. In the case of serious neurosis, this psychological machinery is dysfunctional. Whenever agents try to act, their neuroses gets in the way. There is a pathological waywardness that obstructs their actions. If, however, the insane suffer from a chronic form of weakness of will, they cannot, as Wolf suggests, achieve autonomy.[51]

Considered from an epistemic point of view, the insane suffer from ignorance. Wolf defines sanity as "the minimally sufficient ability to cognitively and normatively recognize and appreciate the world for what it is."[52] Insomuch as the insane lack this ability, they lack knowledge. They are ignorant agents. So they fail at autonomy.

Wolf identifies an objective criterion for human achievement. Yet there are contemporary authors who resist even the most minimal appeal to notions of objectivity. Christman writes: "I would defend the claim that only minimal internal conditions for rationality . . . would be plausible as conditions for autonomy. For to demand more—for example, that one's beliefs . . . be confirmed by objectively relevant evidence—would make the property of autonomy divergent from the idea of *self*-government that provides its intuitive base."[53] But internal consistency, consistency between my beliefs and actions, is not enough for rationality. Wolf reacts against such solipsism, but she does not go far enough. Autonomy entails more than mere sanity. Autonomous agents must act in a manner that is positively praiseworthy; that is, they must achieve moral excellence.

PLOTINUS REVISITED: MURDOCH

While Wolf proposes a sanity requirement for autonomy, Iris Murdoch depicts human endeavor as a movement of return by imperfect creatures toward some ultimate, transcendent idea of the good. Murdoch, who revives many of Plotinus's ethical notions in her own moral writings, argues for the existence of a Platonic conception of the Good. The Good is an idea of perfection that is "forced upon us,"[54] that "floats free from contingent detail and is not at the mercy of history."[55] It is something "real,"[56] which is "everywhere . . . unlike other things."[57] Logically, it "is necessary in some non-tautological, not merely linguistic sense."[58]

Murdoch proposes this idea of the Good as an objective criterion that measures our own achievement. Although the idea of the Good "cannot be detached" from "the conception of being human,"[59] we do not decide what the Good is. We do not invent the Good.[60] Our experience "of the Good is not like an arbitrary and assertive resort to our own will; it is a discovery of something independent of us."[61] We do not judge the idea of the Good; it judges us.

On Murdoch's account, nonautonomous agents fail at perfection, not through ignorance, but through weakness of will. Perhaps surprisingly, Murdoch disagrees with Socrates. Ignorance is not a human possibility. The Good is "clearly seen and indubitably discovered."[62] It "haunts all our activity," no matter how hard "we try to blot it out."[63] The problem is not that agents do not see the Good. The problem is that they are unable to live up to an idea of the Good they plainly see.[64]

Plotinus insists that we move toward the Good, the Beautiful, in *all* our striving. This results in a more generous notion of morality. Murdoch argues, for example, that morality includes aesthetic, artistic achievement.[65] The poet, the painter, and the ballet dancer are inspired by a vision of the Good the way a holy person or a saint is. Anytime we strive toward perfection in our professional or our personal lives, we are motivated by a desire for the Good. Personal achievement is then inescapably moral.

Murdoch is frankly supernatural. In the face of a moral skepticism that separates the moral from the empirical realm (the fact-value distinction), Murdoch falls back on a spiritual account of reality. We do not find perfection in the world. "We know of perfection as we look on what is imperfect."[66]

Our idea of the Good must come from "outside the world."[67] It must derive from "something of a different unique and special sort,"[68] not from God, but from something otherworldly.[69] This mystical side may strike some readers as unconvincing, but it supplies an objective account of human accomplishment, one that transcends a pervasive subjectivism.

In Murdoch's theory, successful self-government means moving toward an objective standard of perfection that exists outside ourselves. Successful agents are not ignorant, nor do they suffer from weakness of will. They reach, in the language of the previous discussion, the third level of achievement.

JUSTICE AS IMPARTIALITY: BARRY

Brian Barry, in championing a notion of "justice as impartiality," has argued against attempts to derive the principles of justice from notions of rational self-interest.[70] Barry elaborates an objective theory of justice, one that equates justice with an impartial distribution of goods that will be acceptable to all reasonable people.

Barry distinguishes between two types of justice theories: those that conceive of "justice as mutual advantage" and those that conceive of "justice as impartiality."[71] On a mutual advantage theory, goods are distributed unequally. The stronger get more because they can force the issue; the weaker get less because they are more vulnerable. On a "justice as impartiality" theory, the stronger and the weaker are treated in an equal manner regardless of their ability to force concessions. The stronger do not get more because they are stronger, the weaker do not get less because they are weaker. Only merit and need are taken into account. The ability of various parties to force their will on others is dismissed as a "morally irrelevant" consideration.

Barry argues that impartiality is "the core of morality."[72] Justice requires that "people should not look at things from their own point of view alone but seek to find a basis of agreement that is acceptable from all points of view."[73] "People [are] to detach themselves from their own contingently given positions and take up a more impartial standpoint."[74] It is not enough that agents serve their own perceived interests. Agents who act justly must satisfy an objective standard of impartiality. They will be judged on their impartiality regardless of their own personal beliefs or predispositions.

Barry alludes to Scanlon's view that the moral motive is "the desire to be able to justify one's actions to others on grounds they could not reasonably reject."[75] To say that I act in a just manner is not simply to say that I approve of my own actions. It is to say that other rational agents will also approve of my actions. Justice is not a matter of subjective whim or inclination. There are standards reasonable people can agree to. This is to advance an objective criterion of fairness that is recognizable as such to other rational agents.

Barry's account of distributive justice avoids solipsism. If one wants to act in accordance with the requirements of justice, it is not enough to further one's perceived interests. Just individuals act in accordance with an *objective* standard of fairness. Agents who successfully govern themselves are not ignorant of what real fairness is, nor do they suffer from weakness of will. They reach, so to speak, the third level of achievement.

Like other authors already discussed, Barry provides an objective account of human achievement. If impartiality means acting "without fear or favor," "it also means the absence of more subtle departures from objectivity."[76] Implicit in Barry's account is an appeal to the idea of an objective world, a world that forces certain beliefs upon us, that imposes standards of true and false, right or wrong. Justice is, like morality, an objective achievement. It means satisfying a criterion for success that exists, in the appropriate sense, independent of ourselves.

NAESS: DEEP ECOLOGY

To practise strong evaluation, to be sensitive to feedback, to be sane, to flourish as an individual human being, to act in accordance with an idea of the Good, to judge impartially—these are various ways of defining what we mean by successful self-government. Normative criteria may be derived from various sources. Once an objective criterion for human action has been formulated, it may be used as a measure of personal autonomy. Consider, for the sake of illustration, how the principles of "deep ecology" might be incorporated into a normative account of freedom.

Environmentalism advances an objective criterion of human achievement. To successfully govern oneself is to live in harmony with the natural world. It is to preserve the natural order, to avoid the wanton destruction of nature. Seen from an ecological perspective, destroying the environment is not only immoral but highly irrational. Even if environmentally irresponsible agents satisfy their own desires and aspirations, they do not successfully govern themselves. They do not qualify as autonomous agents.

Autonomy means successful *self*-government. If, however, we are a part of nature and nature is a part of us, respecting nature means respecting ourselves. According to Arne Naess, the most famous proponent of deep ecology, "To injure nature wantonly would mean injuring an integral part of ourselves."[77] Considered in ecological terms, agents who harm the environment are shortsighted. They do not govern themselves successfully; they are not autonomous.

Contemporary theorists in political theory tend to emphasize the authenticity condition for autonomy. Ecologists, however, define authenticity in terms of a relationship between the self and the environment. In a discussion of environmental ethics, Dovey defines authenticity as "a depth of connectedness between people and their world."[78] To disregard or misunderstand our connection to the natural order is to misunderstand our own identity. It is to live in an unauthentic manner. To be ecologically responsible is to be true to who we really are.

Seen from the ecological perspective, one cannot successfully govern oneself unless one acts in a way that is respectful of nature. Naess identifies individual "self-realization" with the "Self-realization" of all nature.[79] Autonomy, successful self-government, presupposes an intimate connection, a kind of symbiotic relationship, with the rest of nature. If we alienate ourselves from the natural order, we alienate ourselves from our deepest selves; we become false and disingenuous creatures. We betray our own species and our own individual nature.

If environmentalism provides a wider definition of authenticity, it also provides an objective criterion of human achievement and good living. Particular practices do not lead to human flourishing because we believe they lead to human flourishing. They lead to human flourishing because they reflect a caring concern for the order inherent in the natural world. Seen from this value perspective, agents who wantonly destroy nature do something objectively wrong. They fail at self-government.

There are two ways in which agents may fail to be autonomous. Agents who do not understand the importance of ecological responsibility are ignorant agents. They need to be educated. Agents who understand the importance of ecological responsibility but continue to live in ways that are convenient and comfortable but harmful for the environment suffer from weakness of will. In either case, agents who do not act in a manner that is respectful of nature cannot achieve autonomy. Environmentalism provides, in this manner, an objective criterion of successful self-government.

In deep ecology, as in communitarianism, we recognize an underlying motif. Human beings, in order to find meaning, must identify with something larger than themselves. Environmentalists stress an identification with nature, whereas communitarians stress an identification with the political and social structure. But human agents may identify with other descriptions of reality—religious, spiritual, institutional, professional, whatever.

The monk achieves autonomy by being a good monk. The soldier achieves autonomy by being a good soldier. The doctor achieves autonomy by being a good doctor. These agents do not achieve autonomy by isolating themselves from the standards and the techniques of their professional discipline. Implicit in these occupations or professions are various standards of evaluation. These standards can be used to differentiate agents who successfully govern themselves from agents who do not. We achieve autonomy, not by refusing an identification with, but by living up to the ideals embodied in groups or environments that are larger than ourselves.

HUMAN FLOURISHING: MASLOW, SWANTON, NUSSBAUM

On a normative theory, successful agents must satisfy an objective norm of individual achievement. They conform to the natural law, obey the categorical imperative, display heroic individuality, engage in strong evaluation, are sensitive to feedback, possess psychological health, aspire to the Good, act in an impartial manner, and respect the environment. Authors like A. H. Maslow, Christine Swanton, and Martha Nussbaum propose as the standard of human excellence naturalistic accounts of human flourishing.

Maslow presents a psychological account of human fulfillment based on a hierarchy of needs and a library of observations on human behavior.[80] Swanton and Nussbaum are more philosophical than psychological. Inspired by Aristotle, they present accounts of human flourishing that are almost biological in tone. For Nussbaum, human flourishing means being "adequately nourished," having "adequate shelter," enjoying "opportunities for sexual satisfaction," "being able to move from place to place," "being able to use the five senses."[81] For Swanton, human flourishing means engaging in those activities and satisfying those desires that are characteristic of the human species.[82] Though Swanton's theory closely parallels Nussbaum's, she defines human flourishing in terms of the absence of negative traits: individuals who prosper are not suicidal; they are not beset by chronic exhaustion, lassitude, ennui, or boredom; they are not anxious, lonely, or severely stressed; they operate without feelings of worthlessness, terror, fear, or coercion, and so on.[83]

Both Nussbaum and Swanton provide an objective account of human flourishing. Being an accomplished human being does not mean doing what one wants to do. It means satisfying objective criteria of excellence. Christine Swanton brings up the example of an anorexic patient.[84] The anorexic wants to stop eating. Even if she is able to do what she wants to do, even if she is able to stop herself from eating, she does not qualify as an autonomous agent. Successful self-government means measuring up to an objective standard of health and well-being. It does not mean pandering to some neurotic obsession.

In articulating accounts of human flourishing, Nussbaum and Swanton both appeal to normative criteria that are situated outside the individual. Agents who experience self-satisfaction are not invariably autonomous, for some ways of satisfying our own desires do not count as bona fide instances of human flourishing. The anorexic suffers from ignorance. The beauty myth has corrupted her sense of personal excellence. So she is no longer autonomous.

Swanton and Nussbaum elaborate an objective account of human welfare, and both seem to associate human flourishing, along with Maslow, with good living conditions. But this is problematic. Nietzsche would have regarded any attempt to identify human flourishing with good living conditions as monstrously misguided. Nietzsche castigates the herd, the "little" people who "have no respect for great misfortune, for great ugliness, for great failure."[85] Eliminate boredom, loneliness, anxiety, cruelty, terror, hardship and fear, secure good living conditions, make everything painless, easy, and comfortable, and there will be no room for human achievement. Swanton associates human flourishing with the absence of negative experience, but for Nietzsche negative experience is an indispensable part of human flourishing. Those who confuse happiness with comfort do not know the true depths of joy. As Nietzsche expresses the thought: "So rich is joy that it thirsts for woe, for hell, for hatred, for disgrace, for the cripple, for world—this world, oh you know it!"[86]

Swanton associates human flourishing with the absence of adversity, but the overcoming of adversity produces good rebels, heroic men and women. As Nietzsche insists, human achievement entails, in part, the inexplicable transformation of what is grievous and evil into what is healthy and good. Zarathustra tells the virtuous brother: "Once you had wild dogs in your cellar, but in the end they turned into birds and lovely singers. Out of your poisons you brewed your balsam. You milked your cow, melancholy; now you drink the sweet milk of her udder."[87]

The "horticultural model" of human flourishing betrays the freedom ideal. It is not the conditions one inhabits that turns one into a flourishing human being. It is an individual act of will. There is a decisive element of free will, of personal initiative, individual virtue, and morality, that comes into play. Flourishing is not something that automatically happens in response to the appropriate living conditions. Flourishing is an individual achievement.

Nussbaum recognizes, in passing, that human life consists of a struggle against limits and that eliminating all limits would make human striving largely pointless. Still, her theory is open to misinterpretation. One must respect the paradoxical nature of the human condition. One must not divorce flourishing from suffering. Human flourishing must not be understood as a condition of optimal living conditions, but as the accomplishment of good and praiseworthy things in the face of inevitable obstacles.

Autonomy and Succor: Gilligan, Noddings

While Swanton and Nussbaum propose an objective account of human flourishing, feminist authors such as Carol Gilligan and Nel Noddings have proposed a morality based on an ethics of caring. Although the care perspective may be incorporated into a normative account of personal autonomy, feminists sometimes discard, as fundamentally misguided, philosophical notions of autonomy. An ethics of care is purported to be incompatible with autonomy.

Gilligan and Noddings take exception to Lawrence Kohlberg's influential account of moral development. Kohlberg bases his psychological theories on the moral philosophies of Rawls and Kant, dividing moral development into a series of six psychological stages, with each stage representing a higher level of moral awareness.[88] Amoral individuals progress from egocentricity to ethnocentricity until, in the final stage, they come to embrace a morality based on universal ethical principles.

Gilligan, in disputing Kohlberg's psychological system, distinguishes between a justice perspective and a care perspective. The justice perspective characterizes human relationships "in terms of equality." The care perspective characterizes relationships "in terms of attachment." There are two corresponding moral injunctions: "not to act unfairly towards others" and "not to turn away from someone in need."[89] There are likewise two moral faults. We may practice injustice or oppression; that is, we may treat people unequally. Or we may practice indifference or abandonment; that is, we may refuse to care for others. Gilligan and Noddings attribute these two types of moral thinking to gender difference: the care perspective is essentially the morality of women; the justice perspective is essentially the morality of men. Kohlberg is portrayed as the archetypical male theorist, someone who identifies morality exclusively with justice. Gilligan and Noddings want to argue that this is an impoverished moral perspective.

Gilligan dissociates herself from the notion of personal autonomy, but the care perspective and the autonomy perspective are not mutually exclusive options. Successful self-government does not entail a callous disregard for others. When feminists reject the ideal of personal autonomy, they are (rightfully) reacting against a very narrow account of autonomy that goes so far as to emphasize self-affirmation and self-satisfaction at the expense of others. But if autonomy has a moral component, the problem disappears. To be autonomous is to be moral; that is, it is, in large part, to care deeply for other people. A person who does not care for others is, in the deepest sense, a failure. As Gilligan and Noddings point out, they do not successfully govern themselves.

Gilligan distinguishes a care perspective from an autonomy perspective. The care perspective conceives of action "as responsive and . . . arising in relationship."[90] The autonomy perspective champions values of independence and self-sufficiency. If, however, people need to be free to decide for themselves, their decisions need to include a concern for others. As Taylor points out, a self-referentiality of manner need not include a self-referentiality of content. Autonomous agents are, in Haworth's words, sensitive to feedback. To be sensitive to feedback is, in large part, to be sensitive to other human beings. It is to respond to their cries for help. This is an indispensable part of human achievement.

Margaret Moore criticizes Will Kymlicka's assumption "that autonomy and community stand in fundamental opposition to one another."[91] As Moore points out, justice and caring are not opposing ideals. The feminist theory of ethics is a welcome counterpoint to the minimalist, rule-oriented accounts of morality so prevalent today. Environmentalists stress an inalienable attachment to the natural world; feminists emphasize our attachment to other human beings. In this kind of theory, ignorant agents subscribe to a false of ideal of atomistic individuality; weak-willed agents care for others but allow their egoism or other character flaws to interfere with their concern. Both fail at successful self-government.

MYSTICISM: OTHERNESS

I have argued that there is no contradiction between care and autonomy. Successful self-government is sometimes confused with self-centeredness, but this emphasis on the self as the center of preoccupation and the arbiter of value has debilitating consequences. An exclusive preoccupation with self trivializes the human predicament, emptying human life of meaning.

Taylor argues that one can only find meaning by linking up with something larger than the self—a community, a religion, a political cause, nature, history. If autonomy is taken as the epitome of self-fulfillment, human existence only makes sense when it is conceived of as an encounter with the other. My father, a religious man and, at that time, a socialist, used to tell us that the only point of human life was to serve others. But the other may be variously defined. It may be an individual human being, a community, God, a political cause, a body of knowledge, a system of values. Royce's notion that one must be loyal to loyalty is an apt, if incomplete, expression of the same insight. If one is to lead an ethical life, one must devote one's existence to causes or issues that transcend the self.[92] This devotion to the other is what legitimizes human life, and personal autonomy must be defined in such a way that it does not interfere with such legitimizing endeavor.

To understand how human life takes on meaning, we might look to the phenomenon of mysticism. There is a tendency to identify mystical experience with sensational side effects, with phenomena that tend towards the extreme, the spectacular, and the lurid. Grace Jantzen complains that even scholarly investigation of the subject has been transformed into "a study of bizarre states of consciousness," of "voices, visions, levitations, ecstasies, and things that go bump in the night."[93] This is a perennial protest echoed in the writings of Butler,[94] Underhill,[95] Hughes,[96] Hodgson,[97] Egan,[98] Katsaros, and Kaplan.[99] Mainstream scholarly opinion, on the other hand, posits mysticism as an analogue of more ordinary experience. It is "a psychological process which occurs with varying degrees of intensity in everyone's life."[100] Mystics seek out meaning, not through the construction of philosophical arguments, but by following a particular way and through submission to an absolute Other.

The philosopher Martin Buber argues that meaning comes through a close encounter with another subject. The mystical paradox is that one can only find oneself by completely losing oneself in this Other. This revelation of the *totally* intimate in the *totally* foreign provides the impetus for the powerful emotional release popularly associated with mystical endeavor. It is an experience that surfaces, in various ways, in most religions and cultures.[101]

The Other of mystical experience may be variously defined. What is important is that the Other and the mystic possess radically different natures. The mystic is finite, individual, contingent; the Other is infinite, universal, eternal. The mystic is a created agent; the Other is uncreated. The mystic is concrete and specific; the Other is immanent and transcendental. The mystic is human; the Other is divine. Yet in losing themselves in this radically Other, variously described, mystics find themselves.

An important part of the autonomy ideal is the search for authenticity. Meyers, for example, describes autonomy as a search for "one's authentic self." How are we to discover this authentic self? Popular authors propose a relentless search for the inner self, the real self, the authentic self. Mysticism teaches the opposite doctrine. One only finds oneself when one loses oneself in what is "wholly Other."[102] It is the pursuit of that which is foreign that leads to intimate self-discovery. The movement is not inwards but outwards, beyond the self, toward that which is genuinely Other.

Feminist authors like Gilligan and Noddings aptly criticize the individualistic tenor of popular theories of autonomy. Their views are in line with the mystical model in another way. Traditional philosophy tends to privilege propositional knowledge, while mystical experience is ineffable, intuitive, experiential, nonpropositional. Mystics do not translate the truth into words. They "see" the truth directly, without recourse to intermediary images or arguments. If Noddings criticizes authors who reduce ethics to logic, this is in keeping with the mystical doctrine that ultimate truth is not to be obtained within a series of formally-correct propositions but in a loving attention to the Wholly Other.

In mysticism we find ourselves in the Other. The paradoxical nature of the discovery may seem philosophically disreputable. The philosophical impetus is to reconcile the contradiction, to conceive of the self and Other in terms of an underlying sameness. Caroline Whitbeck criticizes the mystical notion of "identity-in-difference."[103] She elaborates, in response, a "feminist ontology" that conceives of the relation between self and Other as "a relation between analogous beings."[104] To conceive of the Other solely in terms of sameness or analogy is, however, to impoverish the very idea of relationship. Consider human love. Do I only love that part of you which is analogous to me? Do I only value your resemblance to me? If I really love you, I will value not merely your sameness but also your difference. I will value that aspect of you which makes you different from me, that part of you which makes you you instead of me. If I only love that part of you which resembles me, my love is narcissism in disguise. Loving you is another way of loving me. Love must entail a recognition, an acceptance, and even a cherishing of difference. Narcissists unwittingly reduce the other to a projection of their own wills, beliefs, and attitudes. In their encounters with others, they only meet themselves.

Gilligan and Noddings denounce the standard view of autonomy because it trivializes the importance of relationship. On a communitarian view, successful self-government will entail solidarity or communion with others. Mysticism proposes, as the true source of happiness, an intimate relationship of care and concern with the genuinely Other. Seen from this perspective, self-absorption is the ultimate obstacle to autonomy. Individuals who do not understand their need for others are ignorant. Individuals who strive unsuccessfully to move beyond their own egotism are weak-willed. Agents who are weak-willed or ignorant do not successfully govern themselves. Because they do not love others, they cannot, in any genuine way, love themselves. They cannot be autonomous.

Conclusion

We cannot make sense of the notion of human freedom without an objective account of personal autonomy. Michael Sandel complains that Rawls values "not the ends we choose but our capacity to choose them."[105] The mere capacity to choose may be turned to evil ends. The exercise of choice is valuable, not as a condition in and of itself, but as a prior condition to the accomplishment of the good. To value our ability to choose, not as a means to good choices, but as a means to unevaluated choice, is not to value our own choices because they are good, but because they are our own. This is only narcissism.

Morality is objective. It is a form of insight, reason, or coherence that we discover operating in the world, in our own consciences and in the lives of ordinary people. To argue that moral standards are objective is to recognize that there are criteria over and beyond ourselves that determine what is sound, reasonable, authoritative, right, or true. One may argue for different views of morality. Gilligan proposes an ethics of care. Taylor emphasizes values of community and human solidarity. Environmentalists tell us that human beings should live in harmony with nature. Mysticism provides a model for autonomy based on Other-centered love. But whatever stance we take, we cannot make sense of morality unless we understand it in objective terms as the primary motivation underlying all human endeavor.

My argument to this point can be summarized. Rationality must not be identified with the advancement of self-interest, but with consistency broadly construed. Morality must not be identified with a restrictive system of social constraints, but with a process of self-realization. And finally, autonomy must be identified, not with agent self-approval, but with an objective standard of morality and rationality. Haworth speaks of objectivity as "a mode of self-transcendence in which individuality is affirmed."[106] Autonomous individuals must move beyond self-interest, solipsism, and self-congratulation and accomplish an objective good. They must affirm and express their own individuality while transcending the narrow limits of a fatal subjectivity.

The good rebel, the noncooperative subject in the Milgram experiment, provides a model par excellence of autonomy. Good rebels do not suffer from weakness of will or from ignorance. They satisfy objective standards of morality and rationality. They do the right thing under duress. They identify with a moral cause. They provide a conspicuous example of human achievement. Let us consider, then, in more detail the concept of good rebellion.

Part III:

Rebellion

8

A Theory of Rebellion

MORE THAN CIVIL DISOBEDIENCE

I have argued, like Kant, that human agents cannot be free unless they are rational and moral. But while Kant conceives of morality, in traditional terms, as a submission to authority, I want to use the good rebel as a conspicuous example of both freedom and morality.

Good rebels oppose authority. They may engage in acts of civil disobedience, breaking the law for a higher moral end. Kant, however, will not countenance civil disobedience even in the case of illegal acts by the government. "Even if the organ of the sovereign, the ruler, proceeds contrary to the law," Kant writes, "subjects may indeed oppose this injustice by complaints but not by resistance."[1] One may voice disapproval, but one may not actually break the law. One may talk, but one cannot, in any robust sense, rebel.

Views have changed. Henry David Thoreau, in his famous pamphlet *Civil Disobedience,* makes an influential case for noncompliance with an unjust state.[2] His opinions have, in large part, prevailed. Contemporary Anglo-American authors generally accept that there are circumstances in which civil disobedience is permissible or even necessary. John Rawls, for example, argues that there is a justification for civil disobedience in a constitutional democracy just so long as it is a nonviolent, selfless act carried out for a just political motive in extreme circumstances when no other alternative is available.[3]

Nicholas Kittrie, in a series of books, has investigated political dissent more fully. Kittrie reviews a host of rebels, good or bad, including such diverse figures as Jean-Paul Marat, Charlotte Corday, Joan of Arc, Marcus Brutus, John Brown, John W. Hinckley, John Wilkes Booth, Andrei Sakharov, and Che Guevara.[4] He formulates a bill of rights based on principles of international law and the doctrine of a higher law that legitimizes justifiable political dissent and distinguishes it from actual crime.[5]

Although this political and legal approach is timely and important, rebellion is not necessarily or even primarily political. Good rebels may engage in acts of political disobedience, but their political activism is ultimately the expression of a personal commitment. Rebellion begins, not with politics, but with morality, understood in its broadest sense as the motivating force behind all successful human achievement. I will present, then, a moral account of rebellion, one that has its roots in individual values.

According to the *Oxford English Dictionary*, the verb "to rebel" means "to rise in opposition or armed resistance"; "to resist, oppose"; "to . . . exhibit opposition, to feel or manifest repugnance." If, however, rebellion entails a struggle against some kind of authority, authority is not solely political. Opinions, ideas, attitudes, social customs, moral principles, institutions, persons, and books may all be viewed as authoritative. Rebellion begins in a movement of opposition to popular conventions that may or may not end in political interventionism.

The youth who repudiates his parents' convictions and becomes a pig farmer instead of an eye surgeon rebels. The business man who leaves the world of high finance and enters a monastery rebels. Artists who repudiate the stylistic conventions of an earlier era rebel. Scientists who set the foundations of a new physical paradigm rebel. Women who combat gender stereotypes rebel. And so on. Rebels, in the words of *Webster's Dictionary*, "put up a fight, show opposition." They may, however, show opposition or put up a fight without entering the political or legal arena, without actually breaking the law.

To present the good rebel as the rebel par excellence is not to glorify uncritically the historical figure of the political rebel. Kittrie condemns, in the strongest possible language, a tradition of immoral rebellion that he traces through human history. Commenting on the darker side of individual rebellion, he tells us that

> While recognizing the rebel's function as a creative hero, . . . [we should] also recognize his or her role as a destroyer. . . . History is replete with these destructive rebels—aggressors, insatiable power seekers, tyrants, and megalomaniacs who abuse authority and pursue, and often tragically obtain, power as an end in itself. For these self-centered and "pseudo-convictional" rebels (the Nebuchadnezzars, Neros, Genghis Khans, Hitlers, and Stalins, as well as for lesser-known victimizers, avengers, and aberrant butchers) destruction becomes more important than creation.[6]

Kittrie proposes a typology of political rebellion. There are, he claims, good rebels and bad rebels, rebels who deserve accolades and rebels who deserve punishment. I will argue, however, that bad rebels are not, on closer examination, rebels at all. For all its spectacle and pretense, immoral rebellion is appearance rather than reality. The good rebel is not only the rebel par excellence; he or she is the only true rebel. Strictly understood, rebellion cannot occur without a decisive orientation toward the good.

Kittrie entitles the prologue in his most recent book "The Eternal Struggle between Authority and Autonomy."[7] If, however, individual autonomy has a moral (as well as a rational) component, there is no struggle between legitimate authority and autonomy. There may be an eternal struggle, but it is a struggle between *evil* authority and autonomy. Insomuch as human history leaves space for evil authorities, good rebels will never cease opposing them.

UNFULFILLED REBELLION

Rebellion has become a popular and conspicuous element of modern culture. One need only think of the popular music industry, where performer after performer displays a practiced and self-conscious nonconformity. Skinheads, punkers, and neo-Nazis rebel. Richard Feynman, the Nobel laureate in physics, depicts himself, in his autobiographies, as the consummate rebel. James Dean was a rebel. The hippies rebelled. Malcolm X, Che Guevara, and Archbishop Oscar Romero rebelled. Animal rights activists and deep ecologists rebel. Gloria Steinem thinks of herself as a rebel. So does Noam Chomsky. And some would declare, with a vigor that reveals the strength of their own convictions, that even Jesus rebelled. Rebellion is a familiar archetype in popular thought. In sorting through the contemporary scene, one runs up against individual after individual who, rightly or wrongly, critically or uncritically, buys into the rebel ideal.

Robert Paul Wolff writes: "Most men . . . feel so strongly the force of tradition or bureaucracy that they accept unthinkingly the claims to authority which are made by their nominal rulers. It is the rare individual in the history of the race who even rises to the level of questioning the right of his masters to command and the duty of himself and his fellows to obey."[8] Wolff, a committed anarchist, celebrates the right to disobey, but it is not enough to disobey. Criminals, the paid assassin, the violent young offender, and naughty children disobey. But these are hardly wholesome archetypes, people we try to model ourselves on. If rebellion is to be a worthwhile ideal, it must entail more than simple disobedience.

A popular mind-set associates rebellion with conspicuous individuality. The moral connection is downplayed, deemed nonessential, even extraneous. This has lead to a widespread degeneration of the rebel ideal. If Kurt Cobain—a rebel icon of the entertainment industry—balanced a shotgun between his knees, placed the barrel in his mouth, and pulled the trigger, it may be the sad but natural consequence of a certain line of thinking.[9] Rebellion without a cause, without moral ideals, leads to nihilism. Divorced from ideas of the good, rebellion tends toward tragedy, unfulfillment, and despair.

Kittrie writes: "Contemporary culture all too often glamorizes [the] destructive or negative rebel. Among our most successful popular culture idols are those who express contempt for the 'establishment' and its values—from America's James Dean, the 'rebel without a cause,' and numerous heavy metal and rap music groups, to Ulricke Meinhof, founding member of Germany's Baader-Meinhof terrorist gang."[10] Kittrie believes that this glamorization of the unqualified act of rebellion, of rebellion for its own sake, has nefarious consequences. In his opinion, "When rebellion is an end-in-itself, when the ascension to power becomes a self-contained objective, the darker side of the rebel prevails. The act of rebellion then tends to become an infliction of nihilistic terror—designed to revenge, to destroy, to disrupt, to frighten, to cow, to shock, and to disgust, rather than to recreate or renew."[11]

If one examines carefully popular novels and cinema, one discovers a literature of unfulfilled rebellion. In celebrating rebellion without a cause, rebellion for rebellion's sake, popular literature demonstrates, in spite of itself, the very poverty of this amoral ideal. We can only examine a small cross-section of these works here. If we consult novels like Kate Chopin's *The Awakening*, Aldous Huxley's *Brave New World*, Jack Kerouac's *On the Road*, J. D. Salinger's *Catcher in the Rye*, Douglas Coupland's *Generation X*, or movies like *Easy Rider* and, more recently, *Sid and Nancy*, we encounter the literary type of the unfulfilled rebel, an individual who, in pursuing freedom apart from the good, is inexorably drawn into scenes of folly, despair, darkness, or futility.

These stories reveal, in living detail, the consequences of rebellion gone bad. Madame Pontellier, the protagonist in Chopin's *The Awakening*, is attracted to the life of bohemian independence. She is, however, married with children. Unable to reconcile her dream of personal liberty with her family responsibilities, she is faced with a rude dilemma. She must choose her children or she must choose emancipation. She cannot have both. Caught between these competing value systems, she collapses into despair and drowns herself.

Madame Pontellier has been portrayed as an archetype of women's liberation. But Chopin's novel tells a story, not of liberation, but of failure. This woman from conventional society cannot express her individuality and maintain her maternal relationship with her children. She cannot be true to herself and true to her children. She must live for herself or she must sacrifice herself for her children. She chooses to rebel against society's norms, but this act of rebellion places her children out of reach. Madame Pontellier is faced with a merciless dilemma. She can be morally good and, as dutiful wife and mother, take care of her family. Or she can embrace freedom and abandon her own. She is driven to rebel, but rebellion without a moral good is a futile endeavor. Suicide, extinction in nature, is the only way out of her quandary. Her death brings to a desperate end an individual life divorced from the good.[12]

Huxley's *Brave New World* (like Orwell's *1984*) is a plea for the right to be an individual. There are three rebels in the novel: John the Savage, Bernard Marx, and Helmholtz Watson. None of these figures conform to society's expectations. Watson becomes a good rebel and Marx, an unwilling rebel; the Savage is the unfulfilled rebel. Although he resolutely refuses to conform to a deeply flawed society, he fails to liberate himself. In the context of the novel, he comes to instantiate bad rebellion, rebellion that fails. Although he is different from others, this difference expresses itself in some nightmarish, retrograde way.

Raised in the wilderness among primitive peoples, the Savage embodies some form of mindless, emotional atavism. He has been corrupted by an irrational, unscientific worldview, a mishmash of totemism, Christianity, and ancestor worship. Transported from a primitive past into a technological future, he is unable to survive the cultural shock, eventually committing suicide, flagellating himself in a mindless penitential rite, in a fury of senseless self-immolation. Huxley depicts his gory death as the epitome of perverseness and futility.

One may contest this negative portrayal. Older, aboriginal worldviews are not as perverse as Huxley suggests. Religious interpretations may provide a meaningful alternative to a facile consumerism. In the context of Huxley's novel, however, the Savage is an ignorant agent. He is superstitious, unscientific, primitive, anything but modern. He is able to critique society, but he is unable to envision any constructive alternative. Because he is an ignorant agent, he cannot realize the good, and because he cannot realize the good, he cannot liberate himself. Detached from any constructive good, his rebellion degenerates into blind, obtuse passion. His protest against a dehumanizing modernity fails, and fails conclusively.

Dean Moriarty, the rogue-hero of Kerouac's picaresque novel *On the*

Road, is another rebel caught in a frantic quest for personal realization that never quite succeeds.[13] Dean is an American Rimbaud, an adult Huck Finn, the "HOLY GOOF,"[14] poet, priest and prophet of the beat generation, someone with an insatiable appetite for experience who almost destroys himself in his faltering but persistent attempts at private liberation. If, however, Dean is a kind of bohemian saint, his life is littered with mistakes, betrayals, broken promises, and unrealized hopes. The thirst that drives him onward is never slaked. The searing ecstasy of isolated moments is inevitably interrupted, punctured, and pierced with incoherence, meaninglessness, and desolation. There are moments of epiphany, but any permanent sense of happiness or peace eludes him.

Kerouac's novel is the signature piece of the beat generation, but the story is no vagabond idyll. Kerouac captures, with gritty honesty, the pathos of failed rebellion. There is a predictable pattern to Dean and Sal's adventures. They hitchhike across the continent, indulging in all the new America has to offer: drugs, sex, jazz, poetry, psychoanalysis, fast cars, and relentless, nonstop, high-speed driving. And yet these feverish, passionate pilgrims never reach the promised land. They begin their journeys filled with hope but return home defeated, exhausted, starving, physically ill, penniless, almost mad. As Sal explains: "You start life a sweet child believing everything under your father's roof. . . . Then comes the day of Laodiceans, when you are wretched and miserable . . . and with the visage of a gruesome grieving ghost you go shuddering through nightmare life."[15] These youthful rebels do not find fulfillment, but misery, emptiness, alienation. The fruit of self-indulgence turns inevitably into the dust of despair.

Dean Moriarty epitomizes, perhaps more than any other literary figure, the type of the unfulfilled rebel. Sal confides to Dean: "I don't have close relationships with anybody anymore, —I don't know what to do with these things. I hold them in my hand like pieces of crap."[16] Dean and his friends are unable, in any lasting sense, to relate to and care about one another. In another scene, the wife of a friend yells at Dean: "For years now you haven't had any sense of responsibility. . . . You have absolutely no regard for anybody but yourself and your damned kicks. All you think about is what's hanging between your legs and how much money or fun you can get out of people and then just throw them aside. . . . It never occurs to you that life is serious and there are people who are trying to make something decent out of it instead of just goofing all the time."[17] Dean, the epitome of a predatory sexuality, cannot dispute the charges. He has moments of raw exaltation, but his attempts at self-fulfillment ultimately fail. He remains an incurable wanderer, someone who unsuccessfully pursues the Holy Grail of his own self-realization.

Kerouac, unwittingly perhaps, supplies a moral lesson. Dean strives after self-realization, but happiness is a moral state. It involves relationships with other people. Dean is too self-absorbed to care for others. He has relationships, but he lacks commitment. He treats his friends as means rather than as ends. This is why he fails. Dean tries to achieve a private self-realization apart from any mutual, communal good. He cannot liberate himself because, for all his passion, he ignores what is morally good.

Holden Caulfield, a student expelled from an American prep school, is the confused hero of J. D. Salinger's *Catcher in the Rye*. Surrounded by people who lack the courage or the wits to be true to themselves, Holden rebels against the "phoniness" of middle America. As he complains about his private school: "Even the couple of nice teachers on the faculty, they were phonies, too."[18] Holden leaves school and sets out on a quest for individual authenticity. But the strain and stress of nonconformism take their toll. Holden eventually breaks down both mentally and physically.

Salinger's novel chronicles the demise of its schoolboy hero. Still, there is a hopeful note to Salinger's prose, for Holden comes to realize, with inchoate but dawning comprehension, the importance of the good. Asked about a future career, he invents a new profession, finding inspiration in a misquote from a Robert Burns poem, "If a body catch a body comin' through the rye." As Holden explains to his sister Phoebe: "I keep picturing all these little kids playing some game in this big field of rye and all. Thousands of little kids, and nobody's around—nobody big I mean—except me. And I'm standing on the edge of some crazy cliff. What I have to do, I have to catch everybody if they start to go off the cliff—I mean if they're running and they don't look where they are going I have to come out from somewhere and *catch* them. That's all I'd do all day. I'd just be the catcher in the rye and all. I know it's crazy, but that's the only thing I'd like to be."[19] To be the "catcher in the rye" is to protect the weak, to save the innocent. It is to care for little children. This is a moral aspiration. At the end of the story, Holden comes to understand the importance of morality. To realize oneself is to help others; to experience true freedom is to achieve a moral good.

Wyatt and Bill, the main characters in *Easy Rider*, rebel against a rigid society, only to lose their lives in the process. They forsake an idyllic life in a rural commune and travel to New Orleans to lose themselves in a frantic bout of dissipation, drugs, and sex that only ends in dejection and discontent. Restless and unfulfilled, they hit the road again but are brutally murdered by country hillbillies, the representatives of a blind, authoritarian society. In *Sid and Nancy*, Sid Vicious and his punk-rocker friends ignore or repudiate the conventions of mainstream society, not because they are evil, but because they are the conventions of mainstream society. What begins as a cry of legitimate protest becomes a febrile exercise in masochism, sex, brutality, and hard drugs. Rebellion becomes mindless, acritical. Sid Vicious becomes ever more brutalized. He ends up as an addict and a murderer, and eventually commits suicide.

Douglas Coupland's *Generation X* is, in many ways, a reworking of Kerouac's *On the Road*.[20] A compilation of stories culled from the largely uneventful lives of a jaded group of twenty-somethings, it explores themes of youthful alienation in a postmodern consumer society. In one episode, Mr. Takamichi, an Americanized Japanese business magnate and a former photographer, shows Andy his most valued possession, "a photo of Marilyn Monroe getting into a Checker cab, lifting up her dress, no underwear, and smooching at the photographer, presumably Mr. Takamichi."[21] Andy is aghast. As he describes his reaction to friends Dag and Claire: "Blood rushed to my ears, and my heart went bang; I broke out into a sweat and the words of Rilke, the poet, entered my brain—his notion that we are all of us born with a letter inside of us, and that only if we are true to ourselves, we may be allowed to read it before we die. The burning blood in my ears told me that Mr. Takamichi had somehow mistaken the Monroe photo . . . for the letter inside of himself, and that, I myself, was in peril of making some sort of similar mistake."[22]

Mr. Takamichi cannot be true to himself. He cannot read the letter engraved in his soul. Why? Because he has been distracted by a tawdry, counterfeit, and distressingly superficial caricature of American popular culture. Mr. Takamichi has rebelled against his traditional Japanese heritage only to embrace the most inane myths of American consumerism. This is, in large part, a moral fault. Morality tells us that watching Marilyn Monroe lift up her dress sans *sous-vêtements* is not an authentic good. To treasure this garish moment, to place it at the center of one's existence, is an aberration. This cannot count as personal liberation.

Coupland's stories do not contain the moments of searing intensity one finds in Kerouac. His characters lead an existence of small achievements, alienated not just from mainstream society but also from strong convictions about the good. And yet their life is redeemed by shared stories, by contact with nature, and by a lyricism of deep feeling. It is this link to goodness, however minimally construed, that sanctifies their rebellion and makes it, in whatever partial sense, worth living.

If we reiterate what happens to these amoral rebels, it makes for a despairing list. Edna Pontellier in *The Awakening* is led to despair and eventual suicide. The Savage in *Brave New World* ends his life in an orgy of self-abuse when he hangs himself in his hermitage. Dean Moriarty in *On the Road* walks out on an ailing friend and is in turn abandoned, in a state of incoherence and near madness, on the cold and bleak streets of New York. Holden Caulfield in *Catcher in the Rye* suffers from a physical and mental breakdown and is committed to a sanatorium. Wyatt and Billy in the movie *Easy Rider* are brutally murdered by two rednecks shortly after Billy warns his friend, in one pithy colloquialism, of their complete failure: "We blew it." Punk-rocker Sid Vicious in *Sid and Nancy* stabs his desperate girlfriend to death and, languishing alone on skid row, dies of a heroin overdose. And finally, Mr. Takamichi, the wealthy businessman in *Generation X*, provides an example of human inanity and failure amid all the trappings of human success. These are all failed protagonists, characters who, because they express their rebellion apart from the good, fail, in some manner or another, to achieve true liberation and genuine self-fulfillment.

LUCIFER

There is evidence that amoral rebellion, rebellion apart from the good, is unsatisfying, disruptive, and destructive. Kittrie criticizes this kind of nihilistic excess, and I want to make an even stronger claim. I want to argue that rebellion for its own sake, rebellion apart from the good, is not rebellion at all. It is, at best, pseudorebellion. As we have already seen, rebels oppose, resist, take up arms against, put up a fight. Rebellion is a muscular act. It takes effort, self-control, willpower. I will argue that bad rebels, on closer examination, are incapable of this kind of effort.

Consider the archetype of bad rebellion, the archangel Lucifer, who, according to the Christian story, was expelled from Heaven for disobedience to God. In *Paradise Lost*, Milton recounts the tale of Satan's fall and the subsequent war on God waged by "all his Host of Rebel Angels."[23] This is rebellion in a traditional sense, rebellion understood as a destructive act, as a determined, spiteful revolt against good authority for the sake of pure evil.

Milton's Satan is an impressive character. Like some Nietzschean Superman, he incarnates the will to power, orchestrating a revolt of the forces of Hell against the forces of Heaven. He is a paradigm of strength, virility, independence, ambition, and autonomy, a larger-than-life figure of brooding magnificence, titanic energy, angelic intelligence, and "unconquerable will." Satan is, in the most powerful sense of the word, a doer, an actor, an agent, but he is, at the same time, an evil agent. He stands as the archetype of the thoroughly bad rebel, the evil agent who knowingly rebels against some incontestable good.

One may contest this interpretation of the poem. The literary critic Northrop Frye has argued that this commonsense view of Satan misses out on a level of irony that pervades Milton's poem. There is a purposeful paradox that divides the dramatic and conceptual elements of the text. Appearances are not reality. According to Frye, "What is actually going on is the opposite of what appears to be going on. Satan, who seems so lively and resourceful, is the power that moves toward the cessation of all activity, a kind of personal entropy that transforms all energy into a heat-death."[24] As Frye explains, Milton subscribed to the Augustinian notion of evil as deficiency or absence. But if evil is literally absence, it must follow that "There is no such thing, strictly speaking, as an evil act." Because "the evil of sin implies deficiency, [it] implies also the loss of the power to act."[25]

For Milton, as for Augustine, the person who "acts" immorally does not act at all. Consider the first human sin. On Milton's account, "What happens when Adam eats the forbidden fruit . . . is not an act, but the surrendering of the power to act. . . . His position is like that of a man on a precipice—if he jumps it appears to be an act, but it is really the giving up of the possibility of action, the surrendering of himself to the law of gravitation which will take charge of him for the brief remainder of his life. . . . A typically fallen human act is something where the word "act" has to be in quotation marks. It is a pseudo-act, the pseudo-act of disobedience, and it is really a refusal to act at all."[26]

If "there is a quality in Milton's treatment of the demonic world that can only be called Wagnerian: in the unvarying nobility of the rhetoric, in the nihilistic heroic action,"[27] this is mock heroism, all pretense, braggadocio, and bluster with no substance. Milton may or may not succeed in his poetic purposes—he does provide a grandiose image of Satan—but the underlying theme, that the even greatest evil is not action but lack of action is in line with the argument defended here.

Milton's Lucifer is unable to control his irrational pride. (It is not just immoral but irrational to consider oneself equal with God.) He is a slave to irrational, unreflective nature. He cannot control his desires. He cannot govern his appetites, his need for acclaim. He is like the man who knowingly jumps off the cliff. The falling man may be moving at a high rate of speed, but he is no longer acting. He is being acted upon. He cannot be said to govern himself. He is giving in, without resistance, to brute nature.

Milton's Lucifer is not a true rebel. To rebel is to resist, to put up a fight, to oppose. Those who give in to unreflective desire do not rebel.

They do not resist, put up a fight, oppose. They do not fight the good fight, they give up; they simply surrender. They conform unthinkingly to the chaotic and meaningless gestures of irrational nature, not with a bang but with a whimper.

We can compare Milton's account of Lucifer to our previous example of the "successful" gunman who robs strangers because he is greedy, angry, or lazy. The gunman may cut a dashing figure with his desperate actions, but he is not an autonomous agent. He cannot be autonomous, for he does not govern himself. It is his refusal to act, his unwillingness to control his anger, greed, or laziness that leads him to a life of crime. The gunman may like to think of himself as a rebel icon, but his rebellion is more appearance than reality.

Frye paraphrases Milton's definition of an act: "An act is the expression of energy of a free and conscious being."[28] That is to say, in modern philosophical terminology, an act is an expression of an *autonomous* being. But only good rebels, rebels who achieve the good, accomplish something. Lucifer's deeds, for all their preternatural dimensions, are a parody of action. They represent, for all their heroic overtones, a kind of sham agency. Satan's actions are destructive rather than creative. They do not add anything to the universe; they annihilate, obliterate, make a void that swallows up the original earthly paradise that was the Garden of Eden.

Immoral agents lack agency. They are, in the profoundest sense, incapable of rebellion. The truly wicked, the Hitlers of this world, may seem, at times, to act with terrifying efficiency, but this is not self-government but a lack of self-government. Self-mastery is, in such contexts, fraud, trickery. The term "action" here denotes a lack of action. This is not resistance but lack of resistance. The seriously immoral may act in the way sticks and stones move (and sticks and stones may, of course, kill people), but sticks and stones do not govern their own movement. They allow themselves to be acted upon by circumstances, by appetites, by greed and ambition, that is all. True rebellion necessitates robust exertion, not simple surrender.

Bad rebels do not rebel. Their ignorance tricks them into inactivity or their weakness of will saps their strength and pulls them down into passivity. True rebellion is a strenuous activity. It necessitates a double action, agency on two different levels. Good rebels direct, control, and marshal their energies in the direction of the good, but they also have to surmount wrongful authority. Good rebels go to heroic lengths in their opposition to evil. They are not only true rebels, but the most rebellious of rebels. We began this book discussing Milgram's experiments on submission to authority. The noncooperative subjects in the experiment do not only do what is right. They do it under duress, in the face of an oppressive external authority. Their behavior provides us with an exemplary model of human freedom.

One sees the dynamic of false rebellion played out not only in Milton but in popular literature. Characters such as Madame Pontellier in *The Awakening*, the Savage in *Brave New World*, Wyatt and Billy in *Easy Rider*, Dean Moriarty in *On the Road*, and Sid Vicious in *Sid and Nancy* are failed rebels. These are individuals who pursue freedom *instead* of the good. Striving for self-realization apart from morality, they do not achieve any lasting form of self-fulfillment. In such cases, rebellion comes to epitomize, not agency, but the lack of agency—despair, futility, meaninglessness, and suicide. As Holden Caulfield comes to realize, autonomy does not only mean expressing one's individuality. Nonconformism, rebellion, and the modern cult of personal autonomy only make sense when construed as a means to a higher good.

CREATIVE REBELLION

Albert Camus defines the rebel as "A man who says no but whose refusal does not imply renunciation."[29] Camus provides a positive account of rebellion. He argues against the traditional image of rebellion as a destructive, negative gesture. If the rebel says no, he "is also a man who says Yes from the moment he makes his first gesture of rebellion."[30] Rebellion is deeply connected to moral sentiment. It "cannot exist without the feeling that, somewhere, somehow, one is right."[31]

I have argued for moral rebellion. If, however, true rebellion requires a positive movement in the direction of an authentic human good, it must be, at the same time, a creative gesture. The most creative act of all is to be able to conceive of the good in a thoroughly evil world. Conformists accept the way things are, but good rebels imagine a better place. They are able to overcome prejudices and conventions and conceive of new possibilities. Paul Marcus, in a study of Nazi death camps, describes the way in which prisoners with set moral commitments were, perhaps surprisingly, able to transcend the inhumanity of the camps.

Marcus, who revives and amends the theories of Bruno Bettelheim, emphasizes the creative aspects of human liberation. He begins by insisting on the importance of moral integrity to personal autonomy. Although he says, "the concept of autonomy has a moral component to it," this is not, for Marcus, a matter of conceptual necessity, but a matter for historical validation.[32] In the human laboratory of the concentration camps, the supposed tension between morality and autonomy, between caring for others and caring for oneself, broke down. As Marcus indicates: "Inmates who tended to fare the best in camps in terms of autonomy, integration and remaining human . . . in general acted in ways that usually did not intentionally harm other 'innocent' inmates and were regarded by most inmates as working against the Nazis and promoting the inmates' life and soul-sustaining interests."[33] In these dehumanizing conditions, "the most effective way of staying psychologically intact" was through an active concern for the welfare of others.[34] Those who were able to preserve their self-identity displayed a healthy selflessness. As Marcus observes, "In the camps, the more you gave to others, the more you received in terms of the psychic income necessary to remain human. That is, responsibility to the Other did not limit the freedom of the inmate. On the contrary it set him free."[35]

In describing the practice of autonomy under conditions of extreme duress, Marcus comments on the creative aspects of good rebellion. He argues that "maintaining autonomy and remaining human . . . requires that individuals have the capacity to imagine a moral order beyond themselves."[36] It is a concern for objective values, for values that *transcend* the desires of the will or the self that empowers this necessary moral imagination. In the case of the concentration camps, "the values and beliefs of those inmates who [acted heroically] were not strictly personal and subjective; they had a reference to something outside the inmate's own immediate experience."[37]

Marcus discusses well-known cases of priests, Jews, Jehovah's Witnesses, and Marxists who stood out as examples of humanity and civility amidst the utter degradation of the death-camps. It was, he claims, their commitment to an objective value scheme that preserved their remarkable humanity. Marcus comments:

> In the case of Catholic priests, religious Jews and Jehovah's Witnesses, these inmates found strength and moral direction in the revealed word of an absolute, objective and omnipotent creator . . . not in personal values meaningful only to themselves. [They] had the inner capacity to imagine a moral order transcending the dehumanizing Nazi world which gave them strength and direction to maintain themselves as human beings and to act morally and autonomously. In a somewhat similar manner, the militant Marxists . . . had a strong set of political beliefs and moral convictions that gave them the conceptual and other resources to transcend themselves, and project themselves into the future, beyond Nazi attempts to break their autonomy and to dehumanize them.[38]

One may dispute the finer points of morality, but the commitment to an objective morality was sufficient, in these cases, to make these good rebels truly autonomous. In the environment of the camps, this concern for others was a novel act. To care about others, to treat others humanely, was to create a new possibility. It was to envision a new world of aspirations and attitudes that was utterly alien to inmate experience. Good rebellion was, then, not just a moral but also a creative act.

Marcus examines Michel Foucault's account of critical practice. Good rebels oppose authority, and Foucault chronicles the all-pervasive nature of authority. Foucault exposes the ways in which the prevailing myths and structures of society subjugate and imprison individuals. Good rebellion is not, on this view, limited to overt political action. Challenging the social, cultural, and intellectual mores that bind and legitimize a particular society is a subversive activity. Marcus writes: "Consciousness of freedom . . . entails dissolving or changing those anonymous, depersonalizing, conformist practices that constitute our conception of ourselves and that we take to be self-evident and 'true' within the context of the mass society."[39] Good rebellion, on this account, entails a deconstruction of authority. The individual must expose and explode the myths and clichés that society unthinkingly accepts as true. It is, on this account, the subversion of the prevailing worldview that fosters liberation.

DISCIPLINARY SOCIETY: FOUCAULT

Marcus points to Foucault's work as a model for intellectual liberation. Deborah Cook, in turn, presents the philosopher's work as model of "emancipatory social practice." Cook argues that Foucault lays the theoretical "framework for resistance against disciplinary society and for the practical possibility of radical social and political change."[40] If the modern subject finds itself imprisoned in a disciplinary society, Foucault, following Nietzsche, supplies "the tools to burst open the bars of the iron cage."[41] Caught within a succession of abrupt and anonymous historical events, conscientious individuals "have the power to constitute themselves through various forms of self-mastery."[42]

Cook presents Foucault, in effect, as the champion of good rebellion, but Foucault's troubled discourse eliminates the possibility of good rebellion. As Marcus indicates, it is the existence of a higher, objective order, outside the reach of society's ideological machinery, that allows for transcendence. Rebellion necessitates a creative leap to a higher possibility. This means turning away from an oppressive society, a society that has gone bad, and finding renewal in an *objective* source of truth or morality. Foucault, because of his ideological commitments, is unable to elaborate an account of objectivity. His theory collapses under the corrosive force of an unrelenting relativism. He is not, as he is often presented, the prophet of liberation. He is instead a chronicler of inevitable, necessary repression.

Foucault may narrate histories of repression, but we are left with an account of inevitable repression, repression without reprieve, repression that can never be overcome. There is no place for the good rebel, the person who in a muscular, creative act overcomes the pressures of social conformity and formulates a new moral perspective. Truth is a thing of the world, a product of social coercion. That is all. There is no objective truth outside society, no lonely promontory away from received opinion, no higher moral view from which the oppressive power structures of the state can be judged.

In Foucault's system, truth is inevitably, irredeemably a product or a manifestation of social control. Truth is "the ensemble of rules according to which the true and the false are separated,"[43] "a system of ordered procedures for the production, regulation, distribution, circulation, and operation of statements."[44] Truth is a form of power, "a thing of this world . . . produced only by virtue of multiple forms of constraint."[45] If, however, truth is a form of social control, acknowledging, expressing, or even dying for the truth can never be a liberation. It must always be a form of submission, of surrender, of oppression.

Foucault's account of oppression is all-encompassing in its scope. It captures everyone without exception. Insomuch as society controls what the truth is, society controls our actions, for our actions are motivated by those beliefs we take to be true. On the traditional account, to act in accordance with the truth is to be free. On Foucault's account, to act in accordance with the truth is to be controlled by society. We all base our acts on beliefs we take to be true, however, so on this account we are all enslaved by society. Indeed, the only way to escape social control in Foucault's state would be to disregard those beliefs that we believe to be true. But this is to equate freedom with sheer madness.

Foucault's account, however flawed, exposes and elucidates more subtle forms of oppression. Foucault views oppressive Western society as a kind of Christianity gone bad. Society takes over as spiritual director, projecting itself into the minds of citizens so that the power structures regulate not only external behavior but also the life of the mind itself. Ideology regulates not just action, but the motivation behind action. Social control is pervasive. It permeates everyday life, categorizing and classifying the individual, marking him with his own personality, "attach[ing] him to his own identity, [and] impos[ing] a law of truth on him, that he must recognize and others have to recognize in him."[46]

To control the way in which people think about themselves is the most insidious form of social restraint. Foucault writes: "Slavery is not a power relationship when a man is in chains, only when he has some possible mobility, even a chance of escape."[47] Slavery that is enforced by whips and chains is a crude affair. But if the oppressors can make the slaves believe that they are slaves, if the slaves become habituated to slavelike thoughts, if they are convinced that they are predestined to be slaves, if they see themselves as essentially slavelike, chains will not be necessary. Leave them far from home and they will return of their own free will, as obedient and submissive as before.

Foucault's explanation of oppression undermines the standard liberal account of freedom as negative liberty. If society predetermines the content of our desires and motivations, if it reaches inside our minds and formulates our very thoughts, we can do what we want without being, in any genuine sense, free. To be an individual subject is, for Foucault, to be twice oppressed. It is to obey the state and, more insidiously, it is to incarnate the self-identity that society foists on the self. On this model of self-repression, individual citizens are tools of the state, unsuspecting stooges policing themselves. In exercising self-affirmation, they are unwittingly extending the limits of social control.

Foucault's theory constitutes a warning. If good rebellion is an act of resistance against the forces of social conformism, the struggle must be directed inward as well as outward. Oppression is within us. It is epistemological as well as political. We have internalized the stereotypes, clichés, and prejudices of the surrounding society. This is why rebellion must be a creative endeavor. In an oppressive society that regulates thought, the good rebel must take a creative leap to a new possibility not envisaged by a repressive social order.

Two Dangers

Marcus writes: "Maintaining autonomy and remaining human in the repressive total mass state and, I would add, the seductive mass society, seems to require that individuals put moral duty above self-interest." [48] There are two ways in which society may oppress. It may brutalize citizens or it may seduce them. It may build torture chambers, or it may distract them with the inanities of mass consumerism. The good society demands individual responsibility, but it does not oppress. The oppressive society preaches blind obedience or self-indulgence. It forces prejudices and stereotypes onto people, either because they are too terrified to think or because they are too self-satisfied and preoccupied to care

Charles De Koninck, in arguing for Canadian federalism in the early 1950s, attacks the concept of a "Master State."[49] Although his preoccupation with communism seems somewhat dated, his analysis bears closer consideration. De Koninck identifies two kinds of Master State: one motivated by totalitarianism principles, the other by consumerism. He protests against both systems, arguing that both worldviews are inimical to individual freedom. Consider first his critique of totalitarianism.

De Koninck (like Karl Popper) identifies Marx and Plato as the two great apologists of this kind of authoritarian regime. Both propose anonymous, abstract political regimes that ignore and deny the particularity of human nature. In Plato's Republic, for example, the state apparatus effectively eliminates the family, purposely concealing the natural link that connects intimate family members.[50] Citizens lose their natural, biological identity and become anonymous citizens in a hierarchical state. Although Marx proposes an egalitarian regime, he recommends a similar deconstruction of human individuality. It is the collectivity, not the individual, that has ultimate value. In both cases, one is left with a faceless, bureaucratic, totalitarian regime that forces its subjects to conform, worships its own political power, stifles individuality, undermines the family and destroys real difference. De Koninck's associates this kind of Master State with communism.

In the totalitarian state, social control is explicit and unforgiving. The army and police are forces of repression. De Koninck condemns modern totalitarianism, but he also criticizes the proponents of free enterprise who propose a more subtle type of social control. In the consumer state oppression is (as authors such as Tocqueville, Ortega y Gasset, Lecky, and Burnham suggest) more insidious. Advertising is used to create superfluous needs that can never be satisfied. The forces of marketing manipulate individuals, changing their outlook on life, orienting their behavior, and, in general, inciting social conformity. Politics, understood as a rational extension of human nature, is set aside for a life of distraction and thoughtless gratification.

De Koninck claims that both types of Master State represent an ultimate betrayal. Communism imposes a life of ideological conformity. Consumerism orders life according to appetites rather than reason. Communism depends upon a centralized and anonymous ruling structure that crushes individuality of any sort. Consumerism relies on the implicit rule of the market, which discourages critical thinking and urges conformity.

Communism controls public opinion and behavior by force, propaganda, and public inculcation. Consumerism controls public opinion and behavior by fashion and advertising, by the surreptitious use of sexuality and state-of-the-art techniques of persuasion.

De Koninck argues that totalitarianism ignores man's origins, whereas consumer society ignores his end. In both cases, politics becomes a generic, quantitative science. One enforces mindless political loyalty by brute physical force or by the slick techniques of salesmanship. De Koninck's criticism of the Master State could be schematically represented as in table 11.

Table 11. Two Types of Master State

Type of Regime	Proponents	Social Problem	Individual Problem	Metaphysical Problem
T=totalitarianism	Marx, Plato	impersonal bureaucracy	mindless conformity	turns man away from his origins
C=consumerism	champions of free enterprise	consumerism	appetites over reason	turns man away from his final end

De Koninck's analysis of the Master State enlarges the scope of oppression in an insightful way. On the standard model, oppression is a disagreeable fate, a painful yoke, an unsavory proposition, that has to be forced on an unwilling population. Recalcitrant citizens must be terrorized into submission. This is, in De Koninck's view, what happens in a communist regime. But there is another, more insidious possibility. Oppression may be seductive and ingratiating. We may embrace it willingly. This is, in de Koninck's view, what happens in a consumer society.

De Koninck proposes a binary model of political repression. Oppression may be repugnant or unctuous, brutal or self-indulgent, bitter or sweet, self-imposed or imposed from without. The state may wield power by harsh threats or sweet promises, by punishment or reward, with an iron fist or a velvet glove. A seductive slavery is slavery nonetheless. An affluent society that promotes self-gratification may, with surprising efficiency, enforce a mindless conformity. Luxury may be a distraction; sensuality may drive out the capacity for critical thought; hedonism may be a corrosive force; prosperity may sap our creative and moral energies. Anything that robs the individual of conscience, of the capacity for reasoned reflection, is oppressive, and anything oppressive is something the good rebel can struggle to overcome.

De Koninck, following Aquinas and Aristotle, emphasizes human rationality. If human agents are to realize themselves, the life of the mind must be paramount. In a consumer society, rational reflection is difficult if not impossible. The needs of the marketplace prevail. Advertisers and public relations agents seduce and pander, proposing as the only legitimate aspiration the satisfaction of appetites. Buyers and sellers institute a tyranny of false belief and uncritical opinion that monopolizes the public arena and even political discourse.

Heidegger argued that Russian communism and American capitalism were metaphysically the same. De Koninck views them as complementary extremes with similar results. In contemporary North America, consumerism may be the biggest threat to freedom. Totalitarianism is conspicuous in its injustice. Consumerism is, in comparison, a sweet poison.

IDOLATRY

De Koninck's Master State is powerful beyond measure. It demands the uncritical submission of subjects. It requires exclusive allegiance or loyalty. It asserts its authority as the arbiter of good and evil and, on Foucault's model, of truth and falsehood. But these are attributes that are traditionally ascribed to God. God is powerful beyond measure, worthy of worship, requiring loyalty, even to the point of death. He is the arbiter of good and evil and of truth and falsehood. Seen in this light, the Master State is a false god, a human institution that arrogates divine authority. The problem with oppression is, in a word, idolatry.

The good rebel is a breaker of idols. Idolatry turns something that is less than God "into a godlike being."[51] It sets up something human, fallible, or finite as the repository and source of absolute value. As Moshe Halbertal and Avishai Margali explain: "Absolute value can be conferred upon many things–institutions such as the state, persons, goals, ideologies, and even a football team. . . . What makes something into an absolute is that it is both overriding and demanding. It claims to stand superior to any competing claim, and . . . provides a program and a cause, thereby demanding dedication and devotion."[52] De Koninck's Master State usurps the role of God. It demands unquestioning loyalty; it claims our undivided attention; it requires unconditional obedience. In declaring war on the Master State, the good rebel breaks the idol.

A religious preoccupation with idolatry may seem to be far removed from the secular concerns of contemporary society. Modern liberalism derives, however, from the Protestant rejection of idolatry. As Paul Tillich explains, Protestantism began as a revolt against a Roman authority that had allegedly set itself up as an idol. Protestant doctrine stipulates that "no individual and no human group can claim a divine dignity for its moral achievements, for its sacramental power, for its sanctity, or for its doctrine." If any group tries to make such a claim, "Protestantism requires that they be challenged by [a] prophetic protest, which . . . denies every claim of human pride."[53] Liberalism operates, in a secular arena, on a parallel principle.

In a contemporary defense of liberalism, Bruce Ackerman writes: "No reason is a good reason if it requires the power-holder to assert that his conception of the good is better than that asserted by any of his fellow citizens, or that, regardless of his conception of the good, he is intrinsically superior to one or more of his fellow citizens."[54] The problem is that superior groups or doctrines may become idols, false gods, setting themselves up as absolutes, demanding the unconditional loyalty of citizens. Denying claims to epistemological or moral superiority is then proof against oppression. It liberates the individual conscience and eliminates tyranny. This is, for Ackerman, the basic strategy behind liberalism.

Ackerman attempts to ground liberalism on a principled relativism. If relativism is sound, however, all beliefs and opinions are equally valid. We are as justified as anyone else in believing whatever we believe. No one has any grounds for disputing our lifestyle or our opinions. But this is to make an idol of our own convictions. It is to safeguard our views from any robust criticism. To argue for liberalism *and* relativism is to champion a public prohibition of idolatry in order to facilitate the private practice of idolatry. And this is incoherent.

The good rebel is, in some genuine sense, the original liberal. Good rebels refuse to prostrate themselves before false gods, be they states, persons, goals, ideas, or ideologies, but good rebellion presupposes an objective scheme of values. If there is no criterion of truth or morality outside ourselves, our own subjective experiences become the final authority. This is to turn the self into an idol. It is to undermine the original rationale behind a long tradition of Protestant dissent and also liberalism.

NARCISSISM

I have argued that rebellion is a muscular effort in a positive direction motivated by a creative insight that transcends the prevailing mind-set of an oppressive society. Oppression may be self-imposed or imposed by force, sweet or sour, epistemological or social. It involves an idolatry of sorts, an uncritical submission to an evil authority. Good rebellion, seen from this perspective, is the toppling or breaking of idols.

Christopher Lasch has argued that the "narcissistic personality type" was the predominant temperament of the late twentieth century.[55] Other well-known social critics such as Daniel Bell,[56] Charles Taylor,[57] Allen Bloom,[58] Gilles Lipovetsky,[59] Richard Sennett,[60] Robert Bellah,[61] Alan Downs,[62] and Robert Coles[63] comment at length on the narcissistic tenor of the age. Though liberalism provides an effective defense against external enemies, against tyrants and dictators who would set up totalitarian regimes, consolidating power to enslave the masses, the liberal stress on individual conscience is vulnerable to a more subtle form of slavery. In a narcissistic age, the self may set itself up as the supreme authority, as the sole source of epistemological justification or moral validity. Individuals may confer absolute value, not on some external authority, but on their own individual selves. But this is to turn the self into an idol. It is to subvert the historical rationale behind liberalism. It is to substitute one form of idolatry for another.

Narcissism is self-idolatry. It is idolatry turned inwards. This is in keeping with the original legend. The Roman poet Ovid retells the ancient Greek story of Narcissus in his *Metamorphoses* (3.339–510).[64] Soon after his birth, the oracle declares that Narcissus will only live to maturity "if he not know himself."[65] In the course of time, he grows into a handsome young man who spurns advances from a variety of lovers. Out hunting one day, he stops to rest by a forest pool and falls in love with the image he sees reflected back at him in the still water. He tries to kiss the beautiful face, but each time he disturbs the water's surface, the image disappears. He plunges in with his arms to embrace the stranger but ends up with nothing in his grasp. He asks the beautiful stranger to come out of the water, but he will not come. Frustrated, unable to gain what he loves, Narcissus lingers, rooted in the shoreline, wasting away, consumed by his yearning for himself. He is eventually transformed by merciful gods into the flower that bears his name.

Ovid's sophisticated poem is a tale of unrequited love with a twist. Although lovers generally desire union with the other, this is the source of Narcissus's misfortune. Only if Narcissus were separated from that which he loves, that is, separated from himself, could he be joined with what he loves, that is, himself. As Narcissus exclaims:

What I desire is with me; my [abundant beauty] has made me poor.
Oh would that I were able to withdraw from my body; and, a strange wish
in a lover, I should like what I love to be apart.[66]

Because Narcissus is the person he loves, he must remain eternally separated from that which he loves. He cannot possess his own beauty because, paradoxically, this beauty already belongs to him. A strange sort of unrequited love!

The Narcissus story illustrates the pitfalls of self-love. Self-fulfillment comes from union with the other. It does not derive from any exclusive fixation on self. Narcissus is, in effect, divided into two people, an interior self and an exterior self. His internal self makes an idol of his exterior self. His psyche, his spirit, worships at the altar of his physical beauty. The problem is that Narcissus misconstrues this external self for another person. The experience of love does not push him outwards toward the world and other people, but inwards inside himself. It is a trivial fate. Narcissus does not perish in an epic struggle, because he takes great risks, because he accomplishes great things. He perishes, strange to say, from inertia. Narcissism is, like bad rebellion, the absence of agency. It is a thing of mere appearances; it is the elimination of accomplishment.

The Narcissus story is a basic archetype of human mythology. Modern writers in the psychoanalytic tradition pick up on the theme. In his 1914 work "On Narcissism: An Introduction," Sigmund Freud distinguishes between so-called primary and secondary narcissism. Primary narcissism occurs in early childhood when the child is mainly concerned with the gratification of its own bodily functions. Secondary narcissism is a neurotic trait in older individuals. It occurs when the sexual energy that drives the psyche, the libido, is withdrawn from external objects and reinvested exclusively or predominantly in the self. Rejected or slighted by the outside world, the traumatized individual takes the self as love object and tries to secure self-worth and well-being through an incestuous, me-to-me relationship.

Psychoanalysts consider secondary narcissism as a personality disorder with discernible symptoms.[67] The *Penguin Dictionary of Psychology* lists the following effects of narcissistic personality disorder: "an exaggerated sense of self-importance, a tendency to over-value one's actual accomplishments, an exhibitionist need for attention and admiration, a preoccupation with fantasies of success, wealth, power, esteem, or ideal love, and inappropriate emotional reactions to the criticisms of others."[68] Narcissus was the progeny of the gods and, through no fault of his own, supernaturally beautiful, but secondary narcissists are just ordinary people. They construct grandiose self-portraits, then fall in love with these inflated images of themselves. Unlike the original Narcissus, they do not view themselves as they are, but as they wish to be.

Authors in the psychoanalytic tradition see narcissism as a personality disorder; authors associated with the Frankfurt School such as Herbert Marcuse and C. Alford elaborate a more positive account of the concept.[69] As Ovid's retelling of the tale makes clear, however, narcissism involves a fatal *exaggeration*. Full-blown narcissism is a disorder, a neurosis. It represents a mistake, an error, a fissure between the mind and reality. It fosters, not an active interaction with the world, but a self-indulgent self-absorption, an exclusive and debilitating self-centeredness.

NARCISSISM DISGUISED AS AUTONOMY

Readers who peruse the modern literature on personal autonomy may be struck by the subjective tone of the discussion. Insomuch as philosophy is an expression of a larger mind-set, a philosophical preoccupation with autonomy may be a manifestation of wider cultural attitudes. In a narcissistic age, this is a real and worrisome possibility.

During the middle 1970s, just as one witnessed an upsurge of interest in the subject of personal autonomy in the academic literature, journalist Tom Wolfe was commenting on an unprecedented outbreak of selfishness and self-concern that was transforming the American psyche.[70] In a celebrated 1976 essay entitled "The Me Decade and the Third Great Awakening," the journalist reported on an implosion of egocentricity that was sweeping across Middle America. Wolfe describes this new and heady fixation on the self in terms of a religious revival, a wave of narcissistic self-consciousness propelled forward by the force of its own egotistical appeal: "Great religious waves have a momentum all their own. . . . And this one has the mightiest, holiest roll of all, the beat that goes . . . *Me* . . . *Me* . . . *Me* . . . *Me* . . ."[71] The theme of the decade? "Let's talk about Me . . . Let's find the Real Me . . . Let's get rid of all the hypocrisies and impediments and false modesties that obscure the Real Me."[72]

Wolfe reports on a burgeoning obsession with personal psychological health that finds an outlet in self-help therapies, psychoanalysis, and group encounter sessions. But what was the appeal of the heart-wrenching, teeth-grinding, primeval scream, no-holds-barred, group therapy sessions? "The appeal was simple enough. It is summed up by the notion: 'Lets talk about *Me*.' No matter whether you managed to renovate your personality through encounter sessions or not, you had finally focused your attention and your energies on the most fascinating subject on earth: *Me*."[73]

The style of the essay is vintage Wolfe: bombastic, baroque, obsessive, glib, funny, incisive, cynical. Part New Journalism, part social commentary, "The Me Generation" is not the work of a philosopher. But Wolfe, because of his flamboyant style or in spite of it, touches on a simple truth. Modern society breeds a narrow self-absorption, an excessive self-consciousness, an unhealthy preoccupation with self. The importance accorded the autonomy ideal conceals, at times, a strident and unhealthy preoccupation with Me.

The egocentric attitudes of the so-called Me generation persist today. Consider a so-called declaration of self-esteem taken from a poster that I observed two years ago in a university setting. The poster is a message from the self to the self, a testimony of self-esteem from the deepest Me to the deepest Me. This internal conversation, from which the rest of us are excluded, begins with a capitalized declaration of one very obvious fact:

I AM ME.

The self goes on to remind itself of its own uniqueness:

In all the world, there is no one else exactly like me.

With protracted insistence, the self proclaims its right to exclusive and complete ownership of itself:

I own everything about me, my body, my feelings, my mouth, my voice, all my actions, whether they be to others or myself—I own my fantasies, my dreams, my hopes, my fears—I own all my triumphs and successes, all my failures and mistakes—because I own all of me.

The self reassures itself of the possibility of self-knowledge and self-exploration:

Because I own all of me, I can become intimately connected with me . . . I can love me and be friendly with me in all parts—I know that there are aspects about me that puzzle me, and other aspects that I do not know—but as long as I am friendly and loving to myself, I can courageously and hopefully look for solutions to the puzzles and for ways to find out more about me.

The self equates authenticity with those choices it makes exclusively by itself:

Everything that comes out of me is authentically mine, because I alone choose it.

The self claims the ability to remake itself in whatever manner it so chooses:

> I own me, and therefore I engineer me.
> If later some parts of how I looked, sounded, thought, and felt turn out to
> be unfitting, I can discard that which is unfitting, keep the rest, and invent
> something new from that which I discarded.

And finally, the self reassures itself of its own self-worth:

> I am me and I am okay.[74]

This poster offers its own theory of personal achievement. I deserve respect, not because I fulfill any objective criteria of goodness, but simply because "I AM ME." The goal of life is to be "authentically me." I become authentically me by doing what, in some single-minded manner, I myself truly choose to do. If, however, I want to be authentically me, I must "become intimately connected with me"; I must "love me and be friendly with me in all parts"; I must "courageously and hopefully look . . . for ways to find out more about me." Life becomes a project of incessant self-exploration. The good life, the life worth living, is a life devoted to a relationship with oneself rather than a relationship to others. One turns away from morality and embraces self-absorption.

In their best-selling study *Habits of the Heart*, sociologist Robert Bellah and his associates have chronicled the rise of narcissistic attitudes toward the self in contemporary America. Bellah describes a society that has been balkanized, broken into pieces, divided and fragmented by "an isolating preoccupation with the self."[75] He and his associates do not reject individualism, which they see as central to the American personality, but criticize "those tendencies that would destroy [a healthy individualism] from within."[76] Though their social criticism is muted by a highly qualified, academic style, they insist that "some of our deepest problems both as individuals and as a society are closely linked to our individualism."[77]

Bellah and associates identify two strands in American individualism: a utilitarian strand that emphasizes the pursuit of material well-being and an expressive strand that emphasizes cultural and aesthetic achievement. Benjamin Franklin, frontier businessman and philanthropist, stands as an example of the first kind of individualism, and Walt Whitman, the romantic poet and eccentric, embodies the second. The first poem in Whitman's *Leaves of Grass* is entitled "Song of Myself." It begins with the line: "I celebrate myself." While this legacy of self-celebration has enriched American culture and made the United States the leading industrial power, Bellah claims that it has also led to a radical impoverishment of moral and social discourse.

Bellah argues that "the two traditions of individualism offer us only the cost-benefit analysis of external success and the intuition of feeling inwardly more or less free, comfortable, and authentic on which to ground our self-approval."[78] But to base our self-esteem on trappings of material success or on warm fuzzy feelings of inner harmony is to live in a moral vacuum. The profit motif and the search for the inner-Me are morally and spiritually "blind."[79] Neither helps us discern "which tasks and purposes are worth pursuing." Even more important, they remove any incentive for selfless action, obscuring notions of duty, obligation, and calling. As Bellah writes: "Why should we do one thing rather than another, especially when we don't happen to feel like it or don't find it profitable?"[80]

Bellah and his colleagues report on the radical subjectivity of popular discourse. According to the authors, "The predominant ethos of American individualism seems more than ever determined to press ahead with the task of letting go of all criteria other than a radical private validation."[81] This is, however, to argue for subjectivity, for narcissism, for moral solipsism. In a society of "self-contained" individuals, "the objectified moral goodness of . . . obeying God's will or . . . following nature's laws turns into the subjective goodness of getting what you want and enjoying it."[82] "Utility replaces duty; self-expression unseats authority."[83] One looks to self-approval or private self-satisfaction as the sole barometer of genuine achievement and healthful living.

Critics of the new narcissism denounce the role psychology plays in the legitimization of self-centered behaviors and attitudes. Authors such as Sennett and Lipovetsky claim that pop psychology diverts the agent's attention away from other people, focusing it on some nebulous inner self. The end result is a permanent identity crisis—in Bellah's phrase, a "nervous search for the true self" that drives the individual inwards away from other people.[84] If the original Narcissus perishes because he discovers his reflection in the forest pool, the new Narcissus perishes trying to find the pool in which his true image will be reflected. As Lipovetsky puts it: "Narcissus is no long immobilized before his fixed image, there is no longer any image, nothing but an interminable search for self."[85] Because knowledge about the self is incomplete or fragmentary, subjects can lose themselves in the project of delving ever inwards. This eternal state of identity crisis justifies a never-ending self-absorption.

Lipovetsky denounces *Homo psychologicus;* Sennett dismisses psychoanalysis as "a trap rather than a liberation";[86] and Robert Coles defines the new psychology as "a concentration, persistent, if not feverish, upon one's thoughts, feelings wishes, worries—bordering on, if not embracing, solipsism; the self as the only or main form of (existential) reality."[87] Coles complains about the "haunting, unsettling refrain of recent years; I am alright, I have figured myself out; I know what I want—and that's all that counts."[88] Even in the most sincere relationship, the focus is on self-identity. As Ann Swidler observes, "The hidden message in modern treatments of love is . . . not self-sacrifice but self-development."[89]

I have presented the good rebel as the archetype of individual freedom. If a contemporary narcissism sets the self up as an idol, the good rebel is a breaker of idols. It does not matter where the graven image is erected, they will refuse to worship at the pedestal. If they critically evaluate the beliefs and practices of surrounding society, they critically evaluate their own beliefs and practices as well. Narcissism is the psychological equivalent of solipsism. Narcissism points inward. Good rebellion, on the other hand, points outward beyond the self. The narcissistic self is preoccupied with its own desires, whims, feelings, aspirations, but the good rebel measures up to some objective standard of achievement.

Narcissism, like bad rebellion, represents a failure to achieve, a lack of agency. Ontologically and metaphysically, it has no substance. Good rebellion, on the other hand, is hard work. Good rebels are motivated by some positive vision of the way things ought to be. Because their rebellion is fundamentally moral, because it aims at an objective good, it rises above narcissism, above eccentricity, frivolousness, whim, affectation.

QUIET REBELLION

Good rebellion may not look like rebellion at all. Suppose I live in a society where everyone breaks the law, where contempt for legitimate authority has hardened into a pervasive social practice. In this kind of society, being a conscientious, law-abiding citizen may be a form of good rebellion. Good rebels oppose wrongful authority. But, as Foucault points out, authority pervades, in the most insidious ways, all our institutions, our discourses and our practices. Authority is not, in any exclusive sense, a political force. Social expectation, peer group pressure, may be the most coercive authority of all. A young man in a ghetto who refuses to join a gang may have to *resist*, to *oppose* with all his might, the prevailing social expectations. The young man does not break the law. If anything, he strives mightily to conform to the law. Nonetheless, in resisting the pressure to join a gang, he is a good rebel.

Good rebellion may take on an internal dynamic. Suppose I suffer from a major character flaw. I am an alcoholic, a kleptomaniac, someone with an unruly temper, a lecher. In this circumstance, moral behavior may entail some kind of strenuous inner struggle. The reformed pederast who conquers his own feelings, is, in this sense, a good rebel. He rebels against misguided thoughts, emotions, attitudes. He strives to conform to the law and to morality, but he does it by resisting the flawed aspects of his own nature. This is obviously not an ideal situation, but it does entail a kind of good rebellion.[90]

In a sociological work on crimes of obedience, Kelman and Hamilton distinguish between rule-oriented, role-oriented, and value-oriented individuals.[91] Rule-oriented individuals are preoccupied with obeying the law; role-oriented individuals act out the role of a good citizen; and value-oriented individuals inquire into the nature of ethics. Although Kelman and Hamilton claim that value-oriented individuals are less prone to crimes of obedience, human agents may obey rules or conform to specific roles conscientiously. It is not obedience to rules or role-playing but the suspension of judgment that kills autonomy.

Socrates' well-known dictum that the unexamined life is not worth living is as much a comment on autonomy as on philosophy. If our convictions and aspirations are to be our own, we must come to them through a process of individual reflection. Henry David Thoreau writes: "The mass of men serve the state thus not as men mainly, but as machines. . . . In most cases there is no free exercise of judgement or of the moral sense; but they put themselves on a level with wood and earth and stones. . . . Such men command no more respect than men of straw or a lump of dirt."[92] Conscientious *obedience* may be a form of successful self-government, if we assent to legitimate authority in some thoughtful way. If we farm out our intellectual responsibilities, however, and let other people decide for us, we lose our individual humanity. Good rebels stand as an exemplary model of individual achievement, for they are isolated by a hostile society. Alone and embattled, they must strike out on their own and make decisions for themselves.

I have proposed the ideal of the good rebel. One could try to articulate the opposite ideal, the ideal of the good conformist, but conformists cannot provide us with a model of individual achievement. Conformists lack agency. The source of their behavior is outside themselves. Good rebels initiate action. Society does not support their endeavors. It condemns, bullies, and even terrorizes them. Good rebels must act on their own, at times, against enormous opposition. They must be moved by an overwhelming sense of personal conviction. This is why the good rebel is such a conspicuous example of individual achievement.

9

Negative Liberty

INSIDE AND OUTSIDE OF NARNIA: A FALSE DICHOTOMY

In C. S. Lewis's *The Chronicles of Narnia*, the question of freedom arises. Narnia, an enchanted land of talking animals and runaway children, has fallen on hard times. The Ape, who pretends he is really a man, has usurped political power and declared himself king, enslaving his subjects and enriching himself from the profits of their labors. As a crowd of discontented animals gathers round, he tries to reassure them:

> "There! You see!" said the Ape. "It's all arranged. And for your own good. We'll be able, with the money you earn, to make Narnia a country worth living in. There'll be oranges and bananas pouring in—and roads and big cities and schools and offices and whips and muzzles and saddles and cages and kennels and prisons—Oh everything."
> "But we don't want all those things," said an old Bear. "We want to be free
> . . ."
> "Now don't you start arguing," said the Ape, "for it's a thing I won't stand. I'm a man: you're only a fat, stupid old Bear. What do you know about freedom? You think freedom means doing what you like. Well, you're wrong. That isn't true freedom. True freedom means doing what I tell you."[1]

Lewis's intentions are ironic. The Ape-King proposes two definitions of freedom: (1) "freedom means being allowed to do what you like," and (2) "freedom means doing what I tell you." The tyrant champions freedom (2), a freedom that is associated with "whips and muzzles and saddles and cages and kennels and prisons." But this is not freedom at all. It is a thinly disguised authoritarianism. True freedom is, for Lewis, freedom (1), the ability to do as one likes, that is, the ability to act in accordance with personal taste and inclination.

Lewis's twofold analysis of the concept of freedom seems to come straight out of the work of fellow Oxford don Isaiah Berlin. Berlin, in the influential essay "Two Concepts of Liberty,"[2] divides political thinkers into two opposing camps. On one side, we have negative theorists who define liberty as freedom from outside interference. On the other side, we have positive theorists who define liberty in positive terms as a condition of self-control or autonomy. Negative theorists argue that "freedom means being allowed to do what you like." Positive theorists argue that freedom involves submission to a higher-order self that, in the course of history, comes to be identified with state authority. Berlin, like Lewis, vigorously attacks the latter approach.

Berlin believes that negative and positive approaches to freedom typify "profoundly divergent and irreconcilable attitudes to the ends of life."[3] Although Berlin presents us with an exclusive disjunction—freedom means negative freedom *or* freedom means autonomy—I will argue that these negative and positive concepts are not opposed or mutually exclusive. The concepts of negative and positive liberty do not offer competing visions of the human condition. They are related to one another as means and end. Negative liberty—construed as the freedom to do as one likes—is a highly valuable attribute. It is highly valuable, however, as a means to positive freedom or autonomy.

Berlin and Lewis attack the Hegelian view that freedom means submission to the state. Their rejection of positive notions of freedom is the expression of a perennial discomfort with a political ideology that can best be summed up in Rousseau's infamous phrase that whosoever refuses to obey the state "will be forced to be free."[4] Their concern is not misplaced, but Lewis and Berlin oversimplify the issue. We do not have to side, in any exclusive way, with Berlin or Hegel. Both definitions of freedom have their limits. Freedom does not always mean doing what we like to do, for we may have disordered appetites. Then again, freedom does not always mean doing what the state tells us to do, for we may live in an evil state. It is not that one definition is wrong and that the other definition is right. *Neither* definition is quite correct. Exercising freedom may mean, at times, ignoring our own likes, and it may mean, at times, disobeying the rules or directives of an evil government.

DEFENDING NEGATIVE LIBERTY: THE USUAL ARGUMENT

In contemporary philosophy, granting negative freedom to other people is often defended as a means of procuring negative freedom for oneself. This argument has two basic premises: (1) that it is in our interest to be allowed to do what we want to do, and (2) that the best way to secure negative liberty for oneself is by granting negative liberty to others. Various versions of social-contract theory hinge on similar premises. Negative liberty is a fundamental value, but these premises are, strictly speaking, problematic. Consider them briefly.

The prevalent view that large doses of negative freedom contribute to human flourishing seems more an article of faith than a verifiable assertion. It may seem scandalous to disagree, but the idea that increases in negative liberty lead, in the long run, to personal success and happiness is not a necessary truth. One has to support this kind of claim with some kind of argument. Otherwise, we beg the question.

When discussing law-and-order issues in society, one might distinguish between a liberal and a conservative view. Contemporary philosophers, influenced by a liberal tradition that derives from Mill, generally assume that negative liberty promotes individual flourishing and the improvement of society. But while liberal optimism tells us that freedom is good for people, a perennial cynicism about human nature surfaces in every culture. Conservative John Keykes lambasts the liberal belief "that people are naturally good."[5] Keykes insists that "vices of selfishness, greed, malevolence, envy, aggression, prejudice, cruelty, and suspicion" are "prevalent in all human societies."[6] In the face of such rampant human evil, the liberal faith in human goodness "is an indefensible, sentimental, and destructive falsification of reality."[7] It "flatters humanity by painting a rosy picture of wonderful possibilities, while neglecting the hard facts it cannot accommodate. It is a sentimental [lie] that substitutes illusion for reality."[8]

The usual argument for negative liberty presupposes the excellence of individual humanity. People are smart enough, prudent enough, and moral enough to make their own decisions. On a more cynical (or realistic) view, granting people large amounts of freedom may mean giving them "enough rope to hang themselves." On a conservative view, individual citizens may need to be coerced for their own good. This view is unpopular, but not entirely implausible. Authors like Keykes, Gaylin, and Jennings emphasize the importance of coercion to good government.[9] Coercive action does not only stop agents from harming themselves. It also protects agents who would be harmed by other agents' actions. The citizens of Aldous Huxley's *Brave New World* or the inhabitants of B. F. Skinner's *Walden II* lead wonderfully happy lives precisely because they *lack* individual freedom. They are, in effect, coerced into being good *for their own good*.

Faith in individual human excellence leads to a certain view of political organization. Outside the economic sphere, we might subscribe to an Adam-Smith-like doctrine of the "invisible hand." If we grant individual citizens large amounts of negative liberty, society will be led "as if by an invisible hand" to an arrangement that will best serve the welfare of its constituent members. But claims that people know what is best for themselves cannot be definitively substantiated. Although one would hope that this is indeed the case, this is not a claim that can be settled philosophically.

Liberals argue against coercion. Because coercion restricts negative liberty, it cannot lead to human flourishing. But this is too simple. Suppose we divide society into the rugged individualists who successfully fend for themselves and the psychological weaklings who continually self-destruct. If the rugged individualists predominate, increasing negative liberty may be a good thing. If, however, the weaklings predominate, *restricting* negative liberty may lead to a general increase in happiness. This latter conclusion can be avoided if there are more rugged types than weakling types in society. But how can we determine which personality type predominates? Liberals believe in human excellence. Conservatives argue that human incompetence is rampant. There is no definitive, foolproof way of settling such questions. Both positions are contentious. Both are inherently problematic.

The second premise in standard arguments for negative liberty is that the best way of securing negative liberty for oneself is by granting negative liberty to others. Again, this is not a foregone conclusion. Even worse, it may be politically naïve. Tyrants have an effective strategy for increasing their own negative liberty. They enslave and oppress their neighbors. Why? Because this allows these tyrants to do—without limits—anything they want to do. In securing negative liberty for themselves, successful tyrants do not grant negative liberty to others. They do away with other people's negative liberty entirely.

If I want to procure large amounts of negative liberty for myself, why should I see to it that my next-door neighbor enjoys an equal amount of negative liberty? If I have friends in high places, if I have money or weapons, if I am, by nature, supremely intelligent, if I am willing to act immorally, I may profit from the systematic oppression of my neighbors. If, by good fortune, I am the sovereign, the prince, *Il Duce*, the chief, the boss, or even the head of the household, egalitarian notions may seriously diminish my negative liberty. They may restrict my ability to do as I will.

The standard argument fails on both accounts. We cannot definitively prove that large amounts of negative liberty are in every agent's self-interest. Nor can we prove that granting other people negative freedom is the best way to secure our own negative liberty. Negative liberty *is* an important aspect of human society. But we need a better argument to show why or how it contributes to human flourishing.

INVESTIGATING NEGATIVE LIBERTY

We have isolated three different aspects of the freedom phenomenon. (1) Agents may possess free will; the ability, in a metaphysical sense, to choose between good and evil. (2) Agents may achieve autonomy—that is, they may, of their own accord, do what they ought to do. And finally, (3) agents may possess negative liberty—that is, they may possess the freedom to do whatever they want to do. We have presupposed the existence of free will and have examined, at length, the concept of autonomy. We must now examine the concept of negative liberty.

We might try to define freedom in purely negative terms. Hobbes, for one, provides a purely negative definition of freedom. According to Hobbes, "LIBERTY or FREEDOME signifieth (properly) the absence of Opposition" to action.[10] A man is free when he "finds no stop in doing, what he has the will, desire, or inclination to doe."[11] If, however, negative liberty provides agents with the freedom to do whatever they want to do, why should we value negative liberty? As the conservative critic points out, agents often desire to act in ways that are wicked, base, foolish, or just plain incompetent. Why should we give them the freedom to accomplish their possibly wicked ends?

I will argue that negative liberty is not valuable because it allows agents, in some unqualified sense, to do whatever they want to do. It can only be valuable because it allows agents to achieve the good. If we never accomplished anything worthwhile, if there was nothing worth possessing or pursuing, negative liberty would be of little consequence. As we shall see, however, negative liberty is a necessary condition for moral achievement. We cannot successfully govern ourselves in the absence of negative liberty.

Contemporary discussions of negative liberty inevitably focus on the way in which the actions of other human agents interfere with our own plans and aspirations, but this is to provide a very narrow definition of negative liberty. My ability to do as I will is also limited by many other factors: the laws of physics, the nature of time, the physiology of my body, the historical context I was born into, the actions of nonhuman agents, and so on. Suppose I am a serious runner. I have the will, desire, and inclination to set a new world record in the mile. But I am hindered in my pursuit. I lack adequate training; I suffer injuries; I fall sick; the day before the race, I lose my spikes; I am bitten by a dog; I run the race into a strong head-wind; I am tripped on the last bend; and so on. These are all impediments, obstacles that prevent me from doing what I want to do. Strictly speaking, they are constraints on my negative liberty, constraints on my ability to do as I will.

Our ability to act may be curtailed or hindered in three different ways: (1) by the metaphysical nature of the universe, (2) by the behavior of other agents, and (3) by habits, psychological factors, and beliefs that characterize our very own selves. Rigorously speaking, freedom may be defined, on the negative liberty model, in terms of a single coherent formula. What is freedom? It is an absence or removal of those obstacles that hinder our ability to act. Which obstacles? Those obstacles that originate (1) from the physical world, (2) from other agents, and (3) from within ourselves. Popular theorists tend to overlook (1); they define negative liberty in terms of (2), and they theorize about autonomy in terms of (3). This exclusive concentration on the behavior of other agents is misleading.

Champions of negative liberty defend the right to decide for oneself. They do not always realize that we can protect and preserve negative liberty in three distinct ways. (1) We may heavily invest in science and technology, producing machines and procedures that allow us to manipulate the physical world in accordance with our own wishes. (2) We may establish a political apparatus that jealously protects our individual rights, warding off unwanted intrusions and interventions into our private lives. And (3), we may remedy those psychological constraints and deficiencies that inhibit self-realization. In popular political discourse, the champions of negative liberty tend to focus on (2). But a society that is completely free in a negative sense will focus on (1), (2), and (3). It will be made up of individuals who exert control over their physical environment, who enjoy negative liberty, and who are psychologically able to choose for themselves.

Physical liberty, negative liberty, and autonomy can all be defined in negative terms as the removal of obstacles to action. In this book I have taken a different approach. I have provided, in line with classical Western philosophy, a positive account of individual freedom. Although negative accounts of freedom are conceptually useful, they are, in a more fundamental sense, seriously misleading. Freedom cannot, in any ultimate sense, be identified with the removal of obstacles to action. Indeed, the exercise of freedom can be construed, in the proper sense, as *the imposition of obstacles to action*. Freedom is not, first and foremost, about negative liberty. The seed of the idea resides in the concept of personal autonomy.

Suppose I freely decide to visit my parents in Calgary. This means that

I cannot spend time with my wife and children in Quebec. Or suppose I decide to go to Quebec. This means that I cannot spend time with my parents in Calgary. In making choices, I place obstacles in the way of ability to act. The erection of these obstacles is not, however, a restriction on freedom. It constitutes the phenomenon of freedom itself.

In acting freely, we choose to impose constraints and limitations on our actions. If I choose to speak in French, I cannot speak in English. If I choose to be in Calgary, I cannot be in Quebec. In choosing to do X, I erect an insurmountable obstacle to the commission of all contradictories of X. This may be a matter of some consequence. Suppose I want to drive to Toronto and be back home before six o'clock. I desperately want to be home by six, but there is heavy traffic on the road and I do not make it home until eight. In doing what I want to do (driving to Toronto) I place an obstacle in the way of doing something else I want to do (arriving home before six). The very exercise of freedom may restrict my negative liberty; it may seriously restrict my ability to do what I want to do.

We must not conflate two separate issues: (1) we may be faced with obstacles that prevent specific choices; (2) we may make an actual choice. Negative freedom has to do with (1). Autonomy has to do with (2). Suppose Carlos is considering doing X. And suppose we remove all obstacles to X. We eliminate all contradictory physical factors, prevent interference from other agents, and help Carlos remedy any psychological problems that might prevent the successful completion of X. A fundamental issue remains. Removing all obstacles to the completion of X leaves Carlos with two alternatives: doing X or not doing X. Carlos must now *choose*. He must *will* to do or not to do X. This is how freedom begins. Freedom is a positive phenomenon. It entails a positive act of choice. Hobbes defines freedom in terms of the removal of obstacles to our ability to act. In explaining the freedom phenomenon, however, he overlooks the act of choosing itself. This results in an account of freedom that is seriously flawed. It is as if the germ of the freedom idea escapes him.

One might object that Carlos can decide not to choose. But this will not do. As modern existentialists insist, to choose not to choose is to choose. We are, in Jean-Paul Sartre's famous phrase, "condemned to be free."[12] If Carlos avoids choosing between X and not X, he has chosen something. In refusing to exercise his ability to choose, he has exercised his ability to choose.[13] It is this unavoidable agency, this inevitable *exercise* of choice, that is the origin of the freedom idea. There may be obstacles to the exercise of choice, but freedom is not simply the removal of those obstacles but the agency, the movement of will, the process of deciding, that must accompany any genuine act of choice.

To be free is not simply to be able to choose. It is, more fundamentally, to actually choose. Hobbes writes that an agent is free insomuch as he "finds no stop in doing *what he has . . . the will to doe.*" But an agent who has the will to do something has *already* chosen. He has already exercised his will. This exercise of will is the sine qua non of freedom. Without the exercise of will, there can be no such thing as freedom. Autonomy is the successful exercise of will. It is not a negative but a positive phenomenon.

At the heart of the freedom phenomenon is a positive act of choice, but even this is not enough. I have argued that autonomous agents must not only choose. They must make the right choices. Understood as the acme of human achievement, freedom must be expressed in moral terms, in terms of the affirmative action of successful choosing. The good rebel is a paradigm of freedom, for good rebels act nobly in the face of injustice. They do not acquiesce. They are anything but passive. They do not simply think about morality. They put it into practice.

Contemporary authors like Babbit, Watson, Frankfurt, and Dworkin define autonomy in terms of the psychological ability to choose. On this account, autonomy means, to borrow Hobbes's expression, that a man finds no *psychological* stop in doing what he has the will, desire, or inclination to do. This definition is remarkably passive. It defines freedom as an ability rather than as the exercise of that ability. It is also solipsistic. To be a successful chooser is not simply to choose for oneself. Agents who choose for themselves may make the wrong decisions. Suppose I choose to be incompetent. If I am a truly incompetent agent, I am a failure as a human agent. I am not a successful chooser.

The focus on negative liberty has been embraced by some modern-day conservatives. But these "negative" conservatives seem to contradict themselves. On the one hand, they want to champion a principle of governmental nonintervention. (As in Berlin's famous *plaidoyer* for negative liberty.)[14] On the other hand, they champion an ideal of rugged individualism. (See, for example, Ayn Rand.)[15] If, however, some sort of robust individual choice is at the very heart of the freedom phenomenon, we cannot equate freedom with government nonintervention. It is not the mere removal of political obstacles to action that makes agents free. It is the exercise of rugged individualism. If agents lack the psychological, intellectual, and ethical skills that contribute to rugged individualism, granting them all the political freedom in the world will not make them free. The conservative preoccupation with rugged individualism entails a covert recognition of the importance of autonomy. Berlin may regard positive notions of freedom with opprobrium, but one cannot make any sense of his own preoccupation with negative liberty without assuming some positive account of the freedom phenomenon.

I want to argue that negative liberty is only valuable as a means to autonomy. There is no point providing people with negative liberty if they are incompetent decision-makers. An ideal society will not only provide negative liberty for its members. It will be a society of competent decision-makers. If growing up in a ghetto turns one into a bad decision-maker, society will do its best to eliminate urban poverty. One may eliminate poverty through redistribution of wealth or through free enterprise. Those on the left argue that redistribution of wealth will not occur without government help; those on the right argue that government interference is costly, self-defeating, and inefficient. That is a different debate. The important point, for our purposes, is that a society that cares about human freedom must focus on human welfare, not just on government noninterference.

Debates between the proponents of positive and negative liberty are often, on closer inspection, debates about negative liberty. Suppose, for example, I am a paraplegic. If I have an electric wheelchair, I will be able to move freely from place to place. This will allow me to do what I want to do. But suppose the equipment is very expensive. Should the government buy me the wheelchair? When the government taxes other citizens to secure the money for the wheelchair, it restricts their ability to do as they will with their money. When the government supplies me with the wheelchair, it increases my physical ability to do as I will. So what should be done? So-called positive theorists argue that we should increase the negative liberty of the handicapped; negative theorists argue that we should preserve the negative liberty of taxpayers.

Debates about positive and negative liberty are not just about money. There is a moral component to successful choosing. If, for example, we can teach children to be moral, they will be more successful choosers. So-called positive theorists may then argue that government should promote, in its broadest sense, moral education. This might include anything from teaching children allegiance to the flag, warning them about sexual abuse, providing obligatory sex education, providing religious training, learning about ecology, inculcating the duties of good citizenship, and so on. So-called negative theorists may argue that any attempt to inculcate moral values is a restriction on negative liberty. This would be a debate about the relative importance of negative liberty and autonomy, properly construed. But generally speaking, in practical politics, lines are not so easily drawn. It might very well be that so-called liberals support sex education while so-called conservatives support religious education. In this case, we would not be faced with a debate between parties who argue for and against negative liberty but a debate about which infringements on the negative liberty of children and families are warranted.

Obviously, negative liberty is important. It provides an arena for human achievement. But negative liberty is a necessary but not sufficient condition for autonomy. As Robert Young puts it: "Autonomy does not merely consist in being unobstructed in one's pursuits. To be thus unobstructed is necessary, but not sufficient."[16] Freedom begins with the possibility for choice and culminates in the act of successful choosing.

Negative liberty is a means; autonomy is the end. Henry David Thoreau complains about an American mania for invention. Why? Because "our inventions are wont to be pretty toys, which distract our attention from serious things."[17] Without a proper conception of the good, "our inventions are wont to be . . . but improved means to an unimproved end."[18] Technology increases negative liberty. It removes obstacles that hinder action. Considered as an end in itself, however, technology may become an expensive and even dangerous distraction. The goal of human society is, in Haworth's words, "that the individual may exist in an environment that nurtures and endorses autonomy."[19] Insomuch as technology detracts from that goal, it is no longer a worthy end. Authors like Thoreau, George Orwell, Rollo May, George Grant, Martin Heidegger, and Albert Borgman remind us, in diverse ways, that technology may pose serious threats to autonomy.

FORMAL THEORIES OF AUTONOMY: JOSEPH RAZ

Richard Lindley writes: "Liberal democratic societies pride themselves on respect for negative liberties such as freedom of expression, freedom of the press and freedom of political association. . . . [All of these] are very important, [but] they are not intrinsic values. Their main worth consists in being necessary conditions for the development, maintenance and exercise of autonomy."[20] Haworth concurs.[21] He maintains that John Stuart Mill valued liberty not as an end-in-itself but as a means to a healthy individuality or autonomy.[22] Liberal philosophers like Joseph Raz and Will Kymlicka elaborate somewhat similar arguments. Raz, in particular, maintains "that a powerful argument in support of political freedom is derivable from the value of personal autonomy."[23]

Raz's argument for the value of negative liberty may, at first glance, resemble the argument we will elaborate here. Raz writes: "In judging the value of negative freedom one should never forget that it derives from its contribution to autonomy."[24] But though Raz tries to secure the value of negative liberty as a means to autonomy, he elaborates a formal rather than a substantive definition of freedom. Raz does not identify autonomy with morality. He identifies autonomy, in negative terms, with freedom of choice.

Formalist accounts of liberalism pervade the literature. On the formalist view, autonomy only has to do with people choosing for themselves.[25] It does not involve making the right choices. If we are going to examine whether a particular agent has made the right choices, we must invoke some partisan notion of the good life. And this is to investigate something different than freedom.

Charles Larmore, a prominent formalist, distinguishes between the "substantial ideals of the good life and the ideals of autonomy."[26] According to Larmore: "Substantial ideals involve commitment to some specific way of life. . . . By contrast, the ideals of autonomy . . . concern the way in which we ought to assume and pursue such substantial ideals. They themselves are not so much ways of life as attitudes."[27] Larmore argues that autonomy is purely a "formal" value. It has everything to do with how we choose, and nothing to do with what we choose. On this account, immoral agents may be autonomous just so long as they are not forced to be immoral by other people. If they themselves decide to be immoral, in acting immorally they are fully autonomous.

Raz, like Larmore, argues that autonomy is a purely formal value. "The autonomous life is discerned not by what there is in it but by how it came to be."[28] But if autonomy only has to do with choosing for oneself, it may lead to wrong choices. Raz himself explicitly states: "A person is autonomous even if he chooses the bad."[29] I will argue, however, that we cannot neatly distinguish between the content of an action and the way it came to be. There is something fundamentally incoherent about the content-procedure distinction.

One cannot define autonomy solely in terms of procedures rather than results, for procedures must be evaluated in terms of their results. Suppose, for example, I were to maintain that I had mastered the art of selecting ripe melons (an endeavor of no little skill). And suppose that every time I choose a melon and cut into it, it is still hard and sour and green. In these circumstances, it would make no sense to argue that I was a good melon-chooser. To use a good procedure for selecting melons is to consistently choose melons that are ripe. More generally, it does not make sense to argue that someone who is making the wrong choices is using good decision-making procedures, for good decision-making procedures are, by definition, those that lead to good results.

Formalists want to evaluate the process of decision-making separate and apart from any evaluation of the actual choices made. If, however, autonomy means choosing in the proper way, choosing in the proper way means making the right decision. On occasion, good decision-making procedures may result in bad outcomes, but to argue that they consistently produce bad results is incoherent. If they consistently produce bad results, then they are bad decision-making procedures. We cannot investigate whether an individual is choosing well without paying attention to the outcome of their decisions. Good decision-making procedures lead to an objective good, a good that is valuable not just because the agent chooses it but because it coheres with what it is reasonable to believe about the world.

Raz comes close to elaborating a moral theory of autonomy. He goes so far as to argue that freedom "is valuable only if it is exercised in pursuit of the good."[30] But while Raz recognizes the importance of morality to successful decision-making, he does not incorporate this concern into his definition of autonomy. On Raz's account, autonomous agents satisfy three separate conditions: (1) they must be "minimally rational"; (2) they must enjoy an adequate range of options; and (3) they must not be coerced by others. A minimally rational agent possesses "the mental abilities to form intentions of a sufficiently complex kind and plan their execution."[31] If a minimally rational agent has a wide range choices and is free from coercion, that is enough. He or she is autonomous.

Raz is an "altruistic liberal." He admits that notions of well-being have a moral content.[32] To experience well-being is to thrive, not just physically, but in a moral and communal sense. Yet Raz does not define autonomy in terms of morality but in terms of freedom of choice. Autonomy is the physical, social, and psychological ability to choose. If one chooses unsuccessfully, one is still autonomous.

Raz, like so many other theorists, advances an amoral account of autonomy, but as he himself intimates, there is more to the freedom phenomenon than negative liberty. Being a successful chooser does not just mean "being able to choose"; it means "being able to choose correctly." Freedom is not, at the most fundamental level of analysis, a purely procedural or formal condition. It entails the achievement of an objective or a substantive good. As Haworth points out, autonomy is the achievement of a complex capacity for *successful* decision-making. Autonomous agents must enjoy freedom of choice, but agents who enjoy freedom of choice are not necessarily autonomous.

NEGATIVE LIBERTY AS A MEANS TO AUTONOMY

I have presented autonomy as the acme of human achievement. Bernard Berofsky rejects this idea as extreme, pejoratively labeling it (in a discussion of Haworth) as "autonomism."[33] Willard Gaylin and Bruce Jenning launch a similar attack on "a powerful and often arrogant culture of autonomy."[34] Keykes, in turn, rails against the liberal emphasis on autonomy. These authors offer trenchant criticism of North American culture, but what these authors label as a cult of autonomy is not, properly speaking, about autonomy. They deplore a false autonomy, the kind of self-centered, egocentric Me-generation narcissism Tom Wolfe criticizes. This kind of obsessive self-absorption has little to do with autonomy, as I have defined it here. Self-absorbed, narcissistic individuals do not want autonomy, the freedom to do what is right. What they want is freedom to do whatever they want. That is, what they want is negative liberty.

Negative liberty may be abused. Nonetheless, I will argue that it is an important aspect of freedom because it is a necessary requirement for morality and therefore for autonomy. Why not take away negative liberty and force people to do what is good? Because, if I force you to be moral, I—paradoxically—do not allow you to be moral, for "being moral" means doing the right thing, not because you have been forced, but because you freely choose to do it. If I force you to act morally, your actions are an expression of my will rather than yours. Moral agents act morally on their own initiative. They do what is good freely, voluntarily, of their own accord. When people are forced to be moral, we no longer allow them to be moral.

Rollo May asks a rhetorical question: "Is not one of the central problems of modern Western man that he experiences himself without significance as an individual?"[35] Once we eliminate negative liberty, we eliminate the opportunity for personal achievement and, consequently, empty individual human striving of its ultimate meaning. If we care about self-achievement, we will not force people to choose the good. We must allow them to choose the good on their own, for themselves. To eliminate all negative liberty, all freedom of choice, would be to imprison agents in a space where they themselves cannot accomplish anything.

If autonomous agents make the right choices, they also choose for themselves. This is the raison d'être of negative liberty. It allows for the existence of responsible agents who can be credited, congratulated, acclaimed, or praised for the goodness of their acts. They can be praised because they chose for themselves. The credit belongs to them, not to some external agency. This is the meaning of individual achievement.

Keykes argues against a liberal view according to which agents can "be held responsible only for their autonomous actions."[36] I have introduced a moral account of autonomy. On this account, autonomous agents should, in a positive sense, be held responsible for their actions. They should be. acclaimed for the worthwhile things they do. But, as Keykes insists, nonautonomous agents should also be held responsible, in a negative sense, for their actions. They should be criticized, censored, or even punished for the evil things they do. Consider, very briefly, the relationship between autonomy and moral responsibility.

There are four different cases. Firstly, there are autonomous agent who act in a moral manner. Autonomous agents do, freely and deliberately, what they ought to do. They should be credited, congratulated, acclaimed, praised, and perhaps rewarded for their behavior.

Secondly, there may be autonomous agents who are coerced or forced to act in an evil manner. These kinds of agents cannot be held responsible for such acts, for they cannot, by definition, freely and deliberately act in an evil manner. Otherwise, they would not be autonomous.

Thirdly, there is the case of nonautonomous agents who, knowingly and willfully, act in an immoral manner. Such agents must be held responsible for the badness of their acts. They deserve to be blamed, criticized, condemned, chastised, and perhaps punished.

Fourthly, there is the case of an nonautonomous agent who is forced or coerced into acting in a moral manner. These agents do not act on their own initiative and cannot be credited with the goodness of their acts.

The relationship between autonomy and moral responsibility may be represented in the form of tables 12 and 13.

Table 12. Moral Responsibility and Autonomy

	acts in a good manner	acts in a bad manner
autonomous agent	can be credited	cannot be held responsible (table 13)
nonautonomous	cannot be credited	must be held responsible

Table 13 expands on the case of an autonomous agent who appears to act in a bad manner.

Table 13. Autonomy and Responsibility for Evil

	acts willfully in a bad manner	forced, coerced, or acts accidentally in a bad manner
autonomous agent "appears" to act in a bad manner	cannot act willfully in a bad manner	cannot be held responsible

Autonomy may be identified with morality. Obviously, agents who are generally autonomous (generally moral) may have their weaker moments. And agents who are generally nonautonomous (generally immoral) may have their better moments. How one judges the vicissitudes of an entire life in some coherent and unified manner is too complex an issue to navigate here. Suffice it to say that insomuch as free agents act morally, they act autonomously. And insomuch as free agents act immorally, they fail to act autonomously.

Why then is negative liberty important? If society forced individuals to act in an exemplary manner, there would be no place for moral responsibility. But moral responsibility, broadly construed, makes personal achievement possible. In a world devoid of moral responsibility, we could not make sense of human striving. We must give people the opportunity to strive, and those who strive will sometimes fail. In preserving the possibility for human success, we also preserve the possibility of human failure.

A Political Theodicy

Hobbes spoke of the state as a "mortal god," and one can generate a political argument for negative liberty that parallels traditional religious arguments from theodicy. Christians are faced with an apparent contradiction. If God is benevolent and all-powerful, why did God create a world in which there is evil?[37] Committed Christians usually respond that evil is a human artifact; it derives from an abuse of free will. Why then did God give human agents free will? Because without free will, human beings could not achieve the good. If human beings could not freely do what was wrong, then they could not freely do what was right. Evil, as it turns out, is a disturbing but necessary side effect of a world that makes moral achievement possible.

We can use the same argument to defend negative liberty. Imagine an all-powerful but benevolent government that grants its citizens negative liberty. And suppose there is a significant crime rate. The conservative might protest: "How could a benevolent government permit the existence of crime?" Why not eliminate all crime-related suffering by abolishing negative liberty? Why not force people to be good? If, however, the state forced citizens to act morally, they themselves could not decide to act morally on their own. In politics as in theology, if individual agents cannot freely do what is wrong, they cannot freely do what is right. The freedom to make bad decisions is, as it turns out, a necessary side effect of the freedom to make good decisions. This is why political states must do everything they can to preserve negative liberty. Negative liberty is, like free will, a necessary condition for individual achievement.

This defense of negative liberty strikes a delicate balance between liberal and communitarian positions. Liberal authors argue for a state that is neutral toward the good. Authors in the communitarian tradition argue that the state should be concerned with the moral self-realization of citizens. It is perhaps more reasonable to argue that the state must (1) play a positive role in the promotion of morality *and* (2) defend the negative liberty of its citizens. This is, in some sense, to join the communitarianism of thinkers like Rousseau, Hegel, and Dewey with the liberalism of authors like Hobbes, Locke and Mill. The resulting political view is a kind of liberalism for it recognizes the ultimate importance of individual accomplishment. But it is a communitarian liberalism in that it understands individual accomplishment in moral terms. On the one hand, individuals are not lost or submerged within the state. On the other hand, individuals are not left to their own devices in a kind of moral vacuum. As communitarians suggest, political practice entails more than the mere preservation of negative liberty. In Haworth's words: "An environment that develops people's capacity for autonomy is achieved not merely by removing restraint from it so that 'everything is permitted,' but, more important, by building appropriate institutions and practices."[38]

Raz goes so far as to write: "It is the function of governments to promote morality."[39] It is often argued that a moral state will (1) restrict the negative liberty of individual citizens and (2) be unable to provide a sufficiently rich account of human fulfillment. Consider, very briefly, these two arguments.

The first argument is based on a misconception. Authors tend to assume that a state that is interested in promoting morality will try to force its individual citizens to do the good. As I have already argued, moral agents must accomplish the good freely, of their own accord. If the state wants to promote morality, it will have to preserve negative liberty as a necessary means to morality. To force people to act morally is to take away their capacity for moral achievement.

The second argument is based on an exceedingly narrow view of morality. The moral impetus expresses itself in a multitude of ways. Tinker, tailor, farmer, sailor: human beings may realize their desires and aspirations in widely divergent ways. The original Puritan tradition separated notions of personal freedom from our deeper spiritual aspirations, but a moral state may embrace a more substantial interpretation of moral practice, one that provides a more diversified account of human happiness.

Insomuch as the state has a moral purpose, this purpose must include the cultivation of diverse roles and ideals of excellence.

How much negative liberty should the state grant individual citizens? Surely the answer is: within reasonable limits, as much as possible. How do we define reasonable limits? Political theory provides various answers, but this is an issue we will not delve into here. Simply note: although a liberal emphasis on negative liberty does constitute an importance safeguard against encroachments on individual agency, the good life cannot be identified with the mere removal of obstacles to action. The state should maintain and protect large quantities of negative liberty, but that is not all there is to good government.

THE VIRTUOUS SLAVE: SWANTON

I have identified personal autonomy with morality. Christine Swanton writes: "It would be a crass error to assume that . . . virtue is synonymous with freedom, as if a virtuous slave or a virtuous inmate is free."[40] But this is a contradiction in terms. Swanton states that it would be a crass error to call a virtuous slave or inmate free. If, however, these are virtuous agents, this means that they have chosen, of their own free will, to do good. This would be impossible unless they were free in three different senses: (1) free to choose between good and evil; (2) free—within severe restrictions—to decide for themselves; and (3) free in the sense that they are autonomous, that they have successfully governed themselves. A virtuous slave or inmate must, by definition, possess (1) free will, (2) a minimal amount of negative liberty, and (3) autonomy.

We can distinguish between two kinds of inquiries. We may ask: "Is this particular agent autonomous?" Or we may ask: "Is society providing this agent with an adequate amount of negative liberty?" In the case of the virtuous slave or inmate, the answer to the first question is a definitive yes; the answer to the second question is a definitive no. If society should value negative liberty as a means to autonomy, surprisingly small amounts of negative liberty are necessary for the achievement of autonomy. Even slaves or inmates may, within extremely narrow constraints, successfully govern themselves.

In one sense, virtuous slaves lack autonomy. In another sense, they do not lack autonomy. On the one hand, they cannot be faulted because they are slaves. They are not to blame for their lack of negative liberty. If slaves manage to be virtuous in such trying circumstances, this adds an undeniable luster to their achievements. It does not detract from their merit. On the other hand, slaves are prohibited from practicing a wide range of activities. In this sense, they lack many opportunities for autonomy. We might distinguish, then, between a criterion of merit and a criterion of opportunity. On the merit criterion, virtuous slaves are not any less autonomous. They may even be more autonomous. On the opportunity criterion, they are less autonomous.

Virtuous slaves are less autonomous in that they enjoy less opportunity for autonomy, but they are not less autonomous in that they govern themselves less successfully. Considered from the viewpoint of the individual slave, virtuous slaves may do everything they can to successfully govern themselves. They may be heroes of autonomy. This is because they exist in less than ideal circumstances. They are supremely meritorious because they overcome a supreme handicap. They manage to be fully human in conditions that are inimical to praiseworthy conduct. They manage to successfully govern themselves *in spite of* the difficult conditions they have to endure.

Though even a slave can be autonomous, we do not need a society made up of slaves. A slave-owning society fails to promote autonomy on two different fronts. Slaves fail at autonomy, for they are not allowed to act autonomously within a very wide sphere of endeavor. But slave-owners also fail at autonomy, for they act in an immoral manner. Good rebels provide an illustrious example of human achievement, but it would be morally unthinkable to suggest that we ought to oppress people in order to harvest a new crop of morally exemplary human beings. Morality applies not just to victims but also to whoever is oppressing them.

INSIDE AND OUTSIDE THE PIT: FRANKL

Joseph Raz argues that individuals who suffer from a serious lack of negative liberty cannot, by definition, achieve autonomy. Raz brings up the example of "The Man in the Pit": "A person falls down a pit and remains there for the rest of his life, unable to climb out or to summon help. There is just enough ready food to keep him alive without (after he gets used to it) any suffering. He can do nothing much, not even move much. His choices are confined to whether to eat now or a little later, whether to scratch his left ear or not."[41] Raz argues that the man in the pit cannot achieve personal autonomy. He lacks "an adequate range of options." He does not enjoy, to a sufficient degree, freedom of choice. He has, for all intents and purposes, no negative liberty. This thought-experiment is, however, seriously problematic.

To begin with, the example is more fanciful abstraction than real empirical incident.[42] But even it was a real-life example, it would not prove the intended point. Suppose, for the sake of argument, that somebody does fall down a pit and must remain there for an extended period of time. Why would we think that this person cannot be autonomous? Suppose the man in the pit remains calm. Suppose he is utterly patient. Suppose he does not lose hope. Suppose he is ready to meet death with equanimity. Suppose he thinks about his past life and forgives all those who have ever offended him. Suppose he says prayers to his God. Suppose he looks up and contemplates the stars. Suppose he admires a butterfly that flutters down into his hole. Suppose he composes Elizabethan sonnets to his wife. Suppose he sings medieval madrigals. Suppose he recites Spenser. Suppose he sings hymns. Suppose he never gives up. Suppose he keeps on trying to get out, to scale the walls, to carve out a crude staircase with a rock, to make a noise or build a fire that would signal authorities. Suppose he does all he can without feeling self-pity, without indulging in useless despair and bitterness. None of us would want to spend any prolonged period of time in a pit. But it does not mean that the man who finds himself in a pit cannot be said to successfully govern himself.

Is it impossible to believe that an agent who finds himself in such a minimalistic physical environment could achieve autonomy? In the past, Christian and Hindu mystics, as well as Stoic and Cynic philosophers, *voluntarily* sequestered themselves for long periods of time in caves, in holes, in barrels, in tubs, or on pillars. These were not slaves. They knowingly and freely chose to sequester themselves in environments that severely restricted their negative liberty. We may (like Hume) choose to believe that such ascetical practices were the product of wild, harebrained religious extremists. Though moderns find such severe ascetical practices outrageous, in previous periods of history, these exotic characters were admired and praised by their contemporaries as conspicuous examples of successful self-government or self-mastery. They were considered to be saints or heroes, for unlike the common run of mortals they had conquered their baser physical natures, devoting themselves, heart and mind and soul, to some higher spiritual purpose.

Examples of severely sequestered ascetics and stylite saints are not hard to find in recorded history.[43] In contemporary Western culture, we still see degenerate examples of this type of extreme asceticism when, for example, someone decides to sit on top of a flagpole for several years so as to earn a place in the Guinness Book of World Records. We may choose to believe that these historical figures were absolutely crazy, but this seems rather ethnocentric. Their own cultures viewed them as heroes of autonomy.

In these times and places, it was generally accepted that severely restricting one's negative liberty forced one to confront one's spiritual weaknesses
and overcome one's lower physical nature. We cannot assume, then, that
people who lack physical liberty cannot achieve autonomy.

One might want to argue that there is an important difference between
the traditional ascetic and the character in Raz's thought-experiment. The
ascetic chooses to live in a pit; Raz's character accidentally falls in. Agents
who voluntarily give up their negative liberty are not prohibited from achieving autonomy, but one might argue that this is not the case for agents who
are forced to give up their negative liberty. There are two problems with
this argument. Firstly, ascetical societies generally believe that involuntary
restrictions on negative liberty provide an even *better* opportunity for testing one's spiritual mettle. Secondly, individuals like the good rebel successfully master themselves in the face of *involuntary* adversity. Raz argues that "the inmates of concentration camps" who have been stripped of
their negative liberty and forced into confinement do not have personal
autonomy.[44] If, however, we investigate the personal experiences of actual
inmates, we may come to a different conclusion.

Victor Frankl, in an autobiographical text originally entitled *From
Death-Camp to Existentialism*, details his own experiences as a prisoner in
Nazi concentration camps like Auschwitz and Dachau.[45] Unlike Raz, Frankl
argues that agents in concentration camps may achieve autonomy. They
may, in some absolutely meritorious sense, successfully govern themselves.
As he puts it, "It is possible to practice the art of living even in a concentration camp, although the suffering is omnipresent."[46]

Raz's views notwithstanding, Frankl argues that even the strictest death-
camp regime does not remove all semblance of choice. To the question:
"Does man have no choice of action in the face of such circumstances?"
Frankl responds: "The experiences of camp life show that a man does have
a choice of action. . . . Man *can* preserve a vestige of spiritual freedom, of
independence of mind, even in such terrible conditions of psychic and physical stress."[47]

Frankl relates his own personal experience: "There were always choices
to make. Every day, every hour, offered the opportunity to make a decision, a decision which determined whether you would or would not submit
to those powers which threatened to rob you of your very self, your inner
freedom; [a decision] which determined whether or not you would become
a plaything of circumstance, renouncing freedom and dignity to become
molded into the form of the typical inmate."[48]

In detailing the life of the ordinary inmate, Frankl speaks of "courage,"[49] "curiosity,"[50] "inner peace,"[51] "right action and right conduct,"[52]

"beauty,"[53] "spiritual life,"[54] and even "humor."[55] In his *Psychiatric Credo* he states, with absolute conviction, that "there is nothing conceivable which would so condition a man as to leave him without the slightest freedom. . . . A residue of freedom, however limited it may be, is left to man in neurotic and even psychotic cases."[56] Frankl concludes his book with a short but fervent manifesto outlining his own unyielding belief in individual freedom. He writes: "*Man* is ultimately self-determining. What he becomes— in the limits of endowment and environment—he has made out of himself. In the concentration camps . . . in this living laboratory and on this testing ground we watched and witnessed some of our comrades behave like swine while others behaved like saints. Man has both potentialities within himself; which one is actualized depends on decisions but not on conditions."[57]

Frankl's conviction is born, not out of abstract philosophical considerations, but out of actual lived experience. As a testimony to the actual concrete experiences real men and women, it gains an authority over and beyond that of "fantastical" armchair thought-experiments.

Raz concludes: "Autonomy requires a choice of goods. A choice between good and evil is not enough."[58] But a choice between good and evil *is* enough. If we can choose good over evil, we can successfully govern ourselves. Even in the Nazi death-camps, there was a room for meaningful choice, not because life was rich in pleasant possibilities, but because, in some deeply pervasive sense, human values could still be retained. Frankl ties the psychological demise of individual prisoners to a characteristic "loss of values": "If the man in the concentration camp did not struggle against this [loss] in a last effort to save his self-respect, he lost the feeling of being an individual, a being with a mind, with inner freedom and personal value."[59] It was, as Marcus argues, a dedication to the ethical dimension, a belief in a transcendent, objective good, that preserved the individual's psychological integrity, leaving open the possibility of autonomous action.

RESTRICTING NEGATIVE FREEDOM

Raz and Swanton are not the only authors who argue that people who possess very little negative liberty cannot be autonomous. Lindley maintains that "a prisoner in his cell"[60] will never be able to realize the potential for autonomy. If, however, the prisoner is thrown into jail because he refuses to cooperate with an oppressive state, he does not only not lack autonomy. He is the very image of autonomy. He is the good rebel, someone who, in adopting a stance of moral noncooperation, exercises an independent capacity for ethical decision-making. In accepting his imprisonment, the conscientious objector is actualizing that potential. Although the scope of his activities has been severely restricted, he secures, in the most conspicuous manner, his status as an autonomous individual.

Even the most repressive political regimes produce saints and martyrs who, to all appearances, achieve a very high degree of personal autonomy. These displays of autonomous living are conspicuous because they occur against a backdrop of such forced conformity. This is not to suggest that the conscientious objector exists in an acceptable environment. As much as we admire the political prisoner's strength of character, we do not (and we should not) envy his predicament. But autonomy may flourish in the absence of many negative liberties we take for granted.

The man in a pit, the ascetic, and the political prisoner can achieve autonomy, but there are ways of eliminating the potential for autonomy. Short of murder, the best way is to attack the mind. Repressive regimes employ various techniques: brainwashing, frontal lobotomies, drug- induced stupors, driving people mad. In Stanley Kubrick's film *Clockwork Orange*[61] a delinquent youth named Alex is psychologically conditioned so that he physically gets sick any time he tries to do anything wrong. Alex becomes a model citizen.[62] But Alex is forced to do good. He cannot do the good freely, of his own accord. He lacks autonomy.

Anything that destroys the capacity for free, rational choice destroys the capacity for autonomy. The psychologists in *Clockwork Orange* turn Alex into a machine that is programmed to act in certain ways. Alex is a slave of society. But as the priest complains: "Goodness comes from the inside. It is the result of a choice. The man who cannot make this choice is no longer a man." In depriving Alex of all freedom of choice, the psychologists eradicate his humanity. Even his newfound goodness is only "pantomime." It is, in the priest's words, mere "monkey-business." It is a counterfeit goodness, for genuine goodness must be a product of some freely willed decision.

Autonomy presupposes negative liberty. In the absence of all negative liberty (some of which is remarkably difficult to extinguish), an agent cannot achieve autonomy. At the same time, autonomy is not the same as negative liberty. The practice of autonomy may lead to a substantial decrease in negative liberty. Ascetics restrict their own negative liberty in the pursuit of autonomy. Athletes discipline themselves severely in striving toward particular goals. Parents, when they bring children into the world, severely limit their freedom to do as they will. Political dissidents may be incarcerated because they refuse to conform. These agents prefer autonomy to negative liberty.[63]

MORALITY AS A RESTRICTION ON NEGATIVE LIBERTY

I have identified autonomy with morality, very broadly construed. Is morality a restriction on negative liberty? As MacIntyre explains, an individual with a well-formed character may find it impossible to perform a bad act.[64] If, however, a moral person cannot commit an evil deed, immoral agents may choose between good or evil. Does it follow that immoral agents, because they enjoy more options, enjoy more negative liberty? Is morality a limitation on freedom?

If I am unable to choose evil, this might be construed as a limitation on negative freedom, except that negative liberty is usually defined as the absence of obstacles to *intended* action. In the case of a moral person, the absence of the possibility to do evil is the absence of an unwanted option. It is not an obstacle to *intended* action. It does not count, then, as a limitation on negative liberty.

Seriously immoral agents do not possess more negative freedom than moral agents. I have defined immorality, in line with Augustine, as absence, as a lack of agency. Immorality is not the act of choosing. It is the loss of the capacity to choose. The Marquis de Sade could not choose to resist his sexual compulsions. He was enslaved by his passions. He was only "free" in that he welcomed this enslavement. If someone who is free is unable to sell himself into slavery, this does not make him less free. The fact that he cannot be a slave provides evidence for his freedom.

There is an asymmetry that characterizes the practice of morality and immorality. We may slip into immorality, but morality takes effort. This does not mean that morality is a restriction on freedom. In the case of a moral person, the obstacle to the performance of wicked acts comes from within. It is something that has been chosen. The fact that we cannot do what we choose not to do cannot be intelligibly construed as a limitation on freedom.

FOUR DEFINITIONS: FEINBERG

According to Feinberg, "The word 'autonomy' has four closely related meanings. It can refer either to the *capacity* to govern oneself . . . to the *actual condition* of self-government . . . to an *ideal of character* . . . or . . . to the *sovereign authority* to govern oneself."[65] We have defined autonomy in line with Feinberg's second definition as the actual condition of (successful) self-government. Other meanings suggested by Feinberg are problematic or derivative.

According to Feinberg's first definition, the term autonomy refers to the mere capacity for self-government. A modicum of intelligence, rationality, self-awareness, and psychological health is required for autonomous living. There are individuals who lack this capacity: "[young] infants, insane persons, the severely retarded, the senile, and the comatose."[66] But autonomy is not a question of raw ability. It is also a question of will. To be autonomous is to freely direct this psychological capacity toward proper ends. It is not to have the ability to do what one ought to do. It is to actually do it.

Feinberg's third definition, that autonomy is "an ideal of character," reduces to his second definition that autonomy is the actual condition of self-government. One may measure human endeavor in terms of the accomplishment of specific acts, as a submission to categorical rules, as a stage of self-development, or as an ideal of character. To describe autonomy as "an ideal of character" is to understand human achievement in terms of virtue ethics. But these different descriptions all refer to the actual state of successful self-government.

Finally, Feinberg refers to autonomy as "the sovereign authority to govern oneself." But to claim that one has the right to govern oneself in line with one's own beliefs and conscience is to argue for negative liberty, not for autonomy. Negative liberty, although a prerequisite for autonomy, does not constitute autonomy. One might, of course, define autonomy in terms of acting in accordance with some higher, sovereign authority within oneself. But this would be to return to Feinberg's second definition, for acting in accordance with a higher-order self is the actual condition of self-government.

LIBERALISM AND COMMUNITARIANISM

In philosophical and popular literature, authors often identify themselves as liberal or communitarian. Contemporary liberal thinkers often defend negative liberty in some value-neutral, amoral way. They shy away from objective notions of the good, for this constitutes a restriction on negative liberty. Communitarians, on the other hand, argue that the community constitutes the ultimate legal and moral source. Those who oppose communitarianism see this as a perilous suggestion, for the historical record reveals that political communities often violate human rights, oppose minorities, infringe on individual freedoms, and so on. If liberals, in some rough and ready way, identify with John Stuart Mill and a host of modern disciples, communitarians identify with the Hegelian tradition and with modern authors such as Dewey and Taylor.

In arguing that freedom has, in its deepest sense, a moral component, I may seem to be taking a communitarian view. That may be to some extent true, for communitarians rightly discern the importance of community to any process of moral evaluation. Liberalism tends, at times, toward a reductionist atomism. But my argument is not, by any means, incompatible with liberalism. We need to avoid a simplified liberalism that rests on an unqualified appeal to negative liberty. Liberalism, insofar as it generates a fierce defense of individual human rights, is the correct political view. Individual freedoms, properly construed, are an essential aspect of the good life, precisely because they are a necessary ingredient of any meaningful account of human flourishing.

The liberal-communitarian debate sidesteps, in a very real way, the issue addressed in this book. Liberals tend to champion negative liberty as an end-in-itself, apart from any objective good. I have criticized this tendency, arguing that negative liberty must be conceived as a means to autonomy understood, in the broadest sense, as a moral achievement. Liberal authors, insofar as they ignore morality, are unable to secure a solid defense of individual liberty.

Modern-day communitarians, on the other hand, tend to champion community values apart from any objective good. My account of autonomy does not presume the moral infallibility of particular societies. It revolves around the figure of the good rebel, someone who critiques society and rises above the going consensus in the name of an objective good. Communities, like individuals, are eminently fallible. An objective account of values can help eliminate human complacency and provide a realistic account of human striving.

I have argued that freedom, in its deepest sense, must include moral aspirations, that morality must be understood as something that motivates all our striving, and that morality provides an objective ideal that has independent validity. We can point to good rebels who epitomize, in the most exemplary manner, the heights of human achievement. The example of their striving can remind us that there is room, in all our lives, for good rebellion.

Notes

INTRODUCTION

1. Milgram reports on the research project in *Obedience to Authority*.
2. Ibid., p. 5.
3. Ibid., p. 13.
4. Dan-Cohen, "Conceptions of Choice and Conceptions of Autonomy," p. 232.
5. Haworth, *Autonomy*, p. 11.
6. Milgram, *Obedience to Authority*, p. 163.
7. Camus, *Rebel*, p. 13.
8. In refusing the experimenter's commands, the good rebel acts out of necessity, in accordance with a coherent scheme of values. Camus writes: "Not every value entails a rebellion, but every act of rebellion tacitly evokes a value." Ibid., p. 14.
9. Milgram, *Obedience to Authority*, p. 132.
10. Self-directed agents see themselves as acting on their own. Ibid., p. 133.
11. Ibid., pp. 134, 146.
12. Ibid., p. 146.
13. Gaylin and Jennings, *Perversion of Autonomy*, p. 9.
14. Ibid., p. 6.
15. Ibid., p. 230.
16. Ibid., p. 232.
17. Ibid., p. 228.
18. Taylor, "What's Wrong with Negative Liberty?" p. 179.
19. Raz, *Morality of Freedom*, p. 381.
20. Plato, *Republic* 9.589, 9.590, and elsewhere.
21. Wilson, *Moral Sense*.
22. Ibid., p. xiii.
23. Ibid., p. x.
24. Ibid., p. viii.
25. "Philosophers have sought to find a rational basis for moral judgements; the dominant tradition in moral philosophy asserts that no rational foundation can be given for such judgements." Ibid., pp. viii–ix.
26. Ibid., p. viii.
27. Ibid., p. vii.
28. "Le meurtre des enfants, meurtre des pères, trafic de voleries, il n'est rien en somme

si extrême qui ne se trouve reçu par l'usage de quelque nation." Montaigne, *Essais* II, XII, "Apologie," p. 654. Montaigne tells us that what is truth on this side of the mountains is falsehood on the other side. (See chap. 3, n. 90.) But he also suggests that local mores, laws and customs diverge because we do not pay sufficient attention to the universal laws of human nature. It is the vanity and the inconsistency of the human spirit that obscures and misconstrues the natural law. (See chap. 3, n. 91.)

29. Sumner, *Folkways*, p. 521.
30. Gass, "Case of the Obliging Stranger."
31. Ibid., p. 198.
32. In his *Summa de bono* (1225–36). See MacDonald, "Philip the Chancellor."
33. John of St. Thomas provides an example of a modal distinction: the difference between Socrates being seated and Socrates being in prison. *Ars Logica*, 2.2.3. See Doyle, "John of St. Thomas."
34. As we shall see, Dewey emphasizes the way in which isolated human acts fit into a large pattern of unified conduct.
35. Nietzsche, *Genealogy of Morals*, Third Essay, in *Basic Writings,* trans. Kaufmann, sec. 12, p. 555.
36. See Leiter, "Perspectivism," for a lengthy bibliography.
37. Santayana, "Problem of Freedom of Will in Relation to Ethics," p. 5.
38. Ibid.
39. James, "Dilemma of Determinism."
40. Ancient peoples did not, on this view, recognize individuality. Feyerabend bases his analysis on a familiar but contentious interpretation of the stylistic conventions of archaic art and poetry. *Against Method*, pp. 211–12.

Chapter 1. Morality and Rationality

1. Gauthier, "Justice and Natural Endowment," p. 3.
2. Schmidtz, "Self-Interest," p. 107.
3. Baier, *Moral Point of View*, p. 1.
4. See Gauthier, *Morals by Agreement;* Schmidtz, *Rational Choice and Moral Agency;* Baier, *Moral Point of View;* Mackie, *Ethics;* Narveson, *Libertarian Idea;* Vallentyne, *Contractarianism and Rational Choice;* Danielson, *Artificial Morality;.* and Viminitz, "Defending Game Theoretic Approaches to Ethics" and "No Place to Hide."
5. In Rawls, *Theory of Justice*.
6. Robinson, *Introduction to Early Greek Philosophy,* p. 250.
7. Ibid., p. 251.
8. Drury, *Political Ideas of Leo Strauss*.
9. In the second book of the *Republic*, Glaucon argues that the only thing that keeps men from injustice is the threat of punishment. He recites a famous legend about Gyges, a shepherd who finds a ring that will make him invisible and allow him, through deceit and murder, to take control of the kingdom of Lydia. As Glaucon puts it: "If you could imagine anyone obtaining this power of becoming invisible, and never doing any wrong or touching what was another's, he would be thought by the lookers-on to be a most wretched idiot." Plato, *Republic,* trans. Jowett, 2.360d.
10. For Hobbes, one's duties to society end when one's life is in danger.
11. Ps. 14:2.

12. Ps. 92:7–9.

13. An agent who considered present utility to be infinitely more useful than future utility might have grounds for deciding in favor of immorality. But this is to reject the basic tenets of the religious system: that there is an afterlife, that this future life forms a continuum with the present one; that the pains and pleasures of this life are but a shadow of the pains and pleasures to come, that we will live in Heaven or Hell forever, and so on.

14. In fact, the situation may be more complex, for sinners may repent. Repenting is an act of morality that so to speak cancels out past wrongdoing. Or again, some might want to argue that God redeems all sinners regardless of what they do, but the point here is not to enter into theological niceties.

15. Matt. 5:29.

16. Plato, *Phaedo,* trans. Tredennick, 63c

17. Ibid., 69d.

18. Ibid., 113e.

Chapter 2. A Different Morality

1. Daly, "Faith, Hope, and Charity," p. 209.

2. Ibid. Seen from a Christian perspective, God's love is not, as Daly seems to suggest, "indifferent to value."

3. *Random House College Dictionary*, rev. ed., 1979.

4. *Catholic Encyclopedia*, s.v. "charity."

5. Cohen, *Everyman's Talmud*, p. 223.

6. Ibid. (*Sukkah* 49b).

7. Ibid. (*Baba Bathra* 9a).

8. Ibid. (*Baba Bathra* 10a).

9. Ibid., p. 224. The Talmud distinguishes between two kinds of charity: almsgiving *(tzedakah)* and a generalized "loving-kindness" or benevolence *(gemiluth chasadim)*.

10. The best type of almsgiving is where 'a person gives a donation without knowing who receives it, and a person receives it without knowing who donated it." Ibid. (*Baba Bathra* 10b).

11. *Holy Qur'an*, trans. Ali., 2:271, p. 118. Again, the Koran compares the unbeliever (who personifies evil) to those "who do [good] to be seen, and [to those who] refrain from acts of kindness!" *Holy Qur'an* 107:7, p. 1212.

12. Carus, *Gospel of Buddha*, "The Sermon on Charity," 76.

13. Ibid., p. 75.

14. Thucydides, *History of the Peloponnesian Wars*, trans. Warner., 2.35–14.

15. Miller, *Questions That Matter*, p. 434.

16. "Hurt not others with that which pains yourself."

17. "Do not do to others all that which is not well for oneself."

18. "We should regard all creatures as we regard our own self . . ."

19. "Do nothing to others which if done to you would cause you pain."

20. "Treat others as you would be treated yourself."

21. "What is hateful to yourself, do not do to your fellow man."

22. Wilson, *Moral Sense*, p. 197.

23. Confucius, *Analects* 14.11. Cited in Noss, *Man's Religions*, p. 273.

24. He considered "evil people unworthy of the mutual consideration prompted by fellow-feeling." Noss, *Man's Religions*, p. 273.

25. Cited in ibid., p. 250. *Texts of Taoism*, trans. Legge, p. 91. According to Noss, "most of the present version [of the *Tao Te Ching*] comes from the fourth century B.C." Noss, *Man's Religions*, 247.

26. Ginsberg, *Reason and Unreason in Society*, pp. 307–8.

27. Lewis, *Abolition of Man*. Lewis considers human morality under eight different headings: 1. The Law of General Beneficence: Negative/Positive; 2. Law of Special Beneficence; 3. Duties to Parents, Elders, Ancestors; 4. Duties to Children and Posterity; 5. The Law of Justice; 6. The Law of Good Faith and Veracity; 7. The Law of Mercy; 8. The Law of Magnanimity.

28. F. Murphy, "Problem of Overridingness." Murphy cites attacks on moral "overridingness" by Foote, Slote, and Scheffler.

29. Augustine, in *Saint Augustine*, ed. Mourant, "Sermon 43," p. 43.

30. Augustine, in *Augustinian Synthesis*, ed. Przywara, p. 59 (*In Joannis Evangelium Tractatus* 40.9).

31. Schmitt identifies the natural attitude with knowing-how, the phenomenological attitude with knowing-that. "Phenomenology," p. 142.

32. Ibid.

33. There is room here for differing interpretations.

34. Of course, these craftspeople could slip into a deep coma or otherwise lose their cognitive abilities, but these extraordinary circumstances need not detain us here.

35. Nozick is not, of course, suggesting that we actually use such a machine. Nozick, *Anarchy, State, and Utopia*, p. 42.

36. "Nothing is ultimately desirable except desirable feelings." Sidgwick, *Methods of Ethics* 2.2, p. 126.

37. Ibid.

38. *Little Flowers of St. Francis*, 8, "How St. Francis Taught Brother Leo That Perfect Joy Is Only in the Cross."

39. Dewey quotes Eliot approvingly. Cited in Dewey and Tufts, *Ethics*, p. 214.

40. Which is again akin to the word "beatific."

41. *Oxford English Dictionary*, "happiness."

42. *Oxford English Dictionary*, "blessed."

43. Aristotle, *Nicomachean Ethics*, trans. Ross, 9.1168a30.

44. Ibid., 9.1168b10.

45. Ibid., 9.1168b16.

46. Ibid., 9.1168b20.

47. Ibid., 9.1168b30.

48. Ibid..

49. Ibid., 9.1168a28.

50. Ibid., 9.1169a10.

51. Ibid. 9.1168b28.

52. Ibid., 9.1169a25. He includes in the same list those who "strive towards what is noble and strain every nerve to do the noblest deeds" (1169a10) and those who "act justly and temperately, or in accordance with any other of the virtues" (9.1168b28).

53. Ibid., 9.1169a10.

54. Butler, *Works*, vol. 2, Sermon 11, "Upon Love of Our Neighbour," 3, p. 187.

55. Ibid., "Preface" (by Butler), 36, p. 27.

56. In discussing the Fall, Augustine distinguishes between "other-love," which he associates with the good angels, and "self-love," which he associates with the bad angels. He concludes: "There are, then, two loves, of which one is unholy, the other unclean; one turned towards the neighbour, the other centred on self. . . . These two loves . . . have marked the limits of the two cities . . . and one is the city of the just, and the other is the city of the wicked." Augustine, *Literal Meaning of Genesis*, vol. 2, bks. 7–12, chapter 15, p. 147.

57. Butler, *Works*, vol. 2, Sermon 1, "Upon Human Nature," 5, p. 38.

58. Ibid., Sermon 11, "Upon Love of Our Neighbour," 14, p. 199.

59. In this "one respect benevolence contributes more to private interest, i.e. enjoyment or satisfaction, than any other of the particular common affections." Ibid., 20, p. 205.

60. Of course, one has to be careful. If I act charitably towards you because it makes me feel that I am a fine fellow, so as to profit from some emotional self-centered high, I am acting, not out of love for you, but out of love for myself.

61. Gauthier, *Morals by Agreement*, p. 8.

62. Schmidtz, *Rational Choice and Moral Agency*.

63. Thalos, "Self-Interest, Autonomy and the Presuppositions of Decision Theory."

64. Chwaszcza, "Anmerkungen zu Funktion und Stellenwert des Eigeninteresses."

65. "Because we are nevertheless not economic men and women, [the rest of us] can be constrained." Gauthier, *Morals By Agreement*, p. 317. In the latter chapters of his book, Gauthier expresses doubts about the why-be-moral project. The book ends on a very cautious note. The last paragraph begins: "Perhaps then [I] have constructed, not a theory linking rationality to moral choice, but a portrayal of moral constraints and maximizing choice in an ephemeral market society." Ibid., p. 354.

66. He continues, in an almost plaintive tone: "But that I have no power to provide." Ibid., p. 317.

67. Strawson, "Social Morality and Individual Ideal," pp. 31, 43.

68. Ibid., pp. 26, 41.

CHAPTER 3. A DIFFERENT VIEW OF RATIONALITY

1. Noddings, *Caring*, p. 1.

2. Ibid.

3. Putnam, *Pragmatism*, p. 69.

4. White, *Social Thought in America*.

5. Dewey, "Present Position of Logical Theory," p. 10.

6. Dewey, *Experience and Nature*, pp. 407–8.

7. Pascal thinks of geometry as the example par excellence of strict logical analysis. To provide a complete proof is, "en une mot, à définir tous les termes et à prouver toutes les propositions" [in a single word, to define every term and to prove every proposition]. Pascal, *L'Esprit de la géométrie*, II, 8, p. 14. According to Aristotle, people who ask for a complete demonstration of the truth "lack education." See Aristotle, *Metaphysics* 4.1006a8.

8. Dewey, *Philosophy and Civilization*, p. 43.

9. James, *Pragmatism and The Meaning of Truth*, p. 31.

10. "Pragmatism agrees with nominalism . . . in always appealing to particulars; with utilitarianism in emphasizing practical aspects; with positivism in its disdain for verbal solutions, useless questions, and metaphysical abstractions." Ibid., p. 32.

11. Dewey, *Philosophy and Civilization*, p. 39.

12. James, *Pragmatism and The Meaning of Truth,* 28–29.

13. Descartes, *Meditations on First Philosophy*, trans. Cottingham, "What Can Be Called into Doubt?" 1, 22:20. The French rendering is: "il n'est pas question d'agir, mais seulement de méditer et de connaître." (This is the original Duc de Luynes translation.)

14. Feyerabend, *Against Reason*, p. 234.

15. Ibid.

16. James, *Pragmatism and The Meaning of Truth*, p. 42.

17. Carus, *Truth on Trial*, pp. 7–8.

18. Ibid., pp. 56–57.

19. Hilary Putnam identifies as the most basic insight of pragmatism the realization that a theory "can be both fallibilistic *and* antisceptical." *Pragmatism*, p. 21.

20. Some authors (such as MacIntyre and Wilson) argue that this is an unfair representation of Hume. Hume himself "derives an 'ought' statement from an 'is' statement scarcely eight pages after asserting that this cannot be done." Wilson, *Moral Sense*, pp. 237–38.

21. Ayer, *Language, Truth, and Logic*, pp. 103, 108.

22. This is to commit "the naturalistic fallacy." As Searle expresses the thought: "No set of *descriptive* statements can entail an *evaluative* statement without the addition of at least one evaluative premise." Searle is here describing a position he argues against. Searle, "How to Derive 'Ought' from 'Is'," p. 43.

23. This is from a critique of moral emotivism. See A. MacIntyre, *After Virtue*.

24. Blandshard, "New Subjectivism in Ethics," p. 504.

25. A. MacIntyre, *After Virtue*, p. 12.

26. Flew, "On Not Deriving 'Ought' from 'Is,'" p. 27.

27. Mackie, *Ethics*, p. 64.

28. One might argue that the early Christians were naïve or gullible. Nonetheless, this is the most natural reading of the text.

29. Aquinas writes: "It is impossible for God to be seen by the sense of sight, or by any other sense, or faculty of the sensitive power . . . for God is incorporeal." *Summa Theologica*, trans. English Dominican Province, Ia.12.3. The positivist attack on theistic belief generally misses the point. It attacks a view of God that most theists do not believe in.

30. "The principle of verifiability cannot itself be verified." Copleston and Ayer, "Logical Positivism," p. 618.

31. See, for example, Barnes, Bloor, and Henry, *Scientific Knowledge*.

32. Pickering, *Constructing Quarks*, pp. 413–14.

33. Think of well-known interviews with criminals like Adolf Eichmann, Ted Bundy, and Jeffrey Dahlmer.

34. See, for example, Aristotle, *Nicomachean Ethics* 5.1143b.

35. Novak, "Comments on K. Nielsen's *God, Modernity, and Scepticism*," p. 2. Theoretical reason was not only present in the art of argument; it was also "present in the grasp of certain truths/essences in a non-discursive way." Ibid., p. 2.

36. See, for example, Boethius, *The Consolation of Philosophy*, book 5, sec. 5; Thomas Aquinas, *Summa Theologiae*, 1a, 1xxxix, 8.

37. As C. S. Lewis explains: "We are enjoying *intellectus* when we just see a self-evident truth; we are exercising *ratio* when we proceed step by step to prove a truth which is not self-evident. A cognitive life in which all truth can simply be seen would be the life of an *intellgentia*, an angel. . . . Man's mental life is spent in [*ratio,*] labouriously connecting those frequent, but momentary, flashes of *intelligentia*." Lewis, *Discarded Image*, p. 157.

38. Ibid.

39. Potts, "Conscience," p. 700.

40. "The opinion which is fated to be ultimately agreed to by all who investigate is what we mean by truth." Peirce, "How to Make Our Ideas Clear," p. 38.

41. James, "The Moral Philosopher and the Moral Life," p. 214.

42. Russell, "Retreat of Pythagoras," p. 256.

43. See Rorty, *Contingency, Irony, Solidarity.*

44. Computer versions of "virtual reality" are only the latest trend in a trompe l'oeil tradition that confuses appearances with reality. If we can be led into this kind of confusion, we can and regularly do distinguish, in an orderly way, between reality and illusion. To speak of "virtual reality" is to distinguish between what only seems to be the case and what really is.

45. Such absolute claims "seem to constitute philosophical overkill." Bonjour, *Structure of Empirical Knowledge*, p. 27.

46. Boethius, *Consolation of Philosophy*, trans. Watts, p. 159. "Everything that is known is comprehended not according to its own nature but according to the ability of those who do the knowing." If God knows the world according to his nature, we know the world according to our nature. But human nature is inferior to God's. Therefore we see the world in an inferior way. Ibid., p. 157. Boethius is very clear on this point. He writes: "[T]he superior manner of knowledge includes the inferior, but it is quite impossible for the inferior to rise to the superior." Ibid.

47. Rorty writes that he wants "to abandon the idea that the aim of thought is the attainment of a God's-eye view." Rorty, *Essays on Heidegger*, p. 12.

48. Bernstein, "One Step Forward, Two Steps Backward," p. 557.

49. The term comes from Taylor's evaluation of Rorty. Taylor, "Rorty in the Epistemological Tradition."

50. Aristotle, *Posterior Analytics* 1.9.76a26. Cited in A. MacIntyre, *First Principles, Final Ends, and Contemporary Philosophical Issues*, p. 13.

51. Aquinas, *Commentary on the Posterior Analytics*, lib. 1, lec. 18. Cited in MacIntyre, *First Principles, Final Ends, and Contemporary Philosophical Issues*, p. 13.

52. Aquinas, *Three Greatest Prayers*, trans. Shapcote, p. 6.

53. Ibid.

54. These passages are cited by Aquinas.

55. Boethius, *Consolation*, trans. Watts, 4.66, p. 141.

56. Ibid., p. 137.

57. Nicholas of Cusa, *On Learned Ignorance*, trans. Hopkins, 1.10, p. 52.

58. Leibniz, *Discourse on Metaphysics*, trans. Montgomery, 5, p. 8.

59. Ibid., 24, p. 42.

60. Ibid., 26, p. 28

61. My translation. The French is: "La raison de l'homme est faible, et se trompe aisément; mais la vrai foi ne peut être trompée." Thomas à Kempis (probable author), *L'Imitation de Jésus-Christ* 4.18, p. 457.

62. My translation. The French is: "La plus solide philosophie n'est que la science de l'ignorance des hommes: elle est plus propre à détromper ceux qui se flattent de leur science qu' à instruire ceux qui désirent apprendre quelque chose de certain." Pascal and Nicole, *Pensées de Pascal suivies d'un choix des pensées de Nicole*, p. 377.

63. Newman, *Apologia Pro Vita Sua*, pt. 7, p. 216. (In some editions, this is chap. 5.)

64. Skeptics may argue that coherence cannot guarantee truth. In making knowledge

claims, however, we are not striving for absolute certitude. We are striving to fulfill various criteria of reasonableness. Human descriptions are fallible but not groundless. They can be overturned by counterevidence, but they are not gratuitous. If I say "this is what the world is like," I mean that there is good evidence that this is what the world is like. I mean that the world is, *to the best of my knowledge*, like this. If we are going to describe the world in intelligible terms, we do not have to provide an infallible proof of what the world is like. All we need is good evidence that the world is like this (and not like that), good evidence of which there is plenty.

65. "[Posidonius] developed a golden age theory of history, describing in detail the time when the wise man ruled originally and men lived happy lives following nature." Hallie, "Stoicism," p. 20. See Kropotkin, *Ethics, Origin and Development.* Kropotkin writes, for example, that "not only does nature fail to give us a lesson of a-moralism; i.e. of indifferent attitude to morality . . . but we are bound to recognize that *the very ideas of bad and good* and man's abstractions concerning 'the supreme good' have been borrowed from nature." Ibid., p. 16. Kropotkin attacks social Darwinism, the idea that all nature—red in tooth and claw—operates according to a "law of struggle for existence."

66. Rorty, "Truth and Freedom," p. 637.

67. Ibid., p. 636. See Hare, *Freedom and Reason*, pp. 157–85.

68. Geras, *Solidarity in the Conversation of Mankind*, pp. 7–8.

69. Ibid.

70. See, for example, Luke 6.

71. Russell writes, for example, that the document called *The Protocols of the Elders of Zion*, a forgery alleged to substantiate claims about a Jewish conspiracy to rule the world, was taught in schools. E. F. L. Russell, *Trial,* p. 19.

72. Ibid., p. 20.

73. Ibid.

74. Streicher was the publisher of *Der Stürmer* (The storm-trooper), a weekly anti-Semitic journal published from 1922 onwards. Ibid.

75. See Taylor, *Sources of the Self,* pp. 53–75.

76. Ibid., p. 57.

77. Ibid.

78. Ibid., p. 69.

79. Ibid., p. 59.

80. Ibid.

81. Ibid. , p. 68.

82. Ibid.

83. Mackie, *Ethics*, p. 15. This is the introductory sentence to a chapter entitled "The Subjectivity of Values."

84. Ibid., p. 38.

85. Narveson, *Libertarian Idea*, p. 111.

86. B. Russell, *History of Western Philosophy*, p. 780.

87. Cited in Monk, *Ludwig Wittgenstein,* p. 142. Wittgenstein, with his mystical side, stressed the ineffability of the good. The early positivists believed that logic provided access to some sort of objective truth, but Wittgenstein, who recognized the importance of ethical, spiritual side of human experience, also came to criticize this positivist notion of objectivity as misguided.

88. Taylor, *Sources of the Self,* p. 74.

89. Ibid., pp. 3–4.

90. "Quelle vérité que ces montagnes bornent, qui est mensonge au monde qui se tient au-delà." Montaigne, *Les Essais* 2.12, "Apologie," p. 653.

91. According to Montaigne, it is the vanity and the inconsistency of the human spirit that obscures and misconstrues the natural law. "Il est croyable qu'il y ait des lois naturelles, comme il se voit ès [dans les] autres créatures; mais en nous elles sont perdues, cette belle raison humaine s'ingérant partout de maîtriser et commander, brouillant et confondant le visage des choses selon sa vanité et inconstance." Ibid., p. 654.

92. Rorty has broadcast these opinions in a wide variety of published texts. See *Philosophy and the Mirror of Nature.*

93. Ibid., p. 335.

94. Ibid., p. 337.

95. LeBoeuf, "How Not to Read Rorty," p. 51.

96. Davidson, "Structure and Content of Truth," p. 305.

97. Leiter, "Perspectivism," p. 349.

98. Peacock, "Knowledge, Opinion, and Rorty," p. 1.

99. Ibid., p. 6.

100. Ibid., p. 7.

101. Rollins, "Solipsism."

102. Kant used the term "moral solipsism," but this usage is now rare in English.

103. *Webster's New International Dictionary.*

104. Metaphysical solipsism, in particular, seems a hypothetical position, perhaps only held seriously by Claude Brunet, a seventeenth-century French physician.

105. M. V. Miller, "How We Suffer Now," p. 43.

106. Rieff, "Victims All?" p. 56.

107. Ibid.

108. Engel, *With Good Reason*, p. 215.

109. Croce, *Philosophy of the Practical*, pp. 69–70. Cited in Engel, *With Good Reason,* p. 215.

110. Ibid.

111. Friedrich Nietzsche, *Genealogy of Morals*, in *Basic Writings,* trans. Kaufmann, sec. 12, p. 555.

112. Ibid.

113. Mannheim, *Ideology and Utopia*, p. 300.

114. Ibid., p. 296.

115. See Leiter, "Perspectivism," for a lengthy bibliography.

116. Clark, *Nietzsche on Truth and Philosophy*, p. 129. Compare her view to that of Thomas Nagel in *The View from Nowhere.*

117. Leiter, "Perspectivism," p. 338.

118. Ibid., p. 355 n. 23.

119. Fish writes: "Some people do philosophy, some people (a lot more) don't and those who do have not ascended to a rarified realm of reflection or critical self-consciousness from which they bring back news to their less-enlightened brothers. They merely have the knack of doing a trick some other can't do and the competence they have acquired travels no further than the very small arenas in which that trick is typically performed and rewarded." Fish, "Truth and Toilets," p. 418.

120. Taylor, *Sources of the Self*, p. 72.

121. Lindley, *Autonomy*, p. 26.

122. Dimock, "Autonomy and Freedom of Action."

123. Ibid., pp. 3–4.
124. Feinberg, "Idea of a Free Man," p. 161.
125. Scanlon, "Theory of Freedom of Expression," p. 215.
126. Wolff, *In Defense of Anarchism*, p. 14.
127. Meyers, *Self, Society and Personal Choice*, pp. 52–53.
128. "Autonomous agents must live in harmony not merely with their selves, but with their 'true' selves." Ibid., p. 198.
129. Feinberg, *Social Philosophy*, p. 14.
130. Locke, *Essay Concerning Human Understanding*, bk.2, chap. 11, 13.
131. Wolfe, "The Me Decade."
132. Bell, *Cultural Contradictions of Capitalism*, p. 19.
133. See Lasch, *Culture of Narcissism*.
134. Lipovetsky, *L'ère du vide*, p. 77.
135. Sennett, *Fall of Public Man*, p. 5.
136. Bellah et al., *Habits of the Heart*, p. 56.
137. Ibid., p. 79.
138. *Encyclopedia of Psychology*, p. 417. This is a reference to Kernberg.
139. Lindley, *Autonomy*, p. 20.
140. Haworth uses the example of a conscientious auto mechanic working on an engine. The mechanic "makes an adjustment, notes the result, and is led by his interpretation of the result to plot his next move." Steps taken to solve the problem are "individually sensitive to feedback." Collectively, they provide a "coherent strategy for solving the problem" at hand. Haworth, *Autonomy*, p. 23. Collingwood uses a similar example to explain the nature of logic. See *Autobiography*, p. 32.
141. Authors like Gauthier, Danielson, and Viminitz use terms like "unconditional co-operator," "reciprocal co-operator," "conditional co-operator," "unconditional defector." Although technically useful, such terms do not adequately capture the state of mind that motivates moral agents.

CHAPTER 4. THE IMMORAL AUTONOMOUS AGENT?

1. Babbit, "Personal Integrity, Politics, and Moral Imagination," p. 114.
2. Ibid., p. 115.
3. Ibid.
4. Meyers distinguishes between moral autonomy and personal autonomy. *Self, Society, and Personal Choice*, p. 8.
5. Hill, *Autonomy and Self-Respect*, p. 50.
6. Christman, *Inner Citadel*, p. 14.
7. Lindley, *Autonomy*.
8. Keykes, *Against Liberalism*, p. 61.
9. I will discuss their work in detail later in the text.
10. Raz also distinguishes between moral and personal autonomy. Raz, *Morality of Freedom*, p. 370.
11. Ibid., p. 380.
12. G. Dworkin, *Theory and Practise of Autonomy*, p. 29
13. Young, *Personal Autonomy*, pp. 31, 83, 109.
14. Keykes, *Against Liberalism*, pp. 30–31.

15.   Benn, "Freedom, Autonomy, and the Concept of a Person," pp. 129–30.

16.   Haworth, *Autonomy*, p. 157.

17.   Rosenbaum, *Coercion and Autonomy*, p. 132. Rosenbaum defines "social autonomy" as "a type of power relation over one's own actions with respect to others." (Ibid., p. 114). This view originates in Felix Oppenheim's *Dimensions of Freedom*.

18.   Young, *Personal Autonomy*, p. 19.

19.   Stove, *Plato Cult*, p. 58.

20.   Watson, "Free Agency," p. 109.

21.   Watson writes, "I do not conceive of my remarks to be a defence of compatibilism," but the general thrust of his argument is to provide a defence of compatibilism—a partial defence perhaps, but a defence just the same.

22.   Wolff provides critical commentary on Kant elsewhere (Wolff, *Autonomy of Reason*). I am interested here in his own theory of autonomy, which he, aptly or inaptly, characterizes as Kantian.

23.   Wolff, *Anarchism*, p. 18.

24.   In fact Aristotle divides the human soul into three parts: a nutritive faculty, a sensitive faculty (the appetites) and a rational faculty, but we will not enter into these details here. In most discussions, ancient and modern, the relationship between the sensitive and the rational faculty is the focus of attention. The nutritive faculty represents, for the most part, the biological and involuntary aspects of human individuality. See Aristotle, *De anima* (On the soul).

25.   Frankfurt, "Freedom of Will," pp. 11–25.

26.   G. Dworkin in *Theory and Practise of Autonomy*, "Acting Freely," and "Autonomy and Behavior Control."

27.   Aristotle, *Politics* 1.2.1253a.

28.   Dworkin speaks of second-order desire. Although Frankfurt speaks of second-order volitions, he defines the word "volition" in terms of desire.

29.   Frankfurt, "Freedom of the Will," p, 12.

30.   Thalberg, "Hierarchical Analyses of Unfree Action," p. 130.

31.   Gauthier, *Morals by Agreement*, p. 3, my italics.

32.   Gauthier speaks, for example, of "considered preferences," preferences "that the rational agent "holds in a considered way."

33.   See, for example, *Nicomachean Ethics* 1.1098a–1098a17.

34.   See Aristotle, *Politics* 1.2.1253a15.

35.   Dewey, *Quest for Certainty*, p. 784. Dewey continues: "Only a child in the degree of immaturity thinks to settle the question of desirability by the reiterated proclamation: 'I want it; I want it, I want it.'" And again: "Values . . . may be connected inherently with liking, and yet not with *every* liking, but only with those that judgement has approved." Ibid., p. 786.

36.   Sandel, *Liberalism and the Limits of Justice*, p. 165.

37.   Gauthier, *Morals by Agreement*, p. 32.

38.   Davidson, "How Is Weakness of the Will Possible?" p. 95.

39.   Young, "Autonomy and the 'Inner Self,'" pp. 86–87.

40.   Thalberg, *Hierarchical Analyses of Unfree Action*, p. 134. Thalberg is protesting against Watson's "equation of genuine desires and moral values."

41.   Keykes, *Against Liberalism*, pp. 16–20.

42.   Ibid., p. 17.

43.   Ibid..

44. Ibid., p. 18.
45. Ibid., p. 19.
46. Ibid..
47. Ibid..
48. "Insofar as [agents] are exerting the kind of control over their actions that these conditions depict, they may be said to be making autonomous choices." Ibid.

CHAPTER 5. COMPREHENSIVE MORALITY

1. Taylor, *Sources of the Self*, p. 3.
2. Augustine, *City of God*, trans. Dods, bk. 16, chap. 8, "Whether Certain Monstrous Races of Men Are Derived from the Stock of Adam or Noah's Sons," p. 530.
3. Noddings, *Caring*, p. 3.
4. Stephen, *Science of Ethics*, p. 155.
5. Lyons and Benson, *Strutting and Fretting*, p. vii.
6. Ibid.
7. Ibid.
8. From Tennyson's "Charge of the Light Brigade," of course.
9. Williams, *Morality*, pp. 17–27.
10. Marquis de Sade, *Œuvres*. For those who do not care to confront Sade's full-length works, one can find selections and intelligent commentary in Shattuck, *Forbidden Knowledge.*.
11. Ortega y Gasset writes: "If you are unwilling to submit to any norm, you have, *nolens volens*, to submit to the norm of denying all morality." But this itself is to submit to a normative standard; that is, it is to practice morality. Ortega y Gasset, *Revolt of the Masses*, p. 189. The book was initially published in 1930.
12. The classic statement of the no-harm principle is, of course, Mill's *On Liberty*.
13. Matt. 5:21–22.
14. Matt. 5: 27–29.
15. Matt. 5:48.
16. Rev. 3:15–17.
17. Mark 9:41–43.
18. Matt. 13: 40–42.
19. Matt. 18:8–9.
20. Mark 9:35.
21. For example, Luke10:26–28; Mark. 12:30–32; Gal. 5:13–15.
22. Matt. 5:38–42; Luke 6:28–30.
23. Associated with such diverse figures as John Milton, John Bunyan, the Cambridge Platonists, the American Pilgrim Fathers and Cromwell, Puritanism was a nonconformist religious movement prominent in England and America at the beginning of the sixteenth century. In America the political and philosophical implications of the Puritan view were developed by lesser-known authors such as John Cotton, Roger Williams, John Wise, and, of course, the later Jonathan Edwards. Hobbes and Locke, the foremost philosophical precursors of liberalism in England, were both deeply influenced by Puritan beliefs. See Curti, "Psychological Theories in American Thought," pp. 16–30.
24. These articles of faith are not listed in the order used in the original declaration. The entire TULIP formula was drafted as a response by the Gomarists to the five-point

Remonstrance drafted by the followers of Arminius. Kingdon, "Determinism in Theology: Predestination," p. 28.

25. Theologians distinguish between "operative" and "cooperative" grace. In the case of operative grace, the individual has no choice but to cooperate. In the case of cooperative grace, the individual may choose whether or not to cooperate. A loving, omniscient God may occasionally force us to act in accord with grace, but God does not always force us his grace upon us. In orthodox theory, the final decision of whether we will be good or evil rests with us.

26. Maurer, "Edwards, Jonathan."

27. Ibid., p. 462.

28. Passmore, "Perfectibility of Man." As Passmore aptly concludes: "The quest for spiritual perfection has led men in some strange directions."

29. Larmore, *Patterns of Moral Complexity*, p. 30.

30. A. MacIntyre, "How Moral Agents Became Ghosts," pp. 305–6.

31. Moore, *Foundations of Liberalism*, p. 4.

32. Moore refers to "the integrity problem" and "the motivation problem." She provides a perspicacious criticism of liberalism.

33. In, for example, *The Scarlet Letter*.

34. Brinton, *History of Western Morals*, pp. 242–43.

35. Hence Luther's insistence that the authentic Christian should get married and live in the world.

36. Cited in Taylor, *Sources of the Self*, p. 22. See chap. 13, "God Loveth Adverbs." Brinton provides a balanced account of the Puritan view of worldly pleasure. Brinton, *History of Western Morals*, pp. 226–27.

37. Taylor, *Sources of the Self*, p. 248. Taylor is commenting here on the Puritan roots of "Lockean Deism."

38. As Peters writes: Hobbes's view "that civil society was based upon some kind of contract or covenant, was a commonplace at this period. . . . A model for this was the Pilgrim Fathers who made a declaration in 1620 solemnly covenanting and combining themselves into a civil society . . . .Hobbes' account was unusual in that he . . . deduced a most ingenuous form of *pactum unionis* which made the acceptance of a sovereign a condition of membership." Peters, *Hobbes*, p. 182.

39. Copleston continues: "He continued throughout his life to appreciate the good qualities of sincere pietists; but it is evident that he reacted rather sharply against the religious observances to which he had to conform at the college." Pietism might be described as a German Methodism. Copleston, *History of Philosophy*, 6:180.

40. A. MacIntyre, "How Moral Agents Became Ghosts," p. 305.

41. Baier speaks of "Hobbesians." Baier, "Moral Reasons."

42. Narveson, *Libertarian Idea*, pp. 124–25.

43. As Brinton reports: "When the strongly Puritanical were in full power, they translated their ideal into . . . sumptuary legislation of all sorts, [into] the laws of a republic of virtue." Brinton, *History of Western Morals*, pp. 224–25. Calvin's own Geneva was regulated by a wonderfully detailed and comprehensive legislative arrangement. As one popular historian relates: "[Even] the allowable color and quantity of clothing, and the number of dishes permissible at a meal, were specified by law. . . . A woman was jailed for arranging her hair to an immoral height. . . . To speak disrespectfully of Calvin or the clergy was a crime. . . . Fornication was to be punished with exile or drowning; adultery, blasphemy, or

idolatry with death. In one extraordinary instance a child was beheaded for striking its parents." Cited in Brinton, *History of Western Morals*, pp. 230–31. The passage originates in Durant, *Reformation* , p. 474.

44. Kant, of course, conceives of morality in terms of reverence for a universal law, the categorical imperative.

45. Hobbes conceives of morality as a submission to rules laid down by an absolute sovereign.

46. A. MacIntyre, "Intelligibility, Goods, and Rules," p. 665.

47. Ibid.

48. Larmore, *Patterns of Moral Complexity*, p. 4.

49. See Aristotle, *Nicomachean Ethics* 6.1140b5, 6.1140b8–10.

50. My translation. "Sans aucun doute la loi, qu'elle soit naturelle ou humaine, même la plus particulière, gardera toujours une certaine généralité confuse . . . où se trouve . . . la raison pour laquelle les juges, qui s'appliquent aux cas particuliers et en observent les nuances, sont indispensables à l'ordre de la justice." De Koninck, *La Confédération*, p. 19.

51. Hence the importance of a concept like "equity" in a legal context.

52. Mill, of course, distinguishes between higher and lower pleasures, but to distinguish between different qualities of pleasure produces, at the very least, an unorthodox utilitarianism.

53. Mill, *On Liberty,* ed. Collini, p. 58.

54. Ibid.

55. Ibid., pp. 56.

56. Ibid., pp. 59–60.

57. Because of his commitment to utilitarianism, Mill does not fully develop this line of thought in his own moral philosophy.

58. There is a fundamental tension in Mill's views and in liberalism more generally. On the one hand, liberals argue that human nature is good; on the other hand, their conception of morality presupposes the Puritan view that human nature is fundamentally depraved. These views are perhaps irreconcilable.

59. The verb "to pervert" derives from the Latin *pervertere*, "to turn the wrong way."

60. Rom. 2:13–16.

61. Taylor takes the term 'authenticity' from Lionel Trilling's book *Sincerity and Authenticity*. His concept of authenticity is roughly synonymous with personal autonomy. See *The Malaise of Modernity*.

62. Taylor, *Sources of the Self*, p. 357.

63. Nagel, *View from Nowhere*.

64. Ibid., p. 6.

65. Ibid., p. 4.

66. Considered "from an external perspective . . . agent and everything about him seems to be swallowed up by the circumstances of action; nothing of him is left to intervene in the circumstances." Ibid., p. 114.

67. "Living well and living right are both things we have reason to want, and while there may be some overlap, those reasons are generally of different kinds and come from different sources." Ibid., p. 197.

68. Ibid..

69. "The impersonal standpoint that acknowledges the claims of morality is only one aspect of a normal individual among others." Ibid.

70. Hunt, *Conquest of Everest*, p. 231.

71. Chic, *Pushing the Limits*, p. 371.

72. Austin, *Rocky Horrors, Frozen Smiles*, p. 93.

73. This is from an interview with Sherpa Ang Nyimi. Ortnerm, *Life and Death on Mt. Everest*, p. 242.

74. This is Hans Gmoser speaking. Dowling, *Mountaineers*, pp. 192–93.

75. The truly moral agent is, of course, the individual who achieves *eudaemonia*.

76. Personalism, understood as a philosophical movement, may be identified with a loose aggregate of authors such as Albert Knudson, Borden Browne, Emmanuel Mounier, and, more recently, Lawrence Blum. Personalists consider the distinction between persons and things to be the ultimate moral distinction. One is to treat objects in one way, people in another. See, for example, Knudson, *The Philosophy of Personalism,* and Blum, *Friendship, Altruism, and Morality*.

77. Nagel, *View from Nowhere*, p. 135. It is "to control the behavior of TN from a standpoint that is not mine qua TN." Ibid.

78. King, "Letter from Birmingham City Jail," p. 290.

79. Moral standards, judgments, problems, and arguments are to be distinguished from standards, judgments, problems, and arguments that are (e.g.) aesthetic or technical. Moral rules are to be distinguished from the rules of etiquette, grammar, etc. Sparkes, in an irreverent and ironic style, provides much interesting discussion on the "words" of politics. Sparkes, *Talking Politics,* p. 162.

80. Ibid.

81. Ibid.

82. Although, it has been suggested that the ancients did occasionally put things like javelins on trial for committing immoral actions. See Sprague, *Older Sophists*, pp. 9, 10 (from the life of Pericles in Plutarch's *Lives*).

83. See Kingwell, *Civil Tongue*.

84. Wolf, "Moral Saints."

85. Ibid., p. 419.

86. Ibid.

87. Ibid.

88. Ibid., p. 437 n. 5.

89. Ibid., pp. 436–37.

90. Wolf writes that "a healthy person" would not "wholly rule and direct his life by [such] abstract and impersonal consideration[s]" as the idea that his life must be "morally good." Ibid., p. 434.

91. Ibid., p. 437.

92. Ibid., p. 434.

93. Merton, *Wisdom of the Desert*, CVI, p. 63.

94. As Diogenes says of the early Stoic Antisthenes, "he held virtue to be sufficient in itself to ensure happiness." The sentiment expressed here is entirely typical. Diogenes Laertius, *Lives and Opinions of Eminent Philosophers,* trans. Hicks, 6.11, p. 13.

95. Erasmus in a letter to Ulrich von Hutten dated 23 July 1519. Bridgett, *Life*, pp. 56–60.

96. Wolf, "Moral Saints," p. 422.

97. Ibid., p. 421.

98. Ibid., p. 422.

99. Ibid., p. 432.

CHAPTER 6. MORALITY AND AUTONOMY

1. The best source for Dewey's ethical ideas is Dewey, *Theory of the Moral Life* (1960). The text is a redaction of "Part II" of Dewey and James Tufts's *Ethics* (rev. ed., 1938). Written as a textbook, the prose does not suffer from the rambling, digressive style that characterizes some of Dewey's other writings. It is a well-organized treatment, concise and straightforward.

2. Dewey, *Theory of the Moral Life*, p. 159.

3. Ibid., p. 149.

4. Ibid., p. 19.

5. Frankena calls "virtue ethics" any attempt to define morality in terms of "being" instead of "doing" . This is the standard view. *Ethics*, p. 64.

6. Dewey, *Moral Life*, p. 15.

7. Ibid., pp. 11–12.

8. Ibid., p. 11.

9. In modern parlance, Dewey could be rightly called a "neo-Aristotelian."

10. Dewey, *Moral Life*, p. 80.

11. Ibid.

12. Ibid.

13. Ibid.

14. Ibid.

15. In Dewey's own words: there are those theories that "attach chief importance to purposes and ends, leading to the concept of the Good as ultimate"; those theories that stress "the importance of law and regulation, leading up to a supremacy of the concepts of Duty and the Right"; and those theories that regard "praise and blame as the primary moral fact, thus . . . making the concepts of vice and virtue central." Ibid., p. 25.

16. Ibid., p. 26.

17. Ibid.

18. Ibid.

19. Ibid.

20. Ibid., p. 27.

21. Ibid. Dewey emphasizes the spontaneous nature of praise and blame. "There is nothing more spontaneous . . . than praise and blame of others." Ibid., p. 90. "Men unconsciously manifest approval and resentment." Ibid., 89.

22. Ibid., p. 26.

23. Dewey himself defines objectivity in pragmatic terms, in line with the coherentist account provided in the first section of this text.

24. Dewey, *Theory of the Moral Life*, p. 67.

25. Ibid., p. 77.

26. Ibid., p. 81.

27. Dewey bases his notion of justice on a notion of the common good. He writes, for example: "If the claim is, then, of the kind which [the agent] himself puts forth, if it serves a good which he prizes for himself, he must, in the degree in which he is fair-minded, acknowledge it to be a common good, and hence binding upon his judgment and action." Ibid., p. 83.

28. Ibid., p. 112. Dewey believes that virtue ethics often tends toward an uncritical conventionalism. He comments, "On the whole the prevalence of a morality based on praise

and blame is evidence of the extent to which customary and conventional forces still influence a morality nominally reflective." Ibid., p. 111.

29. Ibid., p. 109.

30. Ibid.

31. Ibid., p. 101. Alasdair MacIntyre provides (in *After Virtue*, for example).an account of virtue theory that situates "the ideal spectator" within the history and traditions of a particular community.

32. Dewey argues, like the "Hebrew prophets and Greek seers," that moral conduct is not truly moral conduct "unless it springs from the heart, from personal desires and affections, or from personal insight and rational choice." Ibid., p. 3.

33. Ibid., p. 83.

34. See Hart, *Concept of Law*, p. 19 and following. (Hart is engaged in a critique of John Austin's command theory of law, but this need not detain us here.)

35. Alternatively, he might do the right thing in a public, social sense, but, all the while, be frustrated and unable to achieve his goals in a personal, private sense.

36. Shakespeare, *Macbeth,* Oxford Shakespeare, III.2.13–24.

37. Ibid., III.2.43.

38. Ibid., V.5.16.

39. Ibid.,V.5.24–33.

40. Ibid.,V.1.48–49.

41. Ibid., V.1.35–37.

42. Ibid., V.1.38. It is the doctor speaking.

43. Ibid., II.3.123.

44. Hitler's life could be seen in a similar vein.

45. *Macbeth* V.2.25–27.

46. Ibid., V.2.24–25.

47. *Macbeth* V.3.29–31.

48. Richard III, another embodiment of evil in Shakespeare's treasury of characters, declares at the end of his life: "I shall despair. There is no creature loves me, And if I die no soul shall pity me." *Richard III* (Oxford Shakespeare), V.3.200–201.

49. Forester, "The Head and the Feet."

50. Aristotle associates virtue with the golden mean, with an avoidance of excess or deficiency in feelings and action. Virtue "then is a mean." *Nicomachean Ethics*, trans. T. Irwin, 1106b28. "Excess and deficiency are in error and incur blame while the intermediate condition is correct and wins praise." Ibid., 1106b24–27.

51. Ibid., 1103b1–3.

52. If gestures of praise and blame begin "without conscious reflection, . . . reflective morality . . . seeks to discover a rational principle by which they will be justified and rendered coherent." Dewey, *Theory of the Moral Life*, pp. 89–90.

53. For Aquinas, the first principle of the natural law is: "Bonum est faciendum et prosequendum, et malum vitandum" [Good is to be done and pursued, and evil avoided]. *Summa Theologica*, Ia, Iiae. 94.2.

54. Taylor, *Sources of the Self*, p. 42.

55. Dewey, *Theory of the Moral Life*, p. 26.

56. See, for example, Rawls, "Justice as Fairness"; R. Dworkin, ""Liberalism"; Ackerman, *Social Justice in the Liberal State*.

57. "Each time I approached the edge, I felt myself drawn over; . . . I have never felt this anywhere else, even when mountaineering or when I was a tree surgeon, and I won-

dered how many people might have been hypnotized into committing suicide unintentionally." Bernières, "Legends of the Fall," p. 79.

58. See Goleman, *Emotional Intelligence*, chap. 6.

59. See Dykens et al., "Eating Themselves to Death."

60. Murdoch, *Metaphysics as a Guide to Morals*, p. 429. Murdoch continues: "Mothers have many egotistic satisfactions and much power. The aunt may be the selfless unrewarded doer of good. I have known such aunts."

61. Ibid.

62. "But the Lord said to him, 'Pay no attention to how tall and handsome he is. I have rejected him, because I do not judge as people judge. They look at the outward appearance, but I look at the heart.'" 1 Sam. 16:7. See also: Matt 7:1, Luke. 6:37, James 4:12.

63. Swanton, *Freedom*.

64. Plato, *Republic* 588b–589b.

65. Aristotle distinguishes between *akrates*, the morally weak man, and *enkrates*, the man who can resist temptation. This is also translated as the incontinent and the continent man. "The incontinent man, knowing that what he does is bad, does it as a result of passion, while the continent man, knowing that his appetites are bad, refuses on account of his rational principle to follow them." Aristotle, *Nicomachean Ethics*, trans. Ross, 1145b12–15. Socrates denies the possibility of *akrasia*. He argues that one cannot act unvirtuously if one has knowledge of virtue. See: Plato, *Protagoras* 357Cff. Also, Aristotle, *Eudemian Ethics* 1246b34, 1144b.

66. Plato, *Symposium* 202; *Republic* 1.350, 5.478. According to Aristotle, Socrates went around inquiring into the nature of specific virtues because he thought that the end of man was the knowing of virtue. See Aristotle, *Eudemian Ethics* 1216b3–4. The virtues become instances of reason or of prudence. See Aristotle, *Nicomachean Ethics* 1144b17–2, 1144b2.

67. Aristotle's account differs in that the incontinent man is not ignorant. He compares the incontinent and the "wicked" man to two different cities: "The incontinent man is like a city which passes all the right decrees and has good laws, but makes no use of them . . . but the wicked man is like a city which uses its laws, but has wicked laws to use." Aristotle, *Nicomachean Ethics*, trans. Ross, 7.10.1152a 19-24.

68. Arendt, *Eichmann in Jerusalem*.

69. Arendt writes: "His was obviously no case of moral let alone legal insanity. Worse, his was obviously also no case of insane hatred of the Jews, of fanatical anti-Semitism or indoctrination of any kind. He 'personally' never had anything against Jews." Ibid., p. 26.

70. Papadatos, *Eichmann Trial*, p. 28 n. 31. Cf. Arendt, *Eichmann in Jerusalem*, p. 25ff.: "Half a dozen psychiatrists had certified [Eichmann] as normal—'More normal, at any rate, than I am after having examined him,' one of them was said to have exclaimed, while another had found that his whole psychological outlook, his attitude toward his wife and children, mother and father, brothers, sisters, and friends, was 'not only normal but most desirable'—and finally the minister who had paid regular visits to him in prison after the Supreme Court had finished hearing his appeal reassured everybody by declaring Eichmann to be 'a man with very positive ideas.'" Arendt adds, a sentence later: "Mr. Hausner's recent revelations in the *Saturday Evening Post* of things he 'could not bring out at the trial' have contradicted the information given informally in Jerusalem. Eichmann, we are now told, had been alleged by the psychiatrists to be 'a man obsessed with a dangerous and insatiable urge to kill,' 'a perverted, sadistic personality.' In which case he would have belonged in an insane asylum." The rest of *Eichmann in Jerusalem* suggests that Arendt saw these latter comments as an unconvincing attempt to justify Eichmann's execution.

71. Arendt, *Eichmann in Jerusalem*, p. 126.

72. Aquinas, *Summa Theologica,* trans. English Dominican Province, Ia-IIae.76.3. See also IIa-IIae.15.

73. Ibid., q. 76, Third Article.

74. Papadatos, *Eichmann Trial*, p. 29.

75. Ibid., p. 30.

76. Kant, *Foundations of the Metaphysics of Morals*, trans. Beck, 2.421, p. 44.

77. Arendt, *Eichmann in Jerusalem*, p. 136.

78. Ibid., p. 136. And see p. 136ff.: "In this household use, all that is left of Kant's spirit is the demand that a man do more than obey the law, that he go beyond the mere call of obedience and identify his own self with the principle behind the law—the source from which the law sprang. In Kant's philosophy, that source was practical reason; in Eichmann's household use of him, it was the will of the Führer."

79. Dimock discusses this kind of problem in "Personal Autonomy."

80. "The self-indulgent [i.e., the morally ignorant] man is worse than the incontinent." Aristotle, *Nicomachean Ethics*, trans. Ross, 7.1150a30. See also 8.1150b30ff.

81. According to Aquinas (culpable) moral ignorance makes the sinful act "more voluntary and more sinful." Aquinas, *Summa Theologica* Ia-IIae.76: "Of the Causes of Sin, in Particular," Fourth Article.

82. "Incontinence is contrary to choice while vice [immorality through ignorance] is in accordance with choice." Aristotle, *Nicomachean Ethics*, trans. Ross, 8.1151a5.

83. "The self-indulgent man . . . is not apt to repent . . . but any incontinent man is likely to repent." Ibid., 1150b30.

84. "Wickedness is like a disease such as dropsy or consumption, while incontinence is like epilepsy; the former is a permanent, the latter an intermittent badness." Ibid., 1150b33–35.

85. "The self-indulgent man is incurable and the incontinent man curable." Ibid., 1150b33.

86. Aristotle's own view of virtue ethics would seem to support this interpretation.

87. Twain, *Portable Mark Twain*, pp. 448–49. The chapter in *Huckleberry Finn* is entitled "You Can't Pray a Lie."

88. Ibid., p. 451.

89. Cooper, *Value Pluralism and Ethical Choice.* Cooper wants to distinguish moral from personal autonomy. According to Cooper: "Personal autonomy is not moral autonomy." Ibid., p. 116. And again: "Personal autonomy . . . cannot serve as an adequate characterization of an autonomous moral agent." Ibid. On Cooper's account, moral autonomy is personal autonomy plus morality. Cooper's insightful commentary does not present a sufficiently critical exposition of the standard view of personal autonomy.

90. Ibid., p. 115.

91. Ibid., p. 116.

92. "Autonomous people are assumed to be in control of their life, and to be free to choose their own values, life plans, and principles." Ibid., p. 118.

93. Ibid., p. 115.

94. Ibid., p. 116.

95. Ibid., p. 117.

96. Ibid., pp. 116, 117.

97. Feinberg, *Harm to Self*, p. 45. Cooper quotes Feinberg at length. Cooper, *Value Pluralism and Ethical Choice*, p. 116.)

98. It appears that, just before his death, Bundy did recognize that his life was a failure.

99. *The Random House College Dictionary,* first ed., 1979. According to the *Oxford English Dictionary,* to govern is to: "4. Conduct oneself in some way; curb, bridle (one's passions, oneself). 5. Constitute a law, rule, standard, or principle, for; serve to decide (case)."

100. *Oxford English Dictionary.*

101. Nietzsche, *Thus Spoke Zarathustra,* in *The Portable Nietzsche,* trans. Kaufmann, "Third Part: On the Three Evils," 10.2, p. 302.

102. Rand, *Virtue of Selfishness.*

CHAPTER 7. NORMATIVE ACCOUNTS OF FREEDOM

1. The origins of natural law theory seem lost in time. The stela that records the legal code of Hammurabi (c. 1790 B.C.) depicts the king standing before Shamash, the god of justice (with throne, ceremonial costume, wings, ring, and cane), who dictates to him the laws. This seem a very early instance of natural law theory! The basic idea was developed as a philosophical theory by the Stoics Zeno and Chrysippus and was later adopted and developed by Cicero and Aquinas. The notion that human law only derives its moral authority from conformity to some underlying rationale can already be found in Plato's *Statesman* 292e–297c. Aristotle, in a passage from the *Nicomachean Ethics,* distinguishes between rules derived from nature and rules derived from human convention (bk 5, chap. 70). Augustine, in his turn, limits the powers of secular political authority. For a short history of natural law ethics, see Richard Hepburn, "Natural Law." See also Cicero, *De legibus* (On the laws); Aquinas, *Summa Theologia* Ia-IIae.90–97.

2. "Unless perhaps to avoid scandal or riot." Aquinas, *Summa Theologica,* trans. English Dominican Province, Ia-IIae.96–4.

3. In a commentary on obedience, Aquinas writes: "The obligation to obey civil authority is measured by what the order of justice requires. For this reason when any regime holds its power not by right but by usurpation, or commands what is wrong, subjects have no duty to obey, except for such extraneous reasons as avoidance of scandal or risk." Ibid., IIa-IIae.104, 6, "Reply to Objection 3."

4. Cicero, cited in Foster, *Plato to Machiavelli,* 184.

5. "The rational creature has itself a share in the eternal reason and derives from this its natural inclination towards its proper action and end; and this manner of sharing in the eternal law, which is peculiar to the rational creature, is called natural law." (Aquinas, *Summa Theologica,* trans. English Dominican Province, Ia.91.2)

6. Cicero in Foster, *Plato to Machiavelli,* 189.

7. Nietzsche, *Twilight of the Idols,* in *The Portable Nietzsche,* trans. Kaufmann, 29, p.532.

8. Nietzsche, *Untimely Meditations,* trans. Hollingdale, p. 137.

9. Nietzsche, *Ecce Homo,* trans. Kaufmann, p. 258.

10. Mill, *On Liberty,* ed. Rees.

11. Ibid., p.11.

12. Philosophers tend to focus on Mill's utilitarianism when discussing his moral philosophy. Mill himself accepts the narrow official view of morality which has served to obscure the comprehensive nature of value-laden striving. But a morality of romantic liberalism is implicit in his thought. Lancaster, *Hegel to Dewey,* 136–37.

13. Mill, *On Liberty*, ed. Collini, p. 59.

14. Ibid., p. 59.

15. Lancaster, *Hegel to Dewey,* 3:136–37.

16. Mill argues that the ideal person will be characterized by "great energies guided by vigorous reason and strong feeling strongly controlled by a conscientious will." Mill, *On Liberty*, ed. Collini, pp. 65–66.

17. "The amount of vigor contained in a society has generally been proportional to the amount of genius, mental vigor, and moral courage it contained." Ibid., p. 63.

18. "People of genius are, *ex vi termini* [by definition], more individual than any other people." Ibid., p. 61.

19. Ibid., p. 63.

20. The "malaise of modernity" has resulted in an erosion of ethical values, in a "narrowing and flattening of our lives," in "a loss of resonance, depth or richness in our human surroundings." Taylor, *Malaise of Modernity*, p. 6.

21. Ibid., p. 73.

22. This is, in the terminology of another debate on autonomy, to ask questions about procedural independence.

23. "To shut out demands emanating beyond the self is precisely to suppress the condition of significance, and court trivialization." Taylor, *Malaise of Modernity*, p. 40. And again: "Only if I trust in a world in which history or the demands of nature, or the needs of my fellow human beings, or the duties of citizenship, or the call of God, or something else of this order matters crucially, can I define an identity for myself that is not trivial." Ibid., p. 41.

24. Nietzsche tends towards hyperbole. His views are diverse, nonsystematic, and not easily classifiable. Although there may be scholars who would contest this interpretation of Nietzsche, it is, at the very least, a view that is frequently and with serious justification attributed to Nietzsche.

25. Taylor, *Human Agency and Language,* p. 29.

26. If the individual is to be held responsible for his actions, there must be, at some point, an initial binding act of choice. If I can continually engage in radical choice, if I reinstitute new value systems over and over again, I can effectively do anything. This would be mere anarchy rather than value-guided behavior.

27. Taylor, *Human Agency and Language*, p. 29.

28. Ibid., p. 30.

29. As Taylor puts it: "If serious moral claims were created by radical choice, the young man could have a grievous dilemma about whether to go and get an ice cream cone, and then again he could decide not to." Ibid., p. 30.

30. Ibid., p. 35. As Michael Sandel has argued (in *Liberalism and the Limits of Justice*) that liberal theories about the social contract that presume the existence of this kind of self are seriously problematic.

31. Sandel rejects a similar Rawlsean account of "purely preferential choice." Rawls himself writes: "The notion of radical choice . . . finds no place in justice as fairness." Rawls, *Theory of Justice*, p. 568. But despite Rawls' protests to the contrary, purely preferential choice is, in many respects, analogous to radical choice. In Rawls' system, the social contract brings into being principles of justice that are just because they have, in the first instance, been chosen. See Sandel, *Liberalism and the Limits of Justice*, p. 164.

32. Taylor, *Human Agency and Language*, p. 38.

33. This example originates in Taylor.

34. Taylor, *Human Agency and Language*, p. 18.

35. "Strong evaluation is a condition of articulacy, and to acquire a strongly evaluative language is to become (more) articulate about one's preferences." Ibid., p. 24.

36. Ibid., p. 4.

37. In, for example, Perry's *General Theory of Value*.

38. Korsgaard, "Two Distinctions in Goodness," p. 173. This was Perry's position.

39. Ibid.

40. Again, this is Korsgaard's paraphrase of Moore's position. Ibid., p. 175.

41. Rorty, "Truth and Freedom," p. 635.

42. Taylor, *Sources of the Self*, pp. 487–90.

43. Rorty, "Truth and Freedom," p. 639.

44. Haworth, *Autonomy*, p. 23.

45. Dewey, *Philosophy and Civilization*, p. 289.

46. Rubin and McNeil, *Psychology of Being Human*, p. 468.

47. See G. Dworkin, "Autonomy and Behavior Control"; "Acting Freely"; and *Theory and Practise of Autonomy*.

48. In any case, what could it mean to say that a lunatic is acting authentically? That he or she is living as a genuine lunatic, that is, insanely?

49. Wolf, "Sanity and the Metaphysics of Responsibility," pp. 137–51.

50. Ibid., pp. 140–41.

51. Wolf's depiction of insanity as a condition inflicted on a passive individual from the outside seems overly simple. See her example of JoJo, a third-world dictator whose sadistic and brutal ways are to be attributed to an evil upbringing. Ibid., p.143. In Harold's case, we do not have a passive individual molded by his environment. Harold has molded himself.

52. Ibid., p. 145. Wolf also writes: "One's desire to be sane involves...a desire to live in the Real World . . . a desire to be controlled—by perceptions and sound reasoning that produce an accurate conception of the world rather than by blind or distorted forms of response." Ibid., 144–45.

53. Christman, *Inner Citadel*, p. 14.

54. Iris Murdoch, *Metaphysics as a Guide to Morals*, p. 507.

55. Ibid., p. 509.

56. Ibid., p. 508.

57. Ibid., p. 426.

58. Ibid., p. 427.

59. Ibid., p. 426.

60. "Non-philosophical people do not think that they invent good. They may invent their own activities, but the good is somewhere else as a judge of these." Ibid., p. 508. This is perhaps a criticism of Mackie.

61. Ibid.

62. "In our ordinary unmysterious experience of transcendence." Ibid..

63. Ibid., p. 428.

64. It is "continually rediscovered in the course of our daily struggle with the world." Ibid., p. 427.

65. "The good artist is a sort of image of the good man, the great artist is a sort of image of the saint." Ibid., p. 428.

66. Ibid., p. 427.

67. Ibid., p. 508.

68. Ibid.

69. Murdoch marshals a so-called ontological argument for the existence of an idea of the good in the Third Meditation. Ibid., pp. 391–430,

70. Barry, *Theories of Justice*.

71. Ibid., pp. 5–9.

72. Actions which "are morally wrong . . . violate the constraints of impartiality." Ibid., p. 291.

73. Ibid., p. 8.

74. Ibid.

75. Ibid., p. 284. And again: "The motive for acting morally remains . . . the desire to be able to justify our conduct." Ibid., p. 290.

76. Ibid.

77. Naess and Rothenberg, *Ecology, Community, and Lifestyle*, p. 2.

78. Dovey, "Quest for Authenticity," p. 33. Authenticity is, in Heideggerean terms, as "a way of being-in-the-world . . . a spatio-temporal rootedness which enriches our world with experiential depth." Ibid., p. 47.

79. The term is deliberately vague. Naess calls it a T_0 or lowest-level concept.

80. Maslow speaks of a hierarchy of needs: physiological needs, safety needs, belongingness and love needs, esteem needs, the need for self-actualization, cognitive needs, and aesthetic needs. Maslow, *Motivation and Personality*. See chap. 4, "A Theory of Human Motivation," pp. 35–58.

81. Nussbaum, "Human Functioning and Social Justice," p. 222.

82. In Swanton's words: "Individual flourishing is constituted by the satisfaction and development of those needs and capacities which, under good conditions, human beings characteristically desire to satisfy and develop, and whose development and satisfaction they enjoy under those conditions." Swanton, *Freedom*, p. 42.

83. To cite: "Good conditions would be defined by, e.g. conditions conducive to the absence of suicidal tendencies, chronic exhaustion, and lassitude; absence of chronic boredom, ennui, anxiety, loneliness, severe stress, feelings of worthlessness; absence of brainwashing, terror, fear, coercion." Ibid.

84. "For the anorexic who experiences the healthy appetite as opposed to the obsessive desire for slimness as a fetter, 'liberation' is obtained not by eliminating the desire with which she does not identify, but by eliminating the non-temperate [higher]-order desire for slimness." Ibid., pp. 134–35.

85. Nietzsche, *Thus Spake Zarathustra*, in *The Portable Nietzsche*, trans. Kaufmann, "Ugliest Man," 7, p. 377.

86. Ibid., "Drunken Song," 11, pp. 435–36.

87. Ibid., 1, "Enjoying and Suffering the Passions," pp. 148–49.

88. Kohlberg, *Philosophy of Moral Development*.

89. Gilligan, "Moral Orientation and Moral Development," p. 20.

90. Ibid., p. 24.

91. Moore, *Foundations of Liberalism*, p. 184. Moore criticizes Kymlicka's claims that in communitarianism "self-discovery replaces judgement." Kymlicka's views are reductionist. We define ourselves in relation to values. Self-discovery is, every step of the way, a value-laden process. One does not only discover the self. One learns, concomitantly, what is good or bad.

92. Royce, *Basic Writings*, vol. 2.

93. Jantzen, "A Mystical Core of Religion" and "Mysticism and Experience." Jantzen traces this identification of mysticism with the abnormal or the paranormal to William James, himself influenced by the romanticism of Schelling and Schleiermacher.

94. Butler writes, "There is probably no more misused word in these days than 'mysticism.' It has come to be applied to many things of many kinds: to theosophy and Christian science; to spiritualism and clairvoyance; to demonology and witchcraft; to occultism and witchcraft; to weird psychical experience, if only they have some religious colour; to revelations and visitations, to other-worldliness, or even to mere dreaminess and impracticality in the affairs of life; to poetry and painting, and music of which the motif is unobvious and vague." Butler, *Western Mysticism*, p. 3.

95. Underhill writes, "What then do we really mean by mysticism? A word which is impartially applied to the performances of mediums and ecstasies of the saints, to 'menticulture' and sorcery, dreamy poetry and medieval art, to prayer and palmistry, the doctrinal excesses of Gnosticism, and tepid speculations of the Cambridge platonists—even, according to William James, to the higher branches of intoxication—soon ceases to have any useful meaning." Underhill, *Mysticism*, p. 72.

96. According to Hughes, "There is scarcely a phase of pathological existence, physical or mental, that has not been called into service in the effort to show that mysticism belongs to the realm of the abnormal and the aberrant. . . . Many have treated it as due to purely physical causes, the result of disorders of the digestive organs and other aliments. . . . Still others have treated it as pure illusion on a level with the experiences and states produced by drugs and by intoxication, or like the aura which precedes epilepsy and the exaltation induced by nitrous oxide gas . . . Some have treated it as a phase of dissociation and split personality, others have regarded it as akin to the hypnotic condition or pure automatism. To some it is self-delusion, to others hysteria or neurosis, whilst to many it is a case of mono-ideism. . . . Finally there are those who approach the subject from the Freudian point of view, treating it as an aberration or a sublimation of the instinct of sex." Hughes, *Philosophical Basis of Mysticism*, p. 206.

97. In 1926 Geraldine Hodgson was to write: "A theory seems to be growing up . . . [that] the real substance of mysticism is unsound mentality, showing itself in extravagance, eroticism, in visions, trances, extreme asceticism; and more unpleasantly, and at least as disastrously, in swollen, overweening vanity and pretentiousness. According to not a few modern writers these qualities are the whole content of Mysticism." Hodgson is, in fact, responding to Leuba's book *Psychology of Religious Mysticism*. Hodgson, *Sanity of Mysticism*, p. 1.

98. Egan, *Christian Mysticism*, pp. 14–16.

99. Kaplan and Katsaros, *Western Mystical Tradition*, 1:9.

100. Horne, *Beyond Mysticism*, p. iii.

101. Jewish "throne mysticism" may seem anomalous. As the use of the Tetragrammaton indicates, Judaism fosters an absolute reverence for God. The mystic does not so much fuse with God as contemplate the throne, the Place where God sits. This experience can still be interpreted in terms of the discovery of oneself in an Other. Mystics in this tradition find themselves, most precisely, in the contemplation of the Other. Nonetheless, it is in a (more distant) communion with the Other that the mystic finds his real self.

102. See Otto, *Idea of the Holy*.

103. See Stace, *Mysticism and Philosophy*.

104. Whitbeck, "Different Reality," p. 68.

105. Sandel, *Liberalism and the Limits of Justice*, p. 19. And again: "it is not our aims . . .
but our capacity to choose our aims that matters most." Ibid., p. 59.

106. Haworth, *Decadence and Objectivity*, p. 91.

CHAPTER 8. A THEORY OF REBELLION

1. Kant, *Metaphysics of Morals*, trans. Gregor, 49, A, p. 95.

2. Thoreau's work was published in 1849.

3. Rawls, "The Justification of Civil Disobedience."

4. In *Rebels with A Cause*, *Tree of Liberty*, and *War against Authority*.

5. Kittrie, *Rebels with a Cause*, pp. 342–44.

6. Kittrie, *War Against Authority*, pp. 18–19.

7. Kittrie, *Rebels with a Cause*, p. 3.

8. Wolff, *Defense of Anarchism*, p. 16.

9. See Giles, "Poet of Alienation"; Hill, "Rebel without a Clue"; and Strauss, "He
Was a Geek and a God."

10. Kittrie, *War against Authority*, pp. 18–19.

11. Ibid., p. 19.

12. Chopin's novel is sometimes touted as part of a new literary canon. It is an uneven
story that, nonetheless, does demonstrate the searing ambivalence that destroys the main
character.

13. Kerouac modeled Dean Moriarty after the real life character Neil Cassidy (Neal
Cassady) who associated with the likes of Allen Ginsberg, John Clellon Holmes, Ken Kesey,
and Tom Wolfe.

14. Kerouac, *On the Road*, p. 194.

15. Ibid., p. 105.

16. Ibid., p. 213.

17. Ibid., pp. 193–94.

18. Salinger, *Catcher in the Rye*, pp. 167–68.

19. Ibid., p. 173.

20. Coupland's story is largely derivative. It lacks the intensity of an author like
Kerouac.

21. Coupland, *Generation X*, p. 58.

22. Ibid.

23. Milton, *Paradise Lost*, lines 37–38.

24. Frye, *Return of Eden*, p. 21, 22–23

25. Ibid., p. 21

26. Ibid., pp. 21–22.

27. Frye, p. 28.

28. Ibid., p. 21. Frye is referring here to Milton's *The Christian Doctrine*.

29. Camus, *Rebel*, p. 13.

30. Ibid.

31. Ibid.

32. Marcus, *Autonomy in the Extreme Situation*, p. 177.

33. Ibid.

34. Ibid., p. 179.

35. Ibid., p. 180. The commandment to care about others is not just a moral truth. It is

a prerequisite for psychological health. Marcus quotes Eitinger, Auschwitz survivor and psychiatrist, as saying, "It was those people who were capable of showing interest in others who, mentally, had the best chance of retaining their individuality." Ibid. p. 179. Citation from Eitinger, *Concentration Camp Survivors*, p. 80.

36. Ibid.
37. Ibid., p. 178.
38. Ibid., pp. 178–79.
39. Ibid., p. 184.
40. Cook, *Subject Finds a Voice*, p. 138.
41. Ibid., p. 137.
42. Ibid.
43. Foucault, *Power*, p. 132.
44. Ibid.
45. Ibid.
46. Foucault, *Power,* p. 331.
47. Ibid., p. 342.
48. Marcus, *Autonomy in the Extreme Situation*, p. 178.
49. De Koninck, *La Confédération*.
50. Plato, *Republic*, bk. 5.
51. Halbertal and Margalit, *Idolatry*, p. 245.
52. Ibid.
53. Tillich, *Protestant Era*, p.226.
54. Ackerman, *Social Justice in the Liberal State,* pp. 10–11.
55. See Lasch, *Culture of Narcissism*. Lasch bases his account of narcissism on the work of psychiatrists and psychologists such as Heinz Kohut and Otto Kernberg. He provides an ample bibliography.
56. See Bell, *Cultural Contradictions of Capitalism*.
57. See Taylor, *Malaise of Modernity*.
58. See Bloom, *Closing of the American Mind*.
59. See Lipovetsky, *L'ère du vide*.
60. See Sennett, *Public Man*.
61. See Bellah et al., *Habits of the Heart*.
62. See Downs, *Beyond the Looking Glass*.
63. See Coles, "Civility and Psychology."
64. For a comprehensive summary of the story, see Barthell, *Gods and Goddesses of Ancient Greece*, pp. 44–45; see also Ovid, *Metamorphoses I–IV*, trans. Hill.
65. This is a play on the ancient Greek motto "Know thyself" which "was inscribed in Apollo's temple at Delphi and was one of the most famous injunctions of the Olympian religion." Ovid, *Metamorphoses I–IV,* trans. Hill, p. 226.
66. Ovid, *Metamorphoses I–IV* 3.467–68, trans. Hill, p. 113.
67. Shaffer provides a succinct review and an extensive bibliography of literature on narcissism. Shaffer, *Blinding Torch*.
68. *Penguin Dictionary of Psychology*, s.v. "narcissistic personality disorder."
69. See Marcuse, *Eros and Civilization;* and Alford, *Narcissism*.
70. Wolfe, "The Me Decade." The finished essay first appeared in August 1976.
71. Ibid., p. 293.
72. Ibid., p. 288.
73. Ibid., p. 279.

74. Satire, "I am me." One wonders from the pseudonym Virginia *Satire* (printed in minuscule lettering) if the authors take the tract somewhat less seriously than those who hang such posters on their walls. One certainly hopes so.

75. Bellah et al., *Habits of the Heart,* p. 56.

76. "Individualism lies at the very core of American culture. . . . We believe in the dignity, indeed the sacredness of the individual. . . . We do not argue that Americans should abandon individualism—that would mean for us to abandon our deepest identity." Ibid., p. 142.

77. Ibid, p. 79.

78. Ibid.

79. They "reveal nothing of the shape moral character should take, the limits it should respect, and the community it should serve." Ibid.

80. Ibid.

81. Ibid.

82. Ibid., p. 77.

83. Ibid.

84. Ibid., p. 55.

85. Lipovetsky, *L'ère du vide*, p. 80. "Narcisse n'est plus immobilisé devant son image fixe, il n'y a même plus d'image, rien qu'une quête interminable du Soi, un procès de déstabilisation ou flottaison psy à l'instar de la flottaison monétaire ou de l'opinion publique" [Narcissus is no longer immobilized before his fixed image, there is no longer an image, nothing but an interminable quest of the Self, a process of destabilization or psychic floating like fluctuations in the exchange rate or the ups and downs of public opinion].

86. Sennett, *Public Man*, p. 5. Riesman had earlier argued that people were moving from an inner-directed condition in which they pursued goals and commitments they felt within themselves to an other-directed condition in which they pursued goals and commitments they sense within others. Riesman, *Lonely Crowd.* Sennett argues the reverse: that Western societies are moving from something like an other-directed condition to an inner-directed condition.

87. Coles, "Civility and Psychology," p. 189.

88. Ibid., p. 194.

89. Swidler, "Love and Adulthood in American Culture," pp. 107–25.

90. The reformed pederast is, in Aristotle's philosophy, the continent man, the person who must strive against his nature to be moral.

91. These authors speak of "the duty to obey and the duty to disobey." Kelman and Hamilton, *Crimes of Obedience*, pp. 53–76.

92. Thoreau, *Walden and Civil Disobedience*, p. 388.

CHAPTER 9. NEGATIVE LIBERTY

1. Lewis, *Last Battle*, p. 34. The scene ends on a comic note: "'H-n-n-h,' grunted the Bear and scratched his head; it found this sort of thing hard to understand."

2. Berlin, *Four Essays on Liberty*. See, in particular, "Two Concepts of Liberty" and "Introduction," II.

3. Ibid., p. 166.

4. Rousseau, *The Social Contract*. See chap. 7, "On the Sovereign."

5. Keykes, *Against Liberalism*, p. 38.

6. Ibid., p. 40.

7. Ibid., p. 209.

8. Ibid., p. 40.

9. Gaylin and Jennings, *Perversion of Autonomy*.

10. Hobbes, *Leviathan*, p. 110. Action for the materialist Hobbes means motion. Hobbes also defines "A FREE-MAN" as "he, that in those things, which by his strength and wit he is able to do, is not hindred to doe what he has a will to do." Ibid., p. 110. But it is very hard to determine, in any precise sense, what a particular individual has "the strength and wit" to be able to do. It is not just a matter of having the strength and wit to do something. It is also a matter of possessing the appropriate resources. Without sufficient resources, strength and wit count for nothing.

11. Ibid.

12. Sartre, *Philosophy of Existentialism*, p. 41.

13. As Sartre observes, "[T]o make [one]self passive in the world, to refuse to act upon things and upon others is still to choose." Ibid., p. 67.

14. Berlin, "Two Concepts of Liberty."

15. In books such as *Atlas Shrugged, The Fountainhead, The Virtue of Selfishness, Capitalism*.

16. Young, *Personal Autonomy*, p. 109.

17. Thoreau, *Walden and Civil Disobedience*, p. 95.

18. Ibid.

19. Haworth, *Autonomy*, p. 167.

20. Lindley, *Autonomy*, p. 186. Lindley also writes: "The main rationale for favoring a large sphere of negative liberty is that it may be essential for the promotion of autonomy." Ibid., p. 8.

21. "The value of [negative] liberty . . . is that it creates a domain . . . in which one's capacity for autonomous life may both be developed and find expression." Haworth, *Autonomy*, p. 167.

22. Ibid., pp. 165–67.

23. Raz, *Morality of Freedom*, p. 400.

24. Ibid. And again: "Negative freedom, freedom from coercive interferences, is valuable inasmuch as it serves positive freedom and autonomy." Ibid.

25. Raz writes: "The ruling idea behind the ideal of personal autonomy is that people should make their own lives. The autonomous person is a (part) author of his life. The ideal of autonomy is the vision of people controlling, to some degree, their own destiny, fashioning it through successive decisions throughout their lives." Ibid., p. 369. And again: "Autonomy is an ideal of self-creation. . . . An autonomous person's well-being consists in the successful pursuit of self-chosen goals and relationships." Ibid., p. 370.

26. Larmore, *Patterns of Moral Complexity*, p. 73.

27. Ibid., pp. 73–74.

28. Raz, *Morality of Freedom*, p. 371.

29. Ibid., p. 411.

30. Ibid., p. 381. As Margaret Moore points out, one cannot, at the same time, maintain "that the exercise of autonomy is compatible with making worthless choices, . . . [and] that autonomy is possible only through choosing objectively worthwhile options." Moore, *Foundations of Liberalism*, pp. 157–58.

31. Raz, *Morality of Freedom*, p. 372.

32. Raz wants to replace the liberal notion of self-interest with a notion of "well-

being." In his words: "Most regrettable is the fact that the common discussions . . . tend to concentrate on self-interest rather than on well-being. Their well-being, and not their self-interest, is what matters most both morally and to people themselves." Ibid., p. 317.

33. Bernard Berofsky, *Liberation from Self*, p. 246.

34. Keykes, *Against Liberalism,* p. 15.

35. May, *Psychology and the Human Dilemma*, p. 25.

36. Keykes, *Against Liberalism,* p. 46.

37. In *Dialogues Concerning Natural Religion*.

38. Haworth, *Autonomy*, p.168

39. Raz, *Morality of Freedom*, p. 415.

40. Swanton is reacting here to the views of "philosophers such as Taylor and Benjamin Gibbs." Swanton, *Freedom*, p. 83.

41. Raz, *Morality of Freedom*, pp. 373–74.

42. Kathleen Wilkes disapproves of "fantastical thought-experiments," based on abstract idealizations. Her argument occurs within the context of philosophical discussions about personal identity. See Wilkes, *Real People*.

43. See Spidlik. "Stylites."

44. Raz, *Morality of Freedom*, p. 379.

45. Frankl, *Man's Search for Meaning*.

46. Ibid., p. 43.

47. Ibid., p. 65.

48. Ibid., p. 66.

49. Ibid., p. 79.

50. Ibid., p. 14.

51. Ibid., p. 58.

52. Ibid., p. 77.

53. Ibid., p. 38.

54. Ibid., p. 35.

55. Ibid., p. 42.

56. Ibid., p. 135.

57. Ibid., p. 137.

58. Raz, *Morality of Freedom*, p. 379.

59. Frankl, *Man's Search for Meaning*, p. 49.

60. Lindley, *Autonomy*, pp. 68–69.

61. The movie is based on Anthony Burgess's book of the same title.

62. In fact, he becomes someone who is preyed upon by others.

63. It goes without saying that in oppressive societies, morality is a very problematic issue. The boundaries of what is permissible (and what is heroic) may change significantly.

64. In A. MacIntyre, "How Moral Agents Became Ghosts."

65. Feinberg, "Concept of Autonomy," p. 28.

66. Ibid.

Bibliography

Ackerman, Bruce. *Social Justice in the Liberal State*. New Haven: Yale University Press, 1980.

Aegerter, Emmanuel. *Le mysticisme*. Paris: Flammarion, 1952.

Alford, C. Fred. *Narcissism: Socrates, the Frankfurt School, and Psychoanalytic Theory*. New Haven: Yale University Press, 1988.

Ali, Mohammed Maulana, trans. *The Holy Qur'an*. Columbus, Ohio: The Ahamdiyyah Anjuman Isha'at Islam, Lathore,1991.

Anderson, Robert. *Hume's First Principles*. Lincoln: University of Nebraska Press, 1966.

Annotated Tremeear's Criminal Code. Edited by David Watt and Michelle Fuerst. Toronto: Carswell, 1995.

Aquinas, St. Thomas. *De Ente et Essentia (On Being and Essence)*. Translated by Armand Maurer. Toronto: Pontifical Institute of Medieval Studies, 1949.

———. *Summa Theologia*, Translated by Thomas Gilby and T. C. O'Brien. London: Eyre & Spottiswoode; New York: McGraw-Hill, 1972.

———. *Summa Theologica*. Translated by the Fathers of the English Dominican Province. New York: Benziger Bros., 1947.

———. *The Three Greatest Prayers: Commentaries on the Lord's Prayer, the Hail Mary, and the Apostles' Creed*, Translated by Laurence Shapcote. Manchester, N.H.: Sophia Institute Press, 1990.

Arendt, Hannah. *Eichmann in Jerusalem: A Report on the Banality of Evil*. New York: Penguin Books, 1963.

Aristotle. *Nicomachean Ethics*. Translated by T. Irwin. Indianapolis, Ind.: Hackett, 1985.

———. *The Works of Aristotle*. Edited by W. D. Ross. London: Oxford University Press, 1928. Includes *Nicomachean Ethics, Eudemian Ethics, Politics, Posterior Analytics, Topics, Metaphysics*.

Augustine. *City of God*. Translated by Marcus Dods. New York: Modern Library, 1993.

———. *In ioannis evangelium tractatus (Homilies on the Gospel of St. John.)* In vols. 78–79, 88, and 92 of *Fathers of the Church*, translated by J. Rettig. Washington, D.C.: Catholic University of America, 1988–95.

———. *The Literal Meaning of Genesis*. Translated by J. H. Taylor. New York: Newman Press, 1982.

Austin, J. L. "A Plea for Excuses." In *Philosophical Papers,* edited by J. O. Urmson and G. J. Warnock, 175–205. 2d ed. New York: Oxford University Press, 1970.

Austin, Peter. *Rocky Horrors, Frozen Smiles: A Mountaineer at the End of His Rope*. Surrey, B.C.: Heritage House, 2000.

Ayer, A. J. *Language, Truth, and Logic*. New York: Dover,1946.

Babbit, Susan. "Personal Integrity, Politics, and Moral Imagination." In *A Question of Values*, edited by Samantha Brennan, Tracy Isaacs, and Michael Milde, 107–31. Amsterdam: Rodopi, 1997.

Baier, Kurt. *The Moral Point of View*. Ithaca, N.Y.: Cornell University Press, 1958.

———. "Moral Reasons." *Midwest Studies in Philosophy* 3 (1978): 62–74.

Barbour, Ian G., ed. *Western Man and Environmental Ethics*. Reading, Mass.: Addison-Wesley, 1973.

Barnes, Barry, David Bloor, and John Henry. *Scientific Knowledge: A Sociological Analysis*. Chicago: University of Chicago Press, 1997.

Barrett, William. *Irrational Man*. Garden City, N.Y.: Doubleday Anchor, 1962.

Barry, Brian. "How Not to Defend Political Institutions." *British Journal of Political Science* 20 (January 1990): 1–14.

———. *Justice as Impartiality*. Oxford: Clarendon Press, 1995.

———. *Theories of Justice*. Berkeley and Los Angeles: University of California Press, 1989.

Barthell, Edward. *Gods and Goddesses of Ancient Greece*. Coral Gables, Fla.: University of Miami Press, 1971.

Bell, Daniel. *The Cultural Contradictions of Capitalism*. New York: Basic Books, 1976.

Bellah, Robert, Richard Madsen, William Sullivan, Ann Swidler, and Steven Tipton. *Habits of the Heart: Individualism and Commitment in American Life*. New York: Harper & Row, 1985.

———, eds. *Narcissism, Individualism, and Commitment in American Life: Readings on the Themes of Habits of the Heart*. New York: Harper & Row, 1988.

Benedict, Ruth. *Patterns of Culture*. Boston: Houghton Mifflin, 1934.

Benn, S. I. "Freedom, Autonomy and the Concept of a Person." *Proceedings of the Aristotelian Society* 66 (1976): 129–30.

Berger, Peter, ed. *The Other Side of God*. Garden City, N.Y.: Anchor Doubleday, 1981.

Bergson, Henri. *Introduction à la métaphysique; Essai sur les données immédiates de la conscience; L'évolution créatrice*. In *Œuvres*. Paris: Presses Universitaires de France, 1959.

Berkeley, George. *A Treatise Concerning the Principles of Human Knowledge*. In vol. 2 of *The Works of George Berkeley, Bishop of Cloyne*. Oxford, Clarendon Press, 1901.

Berlin, Isaiah. *Four Essays on Liberty*. London: Oxford University Press, 1969.

———. "Two Concepts of Liberty." In *Four Essays on Liberty*. London: Oxford University Press, 1969.

Bernières, Louis de. "Legends of the Fall." *Harper's*, January 1996, pp. 76–80.

Bernstein, Richard. "One Step Forward, Two Steps Backward: Richard Rorty on Liberal Democracy and Philosophy." *Political Theory* 15 (1987): 538–63.

Berofsky, Bernard. *Liberation from Self*. Cambridge: Cambridge University Press, 1995.

Blanshard, Brand. "The New Subjectivism in Ethics." *Philosophy and Phenomenological Research* 9, no. 3 (1949): 504–11.

Bloom, Allen. *The Closing of the American Mind*. New York: Simon and Schuster, 1987.

Blum, Lawrence. *Friendship, Altruism, and Morality*. London: Routledge & Kegan Paul, 1980.

Boethius. *The Consolation of Philosophy*. Translated by V. E. Watts. London: Penguin Books, 1969.

———. *The Theological Tractates; The Consolation of Philosophy*. Translated by S. J. Tester et al. London: William Heinemann; Cambridge: Harvard University Press, 1973.

Bonjour, Laurence. *The Structure of Empirical Knowledge*. Cambridge: Harvard University Press, 1985.

Brennan, Andrew. *Thinking about Nature*. London: Routledge, 1988.

Brentano, Franz. *Psychology from an Empirical Standpoint*. Edited by L. McAlister. Translated by A. Rancurello et al. London: Routledge & Kegan Paul, 1973.

Bridgett, T. E. *Life and Writings of St. Thomas More*. London: Oates, 1891.

Brinton, Crane. *A History of Western Morals*. New York: Paragon House, 1990.

Brody, Baruch A. "Acts and Their Effects." In *Readings in the Philosophy of Law*, edited by J. Arthur, W. Shaw. 2d ed. Englewood Cliffs, N.J.: Prentice Hall, 1993.

Burke, Edmund. *A Philosophical Enquiry into the Origin of Our Ideas of the Sublime and Beautiful*. Edited by J. Boulton. Oxford: Basil Blackwell, 1987.

Butler, Bishop Joseph. *The Works of Joseph Butler*. Edited by W. Gladstone. 2 vols. Oxford: Clarendon Press, 1896.

Butler, Dom Cuthbert. *Western Mysticism*. London: Constable, 1967.

Camus, Albert. *The Rebel: An Essay on Man in Revolt*. New York: Vintage Books, 1956.

Caplan, A. L., H. T. Englehardt Jr., and J. J. McCartney, eds. *Concepts of Health and Disease: Interdisciplinary Perspectives*. Reading, Mass.: Addison-Wesley, 1981.

Carus, Paul. *The Gospel of Buddha According to Old Records*. Chicago: Open Court, 1894.

———. *Truth on Trial*. Chicago: Open Court, 1911.

Chopin, Kate. *The Awakening* New York: Bantam Books, 1992.

Christman, John. "Autonomy and Personal History." *Canadian Journal of Philosophy* 21 (March 1991): 1–24.

———, ed. *The Inner Citadel*. New York: Oxford University Press, 1989.

Chwaszcza, Christine. "Anmerkungen zu Funktion und Stellenwert des Eigeninteresses." In *Ökonomie und Moral*, edited by K. R. Lohmann. Munich: Oldenbourg, 1997.

Cicero, Marcus Tullius. *De Legibus*. Translated by C. W. Keyes. London: William Heinemann; Cambridge: Harvard University Press, 1928.

———. *On the Laws*. In *The Treatises of M. T. Cicero*, translated by C. D. Younge. London: Bell & Daldy, 1972.

Clark, Maudemarie. *Nietzsche on Truth and Philosophy*. Cambridge: Cambridge University Press, 1990.

Cohen, A., ed. and trans. *Everyman's Talmud*. New York: E. P. Dutton, 1949.

Coles, Robert. "Civility and Psychology." In *Narcissism, Individualism, and Commitment in American Life*, edited by Robert Bellah et al., 185–94. New York: Harper & Row, 1988.

Collingwood, R. G. *An Autobiography*. 1939. Reprint, London: Oxford University Press, 1970.

Collins, James D. *The Lure of Wisdom*. Milwaukee, Wis.: Marquette University Press, 1962.

Confucius. *The Analects of Confucius*. Translated by Arthur Waley. 1938. Reprint, New York: Vintage Books, 1989.

———. *The Analects of Confucius*. In vol. 1 of *The Chinese Classics*, translated by James Legge. 2d ed. Oxford: Clarendon Press, 1893–95,

———. *The Wisdom of Confucius*. Edited and translated by Lin Yutang. New York: Random House, 1994.

Cook, Deborah. *The Subject Finds a Voice: Foucault's Turn Towards Subjectivity.* New York: Peter Lang, 1993.

Cooper, David. *Value Pluralism and Ethical Choice*. New York: St. Martin's Press, 1993.

Copleston, Frederick. *Aquinas*. Harmondsworth: Penguin Books, 1955.

———. *A History of Philosophy*. New York: Image Books, 1985.

Copleston, Fredrick, and A. J. Ayer. "Logical Positivism—A Debate." In *A Modern Introduction to Philosophy*, edited by Paul Edwards and Arthur Pap, 586–618. New York: Free Press of Glencoe, 1957.

Copp, David. "Considered Judgements and Moral Justification: Conservatism in Moral Theory." In *Morality, Reason, and Truth,* edited by D. Copp and D. Zimmerman, 141–68. Totowa, N.J.: Rowman & Allanheld, 1985.

Coupland, Douglas. *Generation X.* New York: St. Martin's Press, 1991.

Cranston, Maurice. *John Locke: A Biography.* New York: Longmans, Green and Co., 1957.

Crittenden, Paul. *Learning to Be Moral: Philosophical Thoughts about Moral Development.* Atlantic Highlands, N.J.: Humanities Press International, 1990.

Croce, Benedetto. *The Philosophy of the Practical.* Translated by D. Ainslie. London: Macmillan, 1913.

Curti, Merle. *Dictionary of the History of Ideas*, s.v. "Psychological Theories in American Thought."

Daly, Mary. *Dictionary of the History of Ideas*, s.v. "Faith, Hope, and Charity."

Dan-Cohen, Meir. "Conceptions of Choice and Conceptions of Autonomy." *Ethics* 102 (January 1992): 221–43.

Daniels, Norman. "Two Approaches to Theory Acceptance in Ethics." In *Morality, Reason, and Truth*, edited by D. Copp and D. Zimmerman, 120–40. Totowa, N.J.: Rowman & Allanheld, 1985.

Danielson, Peter. *Artificial Morality: Virtuous Robots for Virtual Games.* London: Routledge, 1992.

Davidson, Donald. "How is Weakness of the Will Possible?" In *Moral Concepts*, edited by Joel Feinberg, 93–113. Oxford: Oxford University Press, 1969.

———. "The Structure and Content of Truth." *Journal of Philosophy* 87 (June 1990): 279–328.

de Koninck, Charles. *La Confédération, rempart contre le grand état.* Québec: Commission royale d'enquête sur les problèmes constitutionnels, annexe no. 1, 1954.

Derrida, Jacques. *On Grammatology.* Translated by Gayatri Chakravorty Spivak. Baltimore: Johns Hopkins University Press, 1974.

Descartes, René. *Meditationes de Prima Philosophia.* Translated by Duc de Luynes. Edited by Geneviève Rodis-Lewis. Paris: Librarie Philosophique J. Vrin, 1963.

———. *Meditations on First Philosophy.* Translated by John Cottingham. Cambridge: Cambridge University Press, 1996.

Desert Fathers. *The Sayings of the Desert Fathers: The Alphabetical Collection.* Translated by Benedicta Ward. London: A. R. Mowbray & Co., 1975.

Dewey, John. "The Evolutionary Method as Applied to Morality." *Philosophical Review* 11 (1902): 107–24, 353–71.

———. *Experience and Nature.* Chicago: Open Court, 1926.

———. *Intelligence in the Modern World: John Dewey's Philosophy.* Edited with introduction by Joseph Ratner. New York: Random House, 1939.

———. *Philosophy and Civilization.* New York: Minton, Balch & Company, 1931.

———. "The Present Position of Logical Theory." *Monist* 2 (1891): 1–17.

———. *The Quest For Certainty.* New York: Minton, Balch & Company, 1929.

———. *Theory of the Moral Life.* New York: Holt, Rinehart and Winston, 1960.

Dewey, John, and James Tufts. *Ethics.* New York: H. Holt and Company, 1938.

Dictionary of the History of Ideas. Edited by Philip Weiner. New York: Scribner and Sons, 1974.

Dimock, Susan. "Autonomy and Freedom of Action." Paper presented to the Annual Meeting of the Canadian Philosophical Association, Calgary. Alberta, 11 June 1994.

———. "Personal Autonomy." Ph.D. dissertation, Dalhousie University, February 1994.

Diogenes Laertius. *Lives of the Eminent Philosophers (De Vitis Philosophorum)*. Translated by R. D. Hicks. London: William Heinemann; Cambridge: Harvard University Press, 1972.

Donagan, Alan. *Encyclopedia of Ethics*, s. v. "Deliberation and Choice."

Dovey, Kimberly. "The Quest for Authenticity." In *Dwelling, Place, and Environment: Towards a Phenomenology of Person and World*, edited by D. Seamon and R. Mugerauer, 33–49. Dordrecht: Martinus Nijhoff, 1985.

Dowling, Phil. *The Mountaineers: Famous Climbers in Canada*. Edmonton: Hurtig Publishers, 1979.

Downs, Alan. *Beyond the Looking Glass: Overcoming the Seductive Culture of Corporate Narcissism*. New York: AMACOM, 1996.

Doyle, John. *Routledge Encyclopedia of Philosophy*, s.v. "John of St. Thomas."

Drengson, Alan R. *Beyond Environmental Crisis: From Technocrat to Planetary Person*. New York: Peter Lang, 1989.

Drury, Shadia B. *The Political Ideas of Leo Strauss*. Basingstoke, U.K.: Macmillan, 1988.

Durant, Will. *The Reformation*. New York: Simon & Schuster, 1957.

Dworkin, Gerald. "Acting Freely." *Nous* 4 (winter 1970): 367–83.

———. "Autonomy and Behavior Control." *Hastings Center Report* 6 (February 1976): 23–28.

———. *The Theory and Practise of Autonomy*. Cambridge: Cambridge University Press, 1988.

Dworkin, Ronald. "Liberalism." In *Liberalism and Its Critics*, edited by Michael Sandel, 60–79. New York: New York University Press, 1984.

———. *Taking Rights Seriously*. Cambridge: Harvard University Press, 1977.

Dykens, Elizabeth, Barbara Goff, Robert Hodnapp, Lisa Davis, Pablo Devanzo, Fran Moss, Jan Halliday, Bhavik Shah, Mathew State, and Byran King. "Eating Themselves to Death: Have Personal Rights Gone Too Far in Treating People with Praeder-Willi Syndrome?" *Mental Retardation* 35 (August 1997): 312–14.

Egan, Harvey. *Christian Mysticism*. New York: Pueblo Publishing Company, 1984.

Eichmann, Adolf. *Eichmann Interrogated*. Edited by Jochen von Lang and Claus Sibyll. Translated by Ralph Manheim with an introduction by Avner W. Less. New York: Farrar, Straus & Giroux, 1983.

Eitinger, Leo. *Concentration Camp Survivors in Norway and Israel*. The Hague: Martinus Nijhoff, 1972.

Encyclopedia of Ethics. Edited by Lawrence Becker. 2 vols. New York: Garland, 1982.

Encyclopedia of Philosophy. New York: Macmillan, 1967.

Encyclopedia of Psychology. New York: John Wiley & Sons, 1984.

Engel, S. Morris. *With Good Reason*. New York: St. Martin's Press, 1986.

Feinberg, Joel. "The Concept of Autonomy." In *The Inner Citadel*, edited by John Christman, 27–53. New York: Oxford University Press, 1989.

———. *Harm to Self*. New York: Oxford University Press, 1986.

———. "The Idea of a Free Man." In *Educational Judgements*, edited by James Doyle, 143–69. London: Routledge & Kegan Paul, 1973.

————. *Social Philosophy*. Englewood Cliffs, N.J.: Prentice-Hall, 1973.

Feyerabend, Paul. *Against Method*. Rev. ed. London: Verso, 1988.

————. *Against Reason: Outline of an Anarchistic Theory of Knowledge*. London: NLB, 1975.

————. *Knowledge without Foundations*. Oberlin, Ohio: Oberlin College, 1961.

Fields, Lloyd. "Moral Beliefs and Blameworthiness." *Philosophy* 69 (1994): 397–415.

Fish, Stanley. "Truth and Toilets: Pragmatism and the Practices of Life." In *The Revival of Pragmatism: New Essays on Social Thought, Law, and Culture*, edited by Morris Dickenstein, 428–33. Durham and London: Duke University Press, 1998.

Flew, Anthony. "On Not Deriving 'Ought' from 'Is.'" *Analysis* 25 (1964): 25–32.

Forester, C. S. "The Head and the Feet." In *The Nightmare*. Boston: Little, Brown, 1954.

Foster, Michael. *Plato to Machiavelli*. Vol. 1 of *Masters of Political Thought*. Boston: Houghton Mifflin, 1941–60. Reprint, Great Neck, N.Y.: Core Collection Books, 1978. (Page citations are to the reprint edition.)

Foucault, Michel. *Power*. Edited by James Faubion. Translated by Robert Hurley et al. Vol. 3 in *The Essential Works of Foucault*, edited by Paul Rabinow. New York: The New Press, 2000.

Francis of Assisi, St. *The Little Flowers of St. Francis*. Translated by Raphael Brown. Garden City, N.Y.: Hanover House, 1958.

Frankena, William. *Ethics*. 2d ed. Englewood Cliffs, N.J.: Prentice-Hall, 1973.

Frankfurt, Harry. "Freedom of Will and the Concept of a Person." *Journal of Philosophy* I (January 1971): 5–20.

————. *The Importance of What We Care About*. Cambridge: Cambridge University Press, 1988.

Frankl, Victor. *Man's Search for Meaning*. Boston: Beacon Press, 1962.

Freud, Sigmund. *Freud's "On Narcissism—An Introduction."* Edited by Joseph Sandler, Ethel Spectator Person, and Peter Fonagy. New Haven: Yale University Press, c1991.

Frye, Northrop. *The Return of Eden*. Toronto: University of Toronto Press, 1965.

Gass, William. "The Case of the Obliging Stranger." *Philosophical Review* 66 (1957): 193–204.

Gauthier, David. "Justice and Natural Endowment: Toward a Critique of Rawl's Ideological Framework." *Social Theory and Practise* 3 (1974): 3–26.

————. *Morals by Agreement*. Oxford: Clarendon, 1988.

Gaylin, Willard, and Bruce Jennings. *The Perversion of Autonomy: The Proper Uses of Coercion and Constraints in a Liberal Society*. New York: The Free Press, 199

Geddes, Gary, ed. *Twentieth-Century Poetry and Poetics*. Toronto: Oxford University Press, 1969.

Geras, Norman. *Solidarity in the Conversation of Humankind: The Ungroundable Liberalism of Richard Rorty*. London and New York: Verso, 1995.

Gettier, Edmund. "Is Justified True Belief Knowledge?" *Analysis* 23 (June 63): 121–23.

Gibbs, Benjamin. "Taking Liberties with Freedom: A Reply to Professor Flew." In *Of Liberty*, edited by A. Phillips Giffiths, 61–72. Cambridge: Cambridge University Press, 1983.

Giles, Jeff. "The Poet of Alienation: Cobain's Corrosive Songs Defined a Generation." *Newsweek,* 19 April 1994, pp. 46–47.

Gilligan, Carol. "Moral Orientation and Moral Development." In *Women and Moral Theory*, edited by E. F. Kittay and D. Meyers, , 19–33. Totowa, N.J.: Rowman and Littlefield, 1987.

Gilson, Etienne. *Being and Some Philosophers.* 2d ed. Toronto: Pontifical Institute of Medieval Studies: 1952.

Ginsberg, Morris. *Reason and Unreason in Society.* London: Longmans, Green, 1947.

Goldman, Alvin, and Holly Smith. *Encyclopedia of Ethics,* s.v. "Action."

Goleman, Daniel. *Emotional Intelligence.* New York: Bantam Books, 1995.

Gordon, J. E. *The New Science of Strong Materials, or Why You Don't Fall Through the Floor.* 2d ed. Harmondsworth: Penguin Books, 1976.

Griffin, John Howard. *Black Like Me.* Boston: Houghton Mifflin, 1961.

Groarke, Louis, and Paul Groarke. "Eichmann Retried: Moral Incapacity and the Defense of Insanity." *South Pacific Journal of Philosophy and Culture* 3 (1998–99): 42–70.

Groarke, Louis, and Lawrence Haworth. "The Relation Between Autonomy and Morality." Papaer delivered at the Canadian Philosophical Society Annual Meeting, Université du Québec à Montréal, Montreal, 3 June 1995.

Halbertal, Moshe, and Avishai Margalit. *Idolatry.* Cambridge: Harvard University Press, 1992.

Hallie, Philip. *Encyclopedia of Philosophy,* s.v. "Stoicism."

Hampton, Jean. *Hobbes and the Social Contract Tradition.* Cambridge: Cambridge University Press, 1988.

Hare, R. M. *Freedom and Reason.* Oxford: Oxford University Press, 1963.

———. *The Language of Morals.* New York: Oxford University Press, 1964.

Hart, H. L. A. *The Concept of Law.* Oxford: Clarendon Press, 1961.

Haworth, Lawrence. *Autonomy.* New Haven: Yale University Press, 1986.

———. *Decadence and Objectivity: Ideals for Work in a Post-Consumer Society.* Toronto: University of Toronto Press, 1977.

Hegel, Georg Wilhelm Friedrich. *Philosophy of Mind.* Translated by William Wallace and A. V. Miller. Oxford: Clarendon Press, 1971.

Hepburn, Richard. *Encyclopedia of Philosophy,* s. v. "Natural Law."

Hill, Stephen. "Rebel without a Clue: The Suicide of Millionaire Pied-Piper Kurt Cobain . . . Left a Generation Bereft of a False Prophet." *New Internationalist* 259 (September 1994): 21.

Hill, Thomas E. *Autonomy and Self-Respect.* Cambridge: Cambridge University Press, 1991.

Hobbes, Thomas. *Leviathan.* New York: Prometheus Books, 1988.

Hodgson, Geraldine E. *The Sanity of Mysticism: A Study of Richard Rolle.* 1926. Darby, Pa.: Folcroft Library Editions, 1977.

Holmes, Richard. *The Transcendence of the World: Phenomenological Studies.* Waterloo, Ont.: Wilfrid Laurier University Press, 1995.

Horne, James. *Beyond Mysticism.* Waterloo, Ont.: Canadian Corporation for Studies in Religion, 1978.

Hughes, Thomas H. *The Philosophical Basis of Mysticism.* Edinburgh: T. & T. Clark, 1937.

Hume, David. *A Treatise of Human Nature.* Edited by L. A. Selby-Bigge. Oxford: Clarendon, 1960.

———. *Dialogues Concerning Natural Religion; An Enquiry Concerning the Principles of Morals.* Edited by Nelson Pike. Indianapolis, Ind.: Bobbs-Merrill, 1970.

Hunt, Sir John. *The Conquest of Everest.* New York: E. P. Dutton, 1954.

Hurka, Thomas. *Principles: Short Essays on Ethics.* Toronto: Harcourt Brace, 1994.

Huxley, Aldous. *Brave New World.* New York: Harper & Row, 1989.

James, William. "The Dilemma of Determinism." In *The Writings of William James,* edited by John McDermott, 587–610. New York: Random House, 1967.

———. "The Moral Philosopher and The Moral Life." In *The Will to Believe,* edited by F. Burkhardt, F. Bowers, and I Skrupskelis. Cambridge: Harvard University Press, 1979.

———. *Pragmatism and The Meaning of Truth.* Cambridge: Harvard University Press, 1978.

———. *The Principles of Psychology.* Vol. 1 of *The Works of William James*: Cambridge: Harvard University Press, 1981.

———. *The Varieties of Religious Experience.* New York.: Longmans, Green and Co., 1902.

Jantzen, Grace M. "A Mystical Core of Religion." *Religious Studies* 26 (March 1990): 59–71.

———. "Mysticism and Experience." *Religious Studies* 25 (September 1989): 295–315.

John of St. Thomas. *Cursus Philosophicus: Ars Logica (Philosophical Course: Logical Art).* Edited by B. Reiser. Vol. 1. Turin: Marietti, 1930.

Jones, William. *Machiavelli to Bentham.* Vol. 2 of *Masters of Political Thought.* Boston: Houghton Mifflin, 1941–60. Reprint, Great Neck, N.Y.: Core Collection Books, 1978. (Page citations are to the reprint edition.)

Kant, Immanuel. *Critique of Pure Reason.* Translated by N. K. Smith. London: Macmillan, 1933.

———. *Foundation of the Metaphysics of Morals.* Translated by Lewis Beck. Indianapolis, Ind.: Bobbs-Merrill, 1959.

———. *The Metaphysics of Morals.* Translated by Mary Gregor. Cambridge: Cambridge University Press, 1991.

———. *Philosophy of Laws.* Translated by W. Hastie. Edinburgh: T & T Clark, 1891.

Kaplan, Nathaniel, and Thomas Katsaros. *The Western Mystical Tradition.* New Haven, Conn.: College and University Press, 1969.

Kazantzakis, Nikos. *Zorba: The Greek.* London: Faber and Faber, 1961.

Kelman, Herbert, and V. Lee Hamilton. *Crimes of Obedience: Toward a Social Psychology of Authority and Responsibility.* New Haven: Yale University Press, c. 1989.

Kerouac, Jack. *On the Road.* New York: Penguin, 1991.

Keykes, John. *Against Liberalism.* Ithaca and London: Cornell University Press, 1997.

Kierkegaard, Søren. *Concluding Unscientific Postscript to Philosophical Fragments.* Edited and translated by Howard Hong and Edna Hong. Princeton: Princeton University Press, 1992.

King, Martin Luther, Jr. "Letter from Birmingham City Jail." In *A Testament of Hope: The Editorial Writings of Martin Luther King, Jr.,* edited by James Washington, 289–302. San Francisco: Harper & Row, 1986, .

Kingdon, Robert. *Dictionary of the History of Ideas,* s.v. "Determinism in Theology: Predestination."

Kingwell, Mark. *A Civil Tongue: Justice, Dialogue, and the Politics of Pluralism.* University Park: Pennsylvania State University Press, 1995.

Kittrie, Nicholas. *Rebels with A Cause.* Boulder, Colo.: Westview, 2000.

———. *The War against Authority.* Baltimore: Johns Hopkins University Press, 1995.

Knudson, Albert C. *The Philosophy of Personalism: A Study in the Metaphysics of Religion.* 1927. Reprint, New York: Kraus Reprint Co., 1969.

Kohlberg, L. *The Philosophy of Moral Development.* San Francisco: Harper & Row, 1981.

Korsgaard, Christine M. "Two Distinctions in Goodness." *Philosophical Review* 92 (April 1983): 169–96.

Kropotkin, Prince. *Ethics, Origin and Development.* Translated by Louis Friedland and Joseph Piroshnikoff. New York: B. Blom, 1968.

Kuhn, Thomas. *The Structure of Scientific Revolution.* 3d ed. Chicago: University of Chicago Press, 1996.

Kundera, Milan. *Risibles amours.* Translated into French by François Kérel. Paris: Gallimard, 1986.

Kymlicka, Will. *Liberalism, Community, and Culture.* Oxford: Clarendon Press, 1989.

Lancaster, Lane. *Hegel to Dewey.* Vol. 3 of *Masters of Political Thought.* Boston: Houghton Mifflin, 1941–60. Reprint, Great Neck, N.Y.: Core Collection Books, 1978. (Page citations are to the reprint edition.)

Langsdorf, Lenore, and Andrew Smith. *Recovering Pragmatism's Voice: The Classical Tradition, Rorty, and the Philosophy of Communication.* Albany: State University of New York Press, 1995.

Larmore, Charles E. *Patterns of Moral Complexity.* Cambridge: Cambridge University Press, 1987.

Lasch, Christopher. *The Culture of Narcissism: American Life in an Age of Diminishing Expectations.* New York: W. W. Norton, 1978.

LeBoeuf, David. "How Not to Read Rorty." *Episteme* 4 (May 1993): 43–57.

Leibniz, Gottlob. *Discourse on Metaphysics, Correspondence with Arnauld, and Monadology.* Translated by George Montgomery. LaSalle, Ill.: Open Court, 1962.

Legge, James, trans. *The Texts of Taoism.* Vol. 39 of *Sacred Books of the East.* Oxford: Clarendon Press, 1991.

Leiter, Brian. "Perspectivism in Nietzsche's *Genealogy of Morals.*" In *Nietzsche, Genealogy, Morality,* edited by Richard Schacht, 334–57. Berkeley: University of California Press, 1994,

Lewis, C. S. *The Abolition of Man.* New York: Collier, 1962.

———. *The Discarded Image.* Cambridge: Cambridge University Press, 1964.

———. *The Last Battle.* London: Harper Collins, 1990.

Lindley, Richard. *Autonomy.* London: Macmillan, 1986.

Lipovetsky, Gilles. *L'ère du vide: Essais sur l'individualisme contemporain.* Paris: Gallimard, 1983.

Locke, John. *An Essay Concerning Human Understanding.* Oxford: Clarendon Press, 1975.

Luther, Martin. *Martin Luther on the Bondage of the Will.* Translated by J. Packer and O. Johnson. London: James Clarke & Company, 1957.

Lyons, Dan, and Jan Benson. *Strutting and Fretting.* Niwot, Colo.: University Press of Colorado, 1991.

MacDonald, Scott. *Routledge Encyclopedia of Philosophy,* s.v. "Philip the Chancellor."

MacIntyre, Alasdair. *After Virtue.* London: Duckworth, 1981.

———. *First Principles, Final Ends, and Contemporary Philosophical Issues.* Milwaukee, Wisc.: Marquette University Press, 1990.

———. "How Moral Agents Became Ghosts, or Why the History of Ethics Diverged From That of the Philosophy of Mind." *Synthese* 53 (1982): 305–6.

———. "Hume on 'Is' and 'Ought.'" *Philosophical Review* 68 (1959): 451–68.

———. "Intelligibility, Goods, and Rules." *Journal of Philosophy* 79 (November 1982): 663–65.

———. "Moral Disagreement Today and the Claims of Emotivism." In *Contemporary Ethics,* edited by James Sterba, 77–82. Englewood Cliffs, N.J.: Prentice-Hall, 1989.

MacIntyre, Jane. "Personal Identity and the Passions." *Journal of the History of Philosophy* 27 (October 1989): 545–57.

Mackie, J. L. *Ethics: Inventing Right and Wrong*. Harmondsworth: Penguin, 1977.
Malantschuk, Gregor. *Kierkegaard's Way to the Truth*. Montreal: Inter Editions, 1987.
Mannheim, Karl. *Ideology and Utopia: An Introduction to the Sociology of Knowledge*. New York: Harcourt, Brace & World, 1936.
Marcel, Gabriel. *Mystery of Being*. Chicago: Henry Regnery, 1969.
———. "On the Ontological Mystery." In *The Philosophy of Existentialism*, translated by Manya Harari, 1–31. Secaucus, N.J.: Citadel Press, 1956.
Marcus, Paul. *Autonomy in the Extreme Situation*. Westport, Conn.: Praeger, 1999.
Marcuse, Herbert. *Eros and Civilization: A Philosophical Inquiry into Freud*. Boston: Beacon Press, 1974.
Martin, C. F. J. *Thomas Aquinas: God and Explanations*. Edinburgh: Edinburgh University Press, 1997.
Maslow, A. H. *Motivation and Personality*. 2d ed. New York: Harper & Row, 1970.
Maurer, Armand. *Being and Knowing*. Toronto: Pontifical Institute of Medieval Studies, 1990.
———. *Encyclopedia of Philosophy*, s.v. "Edwards, Jonathan."
May, Rollo. *Psychology and the Human Dilemma*. New York: Van Nostrand Reinhold Company, 1967.
McNeil, E., and Z. Rubin. *The Psychology of Being Human*. New York: Harper & Row, 1981.
Melden, A. L., ed. *Ethical Theories*. Englewood Cliffs, N.J.: Prentice-Hall, 1967.
Merton, Thomas, trans. and ed. *The Wisdom of the Desert*. London: Hollis and Carter, 1961.
Meyer, Hans. *The Philosophy of St. Thomas Aquinas*. Translated by F. Eckhoff . St. Louis and London: B. Herder, 1944.
Meyers, Diana. *Self, Society, and Personal Choice*. New York: Columbia University Press, 1989.
Milgram, Stanley. *Obedience to Authority: An Experimental View*. New York: Harper & Row, 1974.
Mill, John Stuart. *John Stuart Mill's "On Liberty"*. Edited by John C. Rees. Constructed from published and unpublished sources by G. L. Williams. Oxford: Clarendon Press, 1985.
———. *On Liberty; The Subjection of Women; Chapters on Socialism*. Edited by Stefan Collini. Cambridge: Cambridge University Press, 1989.
Miller, Ed. *Questions That Matter*. 3d ed. New York: McGraw-Hill, 1992.
Miller, Michael Vincent "How We Suffer Now." Review of *I'm Dysfunctional, You're Dysfunctional,* by Wendy Kaminer. *New York Times Book Review*, 17 May 1992.
Milton, John. *Complete Poems and Major Prose*. Edited by M. Hughes. Indianapolis, Ind.: Odyssey Press, 1957.
Miri, Mrinal. "Memory and Personal Identity." *Mind* 82 (January 1973): 1–21.
Monk, Ray. *Ludwig Wittgenstein: The Duty of Genius*. London: Jonathan Cape, 1990.
Montaigne, Michel de. *Essais de Michel de Montaigne*. Edited by Albert Thibaudet. Paris: Gallimard, 1950.
Moore, Margret. *Foundations of Liberalism*. Oxford: Clarendon Press, 1993.
Mourant, John, ed. *Saint Augustine*. University Park: Pennsylvania State University Press, 1967.
Murdoch, Iris. *Metaphysics as a Guide to Morals*. London: Chatto & Windus, 1992.
Murphey, Murray. *Encyclopedia of Philosophy*, s.v. "Peirce, Charles Sanders."

Murphy, Frank. "The Problem of Overridingness." *Southern Journal of Philosophy* 36, no. 2 (June 1998): 255–63.

Murray, Malcolm. "Occurrent Contractarianism: A Preference-Based Ethical Theory." Ph.D. dissertation, University of Waterloo, 1995.

Naess, Arne, and David Rothenberg. *Ecology, Community, and Lifestyle: Outline of an Ecosophy.* Cambridge: Cambridge University Press, 1989.

Nagel, Thomas. *The View from Nowhere.* New York: Oxford University Press, 1986.

Narveson, Jan. *The Libertarian Idea.* Philadelphia: Temple University Press, 1988.

New Catholic Encyclopedia. New York: McGraw Hill, 1967.

Newman, John Henry, Cardinal. *Apologia Pro Vita Sua.* London: J. M. Dent & Sons; New York: Dutton, 1912.

Nicholas of Cusa. *On Learned Ignorance (De Docta Ignorantia).* Translated by Jasper Hopkins. Minneapolis, Minn.: Arthur J. Banning Press, 1985.

Nietzsche, Friedrich. *The Basic Writings of Nietzsche.* Translated by Walter Kaufmann. New York: Modern Library, 1968.

———. *Ecce Homo.* Translated by Walter Kaufmann. New York: Viking, 1969.

———. *The Portable Nietzsche.* (Including *Genealogy of Morals*; *Thus Spoke Zarathustra, Twilight of the Idols.*) Translated and edited by Walter Kaufmann. New York, Viking Press, 1968.

———. *Untimely Meditations (Schopenhauer as Educator).* Translated by R. Hollingdale. Cambridge: Cambridge University Press, 1983.

Noddings, Nel. *Caring.* Berkeley: University of California Press, 1984.

Noss, John. *Man's Religions.* New York: Macmillan, 1980.

Novak, Joseph. "Comments on K. Nielsen's *God, Modernity, and Scepticism.*" Paper presented to the Annual Meeting of the Canadian Philosophical Association, Victoria, B.C., June 1990.

Nozick, Robert. *Anarchy, State, and Utopia.* Oxford: Basil Blackwell, 1974.

Nussbaum, Martha. "Human Functioning and Social Justice: In Defense of Aristotelian Essentialism." *Political Theory* 20 (May 1992): 213–46.

O'Connell, Sean. *Dilemmas and Decisions.* Toronto: Harcourt Brace & Company, 1994.

Ortega y Gasset, José. *The Revolt of the Masses.* Authorized anonymous translation. New York: W. W. Norton, 1960.

———. "Refexiones de Centario." In vol. 4 of *Obras Completas de José Ortega y Gasset.* 4th ed. Madrid: Revista de Occidente, 1957.

Ortnerm, Sherry. *Life and Death on Mt. Everest: Sherpas and Himalayan Mountaineering.* Princeton: Princeton University, 1999.

Otto, Rudolf. *The Idea of the Holy.* 1923. Reprint, London: Oxford University Press, 1970.

Ovid. *Metamorphoses I–IV.* Translated by D. E. Hill. Oak Park, Ill.: Bolchazy-Carducci, 1985.

Paglia, Camille. *Sex, Art, And American Culture.* New York: Vintage Books, 1992.

Papadatos, Peter. *The Eichmann Trial.* London: Stevens & Sons, 1964.

Pascal, Blaise. *L'Esprit de la géométrie et de l'art de persuader.* Commenté par B. Clerté et M. L'hoste-Navarre. Paris: Editions Pédagogie Moderne, 1979.

Pascal, Blaise, and Pierre Nicole. *Pensées de Pascal suivies d'un choix des pensées de Nicole.* Paris: Librairie de Firmin-Didot et Cie, 1891.

Passmore, John. "Perfectibility of Man." In *Dictionary of the History of Ideas,* edited by Philip Wiener, 3:463–76. New York: Scribner, 1973–74.

Patterson, Orlando. *Freedom.* New York: Basic Books 1991.

Peacock, Kent. "Knowledge, Opinion, and Rorty: Non-Conversational Constraints on Inquiry." Paper presented at the Ontario Philosophical Society Conference, University of
Windsor, October 1995.

Peirce, Charles Sanders. "The Fixation of Belief." *Popular Science Monthly* 12 (November
1877): 1–15.

———. "How to Make Our Ideas Clear." *Popular Science Monthly* 12 (January 1878):
286–302.

———. *Philosophical Writings of Pierce.* Edited by Justus Buchler. New York: Dover,
1955:

Penelhum, Terrence. *Survival and Disembodied Existence.* New York: Humanities Press,
1969.

Penguin Dictionary of Psychology. 2d ed. New York: Viking Penguin, 1985.

Perry, Ralph. *General Theory of Value.* Cambridge: Harvard University Press, 1950.

Peters, Richard. *Hobbes.* Harmondsworth: Penguin, 1967.

Pickering, Andrew. *Constructing Quarks: A Sociological History of Particle Physics.*
Edinburgh: Edinburgh University Press, 1984.

Plato. *The Collected Dialogues of Plato.* (Including *Phaedo, Protagoras, Republic, Symposium.*) Edited by E. Hamilton and H. Cairns. New York: Pantheon Books, 1963.

———. *Plato: Complete Works.* Edited by J. Cooper. Indianapolis, Ind.: Hackett, 1997.

Popkin, Richard. *Encyclopedia of Philosophy*, s. v. "Skepticism."

Popper, Karl. *Conjectures and Refutations.* New York: Basic Books, 1965.

Potts, Timothy C. *Cambridge History of Later Medieval Philosophy.* Edited by Norman
Kretzmann, Anthony Kenny, and Jan Pinborg. Cambridge: Cambridge University Press,
1982.

Prado, C. G. *The Limits of Pragmatism.* Atlantic Highlands, N.J.: Humanities Press International, 1982.

Przywara, Erich, ed. *An Augustinian Synthesis.* New York: Harper Torchbooks, 1950.

Putnam, Hilary. "A Comparison of Something with Something Else." *New Literary History*
17 (1985): 61–79.

———. *Pragmatism: An Open Question.* Oxford: Basil Blackwell, 1995.

———. *Realism and Reason: Philosophical Papers.* Vol. 3. Cambridge: Cambridge University Press, 1983.

Quine, W. V. "The Pragmatist's Place in Empiricism." In *Pragmatism: Its Sources and
Prospects*, edited by R. Mulvaney and P. Zeltner, 21–39. Columbia: University of South
Carolina Press, 1981.

Rader, Melvin. "Dickie and Socrates on Definitions." *Journal of Aesthetics and Art Criticism* 32 (1974): 423–24.

Ramsey, Frank. *The Foundations of Mathematics.* New York: Harcourt, Brace, and Co.,
1931.

Rand, Ayn. *Atlas Shrugged.* New York: Random House, 1957.

———. *Capitalism: The Unknown Ideal.* New York: New American Library, 1967.

———. *The Fountainhead.* New York: New American Library, 1971.

———. *The Virtue of Selfishness.* New York: New American Library, 1964.

Rawls, John. "Justice as Fairness: Political Not Metaphysical." *Philosophy and Public Affairs* 14 (1985): 223–51.

———. "The Justification of Civil Disobedience." In *The Right Thing to Do,* edited by
James Rachels, 254–70. New York: McGraw-Hill, 1989.

———. *A Theory of Justice*. Cambridge: Harvard, 1971.

Raz, Joseph. *The Morality of Freedom*. Oxford: Clarendon Press, 1986.

Reith, Herman. *The Metaphysics of St. Thomas Aquinas*. Milwaukee, Wisc.: Bruce Publishing, 1958.

Resnik, Michael. *Choices: An Introduction to Decision Theory*. Minneapolis: University of Minnesota Press, 1987.

Rieff, David. "Victims All? Recovery, Co-dependency, and the Art of Blaming Somebody Else," *Harper's*, October 1991, 56.

Riesman, David, with Nathan Glazer and Revel Denney. *Lonely Crowd*. Garden City, N.Y.: Doubleday, 1953.

Robinson, John Manly. *An Introduction to Early Greek Philosophy*. Boston: Houghton Mifflin, 1968.

Rollins, C. D. *Encyclopedia of Philosophy*, s.v. "Solipsism."

Rorty, Richard. *Contingency, Irony, Solidarity*. Cambridge: Cambridge University Press, 1989.

———. *Essays on Heidegger and Others*. Vol. 2 of *Philosophical Papers*. Cambridge: Cambridge University Press, 1991.

———. *Philosophy and the Mirror of Nature*. Princeton: Princeton University Press, 1979.

———. "Pragmatism, Relativism, and Irrationalism." *Proceedings and Addresses of the American Philosophical Association* 53 (1980): 719–38.

———. "Solidarity or Objectivity?" In *Anti-Theory in Ethics and Moral Conservatism*, edited by Stanley Clark, Evan Simpson, 167–83. Albany: State University of New York Press, 1989.

———. "Truth and Freedom: A Reply to Thomas McCarthy." *Critical Inquiry* 16 (spring 1990): 633–43.

Rosenau, Pauline Marie. *Post-Modernism and the Social Sciences: Insights, Inroads, and Intrusions*. Princeton: Princeton University Press, 1992.

Rosenbaum, Alan S. *Coercion and Autonomy: Philosophical Foundations, Issues, and Practices*. New York: Greenwood Press, 1986.

Rousseau, Jean-Jacques. *Du Contrat social*. Edited by R. Grimsley. Oxford: Clarendon Press, 1972.

———. *The Social Contract*. Translated by J. Masters. Edited by R. Masters. New York: St. Martin's Press, 1978.

Royce, Josiah. *The Basic Writings of Josiah Royce*. Edited by John McDermott. Chicago: University of Chicago Press, 1969.

———. *The Philosophy of Loyalty*. In *The Basic Writings of Josiah Royce,* edited by John McDermott, 2:855–1013. Chicago: University of Chicago Press, 1969.

Rubin, Z., and E. McNeil. *The Psychology of Being Human*. New York: Harper & Row, 1981.

Russell, Bertrand. *History of Western Philosophy*. 2d ed. London: Routledge, 1991.

———. *Mysticism and Logic*. New York: Longmans, Green and Co., 1918.

———. "Retreat of Pythagoras." In *Basic Writings of Bertrand Russell,* edited by Robert Egner and Lester Denonn. New York: Simon and Schuster, 1961.

Russell, Edward Frederick Langley (Lord Russell of Liverpool.) *The Record: The Trial of Adolf Eichmann for His Crimes against the Jewish People and against Humanity*. New York: Alfred A. Knopf, 1963.

Sade, Marquis de. *Œuvres*. Paris: Gallimard, 1990.

Salinger, J. D. *The Catcher in the Rye*. Boston: Little, Brown, 1991.

Sandel, Michael, *Liberalism and the Limits of Justice*. Cambridge: Cambridge University Press, 1982.

————, ed. *Liberalism and Its Critics*. New York: New York University Press, 1984.

Santayana, George. "The Problem of Freedom of the Will in Its Relation to Ethics." In *Physical Order and Moral Liberty*, edited by John Lachs and Shirley Lachs, 5–12. Nashville, Tenn.: Vanderbilt University Press, 1969.

Sartre, Jean-Paul. *The Philosophy of Existentialism*. Edited by Wade Baskin. New York: Philosophical Library, 1965.

Satire, Virginia. "I am me." © 1975, Self-Esteem, Celestial Arts, P.O. Box 7327, Berkeley, California 94707. Poster.

Saytre-McCord, Geoffrey, ed. *Essays on Moral Realism*. Ithaca, N.Y.: Cornell University Press, 1988.

Scanlon, Thomas. "A Theory of Freedom of Expression." *Philosophy and Public Affairs* 1 (winter 1972): 204–26.

Schmidtz, David. *Rational Choice and Moral Agency*. Princeton: Princeton University Press, 1995.

————. "Self-Interest: What's in It for Me?" *Social Philosophy and Policy* 14 (winter 1997): 107–21.

Schmitt, Richard. *Encyclopedia of Philosophy*, s.v. "Phenomenology."

Scott. Chic. *Pushing the Limits: The Story of Canadian Mountaineering*. Calgary: Rocky Mountain Books, c. 2000.

Searle, John R. "How to Derive 'Ought' from 'Is'." *Philosophical Review* 73 (1964): 43–58.

Sennett, Richard. *The Fall of Public Man: On the Social Psychology of Capitalism*. New York: Vintage Books, 1978.

Shaffer, Brian. *The Blinding Torch*. Amherst: University of Massachusetts Press, 1993.

Shakespeare, William. *The Oxford Shakespeare*. London: Oxford University Press, 1914.

Shattuck, Roger. *Forbidden Knowledge: From Prometheus to Pornography*. New York: St. Martin's Press, 1996.

Sidgwick, Henry. *The Methods of Ethics*. London: Macmillan, 1884.

Skorupski, John. "The Ethics of Classical Liberalism." Paper delivered at the University of Waterloo Philosophy Colloquium, 16 September 1994.

Smart, Ninian. *Concept and Empathy*. New York: New York University Press, 1986.

————. *Philosophers and Religious Truth*. London: SCM Press, 1964.

Smith, Adam. *The Theory of Moral Sentiments*. Facsimile edition New York: Garden Publishing, 1971.

Sparkes. A. W. *Talking Politics: A Wordbook*. London: Routledge, 1994.

Sparshott, Francis. "Disputed Evaluations." *American Philosophical Quarterly* 7 (April 1970): 131–42.

Spidlik, T. *New Catholic Encyclopedia*, s.v. "Stylites."

Sprague, Rosamond Kent. *The Older Sophists*. Columbia: University of South Carolina Press, 1972.

Stace, W. T. *Mysticism and Philosophy*. London: Macmillan, 1961.

Stephen, Leslie. *The Science of Ethics*. New York: G. P. Putnam's Sons, 1882.

Sterba, James. Editor. *Contemporary Ethics*. Englewood Cliffs, N.J.: Prentice Hall, 1989.

Stove, David. *The Plato Cult and Other Philosophical Follies*. Oxford: Basil Blackwell, 1991.

Strauss, Neil. "He Was a Geek and a God: The Story behind the Tragic Death of Kurt Cobain." *Rolling Stone,* 26 May 1994, E1.

Strawson, P. F. "Social Morality and Individual Ideal." In *Freedom and Resentment and Other Essays*. London: Methuen, 1974.

Sumner, William Graham. *Folkways*. New York: Dover, 1859.

Swanton, Christine. *Freedom: A Coherence Theory*. Indianapolis, Ind.: Hackett, 1992.

Swidler, Ann. "Love and Adulthood in American Culture." In *Narcissism, Individualism, and Commitment in American Life*. Edited by Robert Bellah et al., 107–25. New York: Harper & Row, 1988.

Taylor, Charles. *Human Agency and Language*. Cambridge: Cambridge University Press, 1985.

———. *The Malaise of Modernity*. Concord, Ont.: Anansi, 1991.

———. *Philosophical Arguments*. Cambridge: Harvard University Press, 1995.

———. *Philosophy and the Human Sciences*. Cambridge: Cambridge University Press, 1985.

———. "Reply to Braybrooke and de Sousa." *Dialogue* 33 (winter 1994): 122–31.

———. "Rorty in the Epistemological Tradition." In *Reading Rorty*, edited by Alan Malachowski, 257–75. Oxford: Basil Blackwell, 1990.

———. *Sources of the Self: The Making of the Modern Identity*. Cambridge: Harvard University Press, 1989.

———. "What's Wrong with Negative Freedom." In *The Idea of Freedom*, edited by Alan Ryan, 175–93. New York: Oxford University Press, 1979.

———. "Why Democracy Needs Patriotism." *Boston Review* 19, no. 5 (1994): 119–21.

Tertullian, "On Idolatry." In *Latin Christianity, Its Founder Tertullian*, vol. 2 of *The Anti-Nicene Fathers*, edited by Alexander Roberts and James Donaldson, 61–76. Grand Rapids, Mich.: W. B. Eerdmans, 1978.

Thalberg, I. "Hierarchical Analyses of Unfree Action." In *The Inner Citadel*, edited by John Christman, 123–36. New York: Oxford University Press, 1989.

Thalos, Miriam. "Self-Interest, Autonomy and the Presuppositions of Decision Theory." *American Philosophical Quarterly* 34 (1997): 287–97.

Thomas à Kempis. (Probable author.) *L'Imitation de Jésus-Christ*. Translated into French by F. de Lamennais. Québec: La Librairie Canadienne, 1941.

Thoreau, Henry David. *Walden and Civil Disobedience*. New York: Penguin, 1983.

Thucydides, *History of the Peloponnesian Wars*. Translated by Rex Warner. New York: Penguin Books, 1954.

Tillich, Paul. *The Protestant Era*. Chicago: University of Chicago Press, 1948.

———. *Systematic Theology*. Volume 1. Chicago: University of Chicago Press, 1967.

Twain, Mark. *The Portable Mark Twain*. Edited by Bernard DeVoto. New York: Viking, 1946.

Underhill, Evelyn. *Mysticism*. 1911. Reprint, New York: Meridian, 1974.

Vallentyne, Peter, ed. *Contractarianism and Rational Choice*. New York: Cambridge University Press, 1991.

Veroff, Joseph, Elizabeth Douvan, and Richard Kulka. "The Inner American." In *Narcissism, Individualism, and Commitment in American Life*. Edited by Robert Bellah et al., 151–62. New York: Harper & Row, 1988.

Vesey, Godfrey. *Personal Identity*. London: Macmillan, 1974.

Viminitz, Paul. "Defending Game Theoretic Approaches to Ethics and Political Philosophy." Paper presented at University of Waterloo Philosophy Colloquium, 15 November 1995.

———. "No Place to Hide: Campbell's and Danielson's Solutions to Gauthier's Coherence Problem." *Dialogue* 35 (spring 1996): 235–40.

Watson, Gary. "Free Agency." In *Free Will,* edited by Gary Watson, 96–111. Oxford: Oxford University Press, 1982.

Whitbeck, Caroline. "A Different Reality: Feminist Ontology." In: *Women, Knowledge, and Reality,* edited by Ann Garry and Marilyn Pearsall, 51–76. Boston: Unwin Hyman, 1989.

White, Morton. *Social Thought in America: The Revolt against Formalism.* Boston: Beacon Press, 1957.

Wienphal, Paul. "Dewey's Theory of Language and Meaning." In *John Dewey: Philosopher of Science and Freedom,* edited by Sidney Hook, 271–88. New York: Dial Press, 1950.

Wilkes, Kathleen. *Real People: Personal Identity without Thought-Experiments.* Oxford: Clarendon Press; New York: Oxford University Press, 1988.

Williams, Bernard. *Morality: An Introduction to Ethics.* Harmondsworth: Penguin, 1973.

Wilson, James. *The Moral Sense.* New York: The Free Press, 1993.

Wittgenstein, Ludwig. *The Blue and Brown Books.* Oxford: Basil Blackwell, 1958.

Wolf, Susan. "Moral Saints." *Journal of Philosophy* 79 (1982): 419–39.

———. "Sanity and the Metaphysics of Responsibility." In *The Inner Citadel,* edited by John Christman, 137–51. New York: Oxford University Press, 1989.

Wolfe, Tom. "The Me Decade and the Third Great Awakening." In *Tom Wolfe: The Purple Decades: A Reader.* New York: Farrar, Straus & Giroux, 1982.

Wolff, Robert Paul. *Anarchism.* New York: Harper Torchbooks, 1976.

———. *The Autonomy of Reason.* New York: Harper and Row, 1973.

———. *In Defense of Anarchism.* New York: Harper & Row, 1970.

Young, Robert. "Autonomy and the 'Inner Self.'" In *The Inner Citadel,* edited by John Christman, 77–91. New York: Oxford University Press, 1989.

———. *Personal Autonomy: Beyond Negative and Positive Liberty.* London: Croom Helm, 1986.

Zaehner, R. C. *Mysticism: Sacred and Profane.* Oxford: Clarendon Press, 1957.

Index